The People's Martyr

The People's Martyr

Thomas Wilson Dorr and
His 1842 Rhode Island Rebellion

Erik J. Chaput

Best Wishes,

Erik J. Chaput

University Press of Kansas

Published by the University Press of Kansas (Lawrence, Kansas 66045), which
was organized by the Kansas Board of Regents and is operated and funded by
Emporia State University, Fort Hays State University, Kansas State University,
Pittsburg State University, the University of Kansas, and Wichita State
University

Library of Congress Cataloging-in-Publication Data

Chaput, Erik J.
The people's martyr : Thomas Wilson Dorr and his 1842 Rhode Island
rebellion / Erik J. Chaput.
pages cm
Includes bibliographical references and index.
ISBN 978-0-7006-1924-5 (hardback)
1 Dorr Rebellion, 1842. 2. Dorr, Thomas Wilson, 1805–1854. 3. Rhode
Island—Politics and government—1775–1865. 4. Suffrage—Rhode Island—
History—19th century. I. Title.
F83.4.C47 2013
974.5'03092—dc23

2013019419

British Library Cataloguing-in-Publication Data is available.

Printed in the United States of America

10 9 8 7 6 5 4 3 2 1

The paper used in this publication is recycled and contains 30 percent postcon-
sumer waste. It is acid free and meets the minimum requirements of the American National Standard for Permanence of Paper for Printed Library Materials
Z39.48-1992.

For Katie, for ever and ever

Contents

List of Illustrations

A photo section appears following page 94.

Acknowledgments

I cannot say enough about Fred Woodward, the editor at the University Press of Kansas. Fred took an interest in my project from the very beginning and had an uncanny knack of offering words of encouragement just when I needed them most. The two anonymous reviewers helped me in incalculable ways. I am extraordinarily appreciative of all their comments and suggestions. The incredible production team at UPK, especially Larisa Martin, Susan Schott, Rebecca Murray Schuler, and Sara White Henderson went above and beyond the call of duty to help me finish the book. Martha Whitt's skillful copy editing greatly improved the final product.

There have been three constants from the beginning of my research that need to be acknowledged up front: Russell J. DeSimone, Raymond J. Lavertue, and Patrick T. Conley. Russ and Ray gave of their time to read sections, answer countless questions via email and phone, and, most importantly, to simply be there for me when I needed them most. I am grateful to Russ for allowing me to reproduce a number of images from his incredible private collection. Pat levied relentless assaults on my illogic, forced me to think deeply about what I had written, and offered insightful ways to improve my story. The same goes for my friend Peter Wallner, the author of a magisterial, multivolume biography of Thomas Dorr's close friend Franklin Pierce. I thank Professor J. Stanley Lemons for graciously sharing his encyclopedic knowledge of the First Baptist Church with me over the course of several phone conversations.

I had the good fortune to be a part of a vibrant intellectual community during my time at Syracuse University. James Roger Sharp was an everlasting source of encouragement from the day I set foot in the Maxwell School of Citizenship and Public Affairs. Roger's devotion to his students and his integrity as a scholar have provided me with a model to follow. Through the research and writing of this book I got to meet James Oakes, the historian whose scholarship made me want to pursue history as a major in college.

Numerous archivists helped to facilitate the research of this book. Special thanks to Andy Moul, Kathleen Brooks, Alison Bundy, Tim Engels, and Ann Dodge at the John Hay Library for their enthusiasm for my project. Holly Snyder, the curator of the American Historical Collections at the John Hay Library, took me under her wing when I was a young, and somewhat lost graduate student. I am especially grateful to the Rhode Island Historical Society, an organization that has been revitalized in recent years thanks to C. Morgan Grefe's able leadership. Jordan Goffin, Katherine Chansky, Phoebe Beane, and Kirsten Hammerstrom helped me navigate through the relevant collections at the RIHS. Thanks to Elizabeth Watts Pope, Ashley Cataldo, and Andrew Bourque at the American Antiquarian Society and Bert Lippincott III at the Newport Historical Society. Ed Galloway at the University of Pittsburg helped me to uncover a rare image of Thomas Dorr in prison and graciously granted me permission to reprint the image in the book.

Andrew Boisvert at the Old Colony Historical Society assisted me with the invaluable diary kept by Providence resident Aurilla Moffitt. I am thankful to the North Smithfield Heritage Association for showing me their collection of letters between Thomas Dorr and Metcalf Marsh. The incredible staffs in the special collections department of the Boston Public Library and at the Gilder Lehrman Institute of American History proved to be a great help in the final stages of the project. Ken Carlson at the Rhode Island State Archives, Paul Campbell at the Providence City Archives, and Andrew Smith at the Rhode Island Supreme Court Judicial Records Center assisted me in mining numerous state records. Frank Mauran III graciously shared his encyclopedic knowledge of the Dorr family, showed me an extraordinary letter from William Bridges Adams to Thomas Dorr, allowed me to use a daguerreotype of Dorr in this book, and gave me a tour of 109 Benefit Street. Henry A. L. Brown enthusiastically helped me to navigate the letters of his ancestor Governor John Brown Francis.

Though we have never met in person I need to acknowledge the insights I gained from several email exchanges with Christian G. Fritz. Professor Fritz's scholarship served as an inspiration as I sat down to write. Mary Zboray graciously answered several questions via email about the incredible diary of Worcester resident John Park at the Boston Public Library. In 2010, I benefited from listening to an engaging and thought-provoking lecture on Thomas Dorr's constitutional ideology delivered by University of Kentucky history professor Ron Formisano at the Fabre Line Club in Providence. My understanding of Thomas Dorr was greatly aided by working with Linda Smith Rhoads, the skillful editor of *The New England Quarterly*. With great patience and fortitude, Linda helped me to craft an article on issues of race connected with the Dorr Rebellion for the *NEQ* in December 2012. I am grateful for the permission to republish portions of the article in Chapters 5 and 6.

Thanks to Janet Castleman, Madeleine Metzler, and Paul O'Malley for affording me with an opportunity to teach in the School of Continuing Education and the Graduate School at Providence College. I have had the good fortune over the last few years to be connected to an incredible digital history project headed by the staff in the Phillips Memorial Library. Mark Caprio, Hailie Posey, and Chris Landry never cease to amaze me with what they can do with technology and the ways in which they can make history come alive. This book was completed during my time as a member of the History and Social Science Department at Northfield Mount Hermon. I owe a debt of gratitude to my incredible students, especially Gwen Umbach, and to my colleagues, Peter Fayroian, Hugh Silbaugh, Charlie Tierney, Rick Wood, Eleanor Conover, Janae Peters, Diane Arena, Chris Edler, Charlie Malcolm, Grant Gonzalez, Jim Shea, Drew Inzer, Ted Kenyon, Margaret Van Baaren, John Walsh, Claude Anderson, Michael Corrigan, Louise Schwingle, Dick Peller, David Dowdy, Kim Sprankle, Ted Thornton, Patricia O'Brien, and Pam Allan. Harry Van Baaren graciously donated his time to help me prepare the cover for the book.

My parents, Gary and Lynne Chaput, have supported me throughout my life and instilled in me a love of the past and a passion for writing. Words could never capture my gratitude to my grandmother Elaine Ward for all that she has done for me throughout my life, however, I feel the need to attempt a heartfelt "thank you." Melva Orzechowski, Charlie Short, Ann Short, and Julie Short have been to just about every talk I have ever given on Thomas Wilson Dorr. Warren and Ann Brown graciously provided me with a place to stay in Washington, D.C., as I conducted research at the Library of Congress. Growing up an only child it has been wonderful to join the large Simon clan in West Seneca, New York. My wife, Katie, read each chapter, raised questions, offered advice, and pressed me to finish the project. Though appreciative of Katie's editorial skills, it has been her love, patience, and friendship that I cherish the most. With gratitude, admiration, and affection, I dedicate this book to her.

Erik J. Chaput
April 2013

Introduction

That the Roger Williams state, the pioneer of religious freedom, should still be governed by the Charter of King Charles II instead of a popular constitution . . . is certainly among the very singular anomalies of this boasted nineteenth century, in which we preach so much republicanism, and practice little of it.

Friend of Man, January 11, 1842

As dusk turned to dark on May 17, 1842, the residents of Providence, Rhode Island, were returning to their homes. But few were preparing for a restful night's sleep. Citizens were on edge, expecting the sound of cannon fire at any moment. Schools, shops, banks, and Brown University on College Hill had been closed all day. The sheriff had closed the court house weeks before.[1] The cobblestone streets were filled with men in uniform, from young recruits engaged in their first military drills to more senior militiamen who might have performed a similar duty a decade earlier when the city was beset by a deadly, multiday riot in an area of rundown dwellings along the Moshassuck River.[2] There was a great commotion in Market Square over rumors that the city might be set aflame.

At first it was mere speculation, but as the night wore on, credible witnesses reported that the People's Governor, Thomas Wilson Dorr, a short, portly man with thick, jet-black hair and piercing, hazel eyes, was planning an assault on the state arsenal on the west side of the city. The other man with a claim to the governorship, Samuel Ward King, had feared this for more than a month.[3] The fifty-six-year-old King, a medical doctor by training, was in his fourth term as governor. Rumors circulated that if he captured the arsenal, Dorr intended to march east across the city to Brown University in order to use the dormitories as barracks for his troops. From there he

1

would order his men to seize public and private property and redistribute it among the poor masses, establishing an "agrarian despotism."[4]

Dorr and his men needed either to acquire the supply of armaments inside the arsenal, or, at the very least, to neutralize the government's control of such a large stockpile of firepower. With only thirty men on hand to defend the state's weapons, the arsenal building was extremely vulnerable. Those Providence residents with a knowledge of history probably made the connection to Daniel Shays's attempt to capture the federal arsenal in Springfield, Massachusetts, on January 25, 1787. Four men died in that attempt. Indeed, the prominent New York Whig editor Thurlow Weed would use the headline "Second Shays's Rebellion" when describing events in Rhode Island.[5]

Born into wealth and privilege, Thomas Dorr was certainly no Daniel Shays. As a young man, Dorr seemed destined to take his place among Rhode Island's upper echelon, using his degree from Harvard and considerable legal training to live a life of leisure and civic pursuits. He was often described by his followers as a gentleman of "amiable temper and strict purity [of] character."[6] Dorr would certainly earn his place in the history books though it was not quite in the way his father, Sullivan, and his mother, Lydia, had hoped. Sullivan and Lydia likely dreamed that their oldest son would become governor one day, but they surely did not imagine he would bypass the sitting government of Rhode Island in order to get there.

In the eyes of the wealthy class of people with whom Sullivan and Lydia associated, their thirty-six-year-old son was a sanctimonious, deluded demagogue bent on destruction. A deacon at the prominent First Baptist Church on North Main Street in Providence expressed a "desire" to see their son's head carried "through the streets on a pole." Another deacon at the same church wished to see the "blood" of Dorr's followers flowing in the "gutters."[7] James McKenzie, pastor of Roger Williams Baptist Church in Providence and Dorr supporter, correctly noted that turmoil among Providence's faithful in the spring of 1842 led to "divisions and enmities in families, neighborhoods, and [churches]—presenting such spectacles of Christian armed against Christian."[8]

In the spring of 1842, in the nation's smallest state, there were two governments—one claiming legitimacy under a 1663 Charter that prescribed no mode for amendment, the other claiming legitimacy from a constitution adopted by the majority of citizens in a plebiscite in December 1841. When eleven of the colonies adopted new constitutions during the Revolution, the

General Assembly of Rhode Island simply crossed out the name of King Charles II and pushed forward. Despite repeated attempts, the state had never adopted a formal written constitution. The Charter afforded those with landed property a monopoly on political power. The changing nature of work and immigration in the early nineteenth century meant that the ownership of property and real estate became an unattainable goal for most workers. The growing laboring class who did not own $134 worth of landed property (figure set in 1798) were unable to participate in government.[9] To make matters worse from the reformers' point of view, mill owners frequently made "voters for a day" by temporarily conveying tracts of land to employees. Since there was no secret ballot, employees were forced to vote the ticket their employer desired. In the spring of 1842, many mill owners scared workers away from supporting Thomas Dorr and his People's Constitution, a liberal document that fully incorporated laborers into the body politic.[10] The always colorful New York labor leader Mike Walsh labeled Rhode Island landholders "a craven, avaricious, and unfeeling gang of sneaking, hypocritical thieves and tyrants."[11]

Drawing inspiration from the democratic religious revivals of the 1820s and 1830s, the disenfranchised plebian reformers hoped to improve their chances of not only finding the Lord, but also finding justice on earth. In the early 1840s, almost 60 percent of all adult white males in Rhode Island were excluded from the ballot. Dorr told Amos Kendall, the intellectual firepower of Andrew Jackson's administration, that in the city of Providence there were only 1,300 voters in a white male population over the age of 21, of about 4,500. The state's political institutions, in Dorr's analysis, were "totally inconsistent with a just regard to natural rights," to the "doctrine of popular sovereignty," to the "Declaration of American Independence," and to the "spirit of the Constitution of the United States."[12] The situation in Rhode Island, as historian Patrick T. Conley has noted, was a "democracy in decline."[13]

After the legislature repeatedly blocked attempts to reform the state's archaic system, Dorr and his followers decided to take matters into their own hands. They took the basic principles of popular sovereignty that emerged during the American Revolution as their North Star. Elisha R. Potter, Jr., a lawyer and conservative Democrat from South Kingstown, succinctly summarized the 1841–1842 constitutional crisis in a letter to his brother. "One of the constitutions commonly called the People's was made in this way: a number of the friends of free suffrage on their own authority called a convention to make a constitution . . . the convention met and made a constitution extending suffrage to all on a residence of one year." A vote was then taken in late December 1841 and the "People's Party now says their constitution has been adopted and that they shall support it by all necessary means."[14] In April 1842, Dorr was elected the "People's Governor."

By May, the months-long war of words was now reaching a critical state, a potentially deadly battle over the meaning of American constitutionalism. Both sides fundamentally disagreed over how the sovereign could express its will. Each side claimed that it enjoyed the support of the relevant popular majority required to govern and, therefore, refused to yield. In late 1841, commentators frequently referred to the state of "civil commotion." Now the "commotion" looked like all-out war as Dorr and his band of devoted followers threatened "violence and conflagration."[15]

The "smallest state of the Union" was now the only one that could "boast of two governors" recorded New Yorker Philip Hone in his diary on April 21, three days after Dorr's election as the People's Governor. Hone, a former mayor of New York City, noted that Dorr and his followers were of the belief "that the State belongs to them, and that they will govern it; whilst the other party swears that it does not . . . and so they are preparing to go to blows about the matter."[16] Providence militiaman William Bailey was convinced that Thomas Dorr was motivated only by "malice and revenge." Dorr's goal, according to Bailey, was to "destroy lives and property." Not taking any chances, Bailey hired a carriage to take his wife and young son out of the city.[17] The elites living in the elegant homes on the east side of Providence, including John Whipple, the state's leading attorney and Dorr's former mentor, had already sent their loved ones to Worcester and Boston.[18]

Many of the nation's newspapers promulgated the rumor that radical Democrats in New York City had been stoking the flames of rebellion by encouraging Dorr's forces to rape and plunder.[19] In mid-May, Dorr spent a number of days in the metropolis gathering support for his cause. He was serenaded by Walsh's Spartan Band, an emblem not just of physical strength, but also of the North's workingmen's movement. The radical editor Levi Slamm used his newspaper, the *Democratic Republican New Era*, to call for weapons to be shipped to Rhode Island.[20] The *New Era* had been attacking Rhode Island's "unjust, unnatural, and disgraceful" political structure for several years, chastising the state's leaders for making property the sole determinate of political rights.[21] A September 1839 memorial in Slamm's paper invoked the language of the guarantee of republican government clause in Article IV, section 4 of the Constitution and urged Congress to interfere in Rhode Island in order to remove the "corporate charter."[22] Dorr was an ardent believer in the paper's radical agenda.[23]

On May 16, upon his return to Rhode Island via the Stonington railroad line, Dorr rode triumphantly into downtown Providence in an open-air coach. There "was quite an escort prepared to receive him [by] those who are in favor of insurrection and sedition," wrote Aurilla Moffitt, the wife of a Providence militiaman.[24] Like Napoleon's return from Elba, Dorr, who slightly resembled the French emperor in height and build and greatly admired his military exploits, intended to take up the reins as the governor of Rhode Island.[25] Dorr, who often walked with the aid of a cane, discovered an element of bravado that he never knew he possessed and gave a fiery address to a throng of supporters and onlookers. For the occasion, Dorr replaced his cane with a sword that had been given to him by a group of radical New York City Democrats.

In most circumstances, Thomas Dorr, referred to as "Wilson" by his family and friends, was not an intimidating man. He was a respectable, well-educated, religious, urbane gentleman with an impeccable pedigree. He was more comfortable with a history or law book than a sword or pistol. Careful observers of Rhode Island's political culture in the 1830s knew that Dorr was a rising star, a firebrand politico of the first order. However, no one could have predicted he would be leading a military brigade in the spring of 1842. Dorr's lifelong effort to improve himself and the world around him led directly to his becoming one of the state's leading reformers. In December 1833, he jotted down a series of notes on what he wanted to accomplish in his lifetime: reforms in the banking, education, and prison system, along with the establishment of an independent judiciary, suffrage extension, and most prominently, constitutional reform.[26] A few years later, the destruction of slavery and political rights for free black Americans were added to the list. Dorr devoted all of his considerable intellectual energy and ambition to public service. Captivated by the revolutions that tore across Europe in the early 1830s, especially the July 1830 Revolution in France and the English Reform Movement of 1831–1832, Dorr believed that he could lead Rhode Island into the modern era.

Just as Americans both before and after the Revolution attempted to regulate and exert popular control over unjust and unresponsive government, Dorr attempted to restore the political and economic system in Rhode

Island to its proper order.[27] In Dorr's analysis, the American Revolution "scattered to the winds" assumptions of "monarchial divinity and infallibility" and enshrined the belief that "all just governments rest upon the substance of natural and inalienable rights and that under God the sovereigns of the People are the People themselves."[28] A recently discovered letter from a group of Rhode Island women loyal to Dorr succinctly illustrates this Revolutionary-era connection. Eliza Shaw, Sarah Davis, Mary Stiness, Ann Buffington, and Maria Gardiner believed that Dorr endeavored "to establish a constitution . . . based upon the principles for which our Fathers bled and died in 1776." Shaw, Davis, Stiness, and Buffington believed that "a longer continuance under, and servile submission to a Government deriving its power from a Royal Charter granted by that reckless and proliferate wretch, Charles the 2nd more than 200 year ago" stamped Rhode Island citizens "with the indelible term of slaves."[29] Lower-to-middle-class women loyal to Dorr were political activists, driven by a deep-seated belief in the power of the people and, most importantly, an unwavering faith in the Democratic Party.[30] In contrast, bourgeois women identified with the Whig Party and took a strong and, indeed, vocal stance against Thomas Dorr.[31]

Adherents to a broad definition of popular sovereignty, the Dorrites claimed that their actions were within the bounds of American constitutionalism. They insisted that the rights of the people did not end with voting and petition but "included the right of the people to pass judgment on or to 'regulate' their alleged rulers."[32] As historian Christian G. Fritz has rightly noted, Dorr's "expansive view of popular sovereignty," which included the belief that the people had a right to both ordain and abolish a form of government, constituted a constitutional "middle ground" between state-sponsored revision and the "ultimate right of revolution based on sheer force."[33] Since he viewed his actions as within the bounds of American constitutionalism, Dorr never used the word "rebellion" when describing any of his actions. His opponents, of course, found it to be an accurate description.

Dorr's understanding of the people as sovereign demonstrates the continued salience of the Revolutionary-era ideology in the antebellum era. During the debate over Michigan's admission to the Union in 1837, Pennsylvania Senator James Buchanan foreshadowed the constitutional crisis in Rhode Island in a speech on the floor of the U.S. Senate. "But suppose the case of a State, whose constitution, originally good, had, from the lapse of time and from changes in the population of different portions of its territory become unequal and unjust," said Buchanan. If repeated calls for constitutional reform fell on "deaf ears," then the people could "invoke" their "sovereign capacity, to remedy" the defects in their form of government. "They are not forever to be shackled" by their representatives. The people "are the source of all power; they are the rightful authors of all constitutions," concluded the future president. Thomas Dorr wholeheartedly agreed.[34]

However, the people also had an electoral role to play, and Dorr's opponents chided him for failing to understand this. They were responsible for electing representatives to work for their interests; otherwise, every issue would force a fundamental debate about the basic workings of government. As a correspondent of New York Governor William Henry Seward noted, "It is a dangerous thing to force the people to resort to first principles, when any real or imaginary evil besets them."[35] According to U.S. Senator James F. Simmons, it was an "unheard of doctrine that the people have a right to change their government whenever they please."[36]

As the night of May 17 deepened and Providence began to resemble a city besieged, a deep sense of fear and trepidation gripped the minds of many of the men who gathered inside the arsenal awaiting orders from Quartermaster General Samuel Ames, who married Dorr's younger sister, Mary Throop, in 1839. Dorr's other sisters, Candace and Ann, had married into the Carrington and Ives families, themselves pillars of the Rhode Island aristocracy. Moses Brown Ives called for "firm, decided action" to stop the suffrage movement's "designing leaders," in particular Thomas Wilson Dorr.[37] Candace's father-in-law, Edward Carrington, Sr., sat on Governor King's executive council. Carrington, once one of the richest men in the state, had suffered huge financial losses as a result of the Panic of 1837 and was likely fearful that Dorr's reform effort would hurt his pocketbook even further.

Dorr's three younger brothers, Henry, Allen, and Sullivan, Jr.—whom he so deeply loved and helped to raise—did not come to his aid the night of May 17. The outspoken Henry Dorr saw his older brother's course of action as one that would incite violence and social disorder—staples of the French Revolution after 1791. Paranoid Rhode Island conservatives feared that Dorr would follow Robespierre's fall from grace and institute a Reign of Terror in the name of defending the people's rights. William Bailey informed his mother that he had been reading Adolphe Thiers's *History of the French Revolution* and had reached the conclusion that there "were many elements" of the French Revolution alive in Rhode Island. Dorr was "Marat, Robespierre, and Danton" rolled into one.[38] When Robespierre was "contending for the same doctrines as advocated by Dorr he drenched France in blood," declared Indiana Whig Caleb Blood Smith on the floor of the U.S. Congress.[39]

Despite desperate pleas from Lydia's prominent brothers, Crawford, Philip, and Zachariah Allen, Jr., Dorr refused to negotiate with representatives from the General Assembly.[40] There was no need. Dorr believed he had the upper hand. Seventy of Dorr's men had successfully stolen two six-pounder cannons in broad daylight from the United Train of Artillery in Providence. He now intended to make use of them.[41] If Dorr's men had dragged the cannons directly to the arsenal, they probably could have taken it without firing a shot. The arsenal, a 50-by-60-foot structure with chip stone walls, was constructed to withstand shot and shell, but its thatch roof could easily be blown off, or worse, ignited, burning those inside.[42] King called for additional reinforcements from the conservative coastal enclaves of Warren, Bristol, and Newport, former centers of the lucrative slave trade. King went to the arsenal to encourage his men to stand their ground. Shortly after two o'clock in the morning, Dorr's men set up an encampment within "musket shot" of the northeast wall of the building. At least five cannons were pointed out windows right back at his position.[43]

Rabble-rousing newspaper editors, poor laborers, and assorted urban rowdies might have clamored for a chance to shed blood, or even to take a few potshots at the arsenal, but the more worldly men of good sense still believed that diplomacy would settle the issue. They quickly discovered, however, that Dorr was not interested in compromise. The People's Governor tended to see challenges to his perception of right and wrong as the product of nefarious conspiracies against the common good of the citizenry. "It can't be possible that your brother intends to fire on this building when he knows that you, his father and his uncles are all in it," remarked a Providence militiaman to Sullivan, Jr., who was looking out a window of the arsenal at his older brother in the darkness. "I guess you are not acquainted with the breed," young Sullivan was said to have replied.[44] If this were to be his final battle, Dorr intended to go out like a cannonade. He would willingly become a "martyr to the cause of Democracy."[45]

From a distance, southern slaveholders followed events in Rhode Island with a close eye. Dorr's past membership in the American Anti-Slavery Society (1837–1839) led to frequent charges that he was a diehard abolitionist. Slaveholders worried that Dorr's intention was to spread his "revolutionary spirit south."[46] Southerners looked with trepidation on anyone who adopted a literal interpretation of the alter or abolish provision in Thomas Jefferson's Declaration of Independence. The extensive coverage devoted to the rebellion in southern newspapers, such as the *Charleston Courier* and the *Southern Patriot*, shows that proceedings in Rhode Island were watched closely. Dorr's attempt at extralegal reform was enjoined with the increasingly heated national debate over slavery. Proslavery southern Whigs and Democrats believed that Dorr's ideology threatened to "convert the numberless blacks of the South into voters, who could vote down the Southern state governments at their pleasure."[47] As the abolitionist David Lee Child noted in the *National Anti-Slavery Standard*, the reform effort in Rhode Island was "precisely" a "movement that Southern statesmen" had "warned" of "as being analogous to slave insurrection in the South."[48] If it was "decided" that the "disfranchised majority" in Rhode Island could "recover" their lost rights, it would be of "great interest" to the "disfranchised majority in South Carolina" declared the *Emancipator and Free American*, a Boston abolitionist newspaper.[49]

In addition to his reliance on Jefferson's Declaration, Dorr often turned to the guarantee of republican government clause in Article IV of the Constitution. Dorr believed that Charter government was simply not republican and therefore needed to be replaced. During this period, abolitionists, most notably William Goodell, began to use the clause to serve antislavery ends. Southern states with their enslaved populations were deemed unrepublican.[50] Providence Congressional minister Mark Tucker, no fan of Thomas Dorr, explicitly linked the political reform movement in Rhode Island with Goodell's antislavery efforts.[51]

Dorr's early political career was in line with what historian Jonathan Earle has labeled "Jacksonian antislavery."[52] Dorr's relationship with prominent antislavery advocates in the 1830s—such as James Birney, Wendell Phillips, Lewis Tappan, Arnold Buffum, and John Greenleaf Whittier—along with his attendance at numerous meetings of the American Anti-Slavery Society in New York City led to frequent charges a decade later that he intended to spread his doctrine of the people's sovereignty to the American South. During the People's Convention in the fall of 1841, Dorr fought valiantly for the rights of black Rhode Islanders—a fight that represented the culmination of the Revolution's values of liberty and equality. However, the majority of the delegates believed a white-only clause was necessary to ensure success at the polls. After learning of the clause, Pawtucket abolitionist Susan Sisson declared that only the abolitionists were the "true champions of freedom" in Rhode Island.[53] Neither "the old charter nor the free suffrage parties have any claim to the sympathies of abolitionists, inasmuch as both are radically wrong . . . the former making property and the latter color the basis of suffrage," proclaimed the *Emancipator and Free American*.[54]

In an intense campaign against the People's Constitution, the ex-slave Frederick Douglass and Abby Kelley, the high priestess of New England abolitionism, descended on Rhode Island to display their polemical brilliance and their ferocious critical bite. It was a revolutionary, chaotic situation in Rhode Island in late 1841. Dorr worked hard to achieve a color-blind democracy in the midst of a deep and abiding division over race, but in the end his fellow delegates opted to define citizenship as the exclusive province of whites. This "glaring inconsistency" could not have "escaped the cognizance of even the most prejudiced minds," wrote a correspondent of the Cincinnati *Philanthropist*, a prominent abolitionist tract founded by the two-time Liberty Party presidential candidate James Birney in 1836.[55]

Dorr's life and the rebellion he led in the spring of 1842 are significant in their own right, but they also provide a window into the turbulent and shifting world of antebellum politics. The intense national interest in Rhode Island created an unparalleled written record, which highlights the partisan debate between Jacksonian views of popular sovereignty and the Whig commitment to the rule of law.[56] As historian Sean Wilentz has argued, Dorr's reform efforts constituted "a striking [and] exceptional case in the history of American democratization before the Civil War."[57] Democrats, according to the party's semi-official organ the *Democratic Review*, gleefully "strove to associate their Whig opponents with the suppression of republican institutions and the repudiation of democratic principles."[58] Dorr argued that the Whigs should "surrender" their "title" which was "stolen in grand larceny from the democrats of '76. Let Whigs call themselves Federalists, Tories, nationalists, native, raccoon republicans anything but Whigs, the glorious title of the men who established our liberty."[59]

The broad-based and far-reaching discussions of the people's sovereignty in Rhode Island also reveals the contention between proslavery and antislavery politics in antebellum America. While northern Democrats nearly universally hailed Dorr's conception of the people as sovereign, Democrats south of the Mason Dixon line were apprehensive. Southern Democrats' disdain for the people's sovereignty in 1842–1844 foreshadows their lukewarm support for Lewis Cass's and Stephen A. Douglas's attempts to use the ideology to settle the dispute over the status of slavery in the western territories. John Calhoun and other southern Democrats could not endorse a theory that on the surface seemed to allow antislavery settlers in the Mexican Cession the right to pass laws prohibiting slavery. Southern Democrats argued that settlers could determine the status of slavery only when they drafted a constitution and sought admission to the Union. This would give southern settlers enough time to move west. As one of Dorr's correspondents correctly noted, although the "sovereignty of the people" was in the "hearts of the great democratic mass" in the North, the idea had met with "limited reception" in the South, especially with the "disciples" of Calhoun.[60]

Finally, this book details the ways in which a strong antislavery politician like Dorr eventually turned away from his principles in the 1850s. A complex man, Dorr's later years were marred by a lack of consistency. In the 1850s, Dorr became increasingly resentful of holier-than-thou abolitionists, who, he believed, threatened the strength of the Democratic Party and, by extension, the Union itself. It was, in some ways, an ironic twist of fate for a man whose ideology had threatened to do the same a decade before.

Chapter 1

Beginnings

The actual, living majority of the day possess the true sovereignty of the country and has a right to investigate, revise and amend its political constitution.

TWD to William Bridges Adams, November 7, 1831

"My efforts from the beginning to the end of my public life have been uniformly for the extension of suffrage & a free constitution," dictated a sick and lame Thomas Dorr in 1847. The bachelor Dorr, two years removed from a stint in the state penitentiary, was living in his father's elegant home on Benefit Street in Providence. After his release from prison, Dorr frequently spent months in bed, suffering from severe "rheumatic troubles." Only his hope in Jesus Christ, maintained the devout Episcopal, "sustained" him in his darkest hours.[1] Dorr's closest friend, Walter S. Burges, and his mother, Lydia, stood by taking notes as he rattled off the history of his public career. Just a few months shy of his forty-second birthday, Dorr offered his thoughts in the hopes that Burges or his mother would find a suitable biographer. He had been trying for two years to find an appropriate person to record the events of his life for posterity. Dorr had already arranged his correspondence, completing an index for the voluminous letters he had saved. Dorr clearly feared that the end was near; he said he was "dangerously ill."[2]

Dorr hoped that Burges would share the intricate details of his life story with John O'Sullivan, editor of the famous *Democratic Review*, a heavily partisan, Democratic-leaning New York political and literary journal. Dorr and O'Sullivan first met each other in the 1830s, when Dorr was living in Brooklyn, frequently summering together in Stockbridge, Massachusetts.[3] O'Sullivan was connected with a group of self-conscious literary nationalists collectively known as Young America. Writers such as O'Sullivan, William

Jones, Jedediah Auld, and Russell Trevett, along with novelists Herman Melville and Nathaniel Hawthorne, ensured Young America's entrance into the literary canon. From its inception in 1837, the central hallmark of the *Democratic Review*, as historian Ted Widmer has argued, was "its unrelenting emphasis on youth." The magazine "sounded this theme" at every turn, exhorting "young Americans" to take an active role in their country's destiny. During the constitutional crisis in Rhode Island in 1842, one commentator proclaimed that as France was called "Young France" after 1830, so Rhode Island would now be known as "Young Rhode Island."[4] In 1853, Dorr helped to ingratiate O'Sullivan with the Young America President Franklin Pierce, who selected him as ambassador to Portugal. O'Sullivan informed Dorr shortly thereafter that he had three portraits hanging in his living room: Nathaniel Hawthorne; Narciso Lopez, the Venezuelan general whose invasion of Cuba in 1857 was supported by O'Sullivan; and Thomas Wilson Dorr.[5]

Even if he had the inclination to undertake a biography of Dorr, O'Sullivan would surely have been selective in discussing the various ways in which his old friend was, as Dorr put it, "devoted to matters of public utility and general improvement."[6] The Irish editor would have focused exclusively on the events of 1841–1842, ignoring or distorting the memory of Dorr's wide-ranging reform efforts, especially his close connection to northern abolitionists in the 1830s. Dorr's early life would have received the same cursory treatment O'Sullivan gave it in his July 1842 biographical portrait in the *Democratic Review*.[7] O'Sullivan and his Young America cohorts were inspired by a messianic vision of democracy, principally westward expansion and manifest destiny. In article after article, O'Sullivan sounded the expansionist creed: "More, more, more will be the unresting cry, till our national destiny is fulfilled and the whole boundless continent is ours."[8] After witnessing the potentially dangerous effects of sectionalism at the 1844 Democratic convention, O'Sullivan and his allies poured their energy into smoothing tensions by promoting popular sovereignty as a panacea for the vexing question of the status of slavery in the western territories. Dorr's reform efforts in the 1830s, especially his friendship with the noted abolitionist John Greenleaf Whittier and his antislavery activism, simply did not fit that agenda.

Thomas Wilson Dorr was born into a privileged social environment in Providence on November 5, 1805. The first families of Providence—including the Carringtons, Browns, Ives, Arnolds, Allens, and Dorrs—attached considerable importance to rank. The class consciousness that pervaded the city was not based on hereditary aristocracy alone, but also on property and material wealth. Birth and property combined to determine class structure. Thomas Dorr's grandfather, Ebenezer Dorr, was a Roxbury, Massachusetts, leather dresser and successful merchant who took a leading role in the American Revolution, working with Paul Revere and the Sons of Liberty. In the 1790s, Ebenezer sailed the globe, trading fur and sandalwood in China in exchange for tea, silk, and chinaware.[9] As his trading empire expanded, it became necessary to have a family member stationed in China. The task fell to Ebenezer's son, Sullivan, who moved to Canton in 1799. In Canton, Sullivan was joined by another prominent New England merchant, Edward Carrington, Sr., who served as U.S. consul and an agent for other American merchants. The two men amassed a sizeable fortune during their time in the Orient. After nearly four years of managing the overseas interests of the family, young Sullivan returned to New England and settled in the expanding town of Providence.[10]

In 1803, Sullivan married the tall and stately Lydia Allen, the daughter of Zachariah Allen, a prominent merchant and a member of one of Rhode Island's oldest families. Lydia's great-grandfather, Gabriel Bernon, was a prominent French merchant who fled that country in 1686 after Louis XIV revoked the Edict of Nantes. Bernon's second wife, Mary Harris, was the daughter of one of the five men who accompanied Roger Williams to Rhode Island in 1636.[11] Bernon founded King's Episcopal Church (later renamed St. John's) in 1722. Based on his family's pedigree, Thomas Dorr was certainly "no interloper" in Rhode Island.[12]

In 1805, Sullivan Dorr netted an incredible profit of $100,000 after months of extensive trading in Europe, which enabled him to hire the prominent architect John Holden Greene to design and build a mansion in Providence that would signal his emergence as one of the state's leading men.[13] Sullivan and Lydia, along with their two young boys, Thomas (age four) and Allen (age two), moved into the stately home on Benefit Street in 1809. The house, which sat atop a commanding hill overlooking the Providence cove, was fittingly built on the original burial site of Roger Williams. In August 1836, Thomas Dorr was a fitting choice to give an oration celebrating the 200th anniversary of the founding of Rhode Island.[14] The remaining Dorr children were all born and raised in the stately mansion, the inside of which was decorated by the renowned Italian artist Michele Cornè.[15] The cosmopolitan Sullivan Dorr commissioned Cornè to paint a life-size fresco of the Bay of Naples in his parlor and front hallway.[16]

The Dorr children grew to adulthood in a society that was undergoing immense and wrenching change brought on by capitalist development, westward expansion, a transportation revolution, a rapidly transforming class structure, and massive immigration. The nation's agrarian society was slowly being overshadowed by a more complex, progressive, and interconnected one in which considerations of the marketplace increasingly took precedence. In the North, the building of canals and the advent of steamboats, and later, railroads set in motion economic changes that created an integrated economy of commercial farms and growing urban centers. Concomitantly, state governments, particularly Rhode Island's, built transportation networks that channeled this development. The first cotton mill in the United States was built by the English immigrant Samuel Slater in the North Providence mill village of Pawtucket in 1790. The Blackstone River quickly became one of the most heavily exploited streams in the northeast. Mills were built in the Blackstone River Valley and its tributaries from northwestern Rhode Island to Pawtucket, five miles from Providence.[17]

In the early nineteenth century, Providence was a low-lying city, dominated by the waterfront. The masts of sailing ships stood higher than anything else erected by man. In the decades before the American Revolution, Providence stood in the shadow of Newport, a coastal city with a deep protected harbor on the Atlantic Ocean. Newport was a bustling seaport and the home of some of the state's leading merchants, including Abraham Redwood and Aaron Lopez. However, after the lengthy British occupation of the city during the Revolution, Providence merchants began to chip away at Newport's hold on the state's economic reins.

In the early nineteenth century, manufacturing slowly replaced maritime activity as the central element in Providence's economy, and industry was now the principal outlet for capital investment and wealth accumulation. Following the establishment of Slater's famous mill, industrialization transformed Providence and its outlying areas into a premier manufacturing center. The four Brown brothers—Nicholas, Moses, John, and Joseph—led the way in Providence with their candle and iron factories. Following the Brown brothers' lead, Sullivan Dorr, like other wealthy businessmen, diversified his activities by entering into cotton and woolen manufacturing, insurance, and banking.

As Providence expanded into one of the most industrialized cities in the country, it acted as a magnet for foreign laborers seeking work and a better way of life. Providence grew to more than 12,000 inhabitants by the mid-1820s. A bridge connected the older east side, where the Dorr mansion sat, to the expanding west side, with banks and businesses lining a central market square, along with a fashionable shopping district known as Cheapside after London's commercial strip. A massive granite arcade, modeled after a Greek temple, built in 1828 on Weybosset Neck symbolized the growing commercialism in the city and provided an alternative to the hustle and bustle of shopping on crowded city streets.[18] In 1835, the railroad came to Providence, winding its way southward from Boston, while one from Stonington reached the west bank of the Providence River in 1837.[19]

According to the 1840 census, the number of mills in and around Providence rose from four to thirty, capital quadrupled, and the labor force expanded seventyfold. Providence, one of five rotating sites hosting the state's capital, now claimed a population close to 24,000, double its number of two decades before, but the proportion of representatives for each town remained as it had been in the eighteenth century, when both population and wealth were concentrated in Newport and the southern regions of the state. Even though these areas were rapidly declining in population as the nineteenth century wore on, the 1663 Charter afforded them great political clout and, according to the Cincinnati *Daily Enquirer*, allowed the "Rhode Island nobility" to continue "an oligarchy of white slaves."[20]

Providence's neighborhoods were structured by class and race, with working-class whites and blacks living in new kinds of housing, such as boardinghouses and tenements. Since fewer than 10 percent of the adult white males in the expanding metropolis had any say in political matters, unrest simmered just beneath the surface. Adding to the segmentation was the more geographically clustered and more assertive black community in the city, who established the African Union Meeting House in 1819. In October 1824, a white mob attacked the predominantly black neighborhood of Hard Scrabble in the northerly section of the city after a group of blacks refused to give way on the sidewalk to a group of whites. City authorities stood by and watched as a war of words turned violent. Though hearings were conducted, none of the rioters were ever punished.[21]

Sullivan Dorr's successful economic ventures allowed him to educate his sons in a pastoral setting, secure from the physical and moral corruptions of the increasingly urbanized Providence. Thomas Dorr, who first attended the Providence Latin Grammar School, went to Phillips Exeter Academy in 1817. Dorr's uncles, Crawford, Philip, and Zachariah Allen, Jr., were all Exeter graduates and likely influenced his parents' decision to send their young boy to the New Hampshire boarding school, which had already developed a reputation as one of the top educational institutions in the country. All three Allen uncles would later attend Brown University and go on to become the foremost industrialists in Rhode Island, constructing mill villages in the northern part of the state and entering into a manufacturing partnership with Sullivan Dorr in 1832.[22] Phillips Exeter Academy was incorporated in 1781 by the wealthy merchant John Phillips, whose nephew Samuel Phillips founded Phillips Academy in Andover, Massachusetts, in 1780.[23] Since dormitories were not built at Exeter until 1855, Thomas Dorr, and later his younger brother Allen, stayed with members of the community in homes that bordered the school's property. The two brothers were members of the Golden Branch, a secret literary and debating society.[24]

The liberal arts education the Dorr brothers received at Exeter provided them with the genteel qualities required of societal leaders. As historian Gordon Wood has noted, this meant "being cosmopolitan, standing on elevated ground in order to have a large view of human affairs, being free of the prejudices, parochialism, and religious enthusiasm of the vulgar and barbaric, and having the ability to make disinterested judgments about the various contending interests in the society."[25] Headmaster Benjamin Abbot wrote to Sullivan Dorr in July 1818 to inform him that his oldest son was making good "progress" in "his studies & his general deportment [has] been quite satisfactory to his Instructors." Dorr had qualified academically to graduate from Exeter in 1818, but the headmaster and his father agreed he should stay on another year to mature socially and to gain some additional learning.[26] During his time at Exeter, Dorr proved himself both mentally and physically by heading a class of intelligent and talented young men. The faculty at Exeter ingrained in Dorr an understanding of the importance of service and working towards the republican notion of the common good.

After graduating from Exeter, Dorr entered Harvard College, along with many of his Exeter classmates, at the tender age of thirteen. In this period, Harvard only averaged about 225 students and about thirty professors. The fact that thirteen- and fourteen-year-olds gained admittance demonstrates that the requirements were not strenuous. The bulk of the curriculum was comprised of Latin, Greek, mathematics, English composition, history, logic, moral philosophy, and modern languages. During Dorr's time at Harvard, most of the instruction was conducted under the recitation system in which a student memorized passages under the direction of a tutor.[27]

Dorr's relatives were very concerned with the effect the allurements of the metropolis of Boston would have on a young teenager. Unruliness had long been a part of all-male colleges, but in the early 1800s undergraduate studies at Harvard were distinguished by multiple episodes of widespread collective resistance to authority. During President John Kirkland's tenure, but particularly during the years Dorr was in attendance, Harvard students followed a course of mischief, dissipation, and riot.[28] Harvard undergraduates often played billiards at Lechmere Point, drank heavily in the Marlboro Hotel, and contracted venereal disease after illicit liaisons with Boston's women of ill repute. Food fights, public drunkenness, and barn fires in Harvard Yard with college property as the combustible were just a few of the antics in which Dorr's classmates took part.[29] Jason Whitman, a friend of Dorr's at Exeter, noted that the "punishments although intended . . . to have a corrective influence on the character of the scholars," generally had the opposite effect.[30] Believing their rights to be violated after sanctions were doled out, students often forcibly remonstrated and committed further acts of insubordination. The administration won every battle, but the victories were not without cost. Numerous students were expelled and Harvard's reputation suffered.

One of the oldest surviving letters in Thomas Dorr's correspondence is from his merchant uncle Samuel Adams Dorr, who wrote to his nephew from Canton, China. Samuel Dorr warned his young and impressionable nephew to pick his friends carefully, to stay clear of trouble, focus on his studies, and "conform" to the rules set forth by Harvard's trustees. Samuel Dorr was well aware that Harvard undergraduates were "apt to raise turmoil & effect combinations in direct hostility to their teachers." Dorr's uncle implored him to keep in mind that "the sons of Harvard must in some fact be considered as public property & those selfish views of individual aggrandizement must give place to more elevated notions of public utility."[31] Dorr took his uncle's advice to heart. The Harvard library records indicate that Dorr spent a great deal of time reading the massive works of Hume and Gibbon, among others, while many of his classmates engaged in drunken, disorderly behavior.

In 1819, Dorr's class consisted of eighty-one students, but less than half that number made it to commencement exercises four years later. On the eve of the 1823 graduation, the Great Rebellion, as it is known in Harvard lore, shook the old Yankee institution of higher learning to its core and led to the expulsion of dozens of students. Dorr's tutor, the twenty-three year old George Bancroft, who would gain great fame as a historian, declared in April 1823 that "the year . . . which should have been perfectly happy and cheerful for me, [had] been the most wretched" of his life.[32] Dorr became close with Bancroft, who had graduated from Exeter in 1813. Dorr often came to Bancroft's aid when disturbances broke out. Apparently being a tutor in this period was risky business.[33]

In October of Dorr's sophomore year, the "rebellious spirit" at Harvard was in full swing.[34] The class had a "severe battle in Commons Hall" with the freshmen "demolishing doors and windows and destroy[ing] all the crockery, china, etc." Two nights later, students ignited a large fire in front of University Hall. The fire was followed by the "dropping" of a "large cannon ball from the fourth story" of a dormitory with an "insulting note" attached and addressed to the proctor of the dorm. After suspending the offending student, the faculty voted "that any student found to have a cannon ball or bomb shell in his possession shall be fined not less than one dollar."[35] The administration apparently had good reason to believe that other students were walking around campus with cannon balls in their knapsacks waiting to drop them on unsuspecting tutors.

While his later actions would lead one to believe that Dorr must have been the leader of the radical fringe, Dorr disapproved of his classmates' rebellious antics. On November 5, 1820, Dorr's fifteenth birthday, fifteen students left campus without permission. Dorr chose to celebrate his birthday quietly in the library. His name was subsequently entered on a "Black List." According to his classmate Pickering Dodge, those on the Black List were "very much irritated at the neglect and coldness they receive from the class," and sought to "avenge themselves by becoming spies and informers."[36]

A satiric poem lambasting those loyal to President Kirkland included a verse about a Thomas Wilson Dorr "of Gothic size, / Whose cheeks are so huge one can scarce see his eyes; / That mighty young mammoth so highly renown'd / For the gift of the gab, though tis all empty sound." Two years later, on the anniversary of the Black List, the opponents of the administration removed Dorr's shower stall and burned it in the yard.[37] Despite the taunting and the threats, the headstrong Dorr did not give in to adolescent pressure. He most likely did not endear himself to his classmates when he decided to dedicate his senior thesis to Kirkland.[38]

In the spring of 1823, several months before the August commencement, James Woodbury made an underhanded bid to take away the coveted position of Latin orator from fellow classmate John Paul Robinson. Robinson was somewhat of an easy target because he had previously been disciplined for "irregular conduct."[39] Woodbury was the brother of Levi Woodbury, a future secretary of the treasury, U.S. Senator from New Hampshire, and U.S. Supreme Court justice. Like Dorr, Woodbury was also included on the published 1821 "Black List." Dorr's surviving correspondence indicates that he was friends with Robinson while they were students at Exeter, with both men serving as cofounders of the Golden Branch Society in 1818. However, during their years at Harvard, Dorr thought of Robinson as a "rival" because he did not "digest," as Dorr put it, "the higher standing assigned" to him by the administration.[40]

Woodbury fabricated a story about Robinson's misuse of the scholarship money that had been awarded to him. An investigation was started, and Robinson was eventually acquitted of any wrong doing. However, Woodbury did not stop. He fabricated another lie that painted Robinson as the sole individual responsible for campus unrest. Another investigation led to Robinson losing his financial assistance, along with his role at commencement, though he was not yet removed from the college.[41] Robinson's classmates rallied to his support and elected him to be the principal orator at the spring exhibition, a semiannual event in which members of the graduating class performed dramatic presentations and orations. A vote was taken to ensure that all members of the class would act appropriately at the exhibition, but Woodbury's performance, according to Pickering Dodge, "was hissed for nearly five minutes."[42] On May 2, thirty-seven students joined Robinson in the ranks of those who would not be receiving a Harvard diploma in August.[43] Due to health issues, Dorr spent the vast majority of his senior year in Providence and therefore had no role in the ensuing spat that eventually led to Robinson's dismissal.

In late August, commencement proceedings took place as scheduled, with Woodbury giving the Latin oration for the remaining thirty students, while Dorr gave a ringing Jeffersonian manifesto (in English) on the nature of human improvement and happiness. Dorr argued that "improvements keep pace with the increased illumination and consequently increased virtue of mankind." The irony of such an address given the degenerate behavior of the majority of the class was surely not lost on those in the crowd. Dorr's speech detailed mankind's progress from darkness into light. Coming out of the tradition of Jeffersonian skepticism and Enlightenment rationalism,

Dorr believed deeply in a linear progression of society towards freedom. Dorr saw Americans standing between a receding heroic past and a wonderful future just beginning to unfold. In language that he would later recycle when talking about the effect of Rhode Island's archaic governing structure on the body politic, Dorr defined "slavery" as the "subjugation of the body" and the destruction of "native independence." As was the case with the American Revolutionaries' commitment to universal liberty and their equally passionate commitment to property rights, Dorr spoke of slavery in broad terms, highlighting the enslavement of men by the false doctrines of monarchical government. Slavery debased not only the bondsmen, but also the slaveholder who was made "despicable" by the institution. The "progress of knowledge [was] connected with the progress of improvement and the increase of human happiness"—both of which were advanced by education. Dorr told his classmates that they could build a new society based on enlightened ideas about the perfectibility of men and institutions.[44]

While many of his Harvard classmates later claimed that their years in Cambridge served them little, Dorr never complained about his experience.[45] Dorr was not about to tarnish his name and embarrass his parents by throwing in his lot with rebellious students. His chosen path was to study law and assist his father with his manufacturing pursuits. However, while Dorr did not side with the Harvard rebels, a part of him admired their devotion to the cause, however foolhardy it might have been. This was a passion, a level of outright audacity, that would have had no place in the conservative Dorr household, but it slowly began to take hold in the young Dorr's mind. For the rest of his life, he would need a cause to champion, a set of principles to devote himself to in order to feel worthwhile.

After Harvard, Dorr attended lectures given by New York Chancellor James Kent, the most prominent state-level jurist in the country.[46] Dorr attended four months in early 1824 as a first course and another six months from November 1824 to April 1825. Kent was in the midst of writing his influential *Commentaries on American Law* when Dorr entered his ten-month tutelage.[47] After concluding his period of study with Kent, Dorr returned to Rhode Island to clerk in the Providence office of John Whipple, Rhode Island's foremost legal craftsman. Whipple was considered by many at the time to be the equal of the great orator Daniel Webster in the courtroom. Dorr was formally admitted to the Rhode Island bar in March 1827.[48] The young lawyer set up shop on College Street and earned income by handling matters for the prominent Boston merchant firm run by Thomas Tappan.[49] Despite his success starting his own legal practice, Dorr put his law career on hold in November 1828 to take a tour of the American South.[50] He had been suffering for the past several years with severe respiratory issues and chronic stomach pains and went on the tour to find a cure for his failing health.[51] At the age of twenty-three, Dorr could not walk without the assistance of a cane.

By March 1829, Dorr was in New Orleans, where he may have walked the streets with a young lawyer from Illinois named Abraham Lincoln, although there is no record that the two actually met.[52] Dorr and Lincoln would both be elected to their respective state legislatures as members of the Whig Party five years later. On his way to and from New Orleans, Dorr would have had contact with slaves who worked on the cotton and sugar plantations along the Ohio and Mississippi Rivers. Dorr had been raised in an aggressively entrepreneurial culture with its railroads, ubiquitous newspapers, and factories. The South was a very different world. Instead of the hum of machinery that Dorr would have heard as he strolled the streets of Providence, the sound of the lash generated the power needed for the southern economy to function. The city of Cincinnati, situated on the Ohio River, was a likely stop on any journey to the South in that period. The city was also a prominent destination for runaway slaves. New Orleans, located on the Gulf of Mexico, was the country's second busiest port and a key city in the internal slave trade market. Dorr's southern journey likely influenced his later antislavery activism in the 1830s. However, while the trip provided Dorr with exposure to the horrors of chattel slavery, it was not his first encounter with the institution of human bondage.

The gradual nature of Rhode Island's 1784 emancipation act meant that during Dorr's childhood there were still slaves in the state, with many living and working in Providence. As historian Joanne Pope Melish has pointed out, the effect of the state's manumission law was to limit the freeing of all but a handful of slaves in their prime work years; the ones most valuable to their owners were the least likely to be manumitted. In 1820, there were still forty-seven slaves in Newport and four in Providence.[53] The father of Dorcas Lippitt, a black nanny in the Sullivan Dorr household, was most likely a slave.[54] Dorr's uncle by marriage, Richard James Arnold, entered into the southern planter aristocracy, acquiring sixty-eight slaves and approximately 1,300 acres of rice and cotton land from his marriage to Louise Caroline Gindrat. A prominent businessman, Arnold split his time between Georgia and Rhode Island, summering in Newport, a city justly considered to be a southern protectorate, with several slaves attending to his needs.[55] Dorr's uncle Zachariah Allen, Jr., inherited nearly $100,000 from his father and invested it in the building of a North Providence textile mill and village in 1822. A portion of Allen's inheritance came from his father's ownership of two slave ships, the brigs *Nancy* and *Susannah*, which made several illegal voyages out of Rhode Island in the mid-1790s.[56]

After his southern tour, Dorr chose not to return to Rhode Island immediately. He settled instead in New York City, where he mainly lived off an allowance from his father.[57] Dorr also spent time in Philadelphia visiting various doctors, seeking medical treatment. Though he was not formally admitted to the bar in New York City until May 1831, Dorr used his legal training to assist his father in various ventures relating to his insurance business.[58] It was during this period that Dorr met the prominent lawyer David Dudley Field, one of the leaders of the codification movement in America. Codification, which was Dorr's "favorite plan" of legal reform, represented a democratic movement for access to justice.[59] A perfect legal code would require no intermediaries between the law and the people. With precedent and practice reduced to principle, everyone could know the law. Field's focus was on reducing the expense, delay, excessive formality, and confusion of common law litigation.[60]

Dorr's intellectual development was also influenced by the revolutions that tore across Europe in the 1830s, especially those in France, England, and Poland. Civil unrest and revolution were endemic to Europe after the Congress of Vienna in 1815, with conservative governments fighting off liberal rebellions. Dorr followed closely the international drama of freedom that was gripping post-Napoleonic Europe. "It seems to be in the order of Providence that crowned heads and aristocratic bodies in whose hands is lodged an unjust portion of political power should learn nothing from history . . . and at last lose everything in the convulsion of revolution," wrote Dorr in 1831. Dorr sincerely hoped that the Poles, whose country was partitioned among three powers, would be able to break away from the "barbarian forces" of the Russian czar and enter the liberal age. Dorr prayed that "changes favorable to the knowledge, virtue, liberty and general improvement of the whole mass of the people may be successfully accomplished where they have commenced, and spreading where they have not been; and that even the regions of Asia and Africa may not long remain unvisited by the genius of gradual reformation." Dorr expressed sympathy for the recent bloodless revolution in France that removed the Bourbons from power. He saw this "battle" as symbolizing the freedom struggle in Europe. On July 26, 1830, King Charles X of France published four arbitrary ordinances which tightened restrictions on newspapers, dissolved the newly elected chamber, and changed the electoral laws so as to eliminate most of the middle-class voters. One thing that he forgot to do, however, was to call for extra troops to guard the capital. As Dorr noted, there was "no other civilized country which [was] so dependent on its capital."[61] Parisians responded as they had so often done before—with armed insurrection. "The lower classes of Paris are not better informed than the mechanics of England, but they have been used to more practical freedom and moreover they have seen kings and nobles kicked about like ordinary men," wrote a close friend of Dorr's.[62] After three days of sporadic street fighting, Charles X abdicated his throne, eventually paving the way for Louis Philippe, the new "King of the French," to take over. Dorr communicated frequently with his mother, Lydia, about the 1830 Revolution in France. "The French blood which flows in our veins entitles us to partake in the public sympathy espoused toward the brave defenders of freedom in France and to hail the glorious result of the late revolution," wrote Dorr to Lydia, a descendant of French Huguenots.[63]

Dorr, like many liberal onlookers, was displeased that the monarchy still remained in France, but he was confident the road was now paved for the transition from a "citizen-king" to a "republican chief." Dorr viewed the July Revolution, which established a more liberal regime dominated by the wealthy bourgeoisie, "as a successful attempt to assert the natural rights of our species." Quoting directly from Thomas Jefferson's letter to Robert Weightman, the mayor of Washington, D.C., a missive that also happened to be the Sage of Monticello's final letter, Dorr proclaimed: "the mass of mankind were not born with saddles on their backs and a favored few booted and spurred ready to ride them legitimately by the grace of God." Dorr was emphatic in what he saw as the march of global liberty that would "encourage the oppressed of all nations in the work of overturning those corrupt and despotic systems, which insult and disgrace the civilizations of the nineteenth century." For the first time, Dorr mentioned the "right of the people to alter or abolish" a form of government that did not conform to democratic ideals. A "recurrence to the popular sovereignty" was "always," according to Dorr, "a right and true remedy." In Dorr's view, the July Revolution had brought the "greatest happiness to the greatest number" and had been directed by energetic "young men."[64] Dorr's notion of the power of youth would be something to which he would return to in a few years when discussing the power of abolitionists in their crusade against slavery.

Dorr's correspondence reveals that his political ideas were forged within a context of transatlantic democratic ferment and, most particularly, the product of cross-pollination between British and American liberal reform ideology.[65] This is clearly spelled out in Dorr's lengthy letters to George Townshend Fox, a British visitor to America, and British railroad engineer and political reformer William Bridges Adams. Dorr and Adams struck up a great friendship, vacationing together when Adams was in the United States. The two men had a great deal in common. In the late 1820s, Adams, whose health was as fragile as Dorr's, lived abroad in South America in order to get away from the damp English climate. Both Adams and Dorr lived off allowances from their wealthy fathers while they spent time together in Brooklyn.[66] When Adams returned to England, Dorr sent him numerous portraits of his ideological hero—the Massachusetts statesman Daniel Webster, who rose to national prominence in 1830 when he delivered a famous speech in reply to South Carolina Senator Robert Hayne during the Nullification Crisis. Responding to Hayne's ardent states' rights interpretation of the Union, Webster famously declared that he favored "Liberty and Union, now and forever, one and inseparable."[67] Adams shared Dorr's reverence for Webster.

The political philosopher John Stuart Mill later praised Adams's writings in his classic work, *On Liberty* (1859).[68] Adams wrote frequently for the *Examiner*, a major radical London weekly paper. The decrees in Adams's *The Political Unionist's Catechism: A Manual of Political Instruction* (1833) would later have a profound effect on Dorr. "It is a manifest injustice, that any one possessed of the requisite knowledge for judging of the merits of legislators, should be deprived of the right of suffrage, because he happens to possess no property," wrote Adams.[69] His 1832 pamphlet, *The Rights of Morality*, which was written under the pseudonym Junius Redivivus, was a lengthy, wide-ranging essay on the political culture of England and the need for reform. In discussing the "best form of government," Adams highlighted a republic's capacity to ensure equality.[70]

Through Adams, Dorr developed a deep interest in English politics. The British reformers that Dorr admired worked to achieve democratic measures, including universal manhood suffrage, a secret ballot, the abolition of property requirements for voting, political reapportionment, and, later, the abolishment of slavery. The hereditary House of Lords in England wielded much influence and the House of Commons was unrepresentative of the masses of the people. Thriving industrial cities like Manchester, Sheffield, and Leeds had no representatives in Parliament. The fact that the system of primogeniture in England resembled the political economy of Rhode Island could not have been lost on the young Dorr, who expressed disgust that in such a "liberal age" a large mass of English citizens were "kept down in the most degraded servility and degraded poverty."[71] Dorr followed the English Reform Bill crisis closely. The political imbroglio eventually ended with the passage of an inadequate, but somewhat liberalizing bill in 1832.

Despite his fondness for Adams, Dorr did not hesitate to disagree with his friend's socialist propositions. Adams was clearly farther to the left on the political spectrum and, perhaps, more closely aligned with the French socialist Charles Fourier. "The aristocracy of talent is now taking its proper station . . . rank and wealth must go down before it," wrote Adams.[72] Dorr fervently believed that Adams' *Rights of Morality* opened him up to charges of "agrarianism," a term referring to political proposals for land redistribution from the rich to the poor or landless. The "poor man, who does not now enjoy his share of the fruits of the earth according to the benign provision of his maker," would, Dorr argued, be led to believe that he had the right to take the property of the rich without waiting for the "slow process of legislation."[73] Indeed, Adams said he was averse to "bit-by-bit and as-little-as-need-be Reforms."[74]

Dorr did believe, however, that the "younger men in England" were steeped in the "republican truth that the actual, living majority of the day possesses the true sovereignty of the country and has a right to investigate, revise and amend its political constitution, and to accommodate it to the just demands and necessities of the people."[75] Dorr argued that "the perverse system" that "assigns to one man, or to a few men, vast tracts of land, to a large body, only such small portions as barely suffice to subsist them, and to the majority, absolutely no share at all of the earth's surface" was undemocratic. A large part of this majority, said Dorr, became "virtually the slaves of the favored few, hewers of wood and drawers of water, feeding upon remnants, ignorant and corrupt." Yet, it was "not the operation of a leveling system for which success is implored," said Dorr "but of an elevating one, that raised men to the feeling of personal worth and independence."[76] When government "ceases to accomplish the purposes or performs them imperfectly, entire change or reformation," was "necessary," in Dorr's analysis. According to Dorr, nothing could "impair the right of the majority to alter and amend government which was originally permitted if not formally constituted for the general good."[77] In 1832, George Townshend Fox issued a strong rebuke to Dorr for repeating this sentiment in a letter. Fox, who believed that Dorr had grown too close to Adams, said he "disapprove[d]" of "radicalism," which would "represent the interest of the people as completely opposed to the government, recommending measures which tend only to anarchy and insubordination."[78] Fox's charges would later be echoed by Dorr's opponents in 1842.

In the years to come, Dorr's commitment to popular sovereignty would only grow stronger, as would his penchant for other reform efforts. As historian Mark Schantz has argued, nineteenth-century males with chronic illnesses frequently "hurled themselves into the heady evangelical work of temperance reform, education, and abolitionism." To be chronically ill in nineteenth-century America often meant that one had "special duties and precise obligations, the fulfillment of which were made all the more imperative by the unpredictability of the disease."[79] Dorr's precarious health gave him a sense of urgency that led him to become one of the most influential reformers of his age. His relationship with William Bridges Adams stoked the reform fire that was burning in his heart and his uncle Samuel's admonishment that he not abandon the principles of republicanism that were imbued in him at Exeter formed his ideological construction.

Chapter 2

Jacksonian Dissident

The time may soon arrive when no man will be permitted to hold a seat in the Congress of the United States either as a Senator or as a Representative . . . who will sit still in his place and hear a Southern aristocrat denounce death to every opponent of slavery who shall cross the line, without one thought of honest indignation and without one word of manly reprove.

TWD to Edmund Quincy, September 29, 1838

After living in Brooklyn, New York, for over two years, Thomas Dorr moved back to Providence in late 1831 and resumed his legal practice on College Street. Dorr arrived in his hometown shortly after a deadly, multi-day riot between white sailors on shore leave and local blacks. Dorr's uncles, Zachariah and Crawford Allen, his uncle-by-marriage, Richard James Arnold, and Edward Carrington, Sr., a business associate of his father, were appointed to a committee to investigate the causes of the riot. The committee was mainly concerned with the threat to private property and the consequences of so many people on the fringe of society living in a tightly knit area. As a result of the riot, the Providence town government obtained a city charter and increased the size of its watch.[1]

Amidst this turmoil, Dorr's younger brother Henry and sisters Mary, Candace, and Ann were surely happy to have their brother back home. Henry, who idolized his older brother, was looking forward to Thomas stopping by Benefit Street to play with Nero, the family's beloved dog.[2] Ann was most likely disappointed that Thomas returned to Rhode Island a single man without any serious prospects for a wife. While he was living in Brooklyn, she pestered him about his dating habits. Despite Thomas's chronic health issues, Ann still deemed her brother a very eligible bachelor.[3] Dorr, however, was too concerned with his legal practice and burgeoning political career to be bothered with dating. Dorr's skills as an attorney led the state's longtime prosecutor to seek his help in a sensational murder trial.

In 1833, Dorr assisted Albert C. Greene in prosecuting David Gibbs and Frances Leach for the murder of Sally Burdick, a wash girl in an inn in Coventry, Rhode Island. Sullivan Dorr had hired Greene's father to build the elegant family home on Benefit Street three decades earlier. The fact that Greene selected the twenty-eight-year-old Dorr to not only co-chair the prosecution but to give the opening argument in an extremely high-profile and complex case shows that Dorr was well versed in criminal law. In the courtroom Dorr squared off against his legal mentor, John Whipple. The prosecution believed that after innkeeper David Gibbs learned that he had impregnated Sally Burdick, he hired Frances Leach, a known abortion-ist, to "doctor off" the unborn child.[4] Gibbs, fearful of exposure, traveled the nearly thirty-mile ride to Providence in the cover of darkness to secure Leach's services, leaving Burdick locked in the inn. Leach journeyed to Coventry disguised in man's clothing to perform the abortion. Her first at-tempt failed; another attempt using a different method killed both the fetus and Burdick. To contemporary observers it was another "Avery" case.[5]

In December 1832, Sarah Cornell, an unmarried thirty-year-old factory worker, was found hanging by the neck near a haystack on a local farm. The suspected perpetrator was Methodist minister Ephraim Avery, and Albert C. Greene set out to prosecute him. Though Dorr was not part of the pros-ecution team he followed the case closely and wrote a lengthy pamphlet about the trial under the pseudonym "Aristides."[6] Ephraim Avery was even-tually acquitted in June. In October 1833, Greene got another opportunity to prosecute a suspected murderer.[7] Greene and Dorr argued that both Gibbs and Leach should be convicted of first-degree murder. However, the jury, despite extensive physical evidence, returned with a manslaughter convic-tion for Leach and let Gibbs go free. As one newspaper proclaimed, Rhode Island's jurors had become "notorious" for "softening down murder to manslaughter."[8] Demonstrating his considerable courtroom skill, John Whipple managed to exploit testimony from several women that described how Sally Burdick had fallen from a carriage shortly before she died and, therefore, the internal bleeding that led to her death was not caused by an abortion.[9]

After the trial, Dorr devoted his energy to his legal practice handling matters for his father's insurance firm. Eventually Dorr's thriving legal career afforded him the opportunity to pursue his growing passion for politics and reform. In the early 1830s, Providence was not lacking in reformers. Labor leaders, such as William Tillinghast, Franklin Cooley, and Seth Luther, were airing their grievances in the streets and in the columns of the city's newspaper calling themselves the "friends of Free Suffrage."[10] In an address to a group of Brooklyn mechanics, Luther attacked the "aristocracy" and claimed that workingmen were "the real and only producers of wealth."[11] In an 1833 pamphlet, Luther, one of New England's best-known labor radicals and uncompromising critic of the emerging industrial order, openly declared what Dorr had privately noted to William Bridges Adams the year before. The People "have a right to assemble in primary meetings, and appoint delegates to a Convention," said Luther. "If the people adopt a constitution in this convention" it would become "the law of the land." Luther also argued that Rhode Island's archaic form of government was "not republican" and, therefore, violated Article IV, section 4 of the federal Constitution, which guaranteed to each state a republican form of government. Interweaving revivalism Christianity with the rhetoric of Revolutionary-era republicanism, Luther attacked Rhode Island's $134 freehold suffrage requirement, informing his readers that the "voice of the People" was "the voice of God."[12] During their careers, both Luther and Dorr fought an uphill battle to ensure that their voices and the voices of the working classes were heard by Rhode Island's ruling oligarchy.

In holding to the rule of law, advocating a cautious interpretation of the people's sovereignty, Rhode Island conservatives, a group that included Whigs and rural Democrats, built a bulwark against the tenets of Jacksonian democracy.[13] Conservative Whigs and Democrats still clung tenaciously to the belief that a freehold demonstrated a permanent interest in the community, along with proving a person's disinterestedness and independence.[14] The 1663 Charter restricted suffrage to those men possessing real estate (figure set at $134 in 1798). The restrictive franchise clauses based on stringent property qualifications prevented new waves of immigrants (mostly Irish Catholics) in the 1820s and '30s from entering the body politic. The political culture of Rhode Island was certainly unique. By the early decades of the nineteenth century, as states rewrote their constitutions yet again, manhood became the most important qualification for voting rights. As Henry Crawford Dorr, Thomas's younger brother, nicely put it, the "dust of antiquity had settled thickly down upon the institutions" of Rhode Island. It was now "time that it was removed—that the clogged political machinery should be lubricated and the improvements of modern times introduced."[15] For the time being, Thomas followed his brother's recommendation to push for reform from within the existing political system.

In the mid-1830s, the political reform initiative passed from the hands of Seth Luther and William Tillinghast to middle-class reformers.[16] From the start of his political career in 1834, Dorr was connected with a third-party effort comprised of middle-class reformers aiming to change Rhode Island's archaic governing structure.[17] Rhode Island is "an anomaly among her sister states much as her government is founded upon a charter granted by a British king while her sister states have established governments founded upon the express consent of the People themselves," wrote Christopher Robinson, a key figure in the Constitutionalist Party.[18] Robinson, Dorr, and other party leaders were businessmen and professionals from the northern industrial towns in the state. In March 1834, Dorr was the principal author of an address to the citizens of Rhode Island on the question of political reform and the "inherent right" of the citizenry to call a constitutional convention.[19] In his first major political tract, the twenty-nine-year-old Dorr argued that no "form of a constitution can be worth much, which leaves to the representative servants of the people the power of determining the rights of the people as voters." Drawing on what he learned from William Bridges Adams, Dorr forcibly maintained that political participation was a "natural right" that could not be abridged. Invoking the Constitution's guarantee of republican government clause, just as Luther had done, Dorr posited that the "very nature" of this elusive clause dealt with the majority of the citizens having the capacity to control their government.[20] However, despite Dorr's concerted efforts, the Constitutionalist Party never enjoyed much success because neither the Whigs or the Democrats, which were still controlled by conservative landowners and businessmen, supported it.

The fallout from the Panic of 1837, the effects of which actually began to be felt a year earlier in Rhode Island, and its severe toll on the mill villages, also served to refocus people's attention away from constitutional reform.[21] As historian Patrick Conley has argued, the Panic of 1837 "had a debilitating effect on the Constitutionalist movement, for the depression placed economic survival ahead of political rights on the average Rhode Islander's list of priorities."[22] The Constitutionalists, consisting mainly of freemen, made little progress in enlisting the active support of the disenfranchised class, and as a result the organization evaporated. A despondent Dorr argued that Rhode Island's "freeman had declined to act in the Constitutionalist cause and now freeholders were entirely indifferent as to its success and seemed quite willing to have the *foot set upon their necks.*"[23] It would not be until the mass democratic politics of the Age of Jackson reached its fruition in the election of 1840, along with the economic recovery that soon followed, that the campaign for a modern constitution would resume in earnest. In the meantime, Dorr dedicated himself to a host of other reform activities.

In April 1834, Dorr was elected as a Whig from Providence's Fourth Ward. The newly created Whig Party was united behind what was known as the American System, a combination of protective tariffs and internal improvements aided by a national bank, that in the mind of Sullivan Dorr would promote the "national interests, agriculture, commerce and manufactures" of the country.[24] The Whigs were strongest in the northeast, the most rapidly modernizing region of the country. Dorr came of age politically as the market revolution and democratic revolutions of the antebellum era reached fruition. During the first of several terms in the state legislature, Dorr attempted multifaceted reform efforts from within the ranks of a small group of "New School Whigs," who unlike many of their cohorts, were not dismayed by the democratic revolutions of the antebellum period.[25] As the editors of the *Rhode-Island Republican* noted in 1835, the young lawyer was "forever hatching some new scheme of improvement."[26]

Dorr's first big success as a legislator came in 1836 when he wrote a bill that mandated that the state invest its share of the surplus from the federal Deposit Act in education. The man who went to an elite private institution became the state's foremost champion of free, public education. Dorr believed that education was the "means whereby the human understanding is gradually enlightened and the disposition of the hand and heart directed." The "public utility of a system of education" consisted in its capacity of informing "youth to the nature of government." This was essential in preserving "free government"; it could only be done by "extend[ing] the advantages of education to all."[27] In an 1836 essay calling for the creation of a high school, Dorr argued that by establishing a "thorough system of education" the children "of the poor will no longer suffer from the want of advantages; those of the more favored in circumstances will be as well taught at less cost than at present; and those of the rich will have an opportunity to partake in instruction for all at the public expense."[28] Beginning in 1834, Dorr devoted considerable energy to the Providence School Committee, a position that required him to visit the city's schools and supervise the hiring of new teachers. In 1841, Dorr served as president of the committee, replac-

ing the longtime head, Samuel Bridgham, who died in December 1840. Dorr
spearheaded a move to complete the construction of a high school for the
city, along with getting approval for the appointment of a superintendant.
Dorr even tackled the problem of delinquency that had been ignored by his
predecessor. Dorr believed that the answer for better attendance lay with
the "People themselves" and he set out on a campaign to educate the citizenry about the importance of public education.[29]

Education was not Dorr's sole focus during this period. He also participated in an investigation into the state's banking practices, the results of
which eventually led to his severing ties with the Whig Party and a switch
to the Democracy.[30] Ready to take their chances in the new capitalist age,
the Whigs did not care about those who might not emerge from the economic maelstrom. "By investigating the banks," Dorr argued that he was
"led to consider the unsound doctrines of Whigs and Federalists on banking." The ruling Whig establishment considered Dorr a pariah due to his
desire to reform the banking system, and as a result he was "denounced, as-
sailed, [and eventually] voted out as representative."[31]

After a six-month investigation in which he examined the books of over
fifty banks, Dorr drafted a pioneering banking reform act in June 1836,
which he later maintained "was the first in any state to establish a thorough
visitation of the banks and to reduce them to their just responsibility."[32] Dorr
believed that numerous Rhode Island banks were engaged in practices that
took "advantage of the stockholders" for the "special benefit" of the bank
directors.[33] The 1836 act established three commissioners with broad, sweep-
ing power to oversee banking operations. The first commissioners were
Dorr, George Curtis, and attorney Samuel Atwell.

The June 1836 act constituted the first serious banking reform measure
in the country, much to the chagrin of Dorr's brother-in-law Moses Brown
Ives, president of the Providence Bank.[34] Rhode Island, thanks in large part
to Dorr's bill, was able to weather the economic crisis that gripped the nation
the following year.[35] The state supreme court was empowered to issue in-
junctions against bank directors who did not comply with the commissioners'
requests for information. The act provided for a ceiling on interest rates and
stipulated the amount of capital that a bank had to have in hand at its inception—$50,000. The act also required that banks recover debts in the same
manner as individual creditors. This provision was a repeal of a notorious
practice called the "bank process," which gave banks first lien on the real
property of the insolvent debtor to the virtual exclusion of other creditors.[36]

In their first report in January 1837, the bank commissioners criticized the practice whereby banks had become "to a considerable extent, mere engines to supply the directors with money." Claiming that banks "were designed to be institutions for the direct benefit of the public" rather than being "devoted chiefly to supply the want of those who managed them," the commissioners called for reform.[37] In the face of this powerful blast, the legislature passed a bill limiting a person to a single bank directorship.[38] By June of that year, however, the General Assembly passed yet another omnibus banking bill, this time over the vehement protest of Thomas Dorr. Among its provisions, the June 1837 act held that directors of savings banks could also be elected director of any other bank.[39] It was soon commonplace for major manufacturing families to have three or four banks under their control.[40] The reversal of the clause limiting directorships demonstrates the character and self-serving greed of the Rhode Island Whigs and foreshadows their behavior during the 1841–1842 constitutional crisis. The fact that Dorr had to stand by and witness the dismantling of his work surely added to his distrust of the ruling Whig elite.

Dorr's faith in the Whig Party was further shaken by the proslavery stance taken by several prominent members. After 1836, Dorr joined a small but outspoken group of northern Democrats who extended the Jacksonian battle against the Money Power to the growing Slave Power, which they deemed no less a threat to the vitality of the American democratic system as the Bank of the United States. Jacksonian rhetoric offered a powerful antislavery odium with which to attack the South's peculiar institution and their undemocratic hold on the reins of power in Washington, D.C.[41] Archconservative Whigs Benjamin Hazard and Richard Randolph, a native Virginian and nephew of General William Henry Harrison, continued the state's longstanding connection to slavery by leading a fight in 1835–1836 to enact a state gag law on abolitionists at the behest of the governors of North Carolina, South Carolina, and Georgia.[42] The acerbic Randolph was married to Ann Maria Wanton, a member of Newport's high society. It was no coincidence that after Hazard and Randolph put forth their resolutions, the Rhode Island Anti-Slavery Society was formed. Dorr led the fight in the General Assembly against the proposed gag rule.[43]

In May 1836, Dorr was appointed chairman of a select committee to consider Hazard's and Randolph's proslavery resolutions and the petitions against them.[44] Dorr called a public meeting at the statehouse in Newport for June 22 in order to allow the abolitionists a public forum to protest the charges that had been brought against them by residents of Newport and the "apologists of American Republican Slavery."[45] Hazard managed to block the abolitionist access to the statehouse on June 22. A subsequent abolitionist memorial to the General Assembly asking for permission to meet after the legislative session had concluded was rejected by a vote of 36–28. Dorr's eloquence in defense of the abolitionist right to petition, however, eventually led Hazard to remove his gag proposal from consideration by the assembly.[46]

In Washington, D.C., a young New Hampshire Congressman named Franklin Pierce, a future ally of Dorr's, proved to be instrumental in helping to steer a federal gag bill through the House of Representatives. The measure, which was proposed by Henry Laurens Pinckney of South Carolina, called for abolitionist petitions to be tabled immediately without discussion. The House approved Pinckney's motion in May 1836 by a vote of 177–68. Most northern Whigs voted in the negative, while the majority of southern Whigs, along with most Democrats, voted in the affirmative. The "gag rule" would be debated each year in Congress for the next nine years.[47]

Dorr's drift to antislavery was a natural and logical outgrowth of the positions he staked out to William Bridges Adams in the early 1830s. As Adams maintained in one of his essays, slavery was preventing America from becoming a "pure" republic.[48] Dorr's antislavery and abolitionist principles brought him into direct conflict with the wealthy merchant families of Providence, who were vehemently opposed to abolitionism. His brother-in-law Moses Brown Ives founded the Providence Anti-Abolition Society in 1835. Ironically, he was the nephew of Moses Brown, who cofounded the Providence Abolition Society in 1789.

Thomas Dorr brought an unusually intense ideological commitment to antislavery politics. Unlike many northerners, he had traveled to the Deep South. He had seen firsthand how slavery corrupted the body politic. The new, militant abolitionist movement that was coalescing in the North helped to focus evolving discussions of freedom on the sharp contradiction between liberty and bondage. A recipient of the finest education that money could buy in the antebellum world, Dorr understood the limits and possibilities that existed under the Constitution in terms of eradicating slavery.[49] Dorr sought to contain the southern hold over the reins of national power by labeling slavery a purely local institution lacking federal protection. He was clearly interested in seeing the institution die a quick, not a slow death.[50] As

was the case with the Democrat Benjamin Tappan, the brother of the abolitionists Lewis and Arthur Tappan, Dorr defined the goal of American society "as liberty for all men to retain the fruits of their labor, to pursue
individual happiness, and to participate equally in governing the community." The only way to achieve this goal was to set both white and black men
"free from the chains that had held them since time immemorial."[51]

The abolitionist crusade rose abruptly in the 1830s, coinciding exactly
with Andrew Jackson's escalating war against the banking aristocracy. The
goals of the abolitionist movement had been enunciated by William Lloyd
Garrison, the brash and bespectacled Boston journalist, in his newspaper
the *Liberator*. In the first issue of the *Liberator*, published in January 1831,
Garrison called for a "revolution in public sentiment." Before Garrison
emerged on the scene, organized antislavery was moderate, gradualistic, and
orientated to grappling with slavery at the state and local levels. Garrison
took the crusade to new levels, calling for the immediate end of slavery.
Building on Elizabeth Heyrick's 1824 pamphlet, *Immediate; Not Gradual
Abolition*, Garrison turned the "idea into a social movement."[52] As the 1835
constitution of a female antislavery organization in Rhode Island noted, the
"object of this society shall be to effect the entire and immediate emancipation of the enslaved people of color within the jurisdiction of the United
States and to obtain for them their unalienable rights as men and women as
guaranteed to the citizens of this country by its Constitution."[53]

Garrison proclaimed a new doctrine of uncompromising radicalism in
the national debate over slavery. It was a doctrine that would soon reshape
the way countless white Americans in the free states thought about slavery,
as well as what they were personally prepared to do to bring it to an end.
"It appears to me that abolitionists have now in some measure to do the work
in our society which the apostles had to do among the Jews—to bring them
up to the standard of truth which they themselves acknowledged, to point
out to them the inconsistency of their principles and practice and to urge
them to act out the doctrines they have so long professed," wrote the south-
ern-born abolitionist Angelina Grimké. "I say in some measure because I
believe the doctrines propagated by the Anti-Slavery Society are far more
grand and comprehensive than those embraced by our fathers 50 years ago,"
concluded Grimké.[54] Angelina Emily Grimké, along with her older sister
Sarah Moore Grimké, were the only white reformers of their generation
who were born into the southern aristocracy but rejected that luxurious
lifestyle to fight against the institution of human bondage.

Abolitionist lecturers were extremely active in Rhode Island in the 1830s. Quaker abolitionist Arnold Buffum helped Garrison found the New England Anti-Slavery Society in 1832. Garrison served as the secretary-treasurer, while Buffum was selected president and the organization's traveling lecturer. Buffum's daughter Elizabeth helped to organize the Fall River Female Anti-Slavery Society. In 1840, Elizabeth and her husband Samuel Chace, moved to the Valley Falls section of Cumberland where they brought the who's who of New England abolitionists to lecture, including Garrison, Sojourner Truth, Lucy Stone, Abby Kelley, and Wendell Phillips.[55] Henry Stanton, one of the fifty abolitionist "Lane rebels" who left the Lane Theological Seminary in 1834, gave over 150 lectures in Rhode Island in 1835–1836.[56] In 1837, Angelina Grimké came to Providence and delivered a fiery antislavery lecture.[57]

The formation of the Ladies Anti-Slavery Society in 1832 in Providence—a year before Providence males formed a society of their own—was encouraging to New England abolitionists. In late 1833, Raymond Potter formed the Pawtucket Anti-Slavery Society, an organization open to both males and females. A lecture by the controversial British abolitionist George Thompson in April 1835 led to the formation of the Providence Ladies' Anti-Slavery Society. Another separate female organization in the city dedicated to abolition was led by Sarah Helen Whitman, the Providence widow who captured the heart of writer Edgar Allan Poe.[58] By 1835, Providence and Pawtucket could boast of multiple, gendered antislavery societies that could help to organize lectures and meetings. Most importantly, Providence and Pawtucket were convenient stops for anyone traveling from Boston to New York or Philadelphia or vice-versa. An umbrella state organization was formed in 1836.

Despite this flurry of abolitionist activity in his own backyard, Dorr was slow to join the movement. In 1834, Dorr actually helped found a local branch of the American Colonization Society (ACS), an organization whose purpose was to "free the United States from their whole colored population."[59] The ACS, which appealed to both northern and southern whites eager to expunge slavery and avert the formation of a free black citizenry, was organized in Washington, D.C., in December 1816. Supreme Court Justice Bushrod Washington was the society's first president; other members included James Monroe, James Madison, John Marshall, Henry Clay, Francis Scott Key, and Daniel Webster—the latter of whom was Dorr's ideological hero in the 1830s. The work of the society—gradual emancipation coupled with colonization—was a key component of Henry Clay's American System and was therefore more commonly endorsed by Whigs than Democrats.[60] Black opposition to colonization was a key catalyst for the rise of immediate abolitionism in the 1830s. The difference between the two approaches to dealing with America's race problem was that colonizationists believed that blacks could never be productive members of society while abolitionists sought to help blacks achieve equal citizenship.

Unlike abolitionists, who saw an evil and wanted to eradicate it as quickly as possible, Dorr saw two issues: the "Evil of slavery [&] our right to interfere" in the states where it already existed, which he believed was limited by the federal Constitution.[61] Dorr expressed a conviction that he would hold throughout his life: The "dissolution of the Union" was "a greater evil than the continuance of slavery in this country."[62] In line with many members of the Revolutionary generation, Dorr believed in an antislavery vision that viewed slavery as morally wrong and inconsistent with American democratic ideals. He understood that the Constitution sanctioned the institution and that sectional understandings on which the Union had been created would be destroyed if the abolitionist agenda was adopted too quickly. However, Dorr also believed that the Constitution did not allow for the westward expansion of slavery and that if the slave states were cordoned off by free states, slavery would die a natural death. Dorr's antislavery convictions in the 1830s were in line with the views expressed by Salmon P. Chase two decades later. In an 1850 letter to Senator Charles Sumner, Chase described his antislavery convictions as entailing the belief that the "original policy" of the federal government was to restrict slavery and that under the Constitution, Congress could not "establish or maintain slavery in the territories." According to Chase, the Constitution had been repeatedly "violated for the extension of slavery and the establishment of the political supremacy of the Slave Power."[63]

The continued effort by southern slaveholders and their political allies in the corridors of power in Washington to stifle free expression eventually pushed Dorr into the abolitionist camp. In the later half of the 1830s, Dorr, an usually rare racial liberal and antislavery advocate in terms of nineteenth-century standards, corresponded numerous times with the abolitionist orator Wendell Phillips, the Harvard-educated Boston Brahmin, who was widely known as the "golden trumpet" of the movement.[64] In his correspondence with abolitionists in the latter half of the 1830s, Dorr praised former President-turned-Congressman John Quincy Adams's condemnation of the congressional gag rule, supported congressional efforts to abolish slavery and the slave trade in the nation's capital (the one part of the country over which the national government had undisputed authority), advocated for jury trials for fugitive slaves, and opposed the annexation of Texas. In terms of abolishing slavery and the slave trade in Washington, D.C.—the central thrust of antislavery action in this period—Dorr was in line with other leading abolitionists.[65] The debate over slavery in the nation's center of political power generated numerous legal briefs, most notably Theodore Dwight Weld's *The Power of Congress over the District of Columbia* (1838). As John Quincy Adams noted, the "adversaries of slavery" saw the campaign to abolish slavery in the nation's capital as the thin end of the antislavery wedge—a measure that would lead to the "final abolition of slavery throughout the Union."[66] The influence of Weld's political tract derived from his argument that Congress had not only the power, but the duty to abolish slavery in the nation's capital. Weld argued that Congress, as the sole legislature for the District of Columbia, had full sovereign authority to enact measures to end slavery within its geographical boundaries.[67] Dorr unequivocally agreed.

In an 1837 letter to William Chace, the corresponding secretary of the Rhode Island Anti-Slavery Society, Dorr maintained that Congress had the power to end slavery and the slave trade in the District of Columbia. Chace had written to Dorr, who was running for Congress under the Constitutionalist Party banner, in order to gauge his antislavery sentiments. Instead of merely petitioning the legislature, Chace and other abolitionists adopted the tactic known as "questioning," the formal interrogation of candidates for office to sound out their position on specific antislavery principles.[68] Dorr did not disappoint in his response, which was widely circulated in abolitionist newspapers, including Garrison's *Liberator.*[69] At a time when most politicians viewed abolitionism as a threat to the Union, Dorr, in line with John Quincy Adams, insisted those that restricted abolitionists' right to petition the national government endangered the liberty of all Americans.

In reference to a question about his position on the "gag rule," Dorr maintained that "the right not only of discussing these subjects freely, but of making known the opinions formed upon them to the representatives in their individual and collective capacities needs no agreement to enforce it." Dorr made it clear that a "candid investigation of American slavery in all its nature and bearings will satisfy most men that it ought to come to an end." Moreover, there was no danger of bringing slavery "to an end immediately," especially in the nation's capital.[70] "When public sentiment is elevated we shall move with effect upon the District," said Dorr. "That is the centre, the capital, the citadel of slavery. The *Young Men* must take it." In solid Jeffersonian fashion, Dorr maintained that when the nation's capital was "taken" back from the slave owners, "slavery in the extremities [would] die a natural death."[71] Unfortunately, abolition in the District had the active support of few Congressmen during the 1830s and never came close to realization at any time before the Civil War. Invoking the views on the potential for human progress that he had laid out in his Harvard commencement address, Dorr told Chace that abolitionists should be "encouraged by the history of the last fifty years in believing that all social evils have an ultimate and sure remedy in the power of public opinion." In closing, Dorr unequivocally affirmed his stance against bringing the Lone Star Republic into the Union.[72]

In addition to protesting slavery generally and the slave trade in the nation's capital, abolitionists in the 1830s worked tirelessly to urge politicians to work against the annexation of Texas. Dorr's antislavery beliefs resembled those expressed by the prominent Bay State Democrat Marcus Morton; however, unlike Morton, Dorr belonged to antislavery societies and served on committees.[73] In 1838, in a letter to the Boston abolitionist Edmund Quincy, Dorr characterized the notion of "republican slavery" and its expansion into new territories as antithetical to American ideals of freedom and equality.[74] During Martin Van Buren's presidency, concerns over slavery had made the annexation of Texas, along with the westward expansion of slavery in general, a particularly thorny political issue. After Mexico won independence from Spain in 1821, land-hungry Americans began to flood into its vast northern territory, which included present-day Texas, New Mexico, Arizona, Nevada, Colorado, Utah, and California. The Mexican government outlawed slavery in 1829, but the passage of the law did not deter settlers who were looking to bring their slaves into the region in order to build a cotton empire. In April 1836, forces under the command of Sam Houston, a former governor of Tennessee, routed the army of Mexican ruler General Antonio Lopez de Santa Ana at the Battle of San Jacinto. Santa Ana was forced to recognize Texan independence from Mexico. Rumors circulated in Washington in the summer of 1837 that the Texas minister to the United States would present a formal proposal for annexation of his country.[75] During his two terms in office Andrew Jackson avoided the annexation issue because he understood the high level of volatility it would create in the political system. He waited until his last day in office before he formally recognized Texas's independence.

Antebellum economic growth and westward expansion of slavery forced Dorr to rethink his understanding of republicanism. In an essay written while a student at Harvard, Dorr concluded that "public virtue and the law of liberty have made us what we are now, and will make us, however extended our territory . . . all that we can hope to be."[76] Dorr now feared, however, that the annexation of Texas would postpone emancipation by giving a "perpetual lease . . . to a noxious and fearful institution." On "such a question both philanthropy and patriotism demand of every free citizen the interposition of a decidedly prompt negative" on the question of admitting Texas into the Union.[77] The Texas Revolution, in Dorr's analysis, was a revolution of slaveholders. He did not see the parallels in terms of economic and constitutional issues between the revolt by Texas landowners and the American revolutionaries. Rather, Dorr saw only the possibility of the destruction of republicanism if the United States government supported the slaveholders' revolution in Texas. Here Dorr was in line with the majority of northern abolitionists. Garrison called Texas "the ark of safety to swindlers, gamblers, robbers and rogues" who only wanted to "extend and perpetuate the most frightful form of servitude the world has ever known and add crime to crime."[78]

It is clear from his correspondence that Dorr shared John Quincy Adams's fear of the growing Slave Power. The Slave Power thesis first appeared in the 1830s as an integral part of an abolitionist ideology that energized and mobilized the antislavery forces. The main argument was that the slaveholding South controlled the levers of federal power. As historian Leonard Richards has persuasively argued, Adams's "claim that the Texas revolution was a criminal act set off by slavemasters and land speculators had instant appeal throughout much of the Northeast."[79] Adams was influenced by the writings of the Quaker abolitionist editor Benjamin Lundy, who gave a young Garrison his first opportunity to attack the institution of slavery in the pages of his newspaper, the *Genius of Universal Emancipation*. In 1836, Lundy began publishing the *National Enquirer and Constitutional Advocate of Universal Liberty* in Philadelphia. In the same year, Lundy also published *The War in Texas*, a pamphlet arguing against the annexation of Texas to the United States. A close follower of Washingtonian politics, Dorr was surely influenced by Adams's speeches on the floor of Congress.

In a December 1837 letter to the former Alabama slaveholder-turned-abolitionist James Birney, who was then serving as the corresponding secretary for the American Anti-Slavery Society (AASS), Dorr proclaimed that the abolitionist cause rested "upon the eternal principles of truth, justice, and humanity" and was the "last hope" of his "enslaved countrymen." Founded in 1833 by Garrison and Rhode Islander Arnold Buffum, the AASS undertook a massive national effort to carry out what a later generation would term consciousness raising to convert white Americans to the notion that slavery was incompatible with republican government. In its Declaration of Sentiments, which was greatly influenced by the efforts of Lucretia Mott, the AASS declared that "all laws which are now in force, admitting the right of slavery, are . . . before God utterly null and void."[80] The society's constitution identified slavery as a moral and political evil, called for the immediate end of the notorious institution, promoted egalitarianism, and, most importantly, advocated for Congress to abolish the interstate slave trade and slavery in the District of Columbia, along with abolishing slavery in the territories.[81]

In the 1830s, the AASS employed paid agents, including the Grimké sisters, to spread its gospel. Agents were generally energetic young men and women charged with carrying abolitionism across the country. Birney, who was arrested in March 1837 for harboring a fugitive slave in his house, desperately wanted Dorr to work for the society, an offer that demonstrates how deeply connected Dorr was to abolitionism. The core of the AASS efforts centered on a brigade of militant traveling agents who were selected to execute vast systematic grassroots campaigns—one of the first in the nation's history. With regard to "Dorr's Abolitionism we have only to say, that he is and always has been the most rabid and ultra Abolitionist in all New England," declared the *Providence Journal*.[82]

Though he declined the offer to serve as an agent for the AASS, Dorr assured Birney that he was not turning it down "from fear of personal consequences." Dorr could have been referring to his fragile health, which often prevented him from traveling great distances; however, he most likely wanted to assure Birney that he was willing to brave the frequent threats leveled against antislavery activists in the antebellum period. Considering that abolitionist editor Elijah Lovejoy was killed in Alton, Illinois, just months before by a shotgun blast to the chest, this was a very real fear. Dorr also made it clear that all his efforts were needed in Rhode Island to counter the strong proslavery element in state. "The blood of martyrs is truly the seed of reformation," wrote Dorr in reference to Lovejoy's violent death at the close of the letter. However, Dorr made it clear that the "harvest will not in this instance be one of men in arms, but of concentrated . . . opinions for the recovery of lost rights, and the extermination of Republican slavery."[83] Dorr was not calling for the forceful emancipation of slaves in the South. His use of the term "republican slavery" signified his belief that Southern slavery was protected by the Constitution.

Despite Birney's heartfelt plea, Dorr thought he could better serve the antislavery cause by working to strengthen the Rhode Island Anti-Slavery Society. In 1838, however, Dorr did travel to New York City to meet with Birney and Lewis Tappan prior to the yearly meeting of the AASS, to which he was serving as a delegate from Rhode Island.[84] Dorr had most likely first met Tappan in November 1837, when the New York abolitionist attended the first anniversary of the Rhode Island Anti-Slavery Society.[85] Lewis Tappan, one of the nation's leading abolitionists, was born in Northampton, Massachusetts, in 1788 and became a merchant, first in Philadelphia, then in Boston. In 1827, he joined his successful brother, Arthur, in New York's silk trade. In 1834 rioters swept through New York City, destroying black neighborhoods and sacking Tappan's house.[86] Though Garrison was instrumental in founding the AASS, operational control passed to the wealthy Tappan, who personally bankrolled most of the society's endeavors.[87] At the AASS meeting, which was chaired by the New York abolitionist Gerritt Smith, Dorr took the floor and gave an impassioned speech against the annexation of Texas, praising the efforts of abolitionists and encouraging them to continue their work for the destruction of "the entire system of Republican Slavery."[88] Dorr served on a committee dealing with state organization in concert with his close friend John Greenleaf Whittier, the abolitionist poet who justly earned the title "the bard of freedom."

During his two failed attempts for Congress in 1837 and 1839, Dorr received strong endorsements from the New England abolitionist press.[89] During the 1839 Congressional election, Dorr ran unsuccessfully as a Democratic candidate, though this time his margin of defeat was not as large as it was in 1837 when he ran as a Constitutionalist. He lost by less than 200 votes in 1839.[90] Dorr was "a most staunch and thorough going abolitionist," declared Garrison in his ringing endorsement in the *Liberator*. The abolitionist editor was pleased to see Rhode Island "hoist the Democratic antislavery standard" by nominating Dorr, who was on the board of the executive committee of the Rhode Island Anti-Slavery Society. "Let them send up a Rhode Island Morris to the National Legislature," proclaimed Garrison in a reference to the Ohio antislavery Democratic Senator Thomas Morris, who earned his antislavery stripes by coining the term "Slave

Power" to describe the undemocratic influence of the slave-holding states.[91] Senator Morris called on "the people" to wage a holy war against the Slave Power just as they had against the "Bank Power."[92]

The course of Rhode Island history would most likely have been radically different if Dorr had won election to Congress. Based on his correspondence and personal papers, Dorr's career might have followed the path of other antislavery Democrats, such as John Parker Hale of New Hampshire.[93] Dorr, however, would not earn his fame in the political corridors of Washington. After his loss in 1839, Dorr blamed the defeat on the "Whig abolitionist vote."[94] This was not an attack on the abolitionists, but rather a political truism—there were few antislavery Democrats in Rhode Island. Despite his endorsements by Garrison's *Liberator* and the *Herald of Freedom*, a New Hampshire abolitionist organ, Rhode Island abolitionists did not trust the Democrats. In May 1839, Dorr, serving once again as an officer, attended his last meeting of the AASS in New York City.[95] There Dorr served on another committee with Whittier, one tasked with devising strategies for fund raising.[96] In 1842, Rhode Island abolitionist A. C. Barstow labeled Dorr a demagogue and unfairly declared that in 1839 Dorr "wished to use [the abolitionist] cause to elevate himself to power." No such charge, however, was leveled against Dorr at the time.[97]

Though his connection to the AASS was coming to a close, Dorr's penchant for antislavery was still very much alive in 1839 and 1840. Dorr took copious notes on an intense debate in the Rhode Island General Assembly on finally eradicating slavery within the state and upon the right to petition Congress to abolish slavery in Washington, D.C. Dorr drafted the skillfully worded petitions, which included provisions for the introduction of rights of due process in fugitive slave cases. The fact that he took over twenty pages of notes on the debate suggests that he was actively involved. Dorr authored a petition to put an end to the gradual nature of the state's attempt to disavow the institution of human bondage. Dorr's petition also called for former bondsmen to be considered legal residents of the town in which they resided.[98]

What is clear from the record is that by the end of the 1830s Dorr believed that slavery violated the moral principle of human equality and to defend the institution was to deny that all men were created equal. Dorr repeatedly maintained that Congress should take steps to eliminate slavery where it had the power to do so—the District of Columbia and the territories. As early as 1833, Dorr recognized the antislavery potential of the elusive guarantee of republican government as expressed in Article IV, section 4 of the federal Constitution. Dorr argued that the clause could be used to prevent the admission of new slave states. Dorr understood that the Constitution protected slavery in the states where it already existed, but he firmly believed that Congress had power to control the spread of slavery into the territories. In Dorr's analysis the revolutionary generation had suffused the Constitution with the bias toward freedom.[99] In 1838, at the fifth annual meeting of the AASS, with Dorr in attendance, abolitionist Alvan Stewart hinted at the power of the Guarantee Clause.[100]

In his correspondence, Dorr reveals that he also favored repealing or modifying the 1793 Fugitive Slave Act and affording writs of habeas corpus and personal replevin (common legal tactics in fugitive cases) for accused bondsmen. Whereas many antislavery Democrats, including William Leggett, did not expound on the constitutional status of slavery in the territories, Dorr clearly thought deeply about the effects of the westward spread of slavery.[101] Finally, Dorr's public record reveals that he thought free blacks deserved a place in the body politic. Dorr insisted that blacks were fellow countrymen, not foreigners or a permanently inferior caste. He ardently believed that free blacks deserved civil and political rights.[102] In "the 'house' of 'many mansions' there will be no negro gallery," wrote Dorr to his mother, Lydia.[103] Extending the Jacksonian equal rights doctrine to include black Americans marked Dorr's departure from mainstream Democrats, not to mention the near-universal white assumption of black inferiority.

The decline in membership in antislavery and abolitionist societies in Rhode Island due to the continued economic fallout from the Panic of 1837 likely had a great deal to do with Dorr's move away from organized abolitionism.[104] Also, Dorr's attendance at the 1839 AASS meeting gave him a front-row seat to the ongoing battle within the organization over the role of women and the debate over the connection between abolitionism and the political process. In 1840, the burgeoning schism within the AASS ranks burst open when Lewis Tappan led more than half of the delegates to form the American and Foreign Anti-Slavery Society.[105] Finally, Dorr surely realized that his antislavery views, no matter how far removed from the fiery rhetoric and sentimental, religious reformism of Garrison, prevented him from winning as a Democrat. He had already switched from the Whigs. If Arnold Buffum's Liberty Party had developed in Rhode Island as it did in Massachusetts in 1840, Dorr would have likely joined their ranks; however, the abolitionist political party did not emerge in Rhode Island until later in the decade.[106] By January 1840, Dorr no longer openly communicated with abolitionists. What was on the minds of most Rhode Islanders in 1840 was not antislavery, but political democracy.

The continued economic depression brought to the surface once again the reality that the majority of Rhode Island's working class lacked the power of the ballot to address their grievances. Dorr followed the expositions on the plight of the laboring classes put forth in Orestes Brownson's *Boston Quarterly Review*, the New England equivalent of John O'Sullivan's *Democratic Review*. Dorr invited Brownson to speak to the laboring classes in Providence.[107] Dorr and Brownson both believed that the rights of workingmen were not being recognized and that the citizenry as a whole had the inherent right to improve its economic, social, and political position.

The political reform movement that had begun to sweep the country in the 1820s and fundamentally reorient the nation's political landscape created the political and societal background for political reform efforts. The emergence of a democratic popular culture was advanced by new mechanisms of party organization and democratic reforms, such as the abolishment of property requirements. Reformers began to praise democracy as the rule of majority, where public opinion governed with as few intermediaries as possible. As Arthur Schlesinger, Jr., noted in his classic work, *The Age of Jackson*, Rhode Island's political economy "provoked mounting discontent, as nonvoters began with increasing vehemence to demand a new constitution in whose creation they would be allowed to participate."[108] The persistence of voting restrictions in nineteenth-century Rhode Island challenged one of the oldest and most cherished assumptions in American political history. This theory is predicated on the belief that there was a universal increase in white manhood suffrage and participatory democracy beginning in the decades after the American Revolution and continuing through the Jacksonian period.

Dorr's new list of correspondents included the Massachusetts Democrat Robert Rantoul, Jr., whom he invited to lecture in Rhode Island.[109] Rantoul and Dorr were both Harvard graduates and multifaceted reformers, sharing a passion for reform in areas of public education, banking, and the prison system.[110] During a banking reform speech in Newport, a bastion of conservatism, Rantoul was greeted by a group of Whigs armed with potatoes. Rantoul kept his humor, merely saying that he had often heard that Whig arguments were small potatoes, but had never felt it so sensibly before.[111]

By September 1840, Dorr had emerged as the head of the state Democratic committee, much to the chagrin of conservative Democrats, such as former governor John Brown Francis and South Kingstown attorney Elisha Potter, Jr., who knew that Dorr was at "open war" with the old hardliners and could not be made to "toe the mark" on the issue of the freehold.[112] Dorr was thoroughly committed to using the party to help reform the state's archaic form of government and to challenge what he deemed to be the ruinous economic policies of the ruling Whig elite and their conservative, rural Democratic allies.

In the 1830s, Dorr's fear of the Money Power led him to offer an intelligent and forthright critique of the growing Slave Power in antebellum America. By 1840, Dorr had once again returned to his fear of the Money Power. Dorr, along with the rest of the Democratic Party, would approach the election of 1840 as historian Daniel Feller has argued, with "the fervor of a religious crusade."[113] Politics was still a zero-sum game for many antebellum Americans. Dorr believed that if the Whigs won the presidential election of 1840, ruin would befall the nation. "There is now no longer any doubt of the measures to be added in case the Whigs succeed, viz. the overthrow of the Independent Treasury, a National Bank for a long term, with an increased capital, & thoroughly interlaced with state interests, internal improvements on a grand scale, and a high tariff," wrote Dorr to the Jacksonian editor Amos Kendall on the eve of the election.[114] Dorr saw Martin Van Buren, who worked hard to return the *Amistad* rebels to the Spanish government, as preferable to William Henry Harrison's and Clay's American System.[115] Dorr now saw the fate of American freedom resting on the banking issue and the outcome of the election of 1840. However, what Dorr did not realize at the time was that his move to the Democrats would eventually lead him to embrace racism and anti-abolitionism at a level he was not comfortable with in the 1830s. Any Democrat who subscribed to these doctrines furthered the interests of southern slaveholders, whether they were consciously aware of it or not. There were many antislavery Democrats who rose to prominence in the 1840s and later joined the Free Soilers and then the Republicans. Dorr certainly demonstrated signs that he, too, would be a Jacksonian dissident, but by 1842 those tendencies had vanished.

Chapter 3

The Abolitionists and the People's Constitution

In regard to the question of free suffrage involved in the Rhode Island matter, we have only to say, that neither the old charter nor the free suffrage parties have any claim to the sympathies of abolitionists, inasmuch as both are radically wrong on the question which more immediately concerns us, the former making property and the latter color the basis of suffrage.

Emancipator and Free America, June 30, 1842

Any hope that President Martin Van Buren might have entertained about entering the race to keep his residence on Pennsylvania Avenue with an improving economy went right out the door when an economic panic turned into a severe depression in early 1840. In the late 1830s, the Democratic Party was struggling to hold itself together as a national coalition. There was a strong call for the president to modify Andrew Jackson's 1836 Specie Circular, which required that all purchases of federal land be made with precious metal rather than paper money. Whigs blamed the panic on Jackson's destruction of the Second Bank of the United States and his efforts to establish an all-specie currency. After the passage of the Specie Circular, hard money flowed from east to west, stripping eastern banks in a critical period of much-needed hard money. In 1837, a dramatic fall in cotton prices and withdrawal of English credit sparked a wave of mercantile failures and the contraction of credit. The next year brought hope of a recovery, but another massive dip in 1839 sent many western and southern states, along with New England communities that depended on southern cotton, spiraling into an economic abyss that threatened to make Van Buren a one-term president.[1]

Factories in Haverhill and textile mills in Lowell, Massachusetts, shut down throwing thousands out of work. An estimated 50,000 were out of work in New York City. In Washington, D.C., Van Buren could see relief centers ladling out soup to the poor.[2] The more pronounced the economic situation became the more attractive the potential Whig nominee would become to ailing Americans. Across the country, economic distress was producing political and social upheaval. The diary of Worcester resident John Park, whose daughter Louisa lived just a few blocks away from the Dorr family mansion on Benefit Street in Providence, reads like a present-day commentary from the *New York Times*: "Business generally depressed. Public confidence every where diminishing—and Congress passing month after month on frivolous, often disgraceful debates—doing nothing on the great questions of national interests."[3] In 1840, as the nation's two major parties launched their respective presidential campaigns, the restoration of prosperity and the salvation of the economy emerged as the central issues.

During the presidential campaign season, the American populace witnessed the brilliant mastery of the new Whig leaders—Thurlow Weed, Horace Greeley, William Henry Seward, and Thaddeus Stevens—who were able to manipulate and control the political process to support their candidate. As historian Harry Watson has noted, the Whigs "needed to shake their image as the party of financial aristocrats and create a vision of democratic capitalism, in which every American, no matter how humble, could work hard, get ahead, improve his family's welfare, and still maintain the advantages of the revolutionary past."[4] In this task they largely succeeded. The political campaigns of 1840 reached unprecedented heights of electioneering and populist-style politics. Public opinion became the almighty lever of the American political system. The communication revolution that led to a profusion of partisan newspapers prodded men to take sides and go to the polls in support of their candidate. The election of 1840 followed on the heels of a steady increase in political participation in the previous decade, as well as long strides in the development of parties as effective political organizations.[5] In December 1839, the Whigs held their first national convention in Harrisburg, Pennsylvania, and, with the help of a strong block of Anti-Masons who had been absorbed into the party, nominated one of the military heroes of the War of 1812, General William Henry Harrison.[6] The elderly military hero was rumored to have lived in a log cabin and have a fondness for hard cider, though neither story was true. In fact Harrison was born into the Virginia gentry. True as it is today, a legend is more powerful than truth, and Whig political leaders quickly printed the legend.[7] Former

Democratic governor John Brown Francis, the grandson of the famed Providence merchant John Brown, quipped that he had "passed several summers" of his life in "log cabins and never considered it a hardship."[8] The irony that Van Buren's early years in Kinderhook, New York, were much closer to the hardship of a life in a log cabin than Harrison's genteel youth was lost on the American populace.

The so-called "Log Cabin and Hard Cider" campaign saw the development of electioneering techniques, such as parades and huge camp meetings, to mobilize the populace.[9] An essential component of the wild and turbulent 1840 campaign was liquor. A new word—booze—entered the American lexicon when E. C. Booz Distillery began to ship huge quantities of "Old Cabin Whiskey." A June 1840 rally for Harrison at the site of the 1811 Battle of Tippecanoe drew over 60,000 people. During the campaign, party managers were able to paint Harrison as everything to everyone. The pro-Whig *New York World* put it this way: "In one quarter of the Union the Whigs represented their candidate as a friend, in another an enemy to a National Bank—here he was an abolitionist, there a slaveholder—in the East a champion of domestic industry, in the South a foe to the Tariff."[10] Rhode Island Whigs were not thrilled with the party's newfound fondness for democracy. "I fear that the Log Cabin & Hard Cider scheme will be carried too far by our friends—there is nothing in that sort of nonsense that is in good keeping with our Rhode Island & Roger Williams character—It is the essence of Locofocoism, and carries with it to most minds the idea of hickory tree days," said Henry Y. Cranston.[11]

The Locofocos, whose name came from a kind of match, were a new political group that sprang up in New York City in the 1830s. The Locofocos despised special privilege, spurned paper money, and promoted equal rights for white males. They believed that the citizenry through majoritarian governance had the right to improve its social and economic position. As William Leggett wrote in 1837, the "right of the majority to rule, is a maxim which lies at the bottom of democratic government; but a maxim of still higher obligation makes it their duty so to rule, as to preserve inviolate the equal rights of all."[12] A pamphlet from the First Social Reform Society in New York headed by Robert Townshend entitled *Address to the Citizens of Rhode Island Who Are Denied the Right of Suffrage* urged Rhode Island reformers to bypass the General Assembly and call a constitutional convention with delegates apportioned on the basis of the population of adult male citizens and open to voting by all males over the age of twenty-one.[13] The "government under which you live as aliens, is at once an usurpation over the rights of man, and a subversion of the sovereignty of the people."[14]

Spurred on by the political fervor connected with the presidential campaign, the Rhode Island Suffrage Association—a conglomeration of urban Whigs, reform-minded Democrats, and radical labor leaders—was formed on March 27, 1840. The passage of a draconian militia law in January 1840, which fixed criminal penalties on all those who avoided military duty, prompted Providence mechanics into action.[15] The association's express goal was "not to shrink from the task" of universal manhood suffrage until it had been "accomplished." "WE KNOW OUR RIGHTS, AND KNOWING, DARE MAINTAIN THEM," read the association's preamble.[16] Prominent Rhode Island Whigs viewed the actions of the Suffrage Association as an attempt to divide the party in order to throw the next election to the Democrats.[17]

John Brown, a botanical physician who made his money manufacturing root beer, founded a paper in Providence to advocate for changes to the state's archaic form of government.[18] On November 20, 1840, the *New Age and Constitutional Advocate* appeared on the streets of Providence, promoting the agenda of the Suffrage Association. Rhode Island's disenfranchised masses were "placed upon a level with the miserable slaves in the shambles of a southern market," declared the *New Age*.[19] Comparisons between the plight of southern slaves and Rhode Island disenfranchised white laborers became a common refrain in the *New Age*: "What sort of freedom is this? It is but one removed from the slavery of the south. Like the southern negro, three fifths of the citizens of Rhode Island have no claim by her laws to any political or judicial right, but to be governed and judged."[20]

The Suffrage Association drew inspiration from the rhetoric of revolutionary republicanism that had been articulated by the northern abolitionist movement. In 1836, Samuel Gould, a delegate to the first meeting of the Rhode Island Anti-Slavery Society, boldly declared: "In other lands the people do not rule. Who rules in America? THE PEOPLE. The matter then is to settle the question whether the people rule, or aristocrats rule among us."[21] For the Suffrage Association and northern abolitionists, the principle of self-government was based on the majoritarian ideal, which was violated both by slaveholders and Rhode Island's ruling oligarchy. New York abolitionist William Goodell, a close observer of political events in Rhode Island, argued that the "authenticated definition of a republican form of Government" was described in the Declaration of Independence—"all men are created equal."[22] New Hampshire abolitionist Nathan Rogers's *Herald of Freedom* equated the "landholders" in Rhode Island to those who "practice[d] the cannibalism called slaveholding" in the South.[23] Rogers was one of the few abolitionists to speak out against northern "wage slavery." His desire was an alliance between labor and the abolitionist movement.[24] In his abolitionist tract, *Friend of Man*, Goodell argued that the "cause of moral reformation in Rhode Island requires the political emancipation of the people."[25] The "sovereignty of ACRES," would not be allowed to continue.[26] Goodell saw in the ideology of the people's sovereignty a way to attack the "Slave Power," something he had been lecturing about for over two years.[27] Goodell would later become one of the foremost proponents of the antislavery implications of the Guarantee Clause as a weapon against the South. As historian William Wiecek has argued, Goodell's "attention to the possibilities" of the Guarantee Clause in terms of attacking the institution of human bondage was "first aroused as a result of his fervent polemical writings on behalf of the Dorrite cause in Rhode Island."[28]

By the fall of 1840, the Suffrage Association had begun to press its call for reform with increased vigor. In practice, the association was a model of democracy in action. It operated in most areas with a minimum of central direction, a maximum of grassroots involvement, and with only one strategic goal: to achieve a modern constitution for Rhode Island. Henry Dorr, who was at this time attending legal lectures offered by Joseph Story at Harvard College, rightly noted that the reform movement emanated from "the people themselves." On "former occasions," said Henry, "a few enlightened persons have endeavored to bring about a change in existing institutions of the people, and as friends of the people." They "forgot," he said, that the people must "accomplish" it for "themselves."[29] Henry Dorr believed that citizens had both a right and a responsibility to agitate for change, provided that they continued to remain loyal to the government and follow the rule of law. Henry had no idea, however, how far his older brother would run with the idea about the power of the people themselves to affect constitutional change against a recalcitrant sitting government.

Despite Thomas Dorr's prediction that "no definite or indefinite quantity of hard cider short of a deluge can float Harrison to the capital," the Democrats were crushed both nationally and locally.[30] When all the ballots had been counted, Harrison won nearly quadruple the number of electoral votes as Van Buren. The incumbent president only carried six states, com-

pared to Harrison's nineteen. Rhode Island went solidly in the Whig column. In addition to the presidency, the Whigs also captured both Houses
of Congress. In November 1840, unprecedented political mobilization tactics produced the highest voter turnout (of adult white males) in the antebellum period. However, whereas the majority of states boasted numbers
of 70 percent or higher in terms of voting participation, the percentage of
the Rhode Island populace that participated in the election of 1840 was less
than 40 percent.[31]

Recognizing the growing groundswell of support for political change
generated by the Suffrage Association and its organ the *New Age*, the General Assembly resolved in February 1841 to call a constitutional convention
in November of that year. Delegates to the convention were to be chosen
on the same basis as the two previous conventions in 1824 and 1834, though
both conventions failed to produce anything close to meaningful reform.[32]
The day after the Landholders' Convention was announced, fearing yet a
third ultra-conservative conclave, the Suffrage Association declared that
the people had a right to assemble in a convention and to enact a republican
constitution for the state.[33] In the coming months the association set out to
convince citizens that its position on a separate constitutional convention
was legal and, above all, in line with the tenets of American constitutionalism.

At a rally on April 17, 1841, nearly 3,000 men and women led by the
prominent Universalist minister William S. Balch marched in procession
around the streets of Providence. The parade started on Benefit Street, just
a few blocks down from the Dorr mansion.[34] Dorr expressed his kinship with
"the nonfreeholders of Rhode Island," who were seeking to "vindicate to
themselves a just and equal participation in political power, and to become
the citizens rather than the subjects of a state now only nominally republican."[35] Dorr's friend, Providence Whig attorney Walter S. Burges, declined
to attend the mass meeting but he, too, expressed warm sympathy for the activities of the Suffrage Association. "When the People Speak . . . they must
be heard—for their voice is the voice of God," said Burges.[36] The Suffrage
Association frequently referred to the "democracy of Christianity." The
"American Revolution was the workings of Christianity, and part of the plan
of Divine government," declared one reformer. Antebellum Rhode Island
reformers were simply following in line with earlier revolutionaries.[37]

On July 5, suffrage supporters met again in Providence, with Balch once
again taking a leading a role. "Ask the hovering spirit of Roger Williams if

liberty is to be measured by dollars and cents, and parceled out by feet and inches to his descendants," proclaimed Balch. For this Protestant minister, "intelligence, virtue, honor, and patriotism" made the man and "not dirt and primogeniture." To those who said that the actions of the Suffrage Association constituted revolution and were therefore illegitimate, Balch invoked the memory of Samuel Adams, Thomas Jefferson, and Patrick Henry. Not one to neglect his own profession, Balch threw Jesus Christ into the list of revolutionaries. The slogan adopted for use at the celebration clearly signaled the lengths the Suffrage Association was willing to go: "WAR FOREVER AGAINST THE TYRANNICAL GOVERNMENT OF RHODE ISLAND." [38]

Thomas Dorr, while still not openly linked to the Suffrage Association, helped write the resolutions, one of which boldly declared that members would carry into effect a new constitution "by all necessary means" and "remove all obstacles to its successful establishment and operation." [39] Dorr was in a difficult political position. As the chairman of the state Democratic committee, he was presiding over a party divided between conservative agrarians, led John Brown Francis and Elisha Potter, Jr., and a newly emerging Equal Rights faction. The old-guard conservative Democrats would not join ranks with the Suffrage Association, though their refusal did little to slow down the reform effort.

Pulling no punches, the *New Age* proclaimed on July 16: "We are arraigned in hostility to the government of Rhode Island and now let us ask if when the day of battle comes, our troops will be found firm, not only against the charge of our opponents but against their smiles, their sophistry and their gold." [40] With the success of the April, May, and July rallies, the association decided to call a constitutional convention, with delegates to be selected on the basis of universal male suffrage at meetings in every town in the state. On August 28, 1841, the selection of delegates to what quickly became known as the People's Convention, fell three days before the selection of delegates to the constitutional convention sponsored by the General Assembly. Dorr was elected to serve as a delegate to both conventions. [41] All twenty-one-year-old male citizens who had resided in the state for one year were urged to attend the People's Convention in October. [42] Due to Dorr's influence, the word "white" was left out of the call for delegates.

The activities of the Suffrage Association had a powerful and uplifting effect on Rhode Island's black community. The democratic fervor created by the election of 1840 and the activities of the association gave Rhode Island blacks hope that they, too, could be included in the body politic. The state's black population constituted roughly 3 percent of a total population of 108,837, including four slaves, according to the 1840 census. By the start of that decade, the black community had lifted itself up sufficiently from its dependency on the white community to establish churches, schools, and civic organizations. In 1820, an African Union Meeting and School-House was constructed on the affluent east side of Providence, just a few blocks from the First Baptist and First Congregational churches.[43] Led by George McCarty, a trader, the church committee restricted pew ownership to blacks.[44] Several blacks owned their homes and could have qualified to vote under the state's stringent property requirements had not a restrictive white-only provision enacted in 1822 prevented them from doing so.

Legally disenfranchised for two decades and enduring segregation in many facets of life, including education, blacks in Rhode Island had been petitioning the General Assembly yearly to regain the franchise.[45] White northerners all too often supported degrading legislation that denied blacks admission into labor unions or public schools, while championing mob violence against black residences.[46] In October 1824, a fight that began on the streets of Providence between a group of black and white men quickly escalated into a riot that led to the destruction of a black neighborhood on North Main Street called "Hard Scrabble." The riot broke out after a failed attempt to reform Rhode Island's archaic governing structure. Changes in the relationship between employers and employees meant that more blacks were moving out of white households where they had worked as servants and were living in tenement houses. As historian John Wood Sweet has noted, the Hard Scrabble riot "was a brutal harbinger of a trend toward widespread antiblack violence in the antebellum North, a crucial turning point in race relations as the region's last slaves were becoming free."[47] After the riot, Providence blacks began to level attacks on racial prejudice and discrimination, calling for equal rights and equal treatment under the law.

At a meeting of the "free colored people" of Providence on January 6, 1831, it was declared that if the city's black populace was to endure a tax burden "the colored people who are liable for these taxes, have a right to vote for town and state officers and ought to have the privileges of sending their children to the free schools."[48] Public schooling for blacks was almost invariably segregated and inferior. Above the elementary school level, few schools admitted blacks.[49] The official petition sent to the Assembly, which was signed by Alfred Niger, George Wyllis, and George McCarty, maintained that the "right to impose taxes, either upon a person or their property necessarily includes the corresponding rights of suffrage and representation." Any law that "authorizes" taxation, but denies representation "must be deemed adverse to the policy and principles of the government," which the petitioners understood to be "based upon the equal rights of all." Moreover, since they were denied access to the "free school system," they should not have to hand over their hard-earned money for the benefit of white children.[50] Niger and Wyllis were very active in interregional black conventions, serving as delegates to the inaugural colored convention in Philadelphia in 1831, but during the 1830s their demands were ignored in Rhode Island.

In early 1841, Niger submitted a remonstrance that argued that the state's suffrage statute was discriminatory against his community. The remonstrance asked the General Assembly to confer upon black Rhode Islanders "the same rights of suffrage enjoyed by their more favored white fellow citizens."[51] Instead of addressing the plea from the black community to accept them fully into the body politic, the assembly simply elected to exempt blacks from town and state taxes on real and personal property.[52] Rhode Island blacks sent another petition to the assembly in June 1841 acknowledging that "they have desired higher privileges and more enlarged rights," but that "they have never asked for them by the passage of an act which while benevolent in form is nevertheless injurious in nature and tendency."[53] The black community was looking to demonstrate its self-sufficiency, not its dependency on the entrenched conservative elite. The assembly elected to leave both the tax exemption and the white-only voting restriction in place.

Throughout 1841, blacks participated in Suffrage Association activities and voted in their elections.[54] However, despite this biracial cooperation, on election day in August 1841 officials in Providence's sixth ward turned away a black man who attempted to cast a ballot.[55] The day before, a letter signed "For the Rights of All" in the *New Age* warned that any attempt to prevent blacks from voting would be considered an "ignoble surrender of inalienable rights" and, therefore, deserved "the severest condemnation of every true friend of the cause and . . . the sure and speedy overthrow of the whole enterprise." Discrimination against blacks, in this analysis, was of the same cloth as discrimination against those without $134 worth of property. The fears of the writer, despite rhetoric from the executive committee of the Suffrage Association that the "great principle of natural universal equality" allows all men "to participate in the affairs of government," were made manifest in the actions of party officials.[56] In September, Alfred Niger was denied a position on the executive committee of the Suffrage Association.[57]

Seizing an opportunity to divide members of the Suffrage Association, Samuel Ames, Dorr's brother-in-law, argued in a sarcastic essay that the initial call for participation in the selection of delegates to the People's Convention "certainly included our colored friends." Suffrage Association announcements ran in newspapers with such statements as: "Let every man who is in favor of a Republican form of government go to the polls." A white-only restriction was never discussed. However, in the end the association "thought it might be too great a shock to public sentiment to allow colored men the privilege" of voting.[58] Ames, writing under the pseudonym "Town Borne," tried to stir the political pot by pointing out the moral failings of the white reformers. If "'all men are born free and equal,' and if 'the right to vote be a natural and inalienable right,' why does the mere accident of color make a difference?"[59] In order to "alleviate" the fears of the black community, but in reality to raise the fears of opponents of political reform, Ames said a revolution akin to the one that took place in Haiti at the end of the eighteenth century was on the horizon.[60]

Dorr's old friend from his sojourn in New York City, John O'Sullivan, wrote to express his support for the "little revolution" in Rhode Island. However, O'Sullivan, who was now editing the influential *Democratic Review*, warned Dorr not to interfere with the "laws of nature," which was a colorful euphemism for black inferiority. Driven both by political pragmatism and racism, O'Sullivan urged Dorr to frame the struggle in Rhode Island purely as involving the question of universal *white* suffrage so as not to incur a backlash. "Before putting my head down the fox's throat, like the silly crane, I must feel perfectly safe about being able to draw it back again," said the Irish editor.[61] Dorr, however, did not share O'Sullivan's racism.

On October 8, in the opening days of the People's Convention held at the Masonic Hall in Providence, Dorr was presented with a memorial from the city's black community that explicitly linked suffrage with the privileges and immunities of citizenship.[62] The prominent Boston abolitionist Lydia Maria Child, the author of *An Appeal in Favor of That Class of Americans Called Africans* (1833), had already railed against the hypocrisy of a potential white-only clause in the pages of the *National Anti-Slavery Standard*, the organ of the American Anti-Slavery Society. "If that ugly, monopolizing word is inserted now, it will . . . most assuredly have to be erased, through much unpleasant conflict."[63] In an era when the rise of political democracy generally went hand-in-hand with racism and black disenfranchisement, Providence's vocal black community was not about to let an opportunity to gain political rights go by without a fight. The goal was to make the Suffrage Association aware of the contradictions between its lofty agenda and its insistence on racial voting qualifications. In so doing they sought to redefine the public discourse on democracy and to ensure their place in it.

The memorial was written by Alexander Crummell, "a respected colored man," and the twenty-two-year-old minister of Christ Episcopal Church in Providence.[64] Crummell had taken up his post in Providence in March 1841. His prominence as a young intellectual had earned him a spot as keynote speaker at the antislavery New York State Convention of Negroes when it met in Albany in 1840. "We know of no system of political ethics in which rights are based on the complexion of the skin," wrote Crummell. The petition made clear that the "annals of nations clearly teach that there is always danger in departing from clearly defined and universal truths, and resorting to unjustifiable invidious partialities."[65] Throwing the political editorials in the *New Age* back into the faces of the delegates, Crummell forcibly argued that racial discrimination was contrary to notions of natural rights and representative democracy. Crummell "cautioned the convention against departing from their principles by all the considerations of justice and moral right, lest the poisoned chalice should in the course of events be returned to their own lips."[66]

Several of the delegates were moved by the eloquent memorial. Delegate Benjamin Arnold moved that the word "white" be stricken from the constitution because it was "inconsistent" with the principles of the Suffrage Association. "Will 15,000 men vote in violation of a principle involving their own rights for the sake of excluding a few hundred?" asked Arnold.[67] The Portsmouth delegate argued that the "enemies" of reform were anticipating that the suffragists would "split" on the "rock" representing the black vote and it would prove to be a "dagger in their bosom."[68] Dorr endorsed and echoed Arnold's arguments. However, Welcome B. Sayles, who would later become one of Dorr's most loyal supporters in 1842, argued for the "greatest good for the greatest number," pointing out that blacks were essentially disenfranchised in the North so why "endanger the whole project."[69] It was better to be inconsistent than to lose at the polls in Sayles's view. Martin Van Buren's 1836 presidential campaign against Whig candidate Henry Clay made it clear that promoting black suffrage was a political liability. Southern opponents repeatedly denounced Van Buren's support for preserving black suffrage, though it was severely diminished because of New York's $250 freehold requirement.[70]

Refusing to give in to the mounting racism, Dorr introduced a resolution in which he argued that excluding blacks from the franchise was a "violation" of the "just principle of suffrage." Moreover, political "expediency" could "never" be justified. Dorr forcibly reminded his fellow delegates that during the American Revolution they "were willing" to allow blacks "to encounter danger and toil and privations, and to shed their blood with us, and lay their bones along the Atlantic shores" in order "to purchase that liberty of which we would now deprive them." The "convention would be inconsistent with their former declaration, with their bill of rights just adopted, and would diverge from the great principles acted out by Roger Williams."[71]

For a moment it seemed that the petition would be well received because Dorr, who had emerged as the intellectual spokesman of the Suffrage Association, openly favored it. Dorr clearly understood that the continued reliance on the theme of the people's sovereignty would appear hollow if blacks were excluded from the franchise. Indeed, a draft of the People's Constitution in Dorr's handwriting does not include a white-only provision.[72] However, former state attorney general and Democratic Congressman Dutee Pearce disagreed.[73] Pearce's hometown of Newport was a favorite spot for vacationing slave masters. Pearce made sure there was no debate on the subject because he did not want the convention to take on the appearance of an abolitionist enclave. Dorr took the principles of the American Revolution to their logical conclusions, while Pearce argued that perceived notions of black inferiority mandated compromise with idealism. It was Pearce's contention that the People's Constitution would not be ratified without a white-only clause.[74] Pearce was not alone in his views. If blacks could vote, "a nigger might occupy" a position of authority in the new government, went the cry from a delegate from the northern mill town of Smithfield.[75] The word "white" was eventually retained by a vote of 46 to 18.[76] Though Dorr failed in his attempt to implement a color-blind democracy, he did manage to win approval for a provision protecting the legal rights of suspected fugitive slaves. Building upon his antislavery activism in the 1830s, the provision Dorr drafted provided legal safeguards for the personal liberty of alleged fugitive bondsmen (as well as free blacks) by providing for a jury trial to determine legal status.

Despite the relegation of blacks to second-class status, the People's

Constitution did remedy numerous abuses that had persisted under the Charter regime. As was to be expected, Article I, section 3 of the People's Constitution emphatically affirmed that "the people have an inalienable and indefensible right in their original, sovereign and unlimited capacity to ordain and institute government and in the same capacity to alter, reform or totally change the same." Other significant features of the People's Constitution included: reapportionment provisions, which increased Providence's representation; annual election of judges; a flexible amendment procedure; a secret ballot; state support of education; a bill of rights, and the increased authority of juries by making them judges both of law and fact. Dorr and his followers believed that an increase in jury power would serve to shield the oppressed. Building on Dorr's banking reform measures in the mid-1830s, the delegates required a popular referendum on every bank bill. Imbued with the ideology of Equal Rights Democrats, delegates prevented the state from incurring debt beyond the sum of $50,000. A local referendum was needed before capital improvements could be made in any city.

The conservative aspects of the document were its denial of a number of important public offices, including those of mayor, to nontaxed citizens, along with a provision whereby no person was allowed to vote on any financial question in cities or towns unless he was a taxpayer or the owner of property (real or personal) of at least $150. Reformers, despite Dorr's advocacy, also failed to abolish imprisonment for debt.[77] Pearce "did not wish any thing should stand in the Constitution which might be used as a scarecrow." Pearce did not want to raise the dreaded specter of agrarianism.[78]

In the end, although all reformers agreed that the people were sovereign and that a majority of the people could abolish their existing government and frame a new one at any time, they were deeply divided over one significant issue: who were "the people"? In the end, racism and the fear of being associated with abolitionism ruled the day. "They complain of inequality! They make an outcry about oppression! While they deliberately disenfranchise a class of citizens guiltless of crime!" declared Lydia Maria Child.[79] In the pages of *The Wampanoag and Operatives' Journal*, the thirty-seven-year-old abolitionist Frances Whipple Greene maintained that in "excluding their colored fellow citizens from the rights and privileges, which they were seeking for themselves," the Suffrage Association "forfeited the esteem and confidence of all the true and consistent friends of freedom." According to Whipple, "the word 'WHITE'" in the People's Constitution was "a black mark against" the suffrage reformers.[80] Similar to Dorr, Greene was a consummate reformer working for temperance, the abolition of slavery, and women's rights.

While the People's Convention was in adjournment, the executive committee of the Rhode Island Anti-Slavery Society, an organization that Dorr had helped to run just two years before, issued a circular condemning the constitution, though significantly it did not signal out Dorr by name. The majority of northern abolitionists understood that Dorr did everything he could to protect the rights of black Rhode Islanders. The circular from the state antislavery society called "on the abolitionists to make a combined and vigorous effort against the proposed Constitution."[81] When an attempt is made "by the pseudo friends of political reform to make the rights of a man dependent on the hue of his skin," abolitionists needed to unite in a "spirited" manner, declared William Lloyd Garrison in the pages of the *Liberator*.[82] The prominent abolitionist editor had a sizeable number of admirers in Rhode Island through his marriage to Helen Benson, the daughter of one of the founding members of the Rhode Island Anti-Slavery Society. Garrison, as he did with so many causes, threw himself into an effort to defeat the People's Constitution.

Only William Goodell looked past the shortcomings in the People's Constitution to the greater good achieved with the extension of suffrage to thousands of propertyless white males. Abolitionism, in Goodell's analysis, was a crusade not only to abolish slavery, but to eradicate all other abuses in society, especially political inequality. Goodell saw political action as an effective strategy and not simply a naive plunge into the world of political compromise as the Garrisonians argued.[83] Goodell reminded his abolitionist colleagues that Dorr was an ardent antislavery man and the white-only clause was not his fault. He clearly saw in Dorr's ideology of the people's sovereignty an antislavery weapon. He chastised his fellow abolitionists who thought a "regard for 'law and order'" required them to "shoulder arms against human rights."[84] Writing to abolitionists, Goodell argued that if they believed in the mission of the "liberty party," they could not stand "aloof" from the cause of freedom in Rhode Island. Though white reformers had failed to implement a color-blind democracy, they could become future allies in the antislavery clause.[85] Goodell also clearly saw the precedent-setting implications of using the Guarantee Clause to settle the constitutional dispute in Rhode Island. Goodell, however, was a voice in the wilderness.

A call also went out from the state antislavery society to Abby Kelley, who was living in nearby Millbury, Massachusetts, to come to Rhode Island to campaign against the document. By the end of her life, Kelley had covered more miles and given more speeches than any other female orator.[86] "Her youth and simple beauty, combined with her wonderful earnestness, her large knowledge and great logical power, bore down all opposition to the end," wrote the ex-slave Frederick Douglass.[87] Born in Massachusetts in 1811, Kelley was educated at the New England Yearly Meeting Boarding School (later renamed Moses Brown School) in Providence. In 1832, she saw Garrison lecture and promptly became an abolitionist. Kelley joined the Lynn, Massachusetts, Female Anti-Slavery Society in 1835, becoming secretary in 1836, and went to New York as a delegate to the Anti-Slavery Convention of American Women in 1837. In 1838, Kelley's first public lecture outside of the Bay State constituted a baptism by fire. Enraged by reports that abolitionists favored amalgamation of the races, residents of Philadelphia stormed Pennsylvania Hall and burned it to the ground.[88] Two years later, at the AASS annual meeting, Kelley broke another cultural rule and effectively split the antislavery movement with her call for gender equality. Reform-minded Quakers like Kelley, along with Rhode Island's Arnold Buffum, often met with more than mere disapproval. Both Buffum and Kelley were disowned by their Meetings for advocating antislavery principles. Shortly after her expulsion from the Uxbridge monthly meeting in early 1841, Kelley told Garrison that the society was, on the whole, proslavery and that she wanted nothing to do with Quakers who worked to support the "bloody system" of slavery.[89]

Thomas Dorr most likely first met Kelley in 1839 when she addressed the annual meeting of the AASS and was appointed to the publications committee.[90] In August 1841, as the voting for delegates to the People's Convention was getting under way, Kelley was preparing to journey to Rhode Island to arouse antislavery forces. "We are looking forward to thy mission here with some anxiety, hoping it may be the means of arousing an antislavery spirit, as I feel confident it will a proslavery one," said Pawtucket abolitionist Susan Sisson, a member, along with Kelley, of the business committee of the Rhode Island Anti-Slavery Society. "The land of Roger Williams is not a land of freedom," proclaimed Sisson. "There is mingling with the life-current here a taint of the Puritan blood, which will course rapidly through the veins of the aristocratical, sectarian and pro-slavery priesthood and their satellites at the bare thought of a woman lecturing."[91] In actuality, Kelley joined in with a long tradition of fiery female lecturers, including Anne Hutchinson, Mary Dyer, and Jemima Wilkinson.

By October 1841, Kelley was in Rhode Island, lecturing in the towns of Westerly and Charlestown in southern Rhode Island, both former sites of large plantations that used slave labor and, in Kelley's words, "strongholds of opposition to the truth." The prominent Providence abolitionist couple Asa and Anna Fairbanks told Kelley they were "pleased" that she had "come to labor in the abolition cause" in Rhode Island. The Fairbanks informed Kelley that they were busy organizing the annual convention of the state antislavery society, which would commence on November 11 in Providence.[92] The "word white, must, if possible be kept out of the Constitution," wrote Kelley to Garrison as she made her way to different abolitionist homes in Westerly in order to raise money for handbills to protest against the placement of a white-only clause in the People's Constitution.[93] Kelley told the readers of Child's *National Anti-Slavery Standard* that a sizeable number of abolitionists supported the Suffrage Association in the past but now would work to defeat the People's Constitution. "They have left the hypocrites, and will now do as valiantly *against* them, as they once did *for* them," proclaimed Kelley.[94] A woman living in the town of Cranston, adjacent to Providence, was converted to abolitionism after hearing Kelley lecture against the People's Constitution. "Thou art accused (like another Socrates) of introducing new gods; of corrupting the minds of the youth; enticing them from the path of rectitude; beguiling them from the church; and so perverting their understandings by thy sophistry, as to lead them to discard all religion," wrote the new convert with considerable pride as she recounted the schism that had erupted in Rhode Island's churches over abolitionist lectures.[95] Kelley probably had no idea at the time that she was in for a "long and severe campaign" in Rhode Island.[96] In the months to come, her life would be threatened numerous times.

While Kelley's lecturing electrified the abolitionist faithful in Rhode Island and drew fire from critics, Dorr was basking in glowing letters of support from political friends. He received encouragement from the Massachusetts statesman Alexander Hill Everett, who wrote him in early November after reading a draft of the People's Constitution that "the code of what may be called American principles of constitutional law has become so familiar to us by more *than fifty years' practice*, that, when the People are permitted to act for themselves, there is no great danger of their being led into any material error."[97]

In the weeks after the end of the first session of the People's Convention, the Suffrage Association undertook an extensive letter-writing campaign to prominent politicians—both Democrats and Whigs—from around the country. Because of his skilled pen, Dorr was selected as the principal draftsman. Through the efforts of the Suffrage Association, "the body of the people has been able to concentrate their action for a reform in our political constitutions," wrote Dorr to John Quincy Adams. Dorr confined his letter to Adams, the former-president-turned-congressman, to the issue of constitutional reform in Rhode Island. He surprisingly chose not to identify himself as an antislavery advocate who had openly opposed the annexation of Texas, a fight that Adams was currently waging in Congress.[98] The "consequence" of this concerted reform effort in Rhode Island was a "convention of the whole People of the State, fairly represented in proportion to the population," said Dorr. He made sure to emphasize that the "non-freeholders" were "compelled to take this course by a just respect to their own rights and after the denial of every application which has been made to the minority government for the establishment of a republic in place of our worn-out system." Echoing language from the *New Age*, Dorr maintained that "the people" of Rhode Island "have a right, in their original and sovereign capacity, to alter and amend their form of government here existing and to render it more conformable to the standard of justice and equality." Dorr attempted to ground this argument with reference to the Guarantee Clause.[99]

Based on his understanding of classical history and philosophy, Dorr's concept of democracy ran afoul of everything that Adams held dear. Adams believed that popular sovereignty would ultimately fail because it was based on the passions and enthusiasms of the people, depriving government of stability.[100] Only Democrats would write in support of Dorr's ideology. As Andrew Jackson, John Quincy Adams's political nemesis, later noted, the people had "a right to alter and amend their system of Government when a majority wills it."[101]

Though they often seemed oblivious to the massive groundswell of support for constitutional change, the Rhode Island General Assembly managed to convene a constitutional convention on November 1, 1841.[102] Dorr and Glocester attorney Samuel Atwell, his old ally from the bank wars of the 1830s, were the only delegates from the People's Convention to attend. A quick glance at the declaration of rights and principles illustrates the ideological differences between the two constitutions. Jeffersonian idealism and ringing endorsements of the people's sovereignty were nowhere to be found in what would become known as the Landholders' Constitution.[103] Henry Dorr warned his brother "not to take a leading part" in the Landholders' Convention because it would only serve to "alarm the freeholders from the country [southern and western regions of the state] with the extreme liberality of your opinions, and thereby to frighten them from such liberal concessions as they might otherwise be disposed to make."[104] The elder Dorr did not heed his brother's counsel. His presence undoubtedly accomplished just what Henry predicted.

The committee on suffrage actually chose Dorr's law office on College Street as a place to convene. Home field advantage, however, did not help Dorr persuade his colleagues that a "landed qualification for voters was unjust and inexpedient."[105] What was expedient to the majority of the delegates to the Landholders' Convention was the retention of the white-only clause for voting. On the last day of the convention, the word "white" was retained by a vote of 51 to 16.[106] Also missing was a provision for jury trials for fugitive slaves enshrined in the language of Article 1, section 14 of the People's Constitution. Charter supporters would later use this clause against Dorr, stating that the "cloven foot of abolitionism" had overtaken Dorr and that his constitution would "dissolve the union."[107] The cloven hoof was a reference to the devil.

Providence's black community sent a memorial to the Landholders' Convention on November 4 protesting the attempt to insert a white-only provision. Having failed so far to persuade the delegates to the People's Convention to live up to their own creed, the leading members of Providence's black community decided to petition the very authorities who had removed them from the franchise in 1822 for the "rights and privileges of citizenship." In a ringing endorsement of color-blind equality, the memorial declared: "We petition the abrogation of that odious feature of the statute, which in making the right of citizenship identical with color, brings *a stain upon the state*, unmans the heart of an already injured people and corrupts the purity of republican faith." They reminded the convention of their service during the American Revolution and the War of 1812, where the "fame" of Captain Oliver Hazard Perry at the Battle of Lake Erie "was gained at the expenses of the bleeding veins and mangled bodies of our neglected and disenfranchised citizens." The memorial detailed how the rhetoric of liberty in the Revolutionary era transformed rights from specific, social, and limited in scope to universal, inherent, and inalienable.

Demonstrating their acute sense of the longstanding anti-Catholic, nativist sentiment in the state, the memorial reminded the delegates that blacks were not "foreign born" nor were they "accustomed to a political creed repugnant to democratic principles." A "foreign birth and adverse usages, that might possibly beget uncongenial political sympathies and sentiments—exists not in our case."[108] The "repugnant" creed was a reference to Roman Catholicism and the widespread conservative fear of enfranchising the growing mass of Irish Catholic immigrants. The population of Providence had grown from 17,000 in 1830 to over 23,000 in 1840, a 35 percent increase due largely to Irish immigration.[109] Henry Bowen Anthony, the nativist editor of the *Providence Journal*, had been writing anti-immigrant diatribes since 1838. He was joined in 1841 by William Goddard, a Brown University professor of rhetoric.[110] References to Catholicism and fear of the foreign-born were not part of the memorial sent to the People's Convention.

With Dorr in the minority, the suffrage committee at the Landholders' Convention argued not only for retention of the landed qualification for voting, but also for new restrictions on naturalized citizens, which would require them to live in the state for three years in addition to the freehold requirement.[111] The convention concluded its business by mid-November. A resolution was passed calling for an adjournment to February in order to let citizens view their unfinished handiwork. A draft of the Landholders' Constitution appeared in pamphlet form. Key sections, including those on suffrage, however, were missing.[112] Aside from an agreement on reapportioning the state on the basis of population rather than on a fixed system, the convention produced no significant reforms. Attention was now focused back on the People's Convention, which was set to reopen on November 16, and the question of black suffrage.

From his home in Boston, Garrison made preparations to wage a verbal war on Dorr and his fellow delegates. Whereas Garrison had supported the abolitionist Dorr as a "democratic anti-slavery" candidate for Congress in 1837 and 1839, he would now journey to Rhode Island to ensure the defeat of a cause dear to Dorr's heart. "Thomas W. Dorr, who while professing to be an abolitionist, is willing to be the representative and head of a party which makes the right to the elective franchise dependent on the complexion of men," proclaimed Garrison.[113] The prominent Boston abolitionist urged Dorr's friend Edmund Quincy to attend the sixth annual meeting of the Rhode Island Anti-Slavery Society convention.[114] It is "really a crisis with our antislavery friends in Rhode Island, and they need all the aid and encouragement we can give them at the present time," said the *Liberator* editor.[115]

Quincy elected not to attend the convention, but other New England abolitionists including Wendell Phillips, Parker Pillsbury, Abby Kelley, Thomas Davis, and the rising star Frederick Douglass, the "fugitive Othello," who was "cut out for" the role of a "hero," made the journey to Providence. Nathan Rogers, who had heard of Douglass's skills as a lecturer, made the journey from New Hampshire to Rhode Island, boarding a "Jim Crow" train in Boston with Garrison and recording the journey for subscribers to the *Herald of Freedom*.[116] This was only Douglass's third lecture outside of Massachusetts. On November 4 Douglass gave a stirring speech on northern racism at the annual convention of the Plymouth County antislavery society.[117] As a lecturer Douglass had "few equals." He "has wit, argument, sarcasm, [and] pathos," wrote Rogers.[118] "He stood there as a slave—a runaway from the southern house of bondage . . . with his back all horribly scared [*sic*] by the lash—with the bitter remembrances of a life of slavery crowding upon his soul—with every thing in his past history, his present condition, his future prospects, to make him a fierce outlaw, and a stern avenger of outraged humanity," proclaimed Garrison.[119]

Generally heralded as one of the finest nineteenth-century orators, Douglass, who stood over six feet tall and had a baritone voice, was a "master of every weapon," using wit, humor, and satire in all his speeches.[120] One white male who identified himself to a local reporter as being a racist left a Douglass lecture on the island of Nantucket with "food for thought" that showered down like "manna from heaven."[121] How "his owner would cower and shiver to hear him thunder in an anti-slavery hall," said Nathan Rogers.[122]

The son of a slave woman and an unknown white man, Douglass was born in February 1818 on Maryland's eastern shore. After escaping from Maryland in 1838 he made his way to New York City where he changed his name to Frederick Douglass and met the black abolitionist David Ruggles, who put him on a ship bound for Newport, Rhode Island. Several weeks later, Douglass moved to New Bedford, Massachusetts. By 1841, Frederick Douglass had spoken several times to audiences in New Bedford—a city that justly earned its title as the fugitive's Gibraltar—about the evils of the colonization movement.[123] In the summer of 1841, Douglass traveled to an antislavery meeting on the island of Nantucket off the coast of Cape Cod. William Coffin, a bookseller who had heard Douglass preach at the African Methodist Episcopal church in New Bedford, invited him to address the Nantucket convention. The second of his speeches on Nantucket so impressed John Collins, who was serving as the general agent of the Massachusetts Anti-Slavery Society, that he invited Douglass to serve as a lecturer for the society on a three-month trial basis. As Collins noted to Garrison, the "public have itching ears to have a colored man speak, and particularly a slave; multitudes will flock to hear one of his class speak."[124] Aside from a brief one-day engagement in Fall River, Massachusetts, the white-only clause in the People's Constitution occupied Douglass's time for the remainder of 1841.[125] The remarkable career of Frederick Douglass, one that would see him emerge as the most important African American leader and intellectual in the nineteenth century, was set in motion.

Douglass was one of six blacks who spoke in favor of resolutions condemning the People's Constitution. To counter the efforts of Douglass and his brethren, the Suffrage Association used the specter of "nigger voting" to arouse racist fears.[126] "We wish the hall had been ten times as large" so "all our 'negro haters' could have heard them." They would have "learned, if they did not know it before, that the 'colored man' had a head to think, a heart to feel, and a soul to aspire to like other men," proclaimed the editor of a Providence abolitionist tract.[127] Robert Purvis, the prominent Philadelphia abolitionist who helped to organize the American Anti-Slavery Society and would later become a central figure in the Underground Railroad, urged the delegates to work against racist northern "doughfaces."[128] In the middle of the antislavery convention's deliberations, John Brown, president of the Suffrage Association, entered the room. In a lengthy address to the convention, Brown argued that the Suffrage Association was charged with advocating for the greatest good of the majority of citizens in the state. Once universal suffrage was achieved for whites, Brown assured that black suffrage would soon follow.[129]

The convention promptly condemned the compromising spirit. To the *Herald of Freedom*, Brown's "political morality seemed about as high as that of a railroad engine with a Jim Crow car to it; or a church with a nigger pew." The "free suffrage doctor [Brown] fell into the merciless hands of Garrison, who tore him limb from limb."[130] Garrison responded to Brown's remarks in what the *New Age* referred to as a stream of epithets. According to Garrison, the suffrage reformers "were engaged in a mean and contemptible business—the dastardly act of the Suffrage men show them to be possessed of mean and contemptible souls."[131] In Garrison's analysis, Brown's argument that the constitution was "the best" that could be achieved rang hollow—"injustice and hypocrisy admit of no excuse."[132] The Rhode

Island Anti-Slavery Society petitioned the People's Convention to allow Douglass and Kelley to argue their case in front of the delegates. This communication was quickly laid on the table by the convention. There is no record of Douglass or Kelley ever presenting their views in person at the People's Convention. On November 18 Dorr did win a motion to have the word "white" revisited in the first election under the new constitution. Only William Goodell viewed this as a significant victory for which Dorr deserved credit.[133] Despite the half-a-loaf offer on black voting, the Boston Liberty Association implored Dorr to speak out against the constitution that he played such a large role in creating.[134] "We condemn unequivocally the compromising spirit which cries half a loaf better than no bread," declared the state antislavery society.[135]

Undoubtedly disappointed that his colleagues did not share his egalitarian views, Dorr refused to throw away all his handiwork. Dorr never hid the fact that the constitution had "imperfections," but on the whole it secured to the white male portion of the citizenry "a measure of political justice and republican freedom."[136] Unwilling to let the People's Constitution flounder on the issue of black suffrage, Dorr papered over the issue of racist elements with raucous, patriotic oratory. Dorr addressed the convention on the day of its adjournment and once again set out to answer the question: Who were the people?[137] He gave a stirring three-hour speech on suffrage, reiterating the principles laid out in the draft of the People's Constitution.[138] In ringing prose, Dorr declared that the Rhode Island "government has degenerated into a freeholding aristocracy; that safety and self respect forbid a longer delay in the work of reform; and that the people are now proceeding, in an unobjectionable and appropriate mode, to adopt such measure as justice requires." Dorr and the rest of the delegates to People's Convention knew that they had arrived at anything but an "unequivocal or decisive" answer, but that is how he painted the convention's final moments.[139]

Ever the student of American politics, Dorr probably did not want to suffer the fate of the radical Pennsylvania Democrat Thomas Earle, who was ostracized by his party for his support of black suffrage.[140] Dorr's viewpoint on black suffrage, circa 1841, was succinctly captured a few months later by a Fall River printer and antislavery supporter. "I regretted at the time of the formation of the People's Constitution that it was not more liberal in some of its provisions and would not then have supported it because it did not secure to colored people the same rights that it does to others," wrote Louis Lapham. However, "when the landholders formed a Constitution still less liberal than the People's," continued Lapham, it "irretrievably shut the door against ever admitting the colored man to vote" convincing "me at once that the Suffrage Party had probably put that question in the most liberal shape that circumstances would at the time render successful."[141]

Susan Sisson saw the opposite taking place. The Pawtucket abolitionist informed Abby Kelley that "professing abolitionists" found the Landholders' Constitution even with its white-only clause "far less objectionable" than the People's Constitution because the General Assembly had the "power of legislating directly on the vexed question without an appeal to the people."[142] Sisson's remarks foreshadowed the growing conflict over the people's sovereignty—democracy and morality did not always go hand-in-hand.

Elisha Potter, Jr., poked holes in the Suffrage Association's conception of who exactly constituted "the people" of Rhode Island. "I might for instance say that the people included women as well as men and that it include persons under twenty one years and according to your principles if I could get a majority of those whom I called the people to adopt it, it would become the constitution of the state," wrote Potter to Dutee Pearce in late 1841 after reading the People's Constitution.[143] The touchstone of conservative ideas about sovereignty was legitimacy and obedience to the laws. Once "you refuse to recognize the authority of the freeholders and those who now constitute the legal voters and undertake to define for yourselves who the people are, there is no knowing where to stop and no possibility of agreeing upon any other limitation."[144] In another letter, Potter connected the Suffrage Association with the radicalism of the northern abolitionist movement. There was a "natural and necessary connection between abolition and doctrines upon which" the suffrage movement was "grounded," said Potter. Foreshadowing the lukewarm support Dorr would later receive from southern congressmen when the legality of the People's Constitution was brought to the floor of the U.S. House of Representatives, Potter declared that "Southern men" would not "give their support to the doctrine that a majority of the people in numbers have a right to get together and upset the government. The consequences of its adoption and promulgation might be dangerous to them."[145] Dorr was simply unfazed by these remarks. He insisted that the people had a constitutional right to revise Rhode Island's archaic governing structure, even if that meant bypassing the General Assembly and writing a new constitution for the state. "He expressed himself <u>entirely</u> indifferent as to the course of the Legislature & laughed the powers that be to scorn," wrote a dismayed John Brown Francis after meeting with Dorr.[146]

Sometime in late December or early January, Thomas Dorr sent his younger brother Henry a copy of the People's Constitution in order to get his opinion. Fifteen years younger than Thomas, Henry had received the equivalent education. Henry was educated at Brown University and then did his legal training at Harvard under the tutelage of Supreme Court Justice Joseph Story. Henry had recently secured employment in New York City in the law office of James Kent, thanks to the efforts of his older brother.[147] After moving to New York from his apartment in Cambridge, Massachusetts, Henry became friends with a young lawyer named George Templeton Strong. The acerbic and thoroughly conservative Strong, whose diary would be made famous by the documentarian Ken Burns, had a powerful influence on Henry's political views. Henry, who was never shy in challenging his older brother, pulled no punches in his ten-page, tour-de-force exposition on the nature of American constitutionalism.

"I am afraid that the Suffrage party are wrong—and that as a matter of expediency their measures have been ill chosen," began Henry, wasting little time in getting to the point. A portion of the state, regardless of the number, had "no right to raise the cry—'peaceably if we can, forcibly if we must.'" Henry did not see "how the disfranchised American citizens of R.I. [could] legally make any forcible alteration in their form of government unless at the same time they publish their first official decree—they proclaim their secession from the Union." For Henry Dorr, the "spirit" of American legal institutions "required that the people should do everything by deputy—that they should not assume to themselves the administration of affairs." According to Henry, the people could "agitate, discuss, and censure at their pleasure, but to take into their own hands the subversion of the government is a matter of the last resort." In terms of the Guarantee Clause, Henry argued that it was "intended to guard against the very attempt which your friends are just now making." Whereas Thomas saw the republican Guarantee Clause in Article IV, Section 4 of the Constitution as justifying his reform efforts, Henry saw it doing precisely the opposite—justifying the federal government's suppression of the People's Government in order to ensure the continued existence of the Charter until the General Assembly took steps to change it. In Henry Dorr's analysis, when Rhode Island ratified the Constitution in 1790, its "republican government" was recognized. Playing the devil's advocate and acknowledging the fact that his older brother might be right, Henry asked what would the effect be at the polls if Dorr's followers became scared because the Charter government threatened to imprison them? In closing, Henry urged Dorr to have the Suffrage Association keep the issue before the people, by writing and protesting peaceably.[148] Henry Dorr clearly had the ability to think things through and to anticipate possible outcomes, a quality his older brother was not blessed with.

Chapter 4

Peacefully If We Can, Forcibly If We Must

In the small state of Rhode Island, with the population of about 100,000, there are at this moment two Governors, two Senates, two Houses of Representatives and other things in proportion—a clear exemplification of Jefferson's maxim that "the world is governed too much."

Charleston Mercury, April 27, 1842

With the printing of the People's Constitution in the *New Age and Constitutional Advocate* on November 26, 1841, and a call for voting to take place December 27–29, the Suffrage Association and the antislavery vanguard entered into a war of words. On December 17, the editors of the *New Age* ran an open letter addressed "To the Abolitionists of Rhode Island." This was an attempt on the part of those members of the suffrage movement who also harbored abolitionist sympathies to provide a rationale for the white-only clause in the People's Constitution. According to Benjamin Arnold, Samuel Wales, and William Wentworth, the final draft of the constitution contained a "direct imperative and positive provision for speedily removing the exclusion and securing to colored men their right of Suffrage." The three authors made clear that at the first session of the People's legislature in May, the question of black suffrage would be put to a vote. Arnold, Wales, and Wentworth acknowledged the racism of many of the delegates to the convention, but pleaded with the abolitionists not to let this prevent them from supporting the overall liberal document.

Anticipating the abolitionist response that a vote for the People's Constitution represented a compromise of principle, the authors answered: "No more than voting for an act to emancipate slaves one year hence, after making every exertion in vain to render their emancipation immediate, is voting to hold them in slavery for one year." The Suffrage Association was "bound to carry out" their "principles to every practicable, but not to every impracticable extent, because principle" would not permit them "to sacrifice a benevolent attainable object to a mere nominal and useless theoretical consistency."[1] Only the New York abolitionist William Goodell agreed with the line of argument put forth by Arnold, Wales, and Wentworth.[2] The majority of northern abolitionists did not see their critique of the document as a "useless" attempt at "theoretical consistency." The abolitionists believed that the delegates to the People's Convention had failed to bring policy into the greatest possible accord with principle.

"A combined and vigorous antislavery effort should be made against the movement . . . attempting to disfranchise the people of color," said Lydia Maria Child in the *National Anti-Slavery Standard*.[3] "We had hoped [for] better things of the land of Roger Williams," wrote Child.[4] The move to insert a white-only provision in the People's Constitution was a "base, cowardly, a hypocritical attempt . . . to gradate the rights of man by the complexion of the skin," declared abolitionist William Aplin's *Suffrage Examiner*, a Providence paper started for the express purpose of defeating the People's Constitution.[5] "It is for you to decide whether this state, early famous as the nursery for free principles, shall now, with the light of truth and liberty beaming upon her, deliberately . . . bow before the dark spirit of slavery," wrote Aplin. It was up to Rhode Island citizens to "determine whether the rights and privileges of the colored people sink or swim with those of white people."[6] On the back page of the paper, Aplin ran a poem from Dorr's friend, John Greenleaf Whittier.

In response to the clarion calls to protest the People's Constitution, the Who's Who of the New England abolitionist movement—including John A. Collins (MA), Stephen Foster (NH), George Foster (MA), Abby Kelley (MA), Parker Pillsbury (NH), and Frederick Douglass (MA)—descended on Rhode Island to protest the People's Constitution. George Foster hoped that a "moral earthquake" would result from their barnstorming.[7] In describing one of Kelley's speeches, the *Providence Journal* noted that never "were such furious denunciations drowned in such honied accents; never were such terrible anathemas spoken with so sweet a smile."[8] Many "a heart must have been touched by the fervid appeal of Kelley, the plain truths of Pillsbury, and the majestic denunciations of Foster," declared the New Hampshire abolitionist organ, the *Herald of Freedom*.[9] Parker Pillsbury's first major speaking tour took place in Rhode Island to protest against the

People's Constitution.[10] Abolitionists, notably Kelley, Douglass, Pillsbury, Stephen Foster, and George Foster, spoke out against the People's Constitution in separate mini-conventions in every corner of the state. There would be no compromise with those who would "trample" upon "inalienable rights."[11] The coastal communities of Newport, Bristol, and Warren—all former major centers of Rhode Island's slave trading ventures—proved to be the most hostile to the antislavery agents.[12]

A tongue-in-cheek resolution passed at an East Greenwich meeting stated that the Rhode Island Anti-Slavery Society has "no objection" to the People's Constitution "only in so far as it is inconsistent with itself, and wars upon inalienable rights."[13] Stephen Foster's remarks in the Freewill Baptist Church in North Scituate, a Dorrite stronghold in the northwestern part of the state, were reprinted in the *National Anti-Slavery Standard*. Foster introduced a resolution condemning the "white Suffrage Constitution" as "more odious and repugnant to the true principles of freedom than the old charter; and cannot receive the support of any true republican or genuine Christian."[14] Mobs of Dorrites sought to break up these abolitionist meetings using the rallying cry of "nigger voting" to inspire violence.[15]

Frederick Douglass's fiery denunciations of the hypocrisy embodied in the People's Constitution served to arouse Rhode Island abolitionists. Douglass later argued that blacks "cared nothing for the Dorr party on the one hand" or the "law and order party on the other." What blacks wanted was "a constitution free from the narrow, selfish, and senseless limitation of the word *white*." The People's Constitution, in Douglass's analysis, was "framed to enlarge the basis of representation so far as the white people of the state were concerned." Dorr was "a well-meaning man" and a "man of broad and progressive views quite in advance of the party [Democrats] with which he acted," wrote Douglass. However, to "gain their support" Dorr "consented to this restriction to a class a right which ought to be enjoyed by all citizens."[16]

George Foster made a special point to highlight the bigotry Douglass had to endure during the rail ride from Providence to the southern regions of Rhode Island. Indeed, at each of the conventions, abolitionists attacked the pervasive racism in the North, calling for a color-blind conception of democracy. The "conductor seized hold of his coat, and ordered him into the 'Jim Crow car' . . . the seats were covered with snow, one door was fastened open, to let in the cold, and produce a free circulation of air."[17] This was nothing new for Douglass. He frequently refused to ride on trains when he was ordered to the Jim Crow car by the conductor; however, he swallowed his pride in this instance in order to lead the charge against the People's Constitution.[18]

Kelley told the *National Anti-Slavery Standard* that the violence directed at her, Douglass, Pillsbury, and her future husband, Stephen Foster, had awakened the state to the importance of antislavery. "Few can see a crowd following a defenseless woman through the streets, hurling missiles at her, and shouting, without inquiry, 'why?'" said Kelley.[19] The courageous abolitionist was pelted with "decayed apples and eggs" in Newport, which she referred to as "one of the strongest, if not the strongest holds of slavery in New England." Despite the "troubled dreams" that stemmed from the abuse, Kelley was able to give numerous speeches on what she labeled "the democracy of antislavery."[20] Her most vocal opponent in Newport was Dutee Pearce, who told the conservative Democrat John Brown Francis that "Kelley and Co." had "acted like mad men," never talked about "compromise," and deserved what they got.[21]

Pearce did not acknowledge that the wild mob that attacked the antislavery meeting in Providence in the midst of the vote on the People's Constitution almost killed Kelley by throwing balls of frozen snow and ice at her head nor that he had given a "proslavery" speech in Newport.[22] William Aplin reported that the final convention in Providence (December 27–28), which was chaired by Dorr's old associate William Chace, "adjourned amidst a scene of confusion and uproar never before witnessed by the friends of free discussion in this city." The "mobocratic elements" reached new heights in Providence. The multiple resolutions praising the slaves on board the brig *Creole*, who successfully revolted against their owners and took over the vessel, surely drew condemnation from conservatives.[23] According to the Pawtucket abolitionist Asa Fairbanks, Thomas Dorr was in attendance at the Providence convention. However, Dorr, a past champion of free speech and defender of the rights of free black Americans, stood silently in the back of the room. He did nothing to stop the hecklers who tried to disrupt the meeting. "Five words from him might have made things all quiet—but, no! He walked silently out," wrote Fairbanks.[24] Ironically, despite the attacks waged by New England abolitionists on the People's Constitution, Dorr's enemies still labeled the document a "horrid abolitionist plot."[25]

When the ballots were finally counted in early January 1842, the People's Constitution was approved by the overwhelming majority. The vote was

13,944 in favor with just 52 opposed.[26] "Dorr's plan has succeeded beyond his most sanguine calculations," declared Elisha Potter, Jr. "The next thing for them to determine is whether they will carry it into effect by force if necessary or whether they will wait and have it done in a peaceable and legal manner."[27] The final vote tally was also remarkably close to the 14,000 vote number that Dorr cited in a letter to Newport attorney Dutee Pearce.[28] In late November 1841, Pearce had suggested to Dorr that aliens be allowed to vote, but Dorr emphatically refused to adhere to this opportunistic position because it contravened the wording of the People's Constitution.[29] When Dorr's personal papers were seized by state authorities several months later, however, Pearce's letter was quoted out of context in order to mount accusations of fraud and deceit.[30] Votes for the People's Constitution were strongest in the northern industrial section of the state. Only 42 percent of support came from the southern agricultural areas. The vote total did, however, include a majority of freeholders in the state (4,960 out of 8,000).[31] The *New Age* boldly declared on January 14 that the People's Constitution "ought to be and is the paramount law and Constitution of the state of Rhode Island and Providence Plantations."[32]

Dorr's ally, Samuel Atwell, a representative to the General Assembly from the town of Glocester, quickly put forth a bill to abolish the Landholders' Convention and to allow the People's Constitution to go into effect.[33] "What the results will be I cannot tell, and do not care," said Dorr. The "will of the People has been decisively expressed . . . if the Legislature [does] not give way, they will be run over by the Government of the People."[34] At the end of the six-day debate, the assembly voted 60 to 7 in favor of passing forceful resolutions against the actions of the Suffrage Association. The first resolution maintained that the Landholders' Convention was "the only body which we can recognize as authorized to form a constitution." The second resolution called for the assembly to "protect and defend the legal and constitutional rights of the people."[35] "Thank God our legislature and the state" are "firm," said federal judge John Pitman after learning of the assembly's resolutions. Pitman acknowledged that the state would "have to give up [the] freehold qualification," but reforms would be made by a "legal convention."[36] Pitman's youngest son would soon join a militia unit in Providence to defend the city against violence.

Taking up his pen once again, Dorr drafted the written response to the actions of the General Assembly. Adopting an 1830s cry from Rhode Island labor radical Seth Luther, Dorr's response was nothing short of militant:

"Peacefully if we can, forcibly if we must." Any attempt to injure or intimidate the citizenry in their endeavor to implement the People's Constitution would be met with "the strong arm of the people."[37] The resolutions called for committees of safety to be created in order to protect those loyal to the cause. Yet, despite this rhetorical reassertion of the Suffrage Association's commitment to the sanctity of the people's sovereignty, Dorr did not attempt to change the curious, and with hindsight, unwise decision to allow the Charter government almost four months to pack up and leave. Article XIV, section 5 of the People's Constitution declared that the Charter authorities "shall exercise all the powers with which it is now clothed, until the said first Tuesday of May 1842, and until their successors, under this constitution shall be duly elected and qualified." Seldom have revolutionaries been so accommodating to an existing government they were trying to overthrow.[38] By waiting until mid-April to hold elections, the Suffrage Association afforded their opponents ample time to mount a counterattack.

Still a delegate to the Landholders' Convention when it reconvened in February 1842, Dorr attempted to convince the delegates to disband and recognize the People's Constitution. His proposal failed miserably, as did a similar one put forth by Atwell that called for a special commission to examine the votes for the People's Constitution.[39] Spurred by the recent, seemingly overwhelming support for the document, delegates to the Landholders' Convention were determined to produce a finished product and not simply a draft as they had in November 1841. This constitution was designed to lure moderates over to the Charter government. As one conservative Whig noted, by "removing" the "governing principle from the possession of the soil" the Landholders' Constitution could be made more palpable to the people.[40]

The constitution did gave the franchise to those white, male native-born citizens who met age and residency requirements, but it retained the real estate requirement for naturalized citizens and actually lengthened the state's residency qualification from one year to three years after naturalization. The document reapportioned seats in the legislature, but less drastically than the People's Constitution. Similar to the People's Constitution, a white-only clause was inserted; however, the Landholders' Constitution did not contain a clause mandating that the white-only provision be revisited. In order to steal the reform thunder from the Suffragists, the General Assembly reversed course on voting provisions.[41] Those white males eligible to vote under the provisions outlined in the constitution would now be allowed to vote on its adoption on March 21–23, though the restriction for naturalized citizens was retained. As Dorr's uncle, Zachariah Allen, Jr., noted, the "Newport members and southern representatives have managed to very adroitly win the favor of the free suffrage party by conceding to them all they asked." Allen was confident of victory.[42]

Worrying little about the olive branch to native-born white males in the Landholders' Constitution, Dorr took on the task of finding candidates to run on what would become known as the People's ticket in the scheduled April elections. Conservatives were simply dismayed with Dorr's decision to push ahead. The Suffrage Association members were acting "like mad men, to persist in the unholy and illegal course of action," noted Governor Samuel Ward King to James Simmons, the chairman of the Committee on Manufacturing in the U.S. Senate.[43] As the April elections grew closer, a growing sense of trepidation crept over the supporters of the Charter government.

As William Goodell highlighted in his pamphlet *The Rights and Wrongs of Rhode Island*, Dorr did not actually want to serve as governor under the People's Constitution.[44] His political instincts told him to seek a prominent Whig in order to garner support outside of the ranks of the Equal Rights Democrats. Dorr's initial choice for governor was Wager Weeden, whom he knew from their days together in the Constitutionalist Party. His second choice was Democrat Thomas Carpenter. Both Carpenter and Weeden wasted little time in refusing the offer. Carpenter would later run as a Democrat in a losing bid to Samuel Ward King.[45] The statewide ticket was eventually headed by Dorr, with Chepachet's Amasa Eddy, Jr., named as his running mate. Dorr and Eddy ran unopposed on the People's ticket.

As the People's ticket was being finalized, a coalition of urban Whigs and rural Democrats dedicated to stopping the People's Constitution from going into effect emerged as the Law and Order Party, or the "legal party," as it was known in conservative circles.[46] Robert Hale Ives, the brother of Moses Brown Ives, believed that old party principles had to be put aside in order for conservatives to come together to protect the state against "incendiary attempts" to overthrow the government.[47] "It must be constantly borne in mind, by every American citizen, that liberty cannot be enjoyed in any country unless it is regulated by law and those laws [must be] enforced," wrote Henry Dearborn, the Massachusetts adjutant general, to a Rhode Island Law and Order man.[48] Prominent Democrats, such as former governors

James Fenner and John Brown Francis, joined ranks with the Whigs, who constituted the majority of the Law and Order Party. Fenner was actually given a seat on King's executive council.

In order to advance their cause, Law and Order men frequently charged that the Suffrage Association intended to implement a "division of property" and an "agrarian despotism," perhaps along the lines advocated by the New York radical labor leader Thomas Skidmore.[49] Francis Wayland, the president of Brown University and a prominent Baptist minister, feared that a "division of property was to be affected as soon as the new government came into power."[50] Congregationalist minister Mark Tucker, who was well acquainted with Dorr from his service on the Providence School Committee, saw it as an "attempt to arm the poor against the rich."[51] In antebellum Rhode Island, church membership often determined political subjectivities. As historian Mark Schantz has noted, Rhode Island's "plebian religious culture" came into direct conflict with "bourgeois" Protestants, most notably Francis Wayland, who valued property, order, "coolheaded deliberation and social cohesion" above all else.[52] According to Dorr, this brand of Protestantism was a "strange religion, from beneath rather than from above, furnishing a convenient mode of serving the devil, under the forms of law and order."[53]

Joseph Peace Hazard, a devout Law and Order supporter and prominent textile manufacturer, was pleased to find that "property holders" in the South recognized that "title deeds" were "at stake" in the Rhode Island controversy. "It makes me believe property everywhere is on our side despite democracy and its father, [the] devil," concluded Hazard, who had recently returned to Rhode Island after a lengthy tour of the South.[54] Many Rhode Island textile firms, especially those led by the Hazard family, had close ties to southern states. Dorr's brother-in-law, Edward Carrington, Jr., spent a considerable amount of time at a Georgia counting-house learning the intricacies of the cotton trade. Dorr's beloved uncle, Crawford Allen, made a fortune as a cotton broker. A rebellion could possibly interrupt the flow of cotton into the state and the so-called "negro cloth" that flowed out.

A circular signed by over fifty of Rhode Island's top businessmen informed the public that the Landholders' Convention had "framed, with extraordinary unanimity, and done in a spirit of magnanimous compromise, a Constitution for the government of Rhode Island."[55] The spirit of "magnanimous compromise," however, was only arrived at because the Suffrage Association had taken matters into their own hands. Dorr told Dutee Pearce that the "big handbill, signed by nearly all the rich aristocrats in Providence, & topped off with [James] Fenner, [John Brown] Francis etc., has done us far more good" in the agricultural regions of the state "than the opinions, charges etc. of the judges have done us harm."[56] This was wishful thinking on Dorr's part.

Joshua Rathburn, a resident of the conservative coastal community of Tiverton, told Dorr that the majority of businessmen would "do anything and everything" rather "than recognize the right of the people at large to make and alter their government at will."[57] Rathburn also outlined the nativist strategy that Law and Order advocates were developing. When Dorr attempted to enfranchise the sizeable Irish Catholic immigrant population with the liberal suffrage provisions for (white) males in the People's Constitution, an epidemic of nativism infected Rhode Island. As historian Patrick Conley has noted, "Irishness was not the obstacle to acceptance in Rhode Island unless the designation 'Catholic' was appended to it."[58] According to Rathburn, the "right to exclude naturalized citizens is strongly insisted . . . and has perhaps operated against us more than any thing else." Citizens were "called upon not to vote for a constitution, but to vote against Irishmen—to support the laws, prevent a civil war, and vote down the Irishmen was the war cry of our opponents."[59] A broadside warned citizens that the People's Constitution would "place your government, your civil and political institutions, your PUBLIC SCHOOLS, and perhaps your RELIGIOUS PRIVILEGES, under the control of the POPE OF ROME, through the medium of thousands of NATURALIZED FOREIGN CATHOLICS."[60]

The nativist fears centering on "Roman Catholic priests" were not the exclusive province of affluent male conservatives. In summing up the differences between the two constitutions under debate, Aurilla Moffitt, the wife of Orson Moffitt, a Providence stable keeper and militiaman, wrote in her diary that the "greatest difference between the two" documents is that "foreigners are admitted to the affairs of the state almost unconditionally" in the People's Constitution and in the Landholders' Constitution "not till they can be supposed to have some interest in its welfare." Moffitt believed that the "free suffrage advocates" would deliver up the state "to the tender mercies of Roman Catholic foreigners who [could] be bought and sold by their employers" and were at "the beck and call of their priests."[61]

Moffitt's views were echoed in the anti-Dorr *Providence Journal,* which utilized the acid pen of editor Henry Bowen Anthony to succinctly state its case against the People's Constitution. In comparing the two constitutions, and offering a view on the superiority of the Landholders' document, editor Anthony argued: "Where will the balance be under Messrs. Dorr, [John] Brown and Company? Where but among 2,500 foreigners and the hundreds more who will be imported . . . Their priests and leaders will say to a political party . . . give us by law every opportunity to perpetuate our spiritual despotism."[62]

Dutee Pearce understood that the Law and Order faction was attempting to drive a wedge into the Suffrage Association ranks by the use of nativist tactics. Pearce had become so desperate that he wanted Dorr to try to regain the trust of New England abolitionists by emphasizing the protection afforded to fugitive slaves in the People's Constitution. In the 1820s, most northern states had passed personal liberty laws designed to guarantee that free blacks would not be taken from the state and that fugitive slaves would not be removed without a fair hearing. Antislavery lawyers used these laws to protect fugitives and free blacks from southern slave catchers. However, the justices on the U.S. Supreme Court took issue with the wording of the statutes.

On March 1, 1842, the U.S. Supreme Court handed down its opinion in the highly contentious case of *Prigg v. Pennsylvania*. The case marked the first time the Court dealt with the 1793 Fugitive Slave Law. Seven justices wrote opinions in the case, the most up to that time in any case that reached the nation's highest court. The justices agreed on four issues, the most important of which were that personal liberty laws that interfered with the rights of slave owners under the Constitution were unconstitutional and that fugitive slaves had no right to due process. Pearce wanted Dorr to try to make political capital by reminding abolitionists how the People's Constitution protected fugitive slaves by providing them with jury trials, while the Landholders' Constitution was silent on the subject.[63] Dorr, recognizing his friend's hypocrisy, did not follow up on the suggestion.

In early March, members of the judiciary prepared a powerful ideological response to the People's Constitution. The Rhode Island Supreme Court issued an advisory opinion that declared the constitution illegal and said any attempt to enforce it would be considered an act of treason.[64] John Brown Francis was confident that Rhode Island's jurists had consulted with members of the U.S. Supreme Court before "coming out so boldly" against the People's Constitution. Francis was certain that southern Supreme Court members, especially Justice Peter V. Daniels—a conservative proslavery Virginian Democrat—would "entertain a common feeling of hostility to" the "radical movement" in Rhode Island because of the threat its ideology posed to the South's peculiar population.[65]

Judge John Pitman hoped that his colleagues in the Rhode Island bar would dedicate themselves to the "great work" they had to do in order to prevent the destruction "of all law and constitutional principle."[66] In January, Pitman authored an anonymous pamphlet addressed to the General Assembly warning against capitulating to the Suffrage Party. Pitman's pamphlet was reprinted in the *Providence Journal* during the debate over Samuel Atwell's motion to have the assembly abolish the Landholders' Convention.[67] If "ever there was a case that called upon a judge to write and speak openly and publicly, it was the very case before you," declared Pitman's close friend, U.S. Supreme Court Justice Joseph Story.[68]

Job Durfee, the chief justice of the Rhode Island Supreme Court, shared Pitman's passion for attacking the Suffrage Association. Durfee turned himself into a stump speaker, going all over the state in April and May to protest the People's Constitution. An 1813 graduate of Brown University, Durfee served several years in the General Assembly before being elected to the U.S. House of Representatives in 1821. After a stint in private practice, he was appointed an associate justice of the Rhode Island Supreme Court in 1833. In 1837, he was appointed chief justice, a position he would hold until his death in 1847. In a letter to Elisha Potter, Jr., Durfee made his feelings clear. "For the United States Congress or the federal courts to recognize the validity" of the People's Constitution "would be the equivalent of establishing constitutionally a principle of disorganization which would eventually annihilate every state in the union," said Durfee.[69] In a widely reprinted charge to a grand jury assembled in Bristol, Durfee declared that if Dorr was allowed to continue, the horrors of the French Revolution would soon take hold in Rhode Island.[70]

According to Joshua Rathburn, Durfee declared in a speech in Tiverton that he was "urged by his official duties as well as by his rights as a citizen to come out and take a stand against . . . what he denominated a lawless combination of a few of the people of the state to put down the legitimate government." Durfee closed with the warning that supporting the People's Constitution was tantamount to treason not only against the state, but also against the United States.[71] Opinion was divided within antebellum legal circles whether state prosecution of treason, which is the only crime defined in the U.S. Constitution, was an infringement of prerogatives exclusive to the federal government.[72] Treason is a political crime in two ways. First, it is political because it is a crime against the state. Second, it can be political in the sense that the sovereign might declare the partisan opposition to be traitors. In 1787, the Founding Fathers hoped to prevent this partisan-political meaning from taking root on American soil. In 1842, Rhode Island's Charter authorities thought differently.

In response to the public statement made by Rhode Island's jurists against the People's Constitution and the purported "treasonous" behavior of members of the Suffrage Association, Dorr, along with Samuel Atwell, Dutee Pearce, Joseph Angell, David Daniels, John Knowles, Aaron White, Jr., Levi Eaton, and Thomas Carpenter, published a "Statement of reasons demonstrating the sovereign Right of the People to make a Constitution," or, the "Nine Lawyers' Opinion" as it was popularly known. What followed was an analysis of the principle of majority rule and its relationship to republican government. Underlying the report was a particular vision of the legacy of the American Revolution.[73]

The opinion from the legal wing of the Suffrage Association opened with the familiar peon to popular sovereignty: If the "majority of the People have in any way lost the power of altering and reforming the government of this state, the Revolution has not made them free, but has only operated a change of masters."[74] In justifying their actions, Dorr and his followers often turned to none other than the father of the country, George Washington. In his famous 1796 Farewell Address, a much beleaguered Washington reminded his countrymen of his fellow Virginian Thomas Jefferson's favorite maxim—the "basis of our political systems is the right of the people to make and to alter their constitutions of government." It was no surprise that Dorr often quoted this line. However, Washington made it clear that citizens had a duty to obey the existing form of government in the following sentence: "The Constitution which at any time exists, till changed by an explicit and authentic act of the whole people, is sacredly obligatory upon all."[75] Dorr preferred to rely on the first part of Washington's statement.

Dorr said he was confident that the "Tories" had "overshot themselves" by coming out so boldly against what he deemed the will of the people.[76] He believed that the "Tory tide" had "reached its height."[77] Dorr found even greater hope when the Landholders' Constitution went down to defeat despite what he considered to be widespread electoral fraud in the buying of votes.[78] The constitution that finally emerged from the convention controlled by the General Assembly was rejected by a vote of 8,689 to 8,013. The slim margin of defeat was made possible only by the two-thirds majority in Providence and the surrounding mill villages—the strongest voting blocks for the Suffrage Association. John Pitman believed "anti-slavery men voted against it because blacks were excluded from voting," though abolitionists did not organize against the Landholders' document as they had against the People's Constitution.[79]

Either because they did not meet the residence, birth, or in the case of naturalized citizens, the property qualifications, over 8,000 people stayed away from the polls. Support for the Dorrite cause declined from almost 14,000 in December 1841 to around 9,000 votes in March because of the Landholders' concession on suffrage for native-born whites. The number would decline even more in April when elections were held under the People's Constitution. The roots of the collapse lay in the division of the Dorrite vote by the extension of suffrage to all native-born white men in the proposed Landholders' Constitution.

Despite the closeness of the vote against the Landholders' Constitution, Dorr labeled it a "complete, and most honorable and gratifying triumph of the People's cause, in the downfall & extinction of the Tory Constitution." He admitted to Dutee Pearce that their "majority [was] not so large as it might and would have been in a fair field," however, the victory was still "decisive, and has struck a dismay into our opponents, which forebodes their final dissolution." It was, in Dorr's analysis, a most "honorable and gratifying triumph of the People's cause."[80] "Popular Sovereignty Vindicated," ran a headline in the *New Age*.[81] However, the close vote on the Landholders' Constitution meant that Dorr's constitution was far from "vindicated."

With the defeat of the Landholders' Constitution, the General Assembly wasted little time in clamping down on the Suffrage Association. The assembly passed a series of resolutions in early April designed to prevent "deluded men" from taking control of the state. The assembly members viewed their role as one requiring them to "protect the citizens by legislation when the laws" were "defective," along with exerting "the means put into our hands to vindicate the rights of government."[82] In order to meet this goal the assembly passed a draconian statute that made it a treasonable offense to assume office under the People's Constitution. The statute, which was referred to by the Dorrites as the "Algerine law" after the tyrannical Dey of Algiers in Africa, had the desired effect of frightening Dorr's supporters. As one Suffrage Party member asked Dorr: "Is not the law this day passed by the General Assembly of binding force on the citizens? Is not the present government of R.I. de facto? Are not the U.S. bound to protect this state in the execution of its laws?"[83]

On April 4, Governor King ordered Samuel Ames, Dorr's brother-in-law and the state's quartermaster general, to fortify the state arsenal in Providence with additional troops. Ames, the husband of Mary Throop Dorr, was then a member of the Providence City Council and would later become Chief Justice of the Rhode Island Supreme Court. King took steps to fortify the Newport artillery in case the military forces in Providence were overrun. He also purchased additional weapons from John Davis, the conservative Whig governor of Massachusetts. King ordered militia commanders in the state to "direct" troops to be in "readiness at thirty minutes warning, armed and equipped to obey" military orders.[84]

King was likely shocked and dismayed when reports started to pour in from militia commanders, especially those in and around Providence, indicating that many units were going to side with Dorr. Elisha Dyer, Jr., the state's adjutant general, said that there was "great disaffection in the whole of the military organization of the state." In "answer to the question will you support the laws of the state if ordered out by the governor, fourteen answered in the affirmative, twenty two in the negative," wrote one commander to Dyer on April 6. Wescott Handy, the commander of a militia unit in the Dorrite stronghold of Woonsocket, a mill village thirteen miles north of Providence, wrote to Dyer informing him that the militia had "unanimously" voted to disregard King's orders.[85]

Dorr drew inspiration from the reports that militia units would support him. He told Levi Woodbury, one of the U.S. Senators from New Hampshire, on April 11 that "if the government at Washington attempts no improper interference with our affair, the People's Constitution will, in all probability, go into effect, without obstruction."[86] By April militia units loyal to the Suffrage Association were forming in and around Providence. Several units drilled just blocks from the Dorr family mansion. Dorr noted to Dutee Pearce on April 4, the same day that the Algerine law was certified, that Woonsocket had "armed & equipped 200 men yesterday; 100 men today." According to estimates, no "more than 150 men of the military order can be found against us in [Providence]. The bulk of the soldiers are for us."[87] Rhode Island was dividing into armed camps.

On April 8, Sullivan and Lydia Dorr, pillars of Providence's elite conservative society, fired off a pleading letter to their oldest son praying that "God in his infinite mercy" would prompt him "to a decision" that would "restore" him "to the good opinion of your friends and fellow citizens." Lydia and Sullivan were obviously following the situation closely in the press, but their daughter Mary Throop kept them apprised of the inner workings of King's administration. Sullivan and Lydia were alarmed that militia units in Providence and the surrounding mill villages were pledging allegiance to their oldest son. They had also gotten word that their son was going to run for governor on the People's ticket. "We hear with great pain that you are about to publish a prox at the head of which you are named for Governor of this state, which is a violation of the lawful authority of the state." Sullivan and Lydia continued: "It grieves us to learn that a man at so mature an age, and so well versed in the laws of his country should be a participant in acts calculated to bring the state into rebellion—produce civil strife with bloodshed and murder." They urged him to stop before he crossed the "Rubicon." It was too late. Their son was halfway across. Blinded by visions of his own success, Dorr was determined to implement a constitution that he himself had largely drafted and which he believed a majority of Rhode Islanders had approved in December 1841.[88]

Clearly alarmed at the divide within the Rhode Island militia ranks, King dispatched John Brown Francis, Elisha Potter, Jr., and John Whipple to Washington, D.C., to make the case for the "interposition" of the federal government for the "protection" of Rhode Island's citizens.[89] The three prominent Law and Order delegates departed for Washington shortly after John Brown, president of the Suffrage Association, left Providence in order to seek an audience with President John Tyler, who was dealing with a major financial crisis.[90] As the war of words in Rhode Island was approaching the field of battle, the federal Treasury almost ran dry because of political infighting over tariff levels.[91] If it continued until the end of June, the country would be without money to pay its creditors. In addition, more and more states were defaulting on their mounting debts as a result of the Panic of 1837.

Before he left, Dorr handed Brown a lengthy letter detailing the history of the reform effort to give to Levi Woodbury, whom Dorr considered a "untiring advocate of popular rights." Brown also carried with him a formal "statement of reasons," which was most likely a condensed version of the

"Nine Lawyers' Opinion." Dorr requested that Woodbury meet with President Tyler to determine what stance the federal government would take in the crisis.

John Tyler took over the presidency in April 1841 after the untimely death of President William Henry Harrison. Tall and slender with a sharply angular face and a distinctive nose, Tyler was the youngest occupant of the White House up to that time and also the first to assume office after the death of a president.[92] Dorr warned that if federal troops were sent he would have no choice but to appeal for aid from neighboring states. "The Tories hold out to Mr. Tyler the promise of the state for the next presidential campaign in which they have no more power to give to him than Satan had to give the Kingdom of the Earth to the Savior," declared Dorr to Woodbury.[93]

Once in Washington, John Brown, who had never traveled outside of New England, visited with numerous politicians, including John Quincy Adams. Brown told Adams that the goal of the Suffrage Association was to see Dorr inaugurated as the governor of Rhode Island on May 3.[94] Brown, accompanied by Ohio Senator William Allen, met with the president on April 9 and came away from the meeting with some hope that federal troops would not be sent to Rhode Island.[95] Much to the displeasure of many senators, especially Silas Wright, Jr., of New York, a disciple of Martin Van Buren and the Democratic leader of the Senate, Brown published an open letter in the *Providence Express* detailing the contents of private conversations and giving the false impression that Senate Democrats were going to advocate for Dorr and the People's Constitution.[96] Brown, who had little conception of national politics, put northern Democrats in a difficult political situation. Dorr's unequivocal faith in the right of the people to alter or abolish their form of government unnerved white southern Democrats. His ideology was deemed one that could lead to the rise of militant blacks, "literally the *bête noire* of proslavery nightmares in the 1840s."[97]

With a growing eye to the presidential campaign of 1844 and winning in his own right, Tyler, without the full support of the diverse coalition that made up the Whig Party that had elected him on a ticket with William Henry Harrison or the Democrats with whom he once associated, was trying to establish an independent base at the time of the Rhode Island constitutional crisis.[98] Since northern Democrats rhetorically supported Thomas Dorr's efforts to change Rhode Island's ruling structure, Tyler could not openly attack the People's Constitution if he wanted to court their favor. As the thoroughly Democratic *Boston Post* maintained, the issue in Rhode Island was "not within the Constitution and a U.S. soldier should not be called on to pollute the soil of RI by shedding blood to uphold a royal charter."[99] In terms of garnering Whig support for a run for the presidency in 1844, Tyler would lose votes if he did not aid the Charter authorities.

History offered Tyler little guidance for how to handle the situation in Rhode Island. President Martin Van Buren had been called upon to provide federal assistance in the so-called Buckshot War in Pennsylvania in 1838, but the situation there was more of the domestic violence variety and not a potentially full-blown insurrection against the sitting government.[100] Many southern newspaper editors wanted Tyler to stay out of the conflict. For example, the editors of the *Southern Patriot*, while acknowledging the dangers of a potential insurrection in Rhode Island, noted that "federal intervention" by the Tyler Administration "would be the death knell of the Constitution" because it would set a dangerous precedent for possible future federal meddling in the South's domestic affairs. John Quincy Adams had been arguing in Congress for years about the power of the federal government to emancipate slaves in war time.[101] Thomas Ritchie, the editor of the *Richmond Enquirer*, was afraid that the use of federal troops to suppress Dorr's forces would set a dangerous precedent for the federal government to consider the republican character of southern state governments.[102] The abolitionist William Goodell saw the slaveholding Tyler's possible interference on the side of the Charter authorities in 1842 as a further manifestation of the "Slave Power" with a "slaveholding executive" destroying the liberties of the people in a "sovereign state."[103]

Tyler weighed this all as he contemplated how to respond to the escalating constitutional crisis. In the first of several letters to Tyler, Samuel Ward King insisted that "the state legislature" could not "be convened in sufficient season to apply to the Government of the United States for effectual protection" as spelled out in the Constitution. Article IV, Section 4 did specify that if the legislature was not in session, the executive of a state could apply for assistance. King said he was obligated as governor to apply "for the protection."[104] In another letter to Tyler, King, who seemed at times to be on the verge of a nervous breakdown, added that a large "deluded" portion of the citizenry had "declared their intention to put down the existing government." King went on to assure Tyler that members of the Suffrage Association were "sufficiently formidable to threaten" the "peace" of the state. King was confident that "a proclamation from the President of the United States and the presence here of a military officer to act under the authority of the United States would destroy the delusion which is now so prevalent." He insisted the protection guaranteed a state by Article IV, section 4 in terms of domestic violence required that "precautionary measures" be taken to "prevent lawless men from breaking out into violence." Finally, King urged Tyler not to wait until there was actual violence before authorizing federal troops.[105]

Tyler elected to wait to reply to King's letter until he met with Whipple, Francis, and Potter, the three Charter emissaries.[106] However, his decision to keep the three men waiting while he attended to other matters caused speculation that he was going to support Dorr. While waiting for the president, Francis paid a visit to the boardinghouse where South Carolina Senator John Calhoun was staying. The former governor wrote his wife that Calhoun was "clearly" with the Law and Order Party in "sentiment as to the illegality of the People's Constitution."[107] Growing impatient, Whipple fired off a hasty letter on April 11 that accused Tyler of supporting "free suffrage." Whipple told Tyler that suffrage reforms would "prevail." Ignoring the concrete and ideological differences between the two constitutions, Whipple assured the president that the documents were practically the same. The freeholders had "yielded" on free suffrage. However, the "question" that Tyler needed to help settle was whether reforms would be carried out "by force of arms" or through another constitutional convention called by the General Assembly.[108] In a joint letter to the president, Whipple, Francis, and Potter offered a one-sided history of suffrage reform. In focusing on the defeated Landholders' Constitution, the three Law and Order officials conveniently glossed over the fact that the convention was unable to produce a document in 1841 because the delegates were divided on suffrage extension. The delegates, of course, only got their act together because it was clear that a majority of Rhode Islanders had expressed their support for the People's Constitution.[109]

Ignoring King's comments in regard to the obligations of the federal government to take preventive measures to protect a state from domestic violence, Tyler took a strong states' rights position—it was not the job of the federal government to come in and settle the constitutional crisis. In terms of the use of federal troops, Tyler insisted that "there must be an actual insurrection, manifested by lawless assemblages of the people or otherwise, to whom a proclamation may be addressed." Tyler informed King that the constitutional crisis in Rhode Island was of the "municipal" variety with which the federal government should play no role. "To throw the Executive power of this government into any such controversy, would be to make the President the armed arbitrator, between the people of the different states and their constituted authorities," wrote Tyler. Tyler argued that the relevant federal statutes did not give him the power to "anticipate insurrectionary movements"—an actual state of war must exist before the President of the United States could act. Tyler, however, assured King that if an insurrection did develop, he would act to protect the government; he would "not look into real or supposed defects" of the Charter regime before committing troops. Tyler insisted that he was required to recognize the authority of the existing government until Congress was notified of a change "by legal and peaceable proceedings."[110]

Decades later Lyon Gardiner Tyler, the president's son and longtime president of the College of William and Mary, used his father's cautious response to Governor King to promote the Southern Lost Cause. Writing in the 1880s, Lyon Tyler lamented that "the doctrine" his father laid out in his letter to Governor King had "not been more respected by some of his more remote successors at the head of the government, when the question came to be one between a Northern president and a Southern community."[111]

Though he refused to do what King asked—send troops to nip the rebellion in the bud—Tyler won over few northern Democrats with his letter. Becoming increasingly obstinate, Dorr declared that Tyler's letter "was the principal cause of the overthrow of the government and constitution of the people of Rhode Island."[112] In a lengthy pamphlet published in 1846, Providence lawyer Dexter Randall rightly argued that Tyler's suggestion of supporting "legal and peaceable proceedings frightened" Dorr, who reacted by "deliberately charging the President with assuming positions he positively disclaimed."[113] Dorr told Pennsylvania Democratic Senator James Buchanan that Tyler's views were at variance "with the American principle of popular sovereignty and set forth the doctrine that no valid change can take place in the institutions of a state without the consent of the authorities and that the National Executive is bound to suppress by military force any attempt by the People at such change."[114] Tyler, of course, said no such thing. At the same time that Dorr and the majority of northern Democrats chastised Tyler for his supposed willingness to commit troops to Rhode Island at a moment's notice, the Whigs were unsatisfied with Tyler's opposition to using force.

Justice Joseph Story informed Secretary of State Daniel Webster that the president's letter was "not sufficient to meet the exigencies which have since risen." Story believed that Tyler had an "unquestionable right to issue orders to the governors of the adjacent states to detail portions of the military so as to have them prepared to be called forth at a moments warning if an insurrection should take place."[115] Story's suggestions of preventive measures were taken almost word-for-word from a letter he received on March 30 from John Pitman, who argued that "the duty of protection . . . requires preventive measures or violence will occur."[116] Story argued that Article IV, section 4 required the federal government to "guard" against "domestic violence" before it is "committed." Because he believed that the "free suffrage constitution" would be "forced upon the people by intimidation and military force," Story urged Webster to have Tyler send troops to Fort Adams in Newport at once.[117] Story also told Webster that Massachusetts Governor John Davis was prepared to mobilize his state's militia on the Rhode Island border. In early May, Davis wrote to his state's adjutant general to inquire about the readiness of the Massachusetts militia.[118]

While he was completely adverse to sending federal troops to Providence, Tyler did authorize the federal commander at Fort Adams to take precautionary steps to ensure the safety of military property.[119] Several companies of U.S. troops also arrived at Fort Adams, but they did not make their way to Providence.[120] This was not really a bold move because Newport was an anti-Dorr stronghold, but it did put the Suffrage Association on notice that federal troops were ready to be deployed for the short ferry ride to Providence. The northern Democratic press swiftly condemned the administration's actions. "Let these Government mercenaries but lift an arm— but draw one drop of blood, and the experiment will soon be tested whether the people of this country or their servants shall rule," proclaimed the *Cincinnati Daily Enquirer*.[121]

After a selective reading of Tyler's letter to King, Dorr fired off a hasty letter to Senator William Allen on April 14 in which he argued that the president believed that "a valid change in a state government" could only be achieved by "the consent of that government." Dorr articulated his belief in the power of the people to alter their form of government with or without prior legislative approval. He linked his doctrine to what he deemed as the true principles of the Democracy, as contrasted with the Whigs (although he did admit many rural Democrats in the state were also against the Suffrage Party).[122] In letters to Senators Woodbury, Allen, Benton, and James Buchanan, Dorr asked if "any friend of State Rights in either House" would do the Suffrage Party "the favor of saying by letter what we are to expect?" Their replies only served to add to what were in many ways delusional and irrational expectations on Dorr's part of possible action by Democrats in Congress.[123]

Each of the letters to Dorr paid homage to the principle of the people's sovereignty. The "people of Rhode Island," said William Allen, "were in the right upon every known principle of public liberty." Moreover, the federal government did not possess the "right" of "interposition" by "force or otherwise."[124] For the rest of the month, Allen would try to no avail to bring resolutions in favor of the People's Constitution to the Senate floor. According to Dorr, another U.S. senator, whose name he had to keep private, wrote to him on April 12 and told him that they need not fear "any force from Washington, whatever may be threatened."[125]

In Levi Woodbury's analysis, if the people of Rhode Island, "who have never yet" made a "Constitution for themselves," have not a "right to do it when and how they please, the whole fabric of our American experiment rests on sand and stubble."[126] Missouri Senator Thomas Hart Benton, a member of Andrew Jackson's "Kitchen Cabinet," promised Dorr that the northern Democracy understood the importance of what was becoming known in Congress as the "Rhode Island Question." Benton said he considered "the majority as having the right to put the new constitution in force."[127]

However, each letter also urged Dorr to shun violence at all costs. Woodbury warned Dorr not to do anything rash. He closed with this admonishment: "But keep calm—cool—yet resolute in right. Shun violence—insubordination—civil war—but move onward like our Fathers—steadily and faithfully to your just and pure objects in constitutional methods."[128] Benton told Dorr that the political issue in Rhode Island could not be settled by the "sword."[129] If this were to occur, it could sink the Democratic Party's chances to regain the White House in 1844. Dorr would have been wise to adhere to the advice imparted to him in a letter from Silas Wright, Jr., the prominent New York Democrat and, like Woodbury, a supporter of John Calhoun. Wright told Dorr that the "great duty now resting upon" him was "caution, caution, caution; forbearance, forbearance, forbearance." Wright urged Dorr to use "discretion" in the weeks ahead and not to come into conflict with the Charter authorities. Wright was fearful of being put in a difficult position if Dorr's attempt at reform should erupt into bloodshed. Wright urged Dorr to properly gauge the current level of support for the People's Constitution. If it differed at all from the December 1841 vote total, Wright admonished Dorr to "cease to press" the "organization" of the People's government.[130]

The fact that on April 18 Dorr received only 6,604 votes for governor under the People's Constitution—a significant decline from the nearly 14,000 who voted for the constitution just a few months before—illustrated this point.[131] Wright also brought to Dorr's attention Allen's failed attempt to bring resolutions in support of the People's Constitution to the floor of the Senate for a vote. South Carolina Senator William Preston led the charge against the resolutions, which related to the "establishment of a constitutional republican form of Government" in Rhode Island. Wright said the "strong vote" should demonstrate to Dorr that it was "clearly best not to attempt to act or agitate unnecessarily."[132] Wright, who had presidential ambitions in 1844, highlighted what was to become the central problem for Dorr and his unwavering belief in the supremacy of the people. The threat of "revolution" would become widespread and for southern Democrats this was simply not a position they could stand behind.[133]

For many conservative New Englanders, such as John Park of Worcester, the farthest thing from their mind was the reaction of the slaveholding South. What they were concerned about was the outbreak of violence in their own backyard.[134] Park was worried about the safety of his daughter Louisa who was married to a Protestant minister in Providence. In order to protect the city's populace, Dorr's uncles, Zachariah and Philip Allen, went as far as concocting a charge that Dorr had failed to deliver some sort of legal service for which they had supposedly already paid him. Zachariah and Philip managed to convince the sheriff of Providence to issue a summons for Dorr to appear before a magistrate on April 29. Albert C. Greene, the former attorney general with whom Dorr worked on the Frances Leach case in 1833, represented the Allen brothers. Dorr acknowledged receipt of the summons, but failed to show up in court.[135] Moses Brown Ives was absolutely convinced that his brother-in-law, whom he considered deranged, intended to "make a martyr out of himself."[136] Later Dorr would welcome the label of a martyr for the people; however in the spring of 1842 his only concern was to implement the People's Constitution.

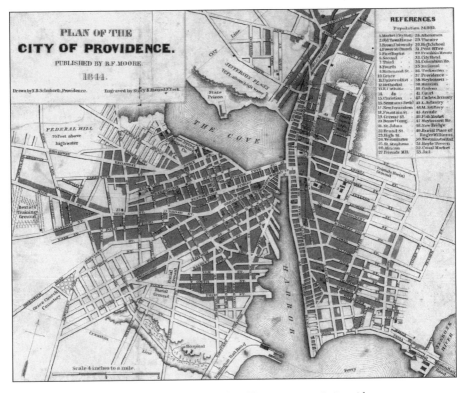

1844 Map of Providence. This detailed map produced by B. F. Moore in Providence depicts the state prison and the militia training area called Jefferson Plain. Dexter's Training Ground, the site of the state arsenal, is located at the left edge of the map. The Dorr family mansion is on the north end of Benefit Street on the east side of the city. Courtesy of Thomas G. Greene.

The attempt on the Arsenal on the night of May 17th

Outside of the State Arsenal (May 17, 1842). This sketch is part of a multipanel illustrated 1842 account of the Dorr Rebellion called "Scenes in Rhode Island." The drawings depict Dorr's return to Rhode Island on May 16, 1842, and subsequent attempt to raid the Cranston Street Arsenal. This particular panel depicts the attempt on the state arsenal on May 17, 1842. Dorr led the charge, but was opposed, and ultimately defeated, by the state militia of Governor Samuel Ward King. Illustrations by Boston artist E. W. Bouve. Courtesy of Russell J. DeSimone.

President John Tyler (1790–1862). Courtesy of the Library of Congress.

Dorr Family Mansion. Built in 1809 the Dorr mansion on Benefit Street was designed by the renowned architect John Holden Greene and was erected on the house lot and original burial site of Providence's founder, Roger Williams. Courtesy of Russell J. DeSimone.

William Lloyd Garrison (1805–1879). Courtesy of the Library of Congress.

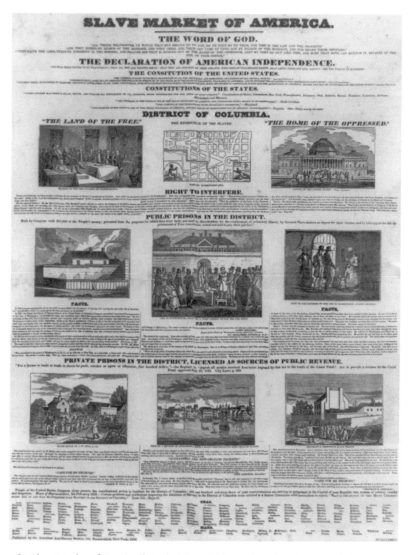

The Slave Market of America (1836). A broadside condemning slavery and the slave trade in Washington, D.C. Courtesy of the Library of Congress.

1841 Suffrage Ribbons. The Rhode Island Suffrage Association held mass meetings to promote its cause, first in Providence on Jefferson Plain on April 17, 1841, then in Newport on May 5, and finally in Providence on July 5. The ribbons shown here were worn at these meetings. Courtesy of Russell J. DeSimone.

Abby Kelley Foster (1811–1887).
Courtesy of the American
Antiquarian Society.

Frederick Douglass (1818–1895).
Courtesy of the American
Antiquarian Society.

1776. 1841.

Adoption of the Constitution of Rhode Island.
PEOPLE'S TICKET.

I am an American citizen, of the age of twenty-one years, and have my permanent residence or home in this State.

I am   qualified to vote under the existing laws of this State.

I vote for the CONSTITUTION formed by the Convention of the People, assembled at Providence, and which was proposed to the People by said Convention on the 18th day of November, 1841.

December 1841 People's Ticket. This ticket is the ballot used in the statewide election on the People's Constitution on December 27–29, 1841. The constitution was approved by a vote of 13,895 to 52. Courtesy of Russell J. DeSimone.

THE PEOPLE'S
Constitutional and State Rights'
TICKET.

(Election Monday, April 18th, 1842.]

FOR GOVERNOR:

THOMAS W. DORR,

Of Providence.

FOR LIEUT. GOVERNOR:

AMASA EDDY, Jr.

Of Glocester.

WM. H. SMITH, *Secretary of State.*
JOSEPH JOSLIN, *General Treasurer.*
JONAH TITUS, *Atttorney General.*

SENATORS.

1st District, ELI BROWN, *of Providence.*
2nd " HEZEKIAH WILLARD, *of Providence.*
3d " JOHN PAINE, *of Smithfield.*
4th " ABNER HASKELL, *of Cumberland.*
5th " SOLOMON SMITH, *of Burrillville.*
6th " (Vacancy.)
7th " JOHN WOOD, *of Coventry.*
8th " (Vacancy.)
9th " NATHANIEL TOMPKINS,
of Little Compton.
10th " JOSEPH SPINK, *of North Kingstown.*
11th " JESSE WILBOUR, JR. *of Hopkington.*
12th " CHRISTOPHER SMITH, *of Barrington.*

April 1842 People's Election Ticket. This ticket appeared in the *Providence Express*, April 13, 1842. Courtesy of Russell J. DeSimone.

Samuel Ward King
(1786–1851). Courtesy of the
Rhode Island Historical Society.

John Calhoun (1782–1850).
Courtesy of the Library of
Congress.

Thomas Wilson Dorr (1805–1854). 1842 daguerreotype. Courtesy of Frank Mauran III.

A HORRIBLE PLOT
To Drench the State of Rhode Island with the Blood of its inhabitants!

A most foul and ferocious plot to MURDER the inhabitants of this State, has recently come to light.

Evidence conclusive, and of the very highest authority can be produced to establish the following statement, viz:

That SAMUEL W. KING did, a short time since, write to John Tyler, of Washington, requesting him to forward to this State, a body of armed men (principally foreigners) to *Shoot down the peaceable inhabitants* of this State, for having dared to exercise the dearest rights of free citizens, in adopting a Constitution, based upon the following *Republican Principles,* viz: "*That all political power and sovereignty are originally vested in, and of right belong to the People. That all free Governments are founded in their authority, and are established for the greatest good to the whole number. That the People have therefore an inalienable and indefeasible right, in their original, sovereign and unlimited capacity, to ordain and institute government, and, in the same capacity, to alter, reform, or totally change the same,* whenever their safety or happiness requires."

For having dared to carry out these principles, SAMUEL W. KING, under the tutelage of a few such men as RICHARD K. RANDOLPH, JAMES FENNER, and SAMUEL AMES, has written to John Tyler, as above.

The PEOPLE of this State feel fully competent to put down any intestine faction, whose object is to subvert their government; but if the plotters of the above conspiracy, succeed in obtaining from abroad a sufficient number of *hired mercenaries,* to wrench the power from the PEOPLE, we shall then, and not till then, call on every patriotic lover of freedom, wherever he may be found, to render us any and every assistance in his power, in opposing such *foreign foes,* and sustaining the government of the PEOPLE.

Providence, May 16th, 1842.

"A Horrible Plot." This broadside was issued by Dorr's supporters just one day before the attempted attack on the Providence arsenal in May 1842. A charter government broadside issued on May 14 proclaimed a "Horrible Plot" of Dorr's men to "butcher the people of Providence." Courtesy of the John Hay Library, Brown University.

Daniel Webster (1782–1852). Courtesy of the Library of Congress.

Dorr Waving a Sword (May 16, 1842). The second panel of the "Scenes in Rhode Island." This sketch depicts Dorr delivering a speech outside of the Burrington Anthony house on Federal Hill. No records of the speech survived. Illustrations by Boston artist E. W. Bouve. Courtesy of Russell J. DeSimone.

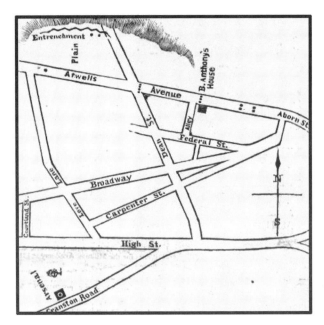

Map of the Arsenal Attack. Providence *Journal*, May 26, 1842. Courtesy of Russell J. DeSimone.

View from Inside the Arsenal. This panel from "Scenes in Rhode Island" depicts the militia gathered inside the arsenal during the raid. Among those defending the arsenal and its weapons were Dorr's father, brother, and uncle. Illustrations by Boston artist E. W. Bouve. Courtesy of Russell J. DeSimone.

Sketch of Dorr Fleeing after the Arsenal Attack. The final panel from "Scenes in Rhode Island" depicts a group of militia cadets pursuing Dorr after his attempt on the state arsenal. Illustrations by Boston artist E. W. Bouve. Courtesy of Russell J. DeSimone.

NOTICE.
CITY OF PROVIDENCE,
Mayor's Office, May 18, 1842.

All citizens friendly to maintaining the peace and good order of the City, are urged to lay aside their business for this day and assemble at 7 1-2 o'clock, A. M. with arms at the Cadet Alarm Post.

THOS. M. BURGESS, *Mayor.*

If any have not arms, they will be provided.

Notice from Providence Mayor Thomas Burgess (May 18, 1842). Courtesy of John Hay Library, Brown University.

Resignation of all the Officers under the People's Constitution.

We the undersigned, elected Senators and Representatives to the General Assembly and to other offices under the People's Constitution not having in accepting those offices, contemplated carrying the Constitution into effect against the power of the General Government of the United States, which has been called upon to act against us, and which the President has signified his intention to grant. Therefore, in consideration of the evils which we think must ensue to our common country from our engaging in a contest with the General Government, although we cannot surrender, nor have altered our views of the right of the people to form and establish a government in the manner in which the Constitution of this State has been framed.

With these views, and first protesting against the course which the President has taken in regard to the controversy between the old and the new government of this State, as being against the fundamental rights of the people of this State, and of the United States, we feel constrained to decline acting further in the several offices to which we have been elected, and which therefore we hereby resign. Neither can we, nor have we, countenanced, in any manner, the late movement of the Governor elected under the People's Constitution, but in every way have endeavored to counteract and prevent so deplorable an act, and one so destructive to the cause in which we have been engaged.

HEZEKIAH WILLARD,
BENJAMIN ARNOLD, Jr.,
WM. M. WEBSTER,
FREDERICK L. BECKFORD,
SAMUEL H. WALES.
PEREZ SIMMONS,

ELI BROWN,
WELCOME ANGELL,
JOHN A. HOWLAND.
WILLIAM COLEMAN.
J. F. B. FLAGG.

Resignation of Elected Representatives under the People's Constitution. Courtesy of Daniel Schofield.

View of Chepachet, Rhode Island (June 1842). This image drawn by Henry Lord, a skilled carriage painter and artisan, is the only firsthand depiction of the events at Chepachet. Courtesy of Russell J. DeSimone.

BY HIS EXCELLENCY,

SAMUEL WARD KING,

GOVERNOR, CAPTAIN-GENERAL, AND COMMANDER-IN-CHIEF OF THE STATE OF RHODE-ISLAND AND PROVIDENCE PLANTATIONS.

A PROCLAMATION.

WHEREAS on the eighth day of June instant, I issued a Proclamation, offering a reward of one thousand dollars for the delivery of the fugitive Traitor, **THOMAS WILSON DORR**, to the proper civil authority: and whereas the said Thomas Wilson Dorr having returned to this State and assumed the command of a numerous body of armed men, in open rebellion against the Government thereof, has again *fled* the summary justice which awaited him; I do therefore, by virtue of authority in me vested, and by advice of the Council, hereby offer an additional reward of four thousand dollars for the apprehension and delivery of the said Thomas Wilson Dorr to the Sheriff of the County of Newport or Providence, within three months from the date hereof.

GIVEN under my hand and the seal of said State, at the City of Providence, this twenty-ninth day of June, in the year of our Lord one thousand eight hundred and forty-two, and of the Independence of the United States of America the sixty-sixth.

L. S.

SAMUEL WARD KING.

BY HIS EXCELLENCY'S COMMAND:

HENRY BOWEN, Secretary of State.

$5,000 Reward (June 29, 1842). Law & Order Governor Samuel Ward King issued a reward of $1,000 for the return of Thomas Dorr in May 1842. Following the events at Chepachet in late June, King raised the reward to $5,000. Courtesy of Russell J. DeSimone.

SENTENCE OF THOS. W. DORR,

Convicted by the FEDERALISTS of Rhode Island of the CRIME of having attempted to CONFER the RIGHT OF SUFFRAGE ON THE POOR,

AS APPROVED BY HENRY CLAY IN THE U. S. SENATE, AND IN HIS RALEIGH SPEECH.

"THAT THE SAID THOMAS W. DORR BE IMPRISONED IN THE STATE'S PRISON, AT PROVIDENCE, IN THE COUNTY OF PROVIDENCE, FOR THE TERM OF HIS NATURAL LIFE, AND THERE BE KEPT AT HARD LABOR, IN SOLITARY CONFINEMENT."

Thomas Wilson Dorr in Chains (1844). This sketch of Dorr appeared on page 8 of *Christian Voters Pause and Reflect: Mr. Clay's Moral Character*, an 1844 Democratic campaign pamphlet. Courtesy of the Darlington Digital Library, University of Pittsburgh (darlington.library.pitt.edu).

DORR LIBERATION STOCK.

I HEREBY CERTIFY,

that _____ has contributed Ten Cents to the Dorr Liberation Fund, for the purpose of carrying, by Writ of Error, the Case of The State of Rhode Island against Thomas Wilson Dorr, to the Supreme Court of the United States. F. C. Treadwell

Counsel for sundry Citizens of Rhode Island.

Countersigned,

A. H. Lord

Providence, R. I. Oct. 28, 1844   President of the Dorr Lib. Soc.

Dorr Liberation Stock. Liberation Stock certificates were sold in 1844–1845 in order to raise funds to bring two separate cases before the U.S. Supreme Court, *Luther v. Borden*, and by writ of error, *The State of Rhode Island v. Thomas Wilson Dorr*. Abby Lord was president of the Dorr Liberation Society. Courtesy of Russell J. DeSimone.

FREEDOM TO DORR!

For President,

JAMES K. POLK.

For Vice President,

GEORGE M. DALLAS.

Democratic Electoral Ticket,

Joseph H. Larwill,	Grenville P. Cherry,
Dowty Utter,	George Corwine,
Clayton Webb,	Cautious C. Covey,
James M. Dorsey,	Isaac M. Lanning,
Robert D. Forsman,	Walter Jamieson,
John Taylor,	Sebastian Brainard,
David Higgins,	James Forbes, Sr.
Gilbert Beach,	Neal McCoy,
John D. White,	Milo Stone,
Thomas Megrady,	Benjamin Adams,
Valentine Keffer,	Stephen N. Sargent.
James Parker,	

1844 Ohio Election Ticket. Courtesy of the John Hay Library, Brown University.

1852 Presidential Campaign Ribbon.
Courtesy of the John Hay Library, Brown
University.

Senator Stephen Douglas (1813–1861). Courtesy of the Library of Congress.

The doctrine of Sovereignty. There is One over all, God blessed for ever; and under him the People are sovereign. His Revealed Word is the higher law, to whose principles and rules of action recourse is had by the framers of Constitutions & by legislators, to impart justice and equity to political institutions. The application of these principles & rules to the Constitutions and legislative acts of States, and to men in their political relations, is what has been called the democracy of Christianity. Rights are the gift of God. The definition and protection of them are the objects of just government.

Thos W. Dorr.

Providence, R.I.
Aug. 10th 1853.

The Doctrine of Sovereignty. Thomas Dorr penned this credo on the doctrine of sovereignty in 1853, the year before his death. In it he states the people's sovereignty is a God-given right and it is the responsibility of just governments to protect this right. Courtesy of Russell J. DeSimone.

Chapter 5

The Arsenal

To the Citizens of Providence!!! You are requested forthwith to Repair to the State Arsenal and Take Arms—Samuel Ward King, Governor of the State of Rhode Island

Broadside, May 17, 1842

On May 9, 1842, a warrant was issued for Thomas Dorr's arrest, though most Providence residents knew he would not be taken without a fight.[1] Many conservatives feared that if Dorr was apprehended a "civil war" would erupt.[2] As the Pawtucket abolitionist Susan Sisson noted in a letter to her close friend Abby Kelley, the "struggle throughout the state between the two parties seems to be approaching a crisis and nothing is heard but the constitution and nothing seen but groups of men with determined looks and flushed faces eagerly contending for their own darling idol."[3] The Potter clan in South Kingstown shared Sisson's fears. "There is quite a respectable revolution going on in our little state . . . men talk of guns and daggers; old women are frightened and the devil only knows what will be the end thereof," wrote one brother.[4] In terms of guns, Samuel Ward King wanted desperately to protect the Charter government's supply. He ordered Dorr's brother-in-law Samuel Ames to add additional patrols around the state arsenal in Providence.[5]

Given the nature of his panic-filled letters to President John Tyler in the month of April, one would have thought that King would have attempted to arrest Dorr the first chance he had. The *Providence Express* and *New Age and Constitutional Advocate* had been running notices for days about Dorr's inaugural parade. On May 3, over 1,500 supporters entered into a lengthy procession behind the People's Governor as he rode in an open carriage through the streets of Providence. The procession, which passed by the Dorr

119

family mansion on Benefit Street, concluded at an unfinished foundry building on the west side of the city. Aurilla Moffitt, the wife of a Providence militiaman loyal to King, noted in her diary on May 3 that Dorr, the "disorganizing governor," had assumed power and she was "fearful" of bloodshed.[6] However, King had ordered Thomas Burgess, the mayor of Providence, to make sure that city forces did not interfere with Dorr's inaugural. King was afraid that any attempt to arrest Dorr would only end in bloodshed.[7]

Rhoda Newcomb, a Providence resident who watched Dorr's inaugural procession go by her home on the east side of the city, informed her son Charles King Newcomb, who was living in the utopian Brook Farm community, that open warfare was on the horizon. Charles had been classmates with Dorr at Harvard. Rhoda Newcomb viewed Dorr's inauguration as an impending apocalypse, an "evil permitted by divine Providence" in order to cleanse the state of its "sins." She did not elaborate on what she meant by "sins." Perhaps she was referring to the state's participation in the international slave trade. Whatever Rhoda Newcomb meant, her real purpose was to mock her son's support for Dorr and help him to see the light. "Don't you see bars fall down, locks give way, see the people rush in, hear the sheriff remonstrate the people, hurrah, down with the government, we are all sovereign?" wrote Newcomb to her son in bitterly sarcastic fashion.[8] In her mindset, the thousands of citizens who came out in support of Dorr were naive at best, dangerous at worst.

It was nearly a universal belief within the Law and Order ranks that Thomas Dorr intended to take over the statehouse on May 3. Dorr's uncle Zachariah Allen, Jr., perceived what he later called a change in "tactics from the ballot box to the cartridge box."[9] Dorr had no intention of shooting anyone, but he did desire to sit in the governor's seat. However, several of his most loyal supporters, including Dutee Pearce, urged caution. Pearce was certainly aware of the two companies of federal troops that arrived at Newport's Fort Adams in Newport the day before.[10] Tensions may have been high on May 3 in Providence, but for the time being the cartridge boxes remained under lock and key. "The long to be remembered 3rd of May has nearly passed by and order still reigns at the seat of war!" declared Providence shopkeeper Joshua Spooner.[11] Conservative onlookers were shocked that there was no violence during the inaugural parade. Indeed, Louisa Park Hall and her minister husband made social calls after the parade, relieved that their city had not been engulfed in flames.[12]

It later became clear to Dorr of this fatal mistake in not occupying the seat of government and "taking possession of the public property."[13] The "fault was in not going far enough, when the demonstration of a purpose to use" the "strength" of the people "would have insured a triumph," said Dorr.[14] The People's Legislature, in Dorr's analysis, preferred quiet acquiescence to the "moderate degree of force which was necessary at this critical point."[15]

While certainly a sizeable crowd, the parade accompanying Dorr on May 3 did not compare with the crowds that attended the rallies in April, May, and June of 1841. One reason is that the support from the middle class, who once joined ranks with the mechanics and artisans in endorsing the People's Constitution, began to erode out of fear of arrest and apprehension for success.[16] The prominent Cranston mill owner William Sprague firmly believed that it would be "good policy for every mill in R.I. to stop" in order that the owners could be "relieved of a very large number of the most desperate characters." If every "operative and mechanic should leave R.I. their places could be filled in 60 days from Scotland and at less price," said Sprague.[17] The wily political operative Sprague actually voted for the People's Constitution in 1841, but he disavowed his connections to the suffrage reform movement a few months later in order to garner enough support in the General Assembly to be appointed U.S. Senator, filling a vacancy created by the death of Whig Nathan Dixon.[18]

Local merchants loyal to the Suffrage Association were often threatened and the "screws were to be put on them without mercy." Landlords turned "tenants out of their houses," along with discharging "men from employment" for bearing "arms in defense of the people's rights."[19] Emily Aplin, the owner of a rental property in Providence left to her by her father, evicted a family after she found out that the father was a Dorrite. "I say without hesitation that were the privilege granted me of choosing a tenant who must be either a Sabbath breaker . . . or a gambler or Intemperate or an understanding Dorrite, though I despise them all, still there would be decided preference for one of the former name," wrote Aplin.[20] After May 3, Charter authorities began to arrest supporters of Dorr indiscriminately under the provisions of the Algerine Law. Bail was set as high as $4,000 in some cases.[21] The editors of the *Providence Express*, a pro-Dorr organ, lost their lease in early June when the building owners threw in their lot with Samuel Ward King.[22] They would not resume publishing until September.

The nativist harangues emanating from Law and Order officials also served to curtail support for Dorr's cause. The intensity of the attacks had escalated greatly from the early spring. "Every Roman Catholic Irishman is a Dorrite," proclaimed one widely reproduced broadside.[23] Another factor in the declining support stemmed from instructions issued by the hierarchy of the Catholic Church. In early May, Elisha Potter, Jr., noted to John Brown Francis that he had received a "report" of "some importance" on the local Catholic population. Father John Corry, one of two priests stationed in Providence, had "interfered to prevent the Irish people from arming in the suffrage cause."[24] Two days later, Francis informed Potter that his "Irishman Patrick" who was "boiling over with fight" told him that James Fenwick, the Bishop of Boston, had put an "injunction upon" Rhode Island Catholics and the measure would be obeyed.[25] Dorr's uncle Philip Allen employed nearly 300 Irish Catholic workers at his print works in Providence and had intimate connections with that community.[26] Bishop Fenwick strenuously urged Catholics not to support Dorr's reform effort. As was the case with abolitionism, since Catholics were a minority everywhere and a suspect minority at that, supporting controversial causes such as a perceived extralegal attempt at constitutional reform or abolitionism would have only incurred the wrath of those opposed to both and would have fed widespread anti-Catholic sentiment.[27] Potter was relieved that the state population of nearly 5,000 Irish Catholics, with more than half living in Providence, would not interfere on the side of Dorr. Potter believed a compromise would be reached that could preserve the power structure of the conservative Democrats. "I wish you could impress it upon the minds of our friends in Providence that the sooner the matter is settled for us the better," wrote Potter to Francis. "Is it not better for us then to concede and so save a revolution than to hold out and have the revolutionary party succeed as I fear they would bye and bye." Is it "not better then to prevent a revolution by conceding the suffrage and having it down in the regular way?"[28]

On May 4, the Charter government declared what was painfully obvious to most Providence residents—a state of insurrection existed. The General Assembly made a formal request to President John Tyler "to interpose the authority and power of the United States to suppress such insurrectionary and lawless assemblages, to support the existing government and laws, and protect the State from domestic violence."[29] Taking every precaution, Samuel Ward King also wrote to Massachusetts Governor John Davis, asking him to have his state's forces stand at the ready.[30] Weeks later Dorr's uncle Zachariah Allen, Jr., took it upon himself to go to Boston to orchestrate an arms deal with the Massachusetts adjutant general.[31] Joshua Spooner was shocked that Dorr's men did not attempt to arrest King when he got off the boat from Newport in Providence harbor to celebrate his fourth term as governor. Spooner was convinced that the Suffrage Association wanted war.[32] Dorr, taking the advice of the Democratic Senators who wrote to him in April, was careful not to do anything that might incite violence.

Fear of arrest and economic reprisals prevented the People's Legislature from meeting for more than two days. In his inaugural address, which was delivered to the elected members brave enough to attend, Dorr acknowledged that "the making and altering of laws, which lie at the foundations of society, should be a work of great care and caution." However, Dorr reaffirmed the core tenet of the Suffrage Association: The "people have a right to change their government when necessary to their welfare."[33] After Dorr delivered his address, the legislature proceeded to nullify the dreaded Algerine Law. A measure was also passed authorizing Dorr to inform President Tyler, the U.S. Congress, and state governors that the People's Legislature was now governing the state.[34] Driven by a fear of going to prison and working in haste, the delegates made the incredible folly of electing as justices of the new supreme court the same judges who had already given their opinion that what they were doing constituted treason. At the end of the brief legislative session, Dorr made the decision to accompany Dutee Pearce and Burrington Anthony, a loyal Providence supporter, to Washington to meet with President Tyler. Two days later Pearce was arrested in Newport under charges of treason. In order to get out of jail he had to post a $5,000 bond. On May 8, Benjamin Arnold, one of the three authors of the address to the abolitionists of Rhode Island, was arrested by Charter authorities. Joshua Spooner reported that over a hundred suffrage men went to the jail to try to break Arnold out.[35]

Initially, Dorr had refused to accompany Pearce and Anthony to the nation's capital because he did not want to leave his precarious government, nor did he want to be accused of hypocrisy. The political high ground that Dorr had staked out for himself was the sanctity of the right of the people to alter or abolish their form of government. He did not want to be perceived as asking the federal government for assistance. However, Walter Burges, Dorr's closest friend, told him that no one could take his place. In Burges's view, the situation called for someone with the gift of rhetorical persuasion.

The president of the Suffrage Association, John Brown, was simply not up to the task.[36] The "principles in all their bearings, all the measures that have been pursued and all the facts from beginning to end of both governments" was something that only Dorr could detail in any type of sophistication to Tyler.[37] On a strategic level, Burges may also have been trying to ensure that his good friend left the state in order to avoid arrest.

As he traveled southward by train to Washington, Dorr wrote a letter from Jersey City to a close associate in Providence. The letter offers a glimpse into Dorr's mind at this crucial juncture. He truly believed that King would step aside. "For God's sake strengthen our men. Let them stand firm. I assure them that we are coming out right," proclaimed Dorr. While more and more Suffrage Association officials were being arrested day after day, Dorr urged that bail not be posted. "Let our men go to jail."[38] This was all well and good for someone like Dorr to say, a man who lived off an allowance from his father for a good portion of his adult life. But for the mechanics and artisans who feared arrest, feared losing their jobs, and feared for their families, this line of reasoning must have seemed outright delusional.

When word reached King that Dorr, Pearce, and Anthony were on their way to Washington, he quickly dispatched Elisha R. Potter, Jr., and Richard Randolph to meet with Tyler. This was the second trip for Potter and Francis to the city in less than a month. John Brown Francis stayed at home in Warwick. The decision to send Randolph as an emissary was a brilliant move on King's part. Randolph was a nephew of William Henry Harrison, a fact that gave him great access to and influence on Tyler. Randolph, a Whig representative from Newport, was also a transplanted Virginian and a former slaveholder. King knew that Randolph would be able to quickly ingratiate himself with Tyler. In the late 1830s, Randolph often went head-to-head against Dorr in the Rhode Island General Assembly, attacking Dorr's antislavery and abolitionist agenda. In January 1838, Randolph argued against Dorr's proposal to instruct Rhode Island's Congressional contingent to work towards emancipation in the nation's capital. It would be "impolitic, unjust, and *dangerous* to emancipate the slaves in the District of Columbia," replied Randolph during a spirited exchange with Dorr on the floor of the General Assembly.[39] Racial fear mongering was not part of the Potter and John Brown Francis pitch to Tyler in April; the substitution of Randolph for Francis changed all that. It was insinuated that Fall River abolitionists, led by Louis Lapham, were going to stream over the border to aid Dorr.[40]

This was certainly ironic and distorted given the abolitionist opposition to the People's Constitution.

According to notes of the meeting with Tyler, Randolph successfully painted Dorr as an abolitionist and the People's Convention an abolitionist cabal. Pro-Dorr supporters believed that U.S. Senator James Simmons had laid the groundwork for these accusations. Simmons, a native of Johnston and owner of several cotton mills, was "daily engaged in whispering into the ears of all the southern Senators to whom he had access, that the suffrage cause was an abolition movement, and that Governor Dorr was one of the leaders of the abolition party."[41] Simmons's goal was to counter the influence of Senators William Allen and James Buchanan, the latter of whom gave a speech the week before in which he denounced the "centralizing" tendencies of the Tyler administration.[42] Whigs in Providence wrote frequently to Simmons to remind him of Dorr's service on the executive committee of the Rhode Island Anti-Slavery Society. "I [urge] you to remember that this man, Thomas Wilson Dorr, who is now the controlling spring of the Rhode Island insurrection and the governor elect under the People's Constitution so called, was in the year 1839, only three years ago, one of the executives of the state committee of the Rhode Island Anti-Slavery Society," wrote a correspondent of Senator Simmons. "The senators from the slave states should understand who it is that made the insurrection against our government here."[43]

Linking Dorr to abolitionism was relatively easy since the *Liberator* and the *Herald of Freedom* had endorsed him for Congress in 1837 and 1839 and his past membership on the executive board of the Rhode Island Anti-Slavery Society and attendance at the annual meetings of the American Anti-Slavery Society in 1837, 1838, and 1839 were no secret. The influential Rhode Island Whig Samuel Man, a member of King's six-man executive council, compared Dorr to Benjamin Tappan, the antislavery Democratic Senator from Ohio and older brother of the abolitionists Arthur and Lewis Tappan. Man said that Dorr's ideology of the people's sovereignty was "no doubt Tappan's favorite measure because thereby he and other hot-headed and dangerous abolitionists [could] accomplish their cherished object in the south, for once established this dogma, together with the principle that all men are free and equal" could destroy the slave system.[44]

However, to say the People's Convention was overrun with abolitionists was another thing entirely. Potter and Randolph did not mention the vehement abolitionist attacks against the People's Constitution. Most delegates did everything possible to exclude blacks from joining their ranks, opting to include a white-only clause in their People's Constitution. Two years later on the floor of Congress, Elisha Potter proclaimed that conservatives in Rhode Island told the Suffrage Association that, "if their principles were carried out, the negroes in the Southern States would have a perfect right to overturn those state governments." In Potter's recounting, members of the Suffrage Association answered "that the negroes" were not recognized by law as persons." However, according to Potter, the Suffrage Association forgot "that the very first principles they set out with, the people, in the exercise of the natural rights, are above all laws whatever."[45] Potter reported that South Carolina Senator William Preston, who was present at the meeting in the White House, maintained that Dorr's ideology would "ruin S. Carolina." If Dorr's ideology prevailed what would prevent the "negroes [from] revolutionizing the South?" asked Preston.[46] Southern politicians saw in the ideology of the people's sovereignty a threat to property rights and white southern society more generally.[47]

Dorr was fully aware of the threat his ideology posed to southern institutions. In a letter to Walter Burges, Dorr acknowledged that "some of the Southern members" of Congress were with the people of Rhode Island, but "not with all People in asserting a principle," meaning popular sovereignty, "which might be construed to take in the southern blacks, and to aid the abolitionists."[48] The result of this doctrine on Dorr's Democratic Party was easy to perceive—it would split the party right down the middle with northern Democrats lining up in support and southern Democrats waiting to hang him in effigy. If the disfranchised majority of Rhode Island under Dorr's instruction "could form a constitution without leave of their masters" then the black "majority of South Carolina might do the same and the peculiar institution would be overthrown." The "northern laborer must therefore be put down, lest the southern laborer should rise," proclaimed the New York abolitionist editor William Goodell.[49]

The perceived threat of Dorr's ideology on the mass of enslaved bondsmen eventually played a significant role in the demise of the revolutionary movement in Rhode Island. Leading northern Democrats, such as Silas Wright, Jr., and Levi Woodbury, who were both supporters of Dorr, began to urge caution once their southern counterparts expressed disapproval. As Alabama Congressman Dixon Lewis correctly noted, the Rhode Island constitutional crisis threatened to divide the Democratic Party along sectional lines.[50] On the one hand, the Democrats were the party of popular sovereignty, drawing a direct linkage to the Jeffersonian idealism that permeated the Revolutionary era. On the other, they were a party of states' rights, strict construction of the Constitution, and upholders of vested rights. Wright and Woodbury were both eyeing potential slots on a ticket with John C. Calhoun in 1844 and openly supporting Dorr would have doomed them in the eyes of southern politicos. Never one to hold his tongue, Calhoun let his displeasure with Dorr become known when the two men encountered each other in a boardinghouse. Calhoun told his friend Dixon Lewis that he gave the Rhode Island agitator "a piece of [his] mind."[51]

Massachusetts politics also had a detrimental effect on Dorr's efforts to secure support for the People's Constitution. Even before William Henry Harrison's inauguration, Massachusetts Democrats had begun talking about who would gain the nomination in 1844. The prominent attorney Robert Rantoul immediately began pushing for Levi Woodbury, the author of several glowing letters of support for Dorr and his cause, as the nominee. However, Rantoul ran into opposition from David Henshaw, who was a Calhoun man. Rantoul acquiesced to Henshaw and began to push for Levi Woodbury to be Calhoun's running-mate. When Rantoul was chosen chairman of the state Democratic committee in May 1842 the Calhoun-Woodbury ticket seemed like a very real possibility.[52] Calhoun's quest for the presidency "attracted a weird collection of the doctrinaire, the disaffected, the mercenary, and the opportunistic."[53] Labor radicals like Orestes Brownson envisioned an alliance between northern workingmen and southern slaveholders. Mike Walsh's gang of Bowery Boys were always ready to fight rhetorically or physically for Calhoun in order to strike at the Tammany Hall politicians who were aligned with Martin Van Buren. Woodbury now had to tread lightly in terms of supporting the revolutionary reform movement in Rhode Island, leaving only Ohio's William Allen as an advocate in the Senate. After spending a week in Washington in early May, Potter reported that Woodbury had come to regret his support for Dorr because "he and Calhoun are said to be negotiating to run on the same ticket for P and VP." According to Potter, Woodbury's previous support for Dorrite principles did not "suit the South."[54]

There was a clear unwillingness on the part of many Democrats to push Dorr's rhetoric where slavery was firmly entrenched. According to Calhoun, the "governments of one half of the States of the Union would not stand the test" of Dorr's understanding of the Guarantee Clause in Article IV, section 4.[55] Calhoun, one of most prominent American statesmen in the first half of the nineteenth century, was also one of the country's leading authorities on the Constitution. His *Disquisition on Government* was one of the most important American contributions to political theory and his *Discourses on the Government and Constitution of the United States* was one of the most thorough treatments of the founding document compiled before the Civil War. In Calhoun's mind, constitutional guarantees and property rights were worthless in the face of Dorr's majoritarian principles. It was inherent in the political process itself that the stronger interest would abuse its power at the expense of the weaker. The only recourse for this, in Calhoun's analysis, was a concurrent veto, state interposition, or secession.

Calhoun's opposition to Dorr's ideology was consistent with his theory of nullification—the fear of majoritarian tyranny. Calhoun was concerned mainly with protecting minority rights under a popular government. Calhoun's friend and fellow slaveocrat Abel Upshur, who was serving as Tyler's Secretary of the Navy, noted that the People's Constitution demonstrated the "very madness of democracy, and a fine example" of the dangers of the "majority principle."[56] Abolitionists, led by *Emancipator* editor Joshua Leavitt, frequently leveled charges that Upshur was building up the U.S. Navy in order to protect the South's peculiar institution.[57] According to Calhoun, "in determining whether the Government of a State be, or not be republican, within the meaning of the Constitution, [the federal government] has no right . . . to look beyond its admission to the Union."[58] The Virginian James Madison argued the same in the *Federalist*. In the forty-third installment of the classic essays on the Constitution, Madison declared that all existing state governments in 1788–1789 were republican and would be guaranteed in their continuance, or in any republican modification, by the federal government. Calhoun argued that the federal right to intervene against a state's rulers was a "high and delicate one." The "forms of the governments of the several States, composing the Union, as they stood at the time of their admission" constituted the only "standard" to go by.[59]

To allow the federal government the option of deciding which government in Rhode Island was republican could set a dangerous precedent to follow for a future (northern) president who wished to interfere with the South's peculiar institution. Under the Constitution, Congress did have the power to decide whom to seat and they would exercise this power during Reconstruction. However, in the antebellum period, southern politicians often feared that giving Congress the option of admitting whichever state delegation they wanted would grant the federal government full control over the admission of new states and, by extension, slavery's expansion. Southern Senators could remember just such an interpretation of the Guarantee Clause urged by antislavery congressmen, including Rhode Island's James Burrill, two decades before in the debates over the Missouri Compromise.[60] Calhoun's counterpart in the Senate, William Preston, viewed the "Rhode Island Question" not in terms of its connection to the ideology of the American Revolution, but rather for its relationship to "the peculiar institutions of the South." Preston believed that if Dorr's ideology won out, then there would "be a dissolution of the Union" because "slaves" could then "alter their laws and govern themselves for they are the majority."[61]

Southern Democratic resistance to Dorr demonstrates the capacity of the "Rhode Island Question" to affect electoral and legislative politics by fostering internal divisions within the party.[62] Highlighting the importance of the "Rhode Island Question" to the politics of the 1840s is the letter writing campaign conducted by Virginia Democratic Congressman William Smith, who later served as Virginia's governor during the Civil War and a Major General in the Confederate Army. In his 1843 letters to potential Democrat presidential and vice presidential candidates, Smith asked a series of six questions that all dealt with the Rhode Island constitutional crisis.

After collecting the views of the leading Democrats on the "Rhode Island Question," Smith's intention was to plead for toleration of "some differences among those who, in general, act and think alike."[63] The "time is rapidly approaching where the Democratic Party will have to select their candidate for the Presidential Election of 1844," wrote Smith to the prominent Massachusetts Democrat George Bancroft, Dorr's former tutor. Differences over the "Rhode Island Question" had to be settled in order to ensure success at the polls. The "sentiments and opinions of those of our prominent statesmen and fellow citizens who may be regarded as within the range of selection by our contemplated convention are, with one exception," said Smith, "satisfactorily known." Smith believed that the "Rhode Island Question" was "deeply interesting to the whole country, involving, in no slight degree, the fate of constitutional liberty."[64]

Smith's third and fourth questions got to the heart of the matter. "After a state shall have been admitted into this Union, have the numerical majority of the people of such state, the right to alter or abolish her constitution, regardless of the mode prescribed for its amendment," asked Smith. Putting his subject directly on the proverbial hot seat, Smith asked should the authorities of a state "deny the right of a numerical majority of her people to alter or abolish her constitution at pleasure," forcing that majority to resort to force, does the minority have a right to call upon the president of the United States for protection?[65]

Along with his letter to Bancroft, Smith wrote similar letters to Martin Van Buren, James Buchanan, and John Calhoun.[66] Buchanan informed Smith that he was a "Suffrage man" and that his "opinion was in accordance with the Northern Democracy" on the "Rhode Island Question." Buchanan, however, urged Smith not to publish the responses out of fear of unnecessarily agitating the Democracy.[67] Buchanan perceptively realized that southern Democrats would refuse to uphold first principles over procedural propriety because of their unwillingness to push the rhetoric of liberty where slavery reigned. Clearly he saw the diverging views on the "Rhode Island Question" offered by northern and southern Democrats.

Martin Van Buren's reply in July 1843 expressed support for the principles behind Dorr's movement. In his letter, the former president quoted from Article III of Virginia's 1776 Declaration of Rights, which states that "whenever any government shall be found inadequate or contrary to these purposes, a majority of the community hath an indubitable, unalienable, and indefeasible right, to reform, alter, or abolish it, in such manner as shall be judged most conducive to the public weal."[68] Van Buren boldly declared that he believed an "armed interposition of the United States" in the "late affairs" in Rhode Island "to defeat the measures deliberately and peacefully taken by a majority of the people" was "a flagrant violation of states' rights and popular sovereignty."[69] Van Buren ran a draft of his letter by his close friend Silas Wright, Jr., who had intimate knowledge of the Rhode Island constitutional crisis through his communication with Thomas Dorr. Wright encouraged Van Buren to add mention of "popular sovereignty" in his reply to Smith in order to connect the reform effort to the American Revolution. Wright was setting up the use of the malleable "popular sovereignty" mantra by the Democrats in future political campaigns.[70] However, the leading southern Democrat for the 1844 presidential nomination did not agree with Wright's interpretation of events nor his attempt to use Dorr's ideology as a political weapon for the party.

According to John Calhoun, the principles outlined in the "Rhode Island Question," if accepted, would constitute the "death-blow to republican forms of government, or, what is the same thing, constitutional democracy."[71] Whereas Van Buren attempted to somewhat couch his argument in generalities, Calhoun's response to Smith's questionnaire was lengthy and clear. In terms of the Guarantee Clause, Calhoun maintained that a precise understanding of its meaning and proper mode of application was of vital importance for the "success and duration" of the American "political system."[72] Rejecting the Dorrite position, Calhoun argued that the Guarantee Clause required Congress and the Executive to protect the *existing* state government. In determining whether the government of a state was republican, the federal government had no right "to look beyond its admission to the Union."[73] In answer to a question about how he would have handled the situation in Rhode Island if he was in the White House, Calhoun maintained that he would have "enforce[d] the guarantee" and protected the Rhode Island Charter authorities.[74]

Calhoun clearly feared that if Dorr's interpretation of Article IV's guarantee of republican government prevailed, it could be used to give political rights to blacks. Under a plausible reading of Article IV, section 4, no state had the right to disenfranchise a quarter or more of its adult free population. Many framers of the Thirteenth Amendment later assumed this very point.[75] As historian William Wiecek has argued, Calhoun "perceived more clearly than most the threat posed to slavery as a system of race control by the constitutional issues raised in the Rhode Island controversy."[76] Calhoun's position favoring "constitutional legitimacy" threatened to erode his political support among northern Locofocos. As Calhoun's friend Robert Hunter noted, his views on the "Rhode Island Question" severely "miscarried" with northern Democrats who were aware of Smith's questionnaire.[77]

There was no doubt Calhoun's "opinions on the Rhode Island controversy" had been "powerfully used to prejudice you in the minds of the Northern Democracy by Van Buren's friends," said Robert Barnwell Rhett in a letter to Calhoun.[78] Hunter did not believe as Dorr did that the "mere number majority of the people . . . had at all times the right of superseding the existing Constitution and Government and establishing another in their place." Northern Democrats, especially Van Buren, were "making capital" of Dorr's constitutionalism.[79] Hunter maintained that the "people" would be "ignorant" of the "principles" of American government if the "Rhode Island Question" was not part of the debate.[80] Smith, however, came to the conclusion that he "should not publish the responses on the Rhode Island Question when received" because it would make glaringly public a wide gulf within the Democratic ranks and hurt the party's chance of capturing the White House in 1844.[81]

According to one report of Thomas Dorr's four-hour May 10 meeting in the White House, the president told the would-be governor of Rhode Island that his "proceedings" were "treasonable against the state and if they committed any overt acts and resisted the force of the U.S. they would then commit treason against the U.S. and as sure as they did so they should be hanged for treason!"[82] Secretary of State Daniel Webster confirmed this. There was no "doubt," wrote Webster to Dorr's former legal mentor, John Whipple, that the "Government of the United States pledges itself to maintain the existing constitution and laws till regularly changed."[83] After leaving the White House, Dorr labeled Tyler and Webster "Tories of the rankest sort." He believed that the Tyler administration feared an "American War of the People against the Government" and would take action against the Dorrites.[84]

Dorr went to Washington in the spring of 1842 with the hope of winning Tyler's support. He left the city with a lesson in sectional politics, along with greater determination than ever to implement the People's Constitution. A letter from the Boston labor radical Orestes Brownson supporting extralegal tactics served to bolster Dorr's psyche and turn him away from any thought of compromise.[85] Dorr's tendency to approach issues theoretically rather than practically and to seek resolution the hard way—on principles—was put to the ultimate test as he made his way back to Rhode Island.

The People's Governor was serenaded by throngs of Democrats in Philadelphia and New York City, two cities where he spent considerable time in during his youth. He was undoubtedly bolstered by this rhetorical support. His closest followers, however, were thinking of one thing only—compromise. The same was true of Elisha Potter, who wrote to President Tyler with news that a compromise could be reached if Dorr would just allow himself to be arrested.[86] Dorr had no intention of giving in. He wrote a lengthy letter on May 13 to the Democratic Connecticut Governor Chauncey Cleveland pleading his case and seeking military aid in case federal forces were sent to Rhode Island.[87] However, at the same time that Dorr's resolve was stiffening, his followers were losing their nerve and looking to compromise.

The meeting that took place in New York City on the morning of May 14, 1842, was unprecedented. For the first time a sitting U.S. secretary of state was attempting to broker a compromise between two warring domestic factions.[88] Wishing to avoid an outbreak of hostilities at all costs, Tyler dispatched Webster to New York after meeting with Dorr. Dutee Pearce, Burrington Anthony, and John Harris, a Suffrage Association official who made the journey south from Providence, represented the People's Government in the meeting with Webster. Aaron White, Jr., had already warned Dorr about the compromise effort: "The charter assembly will give us nothing except apartments in the state prison."[89] Representing the Charter government was John Whipple, Dorr's old legal mentor.[90] In actuality, Whipple did not have authorization from Samuel Ward King to negotiate, but he was privy to Tyler's May 9 letter to King in which the president urged for compromise measures.[91] Whipple had set up the meeting on his own accord because of his friendship with Webster, his past relationship with Dorr, and his desire to prevent bloodshed. Whipple did have some reservations, however, about his chances for success. In late April, he sent his teenage daughter to live with friends in Worcester in order to "escape the troubles."[92] Whipple undoubtedly sensed that Dorr was not about to back down easily.

Just days before their meeting with Webster, Pearce and Anthony had experienced firsthand the power of rumor and conspiratorial talk during their time in Washington. William Preston and James Simmons successfully linked Dorr to abolitionism and, as a consequence, connected the reformer to the most radical and dangerous political creed of the era. Pearce, Harris, and Anthony quickly realized that a brokered peace was their best option. Despite their pleas, Dorr flatly rejected the offer to have the courts decide the fate of the People's Constitution. Dorr did not believe that a verdict supporting the legality of the People's Constitution would come out of a circuit court with Joseph Story and John Pitman presiding.[93] Samuel Man correctly noted that Dorr was "resolved" not to enter into a "compromise that does not recognize the right of a majority to alter and amend or change laws without legislative interposition."[94] Even before the clandestine meeting, Dorr had already made up his mind that it was time "to strike a blow" for the people's sovereignty.[95] Dorr had yielded to his advisors, who cautioned him against occupying the statehouse in Providence on May 3; now he would follow a more militant course.

While Pearce, Anthony, and Harris were attempting to secure some sort of a compromise measure, Dorr was being serenaded by radical New York Democrats and was given a sword used by Andrew Jackson during his Florida Indian campaign in 1813. The New York patrician diarist Philip Hone recorded that Dorr "came to New York a lamb and was sent to Providence a lion by the Tammany sympathizers."[96] New York radicals supported Dorr because he was a principled advocate for the rights of the common man. Radical New York Democrats often demonstrated an intense egalitarianism in their political speeches along with a vibrant interest in the ideology of the American Revolution. Ely Moore, Levi Slamm, Aaron Vanderpoel, Churchill C. Cambreleng, and Mike Walsh had organized numerous large rallies for Dorr.[97] Ely Moore in particular was an outspoken opponent of the "treasonable dogmas advanced by the Landholders' party in Rhode Island."[98] Vanderpoel waxed poetic when he proclaimed at a large rally of New York City Democrats that the constitutional crisis in Rhode Island involved the "great question whether the doctrine of the sovereignty of a majority of the people is, in this, our happy America, a practical principle, or whether it is . . . suspended on the outside of our theory of government."[99] Hone characterized the gatherings as Irish Catholic rallies whose attendants were bent on reducing the "rights of Native Americans."[100]

Mike Walsh and Dorr were certainly strange bedfellows. Walsh was born in Ireland in 1810, the son of a cabinet maker and fomenter of the United Irishman uprising of 1798. At a young age, Walsh emigrated to America. He traveled the country as a young boy, returning to New York City in 1839 where he found work as a journalist. He served as a correspondent for the Democratic *New York Aurora* and then as editor of his own newspaper, the *Knickerbocker*, and later, the *Subterranean*.[101] Walsh spent many a night in his early years sleeping on a park bench while Dorr spent his time in the lavish home of his wealthy parents on the east side of Providence. Whereas Dorr was learned, generally refined, and fiercely loyal, Walsh prided himself on anti-intellectualism, bravado, unbridled arrogance, unscrupulous behavior, and ability to shift allegiances like the wind. Despite Walsh's affinity for John Calhoun, he did profess a firm belief in the doctrine of popular sovereignty. Walsh saw in Calhoun's defense of the South's peculiar institution a bulwark for workingmen against unscrupulous employers and competition from New York City's sizable free black population. Walsh looked past Calhoun's ideas of democracy to the South Carolina statesmen's attack on the banking system and his vehement hatred for Martin Van Buren.[102]

Dorr was "emboldened by the flattery" shown by the New York Democrats; it played to his "vanity."[103] Dorr said he had every intention of bringing "1000 [New York City] volunteers, to act in case a government soldier shall set his foot on" Rhode Island soil after his return.[104] Alexander Ming, an ally of the radical labor leader Thomas Skidmore, and Abraham Crasto, labor radicals who moonlighted as colonels in a New York militia, wrote to

Dorr pledging their support and offering an armed escort to accompany the People's Governor back to Rhode Island.[105] The hero-worship session in New York City led Dorr to concoct a simple plan: his men would attack the state arsenal and deprive the Charter authorities of the weapons they would need to mount an attack and thus force them to capitulate. A correspondent of New York governor William Henry Seward who was traveling in Rhode Island correctly noted that "a number of persons," meaning the followers of Dorr, were "contemplating taking possession of the arsenal, and such arms and munitions of war as they may deem expedient to conquer their own ends."[106] On May 12, 1842, while Dorr traveled to the major cities on the eastern seaboard and was serenaded by thousands, his followers in Providence rallied in support of his right to the governorship. "We will support, protect, and defend Gov. Thomas W. Dorr to the last" was one of the cries.[107]

With the failure of the clandestine, compromise-seeking meeting in New York City, Dorr took a ferry on May 15 to Stonington, Connecticut. The following morning as the three-car train carrying the thirty-six-year-old People's Governor wound its way north from Stonington through southern Rhode Island's fertile farmland, the streets of Providence came alive.[108] Bolstered by the military support he thought was coming from the New York Bowery Lane district and a newfound sense of bravado, Dorr returned to Rhode Island (albeit without the troops promised by Ming and Crasto) determined to implement the People's Constitution. Riding in an open-air coach pulled by a team of four white horses with a shining sword at his side, Dorr led the way through the hilly streets. According to one eyewitness who was at the Harbor Junction depot when Dorr got off the train, the People's Governor "was escorted into the city by a procession numbering about 1,200, three hundred of whom were under arms."[109]

The scene was reminiscent of the crowd of 1,500 men who had escorted Dorr in his inaugural parade. This parade ended at the Federal Hill home of Burrington Anthony, a former federal marshal who had been elected as the People's sheriff for the city of Providence. The short and rotund Dorr "has made his grand entrance today, *a la mode* Napoleon" wrote Samuel Man to James Simmons.[110] As she watched the events unfold, Aurilla Moffitt was dismayed at the sight of throngs of women cheering for Dorr: "Shame on the woman who encourages the lawless proceeding by her presence."[111]

Brandishing and waving his new sword, which he used in place of his traditional walking cane, Dorr used his gift of oratory to inspire a throng of devoted followers. This was a panegyric of the lofty goals of the American

Revolution. No transcript of the speech survives, but in a published proclamation that appeared the next day Dorr maintained that no "further arrests" of his followers would be tolerated. The People's Governor said that "as soon as a soldier of the United States shall be set in motion by whatever direction, to act against the people . . . in aid of the Charter government," he would call for aid from New York.[112] To Samuel Man, Dorr's proclamation amounted "to nothing more than an open declaration of war against the state and also the United States." If President Tyler did not send federal troops to Rhode Island, Man believed the Charter authorities were left with three options: "Arrest Dorr at the risk of a civil war; make a disgraceful compromise with irresponsible persons of the party to which Dorr will not be a party; or abandon the government."[113]

Man had every right to be concerned. Dorr had been signing letters, including one to the U.S. Senate, as "Thomas Wilson Dorr Governor of the State of Rhode Island and Providence Plantations," along with others to the governors of Connecticut and Maine.[114] As news of these letters circulated, Providence residents believed that Dorr's master plan was to "take possession of the colleges for headquarters; the market for provisions; and then to put the city under martial law."[115] It was a near universal, though much exaggerated, belief among the conservative elite that the streets of Providence would be "deluged in blood" and the city burned to the ground.[116]

On the afternoon of May 17, dozens of heavily armed Dorrites raided the Providence Marine Corps of Artillery armory, just blocks from the Dorr family mansion on Benefit Street. George Bennett, the commander of the United Train of Artillery, later testified that the majority of the men under his command were loyal to Dorr. Indeed, one of Bennett's men served as an escort for Dorr as he got off the train from Stonington. Bennett believed that the man in charge of the keys to the armory had handed them over to Dorr's men.[117] Sullivan and Lydia Dorr surely heard the commotion as Lieutenant Josiah Reed and five others stole two Revolutionary war cannons that had been confiscated from British general Johnny Burgoyne at the Battle of Saratoga. Providence shopkeeper Joshua Spooner watched as Reed's men dragged the pieces of field artillery through Providence's cobblestone streets, past his storefront, to Dorr's headquarters at Burrington Anthony's house on Federal Hill.[118] The two cannons, along with several other artillery pieces, were turned and aimed down the hill at the center of the city. The cannons were placed in front of Anthony's home joining the other four pieces of artillery that protected the People's Governor.[119] Crawford Allen,

Lydia Dorr's brother and a close confidant of Thomas Dorr for most of his life, went to the house to try to talk his nephew into leaving the city. The headstrong Dorr did not listen.[120]

Those loyal to the Charter government waited anxiously for Governor King to issue orders. Mayor Thomas Burgess was sure that the "only possible chance for the failure" of Dorr's "undertaking" would be the "refusal of his military to obey." Burgess warned former Governor James Fenner in the early morning hours of May 18 that Dorr's men would attempt to kidnap him and presumably hold him for ransom.[121] After Dorr's men stole the cannons, many "Marines & Cadets stood around and looked upon the exploit with impatience and the greatest anger, but could do nothing without the sanction of the governor who was out of the city," wrote Edward Louis Peckham, a local artist and Charter government supporter.[122] After watching the boldness of Dorr's troops, militiaman William Bailey arranged for a carriage to be ready at a "moment's notice" to take his family out of the city.[123]

Walter Simmons, who was in Providence conducting business on his father's behalf, believed he was observing the beginnings of mob rule. The young Simmons implored his father to seek counsel with the president in order to gain assurance of federal assistance to put down what he feared was sure to become an open rebellion.[124] Governor King was actually en route to Providence from Newport. Spies for the Charter government, including Edward Carrington, Sr., infiltrated Dorr's headquarters and reported to King and his executive council that the People's Governor had resolved on a drastic course of action. At 6 p.m. on May 17, King issued an order calling for citizens to arm themselves and prepare for battle. Alarm bells sounded across the city.[125]

Troops loyal to Dorr were pouring into Providence from the northern mill villages and towns of Woonsocket, North Providence, Glocester, Smithfield, and Johnson. If Dorr had acted decisively in the evening of May 17, he could have easily taken the arsenal. His forces outnumbered the Charter forces ten to one. According to Edward Peckham, who went to the arsenal shortly after the theft of the cannons, there were only thirty men defending the state's cache of weapons and most were not members of regular militia organizations.[126] King ordered that messengers be sent to Newport, Warren, Bristol, and East Greenwich—bastions of conservatism—to gather reinforcements, though it would be impossible for them to arrive in time if Dorr decided to attack. Dorr's delay allowed time for additional militia groups in the city to make haste to defend the arsenal. Included in the ranks of those who went to defend the city was Dorr's father, his brother Sullivan, Jr., his uncle Zachariah Allen, and his brother-in-law Samuel Ames. Trying to come to grips with the fear and trepidation he felt on the night of May 17 when he took up a musket and went to defend the arsenal, Joshua Spooner wrote that Providence militiamen went "to protect their property [and] to protect their families."[127] All talk of compromise and calls for a new constitutional convention, despite concerted efforts led by conservative Democrat Charles Jackson, had failed.[128]

The state arsenal, a two-story building, was situated on the open fields of the Dexter Training ground on the west end of Providence. Quartermaster General Samuel Ames commanded the lower story cannons, while Colonel Leonard Blodget organized the troops in the second-floor windows.[129] The troops in the arsenal loaded the five cannons inside with grapeshot and positioned them near each door and the first-floor windows. While it was certainly well guarded, the arsenal was extremely vulnerable to attack because its roof could be burnt and its doors could easily be blown off by short-range cannon fire.

Around one o'clock in the morning on May 18, reports put Dorr's strength at anywhere from 300 to 400 men at his headquarters on Federal Hill.[130] A young and frightened Henry Hodges heard a cannon, signaling that the "Free Suffrage [men] were attacking the arsenal."[131] The cannon shot young Hodges heard was not actually aimed at the arsenal. It was a signal from Dorr's headquarters for his men to march to the arsenal on Cranston Street. With the street lamps veiled by a heavy fog that had arisen suddenly from Narragansett Bay, Dorr's men used torches to light their way from Federal Hill.[132] Providence elites living in the large homes on the hills of the east side of the city saw a long column of flickering lights marching off into the darkness. Lydia Dorr likely watched with trepidation as her husband went off to defend the city and her son, Sullivan, Jr., went to join her brothers in the arsenal. Lydia's family was coming apart at the seams and taking the city with it.

Somewhere between one o'clock and two o'clock in the morning alarm bells, three strokes from one steeple top and then three from another, began to arouse Providence's sleeping inhabitants, warning them of an impending attack. "Church bells began their successive stroke at short intervals in order to arise the sleeping inhabitants," wrote one Providence militiaman who was stationed in an armory on Meeting Street, about a mile away from the arsenal.[133] Perhaps Dorr recognized the sound of the bells atop St. John's Episcopal Church on North Main Street, where his family owned a pew.

Dorr's hope was to arrive at the arsenal with an overwhelming force and convince its defenders to surrender. However, the troop numbers were not in Dorr's favor. Around midnight, as he planned his attack in Anthony's house, Dorr had had close to four hundred supporters; two hours later as he began his march, those numbers were cut nearly in half. At the same time, more and more Charter troops began to pour into the arsenal. Once his remaining men were in position, Dorr sent his loyal lieutenant Charles Carter to the door of the arsenal with a message for the commanding officer inside. Signal bells began to ring in the city. Carter warned the colonel in charge of the arsenal's defenses that the Dorrites had them outnumbered despite the defections in their ranks. Carter said he intended to take the arms. "Take it be damned" was the reply.[134]

When Carter returned to the Dorrite camp and informed his superiors that military action was necessary to take possession of the arsenal, Dorr took control of the remaining troops himself. Dorr, who had no military training to speak of, placed Carter in charge and ordered the remaining fifty or so men to hold their ground. The forty-seven-year-old labor leader Seth Luther was at Dorr's side, along with Lidea Rodgers, a fiery female supporter.[135] Someone, possibly Dorr, attempted to light the cannons, which flashed, but failed to hurl any projectile toward the arsenal. Hiram Hill, a resident of Cumberland who was in Providence on the night of May 17, said he expected to hear the "volley" of cannons and muskets.[136] One of Dorr's men plugged the cannons so they would not ignite.[137]

For the rest of his life Dorr never discussed his role in what went on in his camp. He never definitely said if he attempted to light the cannons or not. John Burke, a Providence militiaman, did not care who tried to light the cannons. All he wanted was to see "40 to 50" of Dorr's "rascally fellows" shot after the "vagabond" Dorr escaped. The fiery Rhoda Newcomb was equally dismayed that the Charter men did not attack Dorr's forces. She was disgusted with the tactic of "using no violence."[138] John Brown Francis, however, was relieved that Dorr was not killed. "Why make a martyr out of [a] parricide," said Francis.[139]

The attempted attack on the arsenal, despite Dorr's assertion that it was a mere "casual defeat," was a foolhardy endeavor that cost him major support in Rhode Island.[140] One supporter wrote to a friend in New York a few days after the attempted attack expressing how his emotions first delved into anger at the failure, but then came full circle to the realization that the result of "an armed attempt to achieve their rights would have been attended with disastrous results."[141] After the failed attempt on the arsenal, Dorr had few supporters left. Senators and representatives elected under the People's Constitution had "determined to resign instantly" because they "disapprove[d] of the proceedings, our men will not kill . . . our citizens."[142] The numerical strength that Dorr enjoyed early in 1842 had completely evaporated. Yet, the headstrong Dorr was not about to turn himself in or back down. His successful escape out of the city ensured that the fight was not over. Though Dorr's support was dwindling, the citizens of Rhode Island would remain on edge, fearful of what the People's Governor might do next.

Chapter 6

An Abolitionist Plot

The abolitionists would only have to creep through the southern states, take down the names of all the blacks over 21 years of age, and all the reckless, miserable white fanatics—men who have nothing at stake, and would, at a moment's warning, engage in any lawless enterprise promising booty—and then, at a concerted signal, throw up the black flag of insurrection, and proclaim the laws extinct.

Madisonian, May 21, 1842

By daybreak on May 18, 1842, Providence's upper echelon, including Thomas Dorr's brother-in-law Moses Brown Ives and U.S. District Attorney Richard W. Greene, were leading military units through the streets. Ives told a family friend that the night of May 17 was the most "terrible night" he ever witnessed.[1] For those who understood the gravity of the situation, the fact that no blood was shed was the result of Divine Providence and not Dorr's ineptness in leading a military operation. Aurilla Moffitt was filled with joy when news reached her that the skirmish at the arsenal "ended without bloodshed" and her husband was safe.[2]

Socialite Anna Herreshoff, the granddaughter of the wealthy merchant and perpetrator behind the burning of the *Gaspee*, John Brown, recorded how the "electrifying" news of Dorr's failed attack on the arsenal brought the ladies of Providence "out into the streets." All Dorr's "relatives were in the arsenal that dreadful night when the demon [Dorr] with his own hand put the match to the cannon; he might have destroyed his own father," said Anna in disbelief. A few days after the attack, Anna and a group of women went to Federal Hill in order to get a look at Burrington Anthony's home. "I saw the house where Dorr was protected . . . how unlike his own elegant home!" said Anna to her brother Charles Herreshoff, a gentleman farmer.

141

"Here we see the effects of a domineering temper; he has lost all," said Anna "by desiring too much." She also shared the widespread belief that "the lower classes were not looking for suffrage alone." Dorr had "promised" his men, according to Anna, "a division of property." She recounted how a friend of hers went to a dressmaker a few weeks before and the woman told her "she would not work many days longer." When asked why, the dressmaker replied that she was going to get a portion of the "Brown and Ives" property.[3]

Harriet Bailey, the sister of Providence militiaman William Bailey, shared Anna Herreshoff's fears of a social revolution. In the spring of 1842, the most powerful and contagious rumor in Providence's elite circles had the "traitor Tom Dorr" implementing the economic philosophy of the New York labor radical Thomas Skidmore. In a letter to her mother, Jane Keeley, Harriet recounted how one poor woman she talked to informed her that once Dorr succeeded, her son would be as rich as John Whipple, the leader of the Rhode Island bar.[4] Wealthy citizens expressed "gratitude to God" for his "preserving power on that awful night."[5]

A correspondent of Senator James Simmons captured the great sense of fear and trepidation among Providence's elite that something horrible could have occurred the night of May 17. Had Dorr "carried his first point—the arsenal—the city and state [might] have been for several days at least under a military despotism." Dorr's plan, according to a report that leaked out from one of his men, was to "take the arsenal and place the 2,000 stands of arms there in the hands of his mob" then "to march up to the College, drive out the students and make them into barracks for his men then to take the armories of the independent and charted companies—disarm the citizens and arm his own men." If Dorr was successful, said Walter Watson, "he would have this day without doubt compelled a loan of $100,000 or more from the banks." Only "God and the strong light arms of her true hearted men has saved our state from this fearful and deplorable state of things."[6]

Many of Rhode Island's Protestant ministers shared Watson's sentiments and used their pulpits to express them. On May 22, Francis Wayland delivered a powerful thanksgiving sermon in the First Baptist Church. Wayland told his flock that they needed to thank the Lord for his "merciful" deliverance. Never in the "whole course of my life have I seen so clearly, as in this instance, the indubitable evidence of Divine interposition," said Wayland. The Protestant minister considered Dorr's efforts to take the arsenal as nothing less than the resurgence of the "horrors of Revolutionary

France." The true principle involved in the contest was not, in Wayland's analysis, suffrage extension in the abstract, but rather the choice of violence to achieve it. Dorr had made force, not law, the preferred method of addressing grievances. "He who undertakes to affect a revolution by force," said Wayland, "puts to the extremist hazard all the present interests of the community, [and] renders it perfectly uncertain in what manner it will ever again be organized."[7] Wayland's Baptist community, along with the Congregationalists and the Dorr family's Episcopal brethren, threw their lot in with the Law and Order Party.[8] Wayland's sermon did little, however, to calm tensions.

William Adams, a prominent abolitionist from the North Providence mill village of Pawtucket, wrote to his sons, who were working in the textile factories in Fall River, Massachusetts. "There is still surmises of war . . . Governor Dorr is a great terror to all the great folks," wrote Adams, referencing the continued fear of the upper echelon of Rhode Island society.[9] The diary of Aurilla Moffitt succinctly captures this ongoing paranoia: "Preparations are being made all about the city for the reception of Dorr and his insurgent followers. I fear that there is not much reason to doubt that he will come. We are in the hands of God."[10] Susan Backus told her cousin in New York that "Gov. Dorr [was] coming back with troops sufficient to . . . kill" those who did not summit to his rule.[11]

Harriet Bailey lamented that "husbands and fathers and brothers" were "compelled" to "spend their evenings in laborious military exercises . . . while we poor helpless women are penned up at home deprived of their society and in constant fear." Harriet was a close friend of Charlotte Goddard, the wife of William Goddard, one of the leading voices of the Law and Order Party through the pages of Henry Bowen Anthony's *Providence Journal*. Harriet told her mother, Jane, that she "felt much alarm," but had decided to put her faith in the Lord to deliver her. Harriet also informed her mother that only Lydia Dorr supported her son. The rest of the Dorr clan had turned against the apostate.[12] Dorr's family were not the only ones to turn against him.

In the chaos that developed after the fiasco at the state arsenal, when most of his drunken followers scrambled for their lives, Dorr somehow made his way to his headquarters. His men later dragged the two cannons from their position near the arsenal and placed them outside the front door of Burrington Anthony's home. Wholesale resignations of officeholders in the People's Government poured into headquarters as night moved towards dawn. Once they became aware that William Blodget, who exhibited no qualms about firing into crowds during the 1831 Providence race riot, was put in charge of the Charter militia, Crawford Allen and his brother Philip, fearing for their nephew's life, assisted him in escaping the city. The Allen brothers went against the wishes of Governor King, who personally went to the Anthony house with the warrant for Dorr's arrest that had been issued a week before by Thomas Burgess, the mayor of Providence.[13]

On May 18, Dorr rode with Crawford Allen to Cumberland, possibly staying with his brother Allen, who assisted in managing a mill there. Zachariah, who was clearly upset that his nephew had tried to blow him up on the morning of May 18, publicly declared that he did not aid his "ambitious and desperate" nephew and was prepared to take up arms against him.[14] Dorr crossed state lines with Crawford Allen and stayed in Bellingham, Massachusetts, for several days. While in Bellingham, Dorr was visited by the New York editor Levi Slamm.[15] Rumors quickly spread that Slamm's fellow labor radicals would soon be traveling to Rhode Island to aid Dorr in another attempt on the arsenal. "Our city is on the look out for the return of Dorr with a band of ruffians . . . God in mercy grant that our apprehensions may be groundless," wrote Moffitt.[16] For the next ten days, patrols of forty or more armed Charter militiamen walked the streets of Providence in anticipation of Dorr's return.[17] Dorr had made it clear, said Samuel Man, that "all the Allens' money" could not "buy him off." Dorr was set to be "Governor of Rhode Island or die in the cause," declared Man.[18]

With help from the abolitionist Aaron White, Jr., Dorr moved from Bellingham to Thompson, Connecticut, before being escorted by Slamm back to New York City on May 24.[19] King had requested Governor Chauncey Cleveland to intercept Dorr, but the Democrat Cleveland refused to comply.[20] In order to elude bounty hunters in New York City looking to collect the $1,000 price tag on his head, Dorr was shuttled from one safe house to another for several weeks by Mike Walsh's men. In one instance, his pursuers got close to their target but were seized by bodyguards. One was captured, roughed up, and released. After that, the Bowery Boys never let the People's Governor out of their sight.[21]

Before he escaped Providence, Dorr left Henry D'Wolf, a resident of nearby Uxbridge, Massachusetts, in charge of his men. The "Commander of the Patriot Forces," as Dorr put it, harassed the Charter militias in Providence for most of the day on May 18 before fleeing the city. Dorr told D'Wolf to "disregard the resignations of timid members of our legislature

and all attempts to deride our friends and to compromise our rights." Dorr
hoped that D'Wolf could lead another attack on the arsenal to secure the
cache of weapons inside. Dorr instructed D'Wolf to collect "provisions and
munitions of war as fast as possible; and make every exertion to obtain the
aid of men, munitions from other states."[22]

At the same time that the issue in Rhode Island was moving from a war of
words to the field of battle, disunionist resolutions were advanced at the annual meeting of the American Anti-Slavery Society by Dorr's old associate
Edmund Quincy.[23] William Lloyd Garrison first demanded disunion in
April, building upon the petition sent by the citizens of Haverhill, Massachusetts, to Congressman John Quincy Adams in early 1842.[24] Instead of
focusing narrowly on slavery, the petition asked Congress to "adopt measures peaceably to dissolve the Union of these states."[25] Soon Garrison was
joined by a vocal abolitionist minority—including Wendell Phillips, Maria
Weston Chapman, Henry Clarke Wright, and Edmund Quincy—who
agreed, as Wright told the *Liberator*, that "we ought to have laid before the
slaveholders, long ago, this alternative. You must abolish slavery, or we shall
dissolve the Union."[26] Beginning in May, the *Liberator*'s masthead called for
"A REPEAL OF THE UNION BETWEEN NORTHERN LIBERTY AND SOUTHERN
SLAVERY." There "was no moral horror, or political treason . . . in advocating
disunion," noted the New York Quaker abolitionist James Gibbons.[27] Despite the Dorrites' disavowal of black suffrage and Dorr's three-year hiatus
from attendance at the annual meeting of the AASS, the extralegal reform
effort in Rhode Island seemed analogous to Garrison's discussion of disunion. The inflamed rhetoric emanating from abolitionist circles, along with
their apparent willingness to disrupt sectional harmony in pursuit of their
cause, was deemed by lovers of liberty on both sides of the Mason-Dixon
line to be treasonous behavior. As historian Daniel Feller has argued, "like
no other cause or crusade, abolitionism threatened white Americans' peace
of mind."[28]

Dorr's attempt at constitutional reform raised issues about race and slavery at a time when the South was feeling increasingly vulnerable to abolitionist attacks upon their peculiar institution. The ideology surrounding
Dorr's attempt at extralegal reform captures not only the continued salience
of revolutionary constitutionalism in the antebellum period, but also the
continued problem of a sizeable dependent population in a republican body

politic as well as the growing antebellum sectional tensions. The *Charleston Mercury* devoted extensive coverage to the arsenal attack.[29] The editors of the *Madisonian*, the organ of the Tyler administration, linked Dorr's "evil purposes" to abolitionism. Dorr's "doctrine" focusing on the sanctity of "numbers" would "at once convert the numberless blacks of the South into voters, who would vote down the southern state governments at their pleasures." Reportedly pulling the strings was Joshua Leavitt, the editor of the *Emancipator and Free American*.[30]

Southerners were convinced of two things in May 1842: that Thomas Dorr was ready to die for his cause, and supposedly aiding him in his efforts were New England abolitionists.[31] In November 1841, the same month that the People's Convention was meeting in Providence, slaves on board the *Creole*, which had left Virginia bound for New Orleans in October, rebelled on board. After taking command of the vessel in a bloody uprising, the slaves sailed for Nassau in the Bahamas, a British port that had outlawed slavery a decade earlier.[32] There they found refuge when British officials refused to extradite them or charge anyone with manslaughter.

The rebellion aboard the *Creole* occurred during a volatile time in Congress. Sectional interests began to overshadow party loyalties, as southerners and northerners tended to vote in regional blocks on issues concerning slavery. Ohio antislavery Congressman Joshua Giddings was censured in March 1842 by the House of Representatives for introducing resolutions relating to natural rights and the action of the slaves on board the *Creole*. Having been censured by the House, Giddings resigned from Congress and went back to Ohio, where he ran for reelection and won by a landside vote.[33] Southern papers would later make the connection between Dorr's ideology and the slave revolt on board the *Creole*. The editors of the *Madisonian* declared that they were "thoroughly convinced that the wire workers who endeavor to get up a violent and bloody scene in RI, are a band of desperate abolitionists." Those who "encouraged the commission of outrage against the existing government" in Rhode Island were said to be "of the same class that instigated the slaves on board the *Creole* to commit murder and mutiny."[34] The report linking Dorr with a revolt on board a slave ship enraged reform supporters in Rhode Island because they had taken steps *not to* enfranchise blacks. "The sagacious *Madisonian* will stick to it that it was an 'Abolition Plot' in Rhode Island to adopt a Constitution which prohibited colored people from voting!" declared the *Providence Express*.[35]

In one of his numerous retirement speeches, the perennial Whig presidential candidate Henry Clay warned that the principles of Dorrism "would overturn all social organization, make Revolution, the extreme and last resort of an oppressed people—the constant occurrence of human life, and the standing order of the day." Clay believed that Rhode Island had "rendered an important service to the cause of order, stability, and free institutions." Echoing fears of the threat that the doctrine of the people's sovereignty posed to southern society, Clay asked how "such a principle would operate in a certain section of this union, with a peculiar population?"[36] In a speech in Richmond, Indiana, Clay took the opportunity to publicly answer an abolitionist petition urging him to free his slaves. Clay had to tread carefully because the petitioners grounded their plea in the ideology of the Declaration of Independence. Interestingly, Clay drew on events in Rhode Island in the spring of that year to finesse the issue. If slaves were suddenly free, Clay warned, they would "insist upon another part of the same Declaration"—the right to alter and amend their form of government, as Dorr "and his deluded [white] democratic followers recently did in Rhode Island; according to which, an undefined majority have at their pleasure, the right to subvert an existing government, and institute a new one in its place, then the whites would be brought in complete subjection to the blacks!"[37] Clay reiterated these thoughts in a major speech in Raleigh, North Carolina, in 1844, during the height of the presidential campaign. "You can readily comprehend and feel what would be the effects and consequences of Dorrism here at the South," proclaimed Clay, "existing governments" would be "overturn[ed]" and the "black" population would run wild.[38]

Dorr's attempted attack on the arsenal on the morning of May 18 surely reminded southerners of Denmark Vesey's abortive attack two decades earlier, when it was said that nearly 9,000 blacks were ready to join Vesey in his attempt to seize the arsenal at Charleston and exterminate the white male population.[39] In August 1831, two years after the black abolitionist David Walker issued his fiery *Appeal to the Colored Citizens of the World*, some of these fears came to fruition when Nat Turner took to the sword and killed over fifty white Virginians. "We are all aghast about the rebellion in Rhode Island," wrote North Carolina Whig Congressman William Graham. "Every mail is looked to for news of bloodshed and outbreak of war." Graham continued: "The pretended governor has organized a government and is guarded constantly. By the last account he has seized several pieces of artillery, and attempted an attack on the arsenal." According to Graham's information, Dorr was a past "president of an abolition society" and was a supporter of "the doctrine" that "a majority, without regard to color or condition," had "at any time a right to overturn the existing government."[40]

Ironically, hours before Dorr's abortive attempt on the arsenal, William Allen, the "Jacobin of the Senate," finally was able to give a speech on the Senate floor after John Calhoun and William Preston gave in on their steadfast opposition to discussing the constitutional crisis in Rhode Island. Calhoun's irritation is even evident in the bland text of the *Congressional Globe*. Allen had managed to trick the president *pro tem* of the Senate into giving him the floor in order to offer new resolutions on the "Rhode Island Question" even though the Senate had voted to lay his resolutions from April 18 dealing with purported interference from the executive branch on the table.[41] Calhoun had clearly had enough. No matter what the cost to his hopes for winning over northern Democrats in 1844, he could stay quiet no longer. It appeared that he might come to blows with northern Democrats.

Allen insisted that there "was no constitutional form of government in Rhode Island" until Dorr's inauguration on May 3. The Ohio Senator attempted to introduce two resolutions. The first focused on the absolute sovereignty of the people; the second prohibited federal interference on the side of the Charter authorities. The resolutions came from the memorial John Brown handed to Levi Woodbury in early April.[42] Unfortunately for Allen, events in Rhode Island played directly into the hands of Calhoun and Preston. Whatever support Dorr had in Congress was gone by the afternoon of May 18. Southern Democrats joined their Whig colleagues in voting down Allen's resolutions, while northern Democrats, most notably Thomas Hart Benton, James Buchanan, and the antislavery Democrat Benjamin Tappan voted in the affirmative. Allen's resolutions were defeated 28 to 18.[43]

Despite the setback in Congress, Levi Slamm's *Democratic Republican New Era* helped to keep Dorr's cause alive. The People's Governor published a letter in Slamm's paper ten days after the abortive attempt on the arsenal explaining what went wrong. Dorr blamed the fiasco on sabotage and attempts by Pearce, Anthony, and Harris to broker a compromise without his authorization.[44] Despite all the ridicule he was receiving, Dorr remained resolute in his conviction that even though the "arsenal was not captured on the 18th of May," the People's Constitution had not "been disposed of by the fate of arms." The document had "the same validity that it ever had." Dorr made it clear that he did not consider himself an "expatriate"; he was still the rightful governor of Rhode Island. The People's Constitution "was now the property of the individual members of the state, until dispensed with by the whole People." Dorr reminded his friends in Rhode Island that they were "successful" in electing representatives under the People's Constitution. Dorr acknowledged the resignation of a number of representatives, but he maintained that the vacancies could easily be filled. As was the case from the very beginning of the reform enterprise, nothing short of the "principles of the American Independence" was at stake.[45] For Levi Slamm and other partisan Democrats, the more immediate issue was the health of the party.

Slamm, still holding out hope for a Calhoun run at the Democratic nomination, tried to assure the South Carolinian statesman that he had nothing to fear from Dorr's newfound bravado.[46] An editorial by Slamm in the *New Era* tried to convince Calhoun that the "Northern Democracy have sense enough to distinguish between Northern freemen, struggling for their political rights, and Southern slaves, between whom and their masters it is our creed not to interfere." Dorr clearly understood, Slamm assured Calhoun, the differences between his cause and the "voting and disenfranchised classes in the South."[47] Nevertheless, Calhoun was prepared to challenge Dorr's ideology in the Senate.[48] The "doctrine that a majority has a right at all times, according to its will and pleasure, to subvert the Government of a State, and to alter or change its constitution without observing the forms prescribed for its amendment, is revolutionary in its character, and inconsistent with all ideas of Constitutional government," argued Calhoun in a draft of a resolution he prepared, but never offered on the Senate floor, because his associates warned him that it would cost him too much support.[49] As Calhoun's most thorough biographer noted, Dorr's doctrine of the people's sovereignty with its emphasis on majority rule represented the essence of "tyranny" of the majority in Calhoun's mind, "destroying all that was unique and valuable in the structure of American government."[50] News of Calhoun's opposition to Dorr was reprinted in numerous northern Democratic newspapers, destroying Calhoun's hopes of a political alliance between southern slaveholders and northern labor.[51]

By the end of May, Henry D'Wolf was drilling men from the northern towns and villages of Woonsocket, Smithfield, Burrillville, and Chepachet. The countryside was now where Dorr was going to find support. His "city friends" were only interested in compromise.[52] Charter supporters believed that Dorr did indeed have "the promise of men, money and things necessary to carry" his government into effect.[53] Edward Carrington, Sr., very much doubted that the Charter forces could sustain themselves against an army of "loco focos" from New York.[54] Rumors about additional forces and weapons coming by train from New York continued throughout May and June.[55]

Samuel Man believed that Dorr was "<u>fully, fully</u> determined" to attack Providence. The "lives and property" of Rhode Island citizens were still very much "in danger."[56] Man was certainly right about Dorr. "Why should any patriot in Rhode Island throw away his arms," wrote Dorr to his close friend Aaron White, Jr.[57] Militiaman William Bailey believed that Dorr would "never abandon his evil purposes so long as the slightest hope remains of his being aided or abetted in his treason." If he "can muster a sufficient number of men and a sum of money enough to keep them together, said Bailey "he will march into this state and we must meet him before he scorches the city and one or the other party will be nearly exterminated." Bailey was happy to see that men of "wealth and worth," including the Allen, Brown, Ives, and Whipple families, were shouldering arms.[58]

Massachusetts governor John Davis and his New York counterpart, William Seward, complied with King's request to assist in capturing Dorr.[59] In late May, King fired off another letter to President Tyler detailing the "bands" of men which were organizing in Massachusetts, Connecticut, and New York. Should these forces combine with loyal Dorrites in Rhode Island, "we have reason to apprehend a civil war of the most destructive and vindictive character," said King.[60] Tyler dismissed King's hysterical fears of a New England Democratic invasion of Rhode Island, but he did order Secretary of War John Spencer to write to the commander at Fort Adams in Newport asking him to employ a spy to look into the possibility that militias from neighboring states might come to Dorr's aid. Tyler also instructed federal officers in Connecticut and Massachusetts to gather information on possible insurgent groups loyal to Dorr.[61] Tyler was clearly monitoring the situation in Rhode Island carefully, quietly augmenting and supplying his available military resources when necessary, but also displaying a great reluctance to use force until absolutely necessary.

Hiding out in New York City, Dorr was seemingly oblivious to the political reality that he had created for his followers in Rhode Island. The heavy hand of the Charter government was beginning to take its toll. On June 2,

Chief Justice Job Durfee delivered a charge on the law of treason to a grand jury and several members of the People's Legislature were subsequently charged with the crime.[62] U.S. Supreme Court Justice Joseph Story delivered a charge to a federal grand jury in which he outlined the law of treason on both the state and national level. Story informed the jury that if an "assembly is arrayed in a military manner" with "the express purpose of overawing or intimidating the public," such action constituted treason against the state.[63] Story argued that a federal physical presence was necessary before treason became national in scope.[64]

Dorr's unwillingness to compromise was clear because the General Assembly was flooded with petitions calling for yet another constitutional convention.[65] Elisha Potter informed Tyler that the "effect of the passage" of the convention bill helped to consolidate the Law and Order faction and "draw off the more reasonable and peace loving portion of Dorr's supporters."[66] Even the conservative John Brown Francis realized that suffrage needed to be extended, or "civil war" would surely arise.[67] The passage of the convention bill on June 23 gave off the "appearance at least of being democratic."[68] Several of Dorr's principal supporters, including William Simons and Walter S. Burges, now believed that "Law and Order justice and political equality" were "no longer enemies to each other." Simons and Burges could not "for a moment countenance the use of force in maintaining the People's Constitution." Who "will fight for any form when the substance can be gained by peace" asked Simons and Burges.[69]

Learning from the defeat of the Landholders' Constitution back in March, conservatives permitted all adult native-born males, regardless of property ownership, to vote for delegates to the convention. However, the apportionment of delegates remained the same as it was for the Landholders' Convention, under-representing the northern industrial regions. According to the memoir of the black shoemaker William J. Brown, Providence's black community agreed to join militia units in exchange for the right to vote for delegates to the approaching constitutional convention.[70]

Dorr was dismayed that Suffrage Association members could be swayed by "the mere call of a convention" that excluded "a large portion of their fellow citizens from the choice of delegates."[71] He hoped that none of his political supporters would "suffer themselves to be deluded by specious pretenses of compromise." From the safety of Levi Slamm's home in New York City, Dorr labeled the sizable number of his followers in Rhode Island who were willing to compromise as "no force men." Instead "of getting on their knees . . . and asking from them some portion of their rights—they ought to unite with those who do not confine themselves to moral persuasion as the only necessary means for sustaining the Constitution." Dorr was certain that if the People's Constitution could be kept alive until the August election for Congress, the delegates would be received and recognized in Washington, D.C. He was clearly willing to attempt another military operation in Rhode Island to make this happen. The problem was that the majority of his followers were scared and directionless. Their leader was nearly two hundred miles away in New York City, while they ran the risk of imprisonment if they tried to support him. Dorr's encouragement to hold fast and think of "better times" fell on deaf ears.[72]

Despite the mollifying effect of the call for a new constitutional convention, tensions in Rhode Island began to escalate by mid-June. Law and Order militias patrolled Providence's cobblestone streets day and night. Even with a $1,000 bounty on Dorr's head, and agreement among the Law and Order coalition that a convention was necessary to mollify the situation, King was still uneasy. He ordered Samuel Ames to remove from the state arsenal all the heavy artillery in order to deter another attack. The weapons were to be hidden throughout the city. King also sent Ames to Boston to procure additional weapons.[73] When he heard that Colonel James Bankhead, a federal commander in Rhode Island, was leaving the state for New York, King boarded a train to Connecticut to track him down and urge him to return to Rhode Island.[74]

The embattled King wrote yet another letter to President Tyler requesting aid and describing how the "civil authority" in the northern regions of the state was "disregarded and paralyzed." In his reply dated June 25, Tyler chastised King for failing to understand that requests for aid must come from the state legislature (because it was in session) and not the executive.[75] Tyler, perhaps correctly believing that the threats King outlined were overblown, was trying to buy time for cooler heads to prevail. Even after receiving King's report that Dorr's men had secured seventy-five muskets from Boston and eighty more from New York City, along with stolen powder kegs, Tyler remained resolute in his conviction not to use force.[76]

On June 25, the Rhode Island General Assembly also arranged for William Gibbs McNeill of New York to serve as the major general of the Charter forces. McNeill, a West Point graduate and a civil engineer in the U.S. Army, was a fixture in Tammany Hall politics in New York City and a close ally of the president.[77] Dorr had met McNeill while hiding out in New

York City in late May and asked him to head his own forces in Rhode Island. Not sharing Dorr's ideology, McNeill promptly declined the offer.[78] The fact that the Charter authorities selected McNeill when there were certainly military commanders in the various militias who could have led the state's troops suggests that either Tyler or Secretary of State Daniel Webster had the ear of members of King's executive council. As his actions would show, McNeill was by nature cautious. He was not out to shed blood. This approach was in line with Tyler's overall strategy—buy time and hope for reconciliation.[79] Perhaps not trusting Tyler, New York Whig governor William Seward sent Thurlow Weed and another administration official to Rhode Island to keep an eye on McNeill.[80]

With Providence thoroughly under the control of the Charter authorities, Dorr joined a small military force assembled in the Glocester village of Chepachet early in the morning of June 25.[81] The small village was also the home of Dorr's lieutenant governor, Amasa Eddy, and Samuel Atwell, both key players in the Suffrage Association activities for the past two years. Aware of the small number of troops assembled, Dorr returned to the state not to fight, but to reconvene the People's Legislature, which had been in adjournment for over a month.[82] The small village was also ideally positioned just five miles from the Connecticut border in case another retreat was in order. Given the resignations from the People's Legislature that had poured in, along with Dutee Pearce's, Burrington Anthony's, and Walter Burges's disavowals of his course of action, Dorr surely made note of every road, path, and trail out of the village.

Ester Smith, a resident of Greenville, just eight miles southeast of Chepachet, wrote to her sister in Massachusetts informing her that "Governor Dorr" was protected by "an armed force with a guard to the entrance and no one can go to, or come from the place without giving an account of himself." Paraphrasing the Gospel of Matthew (10:21), Smith said she was witnessing the "fulfillment of that passage of scripture, where it says, parents shall rise against their children and children against their parents in the last day."[83] Smith's worst fears played out a few days later as 500 armed troops from Providence set up camp near her house as they prepared for an assault on Chepachet.

Upon his arrival in Chepachet, Dorr found that forces loyal to him had fortified a small parcel of land known as Acote's Hill. The fortifications, according to witnesses, consisted of embankments on the south and west sides of the hill about four feet high made of dirt and brush. Even though

Dorr's men had captured several cannons, their camp was far from a military stronghold.[84] Only about 250 men, whom Dorr referred to as the "sons of the soil, the mechanics and workingmen," came to his defense and most of them were unarmed.[85] As novelist James Fenimore Cooper, the author of *The Last of the Mohicans*, wrote at the time, it was "uphill work" for a "popular revolution" to continue once the majority of the citizenry had abandoned the cause.[86] Dorr had been repeatedly told for weeks that he could expect upwards of a thousand supporters. It "seems that Governor Dorr is by no means sustained in what he is doing by the party which elected him," declared William Cullen Bryant's New York *Evening Post.*[87]

It is not clear how much Dorr knew in advance about the gathering of the troops in Providence or of military preparations that had been under way for several days. His trusty military commander, Henry D'Wolf, had abandoned his post in early June, only to return shortly before Dorr's arrival.[88] Dorr did not sanction the seizure of four Charter troops on June 22, which caused a great stir in Providence. Dorr was in nearby Norwich, Connecticut, when the men were taken. The troops were on a reconnaissance mission on the outskirts of Chepachet when Dorr's forces ambushed the patrol and brought the men tied hand and foot in a carriage to Sprague's Tavern in Chepachet, the soon-to-be site of Dorr's headquarters.[89] The men were eventually marched twelve miles northeast to the stronghold of Woonsocket. The younger sister of one of the captured men believed that Dorr's men would kill her brother, but Eliza Peckham's brother Samuel was released several days later unharmed. Eliza's other brother, Edward, who was on duty the night of the arsenal attack, marched to Chepachet a few days later. The sentiments in Providence remained unchanged after Samuel Peckham's release. Worcester resident John Park feared for the life of his daughter Louisa and his grandchildren in Providence. He noted that women and children were fleeing the city and boarding trains northbound to Boston and Worcester.[90] There was still a widespread belief that there would be "bloodshed and revolution."[91]

According to more than one eyewitness, Dorr dispensed with the sword he had displayed in Providence in May and inspected his troops in Chepachet with a brace of pistols at his side. In order to keep the men sober, which was clearly a problem during the attempted attack on the arsenal, Dorr ordered Jedediah Sprague to close the bar in his tavern. Dorr spent most of his time either at the tavern with his officers, including Charles Carter and Henry D'Wolf, or in the camp with his troops. Addressing the troops in the village square, Dorr told them that they had been gathered to prevent interference with the People's legislature. Dorr issued an order "directing the military of the state in favor of the People's Constitution" to make haste to Chepachet to help defend the position.[92] Cheering him on was the fiery labor leader Mike Walsh, who made the journey from New York City with twelve of his Bowery Boys. Dorr was surely dismayed that for all his bombast Walsh had shown up with only a dozen men. However, many living in Providence thought a whole army had made the journey from New York to Rhode Island.

"Nothing but gun powder will have any effect upon these desperate men who are mostly from other states" who live to "rape and plunder," wrote one Providence resident to James Simmons.[93] Henry Bowen Anthony, the acerbic editor of the *Providence Journal*, told Senator Simmons that militia units were "anxious to be led and to settle the question, one way or the other, whether law or violence shall rule."[94] Walter Simmons, who was again drilling with a Providence militia, reported to his father that "everything" looked "warlike" in the city—"our guns are ready for action, baggage magazines are filled with ammunition, and all are ordered to be ready to march at the ringing of the alarm bell."[95]

Wealthy women on the east side of Providence were in absolute hysterics. Providence was in "great commotion—families leaving, merchants sending off goods for fear of conflagration . . . mothers and wives and sisters are left behind in the most trying suspense," wrote Louisa Park Hall. She was afraid for her husband's safety. There were reports of Dorr's men once again gathering on Federal Hill as they had on the night of May 17. "You will receive this on the anniversary of your wedding day," wrote Louisa, "an anniversary ever to be gratefully remembered by your daughter; and I do remember it in the midst of distractions of no ordinary kind." It was now apparent that the conflict was "between those who [had] nothing to lose, and those who are blessed with character and property." She noted that Captain William Brown, a key military commander in Providence, sent his wife to Worcester because he feared the worst. She prayed that Dorr's men could be induced to "surrender" without "firing upon" citizens. She was thankful that she was "spared the misery" of losing her minister husband to a militia company. Louisa told her parents of her hope that Governor King would issue a declaration of martial law to protect citizens.[96] She got her wish the next morning. On June 25, the Rhode Island General Assembly issued a blanket order that placed the entire state under military rule. Ironically, Law and Order officials based their actions on the issuance of martial law in New Orleans in 1815, an act that was ordered by the ideological leader of the Democratic Party, Andrew Jackson.[97]

Stephen Newman, a Connecticut resident who was traveling to New Hampshire during this period, commented on the sense of fear and trepidation he found in many towns, including Coventry and Foster, as he wound his way north through the state on June 26–28. Newman saw troops marshalling in support of the Charter government in one town and in support of the People's Government in the next. "King alcohol," said Newman, stood ready to conquer both sets of troops. Despite high levels of intoxication, Newman recognized that things could still escalate out of control. The "events of the day were well calculated to shake the confidence in the permanence and durability of American institutions—it seemed as if the foundations of well-ordered society were being broken up and anarchy, confusion, and discord were about to rear their triumvirate throne on the ruins of constitutional liberty," wrote Newman in a log of his journey.[98]

By the end of the day on June 26, a force of over 1,000 men had arrived in Providence from Newport, Bristol, Warren, and the southern regions of the state. According to one militiaman from Warwick, many soldiers wanted to see nothing "short of Dorr's liver on the point of a bayonet."[99] In order to cover the cost, the state withdrew money from the school fund that Dorr had helped to set up several years earlier.[100] Small arms and ammunition had been secretly shuttled out of Providence to the northern regions of the state for weeks.[101] The troops were quartered with private families or in recently vacated dormitory rooms at Brown University.[102] On Sunday, armed men paraded in the streets of Providence. The shops and the churches remained closed.[103] City residents feared the worst.

Governor King authorized troops to "destroy in any manner you may think proper all the bridges over the Blackstone river if necessary . . . for the safety of the state."[104] McNeill dispatched a force of more than 500 men to Greenville to serve as an advance guard. Another 350 men, composed largely of troops from Newport and Warren, proceeded to the town of Scituate. During the night, word reached the troops in Greenville that Dorr's men had fled in all directions. The fortifications on Acote's Hill had been largely abandoned.[105] Edward Peckham's unit marched from Greenville to Chepachet in the pouring rain shortly after midnight on June 28. William Rodman, a member of the Providence Marine Corps of Artillery who followed behind Peckham, noted that "while marching from Greenville" toward Dorr's "encampment" we heard at irregular intervals the roar of cannon, which we naturally supposed to be the guns of the enemy . . . but which proved to be the firing of blank cartridges from Dorr's fort for the purpose of intimidating the troops."[106]

In Chepachet, Dutee Pearce informed Dorr that McNeill's forces numbered at least 1,500, giving the New Yorker at least a 3–1 advantage. He told the embattled People's Governor that the call for a convention had all but squashed hope that suffrage supporters would flock to his side. Otis Hawkins, who kept a tavern and toll gate on the Putnam Pike four miles east of Chepachet, later testified that Sullivan Dorr "passed his house towards Chepachet, and when he returned told him he believed the matter was to be settled."[107] Sullivan Dorr likely advised his son to flee the state as fast as possible.

Realizing that his position was hopeless, Dorr drafted a note to Walter Burges notifying him that he was going to order a full evacuation of military personnel in Chepachet. Dorr believed that "a majority of the people who voted for [People's] constitution" were "opposed to its further support by military means. I have directed that the military here assembled be dispersed."[108] After receiving the letter, which was hand-delivered by Amasa Eddy on June 27, Burges brought the letter to McNeill's headquarters. Dorr intended for the letter to be published in order to demonstrate that he was not going to have a repeat of May 18. However, the heavily mobilized Charter government suppressed publication of the letter for twenty-four hours in order to justify a strong show of force at Chepachet.[109] As Governor King's troops were easily routing Dorr's remaining forces, President Tyler ordered Secretary of War Spencer to proceed immediately to Rhode Island. Tyler gave Spencer full authority to procure forces from Connecticut and Massachusetts. But when Spencer arrived in Rhode Island, there was little for him to do.[110]

Before leaving Chepachet, Dorr ordered that all weapons be removed from Acote's Hill. However, in the confusion, several artillery pieces were left and fired off in the night by drunken soldiers and small children.[111] To Edward Peckham and William Rodman, the sounds of cannon fire signaled that a battle might yet occur. When they entered the small village they found only forty or fifty men near Acote's Hill, all of whom fled when they saw the large force approaching. By nine o'clock in the morning on June 28 there were close to 1,000 troops, including a sizable number led by the commander of the Newport Artillery.[112] Many of Dorr's followers lingered and fired off shots at the Charter troops. Peckham reported a bullet narrowly missing him as he moved through the village. John Pitman, Jr., chased Amasa Eddy's son into Sprague Tavern's and demanded his surrender. When the young Eddy refused, Pitman shot him through the key hole. Luckily for Eddy, the bullet missed the major artery and he survived the wound.[113]

As he did the night of the failed attempt on the arsenal, Dorr once again fled the state, leaving his followers to fend for themselves. He left Chepachet with Charles Carter, one of the few men who had stayed with him since the arsenal fiasco, and made his way to nearby Thompson, Connecticut, where he stayed in Vernon Stiles Inn. A correspondent of Mississippi senator Alexander H. Stevens, future vice president of the Confederate States of America, who was traveling in New England during the period, was glad to hear that Dorr, "a poor miserable outlaw" with his "utterly subversive principles" was on the run.[114] Reading the news of the People's Governor's escape, the acerbic New York attorney George Templeton Strong, a close friend of Henry Dorr, remarked, "If I were a Rhode Islander, I'd expatriate myself in disgust; I wouldn't degrade myself by belonging to a state that can't get up better rebellions." After all the "fuss and preparation, hourly bulletins and as much parade and show as there was in Paris when Napoleon was coming back from Elba," said Strong, nothing became of it. But what was to be "expected from such a little state? If it were all to sink in the earth, one would be puzzled to find a hole."[115]

There were no military casualties at Chepachet for the simple reason that only one shot was fired. The only recorded deaths were Robert Gould, who was shot in the face by his deranged brother-in-law over a matter that had nothing to do with the military campaign and an innocent bystander who was killed the next day in Pawtucket. The majority of the prisoners taken into custody between June 28 and 30 were curious onlookers who were simply in the wrong spot at the wrong time. In all, over 225 prisoners were rounded up and marched back to Providence where they were thrown in jail for a number of days until they were questioned in mid-July.[116] Those not released after interrogation were sent to Newport to stand trial for treason against the state. Edward Peckham described the parade of Dorrite prisoners as they entered Providence as the arrival "of the scum of the earth . . . the women trembled with horror, while beholding them, and thought of the fate which would have awaited them, had these devils been the victors."[117]

When the Charter government called out its militia companies to put down the insurrection, Providence's black community was willing to cast their lot with the established government, the same government that had denied them the franchise for the past twenty years. More than 200 black men joined the nearly 3,500 men who comprised militia and volunteer companies.[118] Louisa Park Hall was grateful that "the colored population have shown an excellent spirit . . . and will probably now help us as well as the abolitionists."[119] The latter point was wishful thinking, but the black residents of Providence were willing to help fill the ranks of the militias. Thanks to the skillful negotiations of shoemaker William J. Brown, the call for the selection of delegates to a constitutional convention first announced on June 25 was egalitarian in nature.

A reporter for the Boston newspaper *Emancipator and Free American* noted that blacks in Rhode Island were "placed in the ranks according to their height and I saw no manifestation of disrespect toward either one of them, by any member of the company, but on the contrary all praised and honored them for their noble devotion to the interest of the great cause of regulated civil liberty which they were now called to defend."[120] According to Brown, Dorr supporters argued that "if it were not for the colored people, they would have whipped the Algerines, for their fortifications were so strong that they never could have been taken." Why "then did you surrender your fort," Brown asked. One Dorrite was said to have replied, "Who do you suppose was going to stay there when the Algerines were coming up with four hundred bull niggers?"[121] There were not 400 black troops at Chepachet, but there were a handful of soldiers attached to white units who assisted in rounding up Dorrites.

Regardless of the Charter government's motivation for incorporating black volunteers into its defense, Providence's white community began to take notice. Just one day after King's government deployed its forces to Chepachet, the *Providence Journal* noted approvingly: "THE COLORED POPULATION of our city have come forward in the most honorable manner, and taken upon themselves the charge of the fire engines." The city's male black populace had "pledged themselves to assist in the protection of property from fire and plunder, while the other inhabitants are engaged in the defense of the State."[122] The week following Dorr's defeat at Chepachet, the city's black community was represented in the July 4 parade by its own marching band, complete with musical instruments supplied by the state from items confiscated at Chepachet.

In the days following Dorr's retreat, those unfortunate enough to be arrested, including Dorr's friend Nicholas Powers, were promptly thrown in jail. Hundreds of people were incarcerated in what must have seemed to many a period of fear, intolerance, and oppression. After he was released from prison Powers found that he was "debarred" from most churches in Providence.[123] In July, members of the First Baptist Church charged John Barton, the son of the Revolutionary war hero William Barton, with conduct "dishonorable to the cause of religion, particularly in sustaining the movement of Thomas W. Dorr in his late treasonable designs."[124] Barton refused to back down and was promptly expelled.

Despite the abuse his followers were enduring on a daily basis, Dorr was not yet ready to turn himself into a martyr by rotting in a jail cell. He intended to keep up what his opponents labeled his "gubernatorial charade" as long as possible.[125] In order to do so, Dorr would come to rely on the efforts of a handful of courageous women loyal to the Suffrage Association. Dorr's faithful supporter Catharine Williams journeyed to the nation's capital to meet with President Tyler in order to try to accomplish what Dorr failed to—federal recognition of the People's Government.[126]

In the months to come, suffrage women served as Dorr's only conduit for information from Rhode Island. Williams compared the activities of female Dorrites in smuggling out information to the clandestine operations of the abolitionist "underground railroad."[127] As male Dorrites languished in prison, the torch of political reform was passed to their female counterparts to keep the reform cause alive and to defend Dorr's honor. "Had they taken up the cudgels in 1842, and kept the men at home to do the chores, affairs might have ended differently," Dorr later wrote.[128] During his self-imposed exile, Dorr's "warmest friends" were a cohort of fiery Democratic-leaning females.[129] A "blend of kin and neighborhood affiliation, party loyalty, and rational judgment of current economic and political issues motivated" the Dorrite women.[130]

The sight of women lecturing in public to mixed male-female audiences and taking part in public debate on political questions aroused considerable criticism. The suffrage movement enabled women to carve out a place in the public sphere. They began to deliver popular lectures that offered a scathing condemnation of the Charter government from the perspective of those who had witnessed its machinations firsthand. Like the women who steadfastly came to his aid, Dorr harbored no regrets about his actions. When a political supporter from Cumberland, a Dorrite stronghold, asked if he thought he had gone too far with his actions, Dorr replied: "You err in charging upon the People of this State that they went too far in 1842." Their "fault was in not going far enough, when the demonstration of a purpose to use their strength would have ensured a triumph without bloodshed."[131] For Rhode Island authorities, of course, Dorr had gone far enough. He was indicted by a grand jury assembled in Newport on a charge of treason against the state for "waging war" against the state.[132] By the end of the summer, members of the Rhode Island Suffrage Association apologized for Dorr's resort to arms and assured Providence city officials that the "sober second thought of the people had decided upon a more conciliatory" and "peaceable means" to achieve constitutional reform. Members of the Suffrage Association were willing to compromise, though their exiled leader was not.[133]

Chapter 7

Grist for the Political Mill

The cause in the state of Rhode Island, though cast down, is not destroyed; and I believe that no man worthy of the name, who has been engaged in the suffrage ranks, will abate either heart or hope, or remit his exertions, until the Constitution adopted by the free votes of the great majority of the whole People, shall become in fact, as in right, the paramount law of the state.

Thomas Dorr to New Hampshire Democrats, December 7, 1842

After Dorr disbanded his forces at Chepachet in northern Rhode Island, he hid out in Thompson, Woodstock, and then New Boston, Connecticut, with the abolitionist Aaron White, Jr. He then moved for a time to Guilford, Vermont, before settling in Westmoreland, New Hampshire, on July 8.[1] Political considerations directed where Dorr went. The Whig Party was in firm control of Vermont politics and, as a result, Dorr did not stay long in Guilford for fear of arrest. "Incredible as it may appear . . . but a few months have elapsed, since, almost in our own neighborhood, sons have been armed against fathers, and brothers against brothers, and trains of artillery have been pointed with deadly intent, while accident alone has prevented the lighting of the match which might have deluged our whole country in blood," declared the Whig Charles Paine, who served one term in office as Vermont's chief executive.[2] While many of his Rhode Island followers had gone into hiding for fear of arrest and imprisonment, Dorr found new allies in the Granite State.[3] In New Hampshire, Dorr first stayed at the home of abolitionist Erasmus Buffum in Westmoreland, until December 1842 when he moved to the capital city of Concord.[4]

Dorr's remaining followers in Rhode Island knew he was in good hands with the "liberal men of New Hampshire."[5] To his followers still on the run,

Dorr told the editor of the *Republican Herald* to spread the word that "treason against the charter of Rhode Island is not a crime recognized in the state of New Hampshire, either by the government or the people."[6] The June 1842 New Hampshire Democratic platform not only attacked the Whig economic measures, it also charged President John Tyler with committing a "flagrant act of usurpation" when he lent moral support to the "tyrannical" overthrow of the People's Government.[7] Home to the Jacksonian machine originally built by editor Isaac Hill, the Granite State was the most reliably Democratic northern state. The party's state chairman, Franklin Pierce, a former U.S. senator who had returned home in 1842 to resume his legal practice, was in firm control of the state's political forces.[8]

Recently elected, New Hampshire governor Henry Hubbard welcomed the exile Dorr with open arms and used the powers of his office to protect his fellow Democrat from kidnapping. Hubbard had previously served stints in both the U.S. House of Representatives and the U.S. Senate. Shortly after Dorr arrived in New Hampshire, one conservative newspaper quipped: "Dorr, in his retreat, at Westmoreland, appears to be under the peculiar protection of His Excellency Governor Hubbard!—They are 'birds of a feather,' and no doubt, if worse comes to worse, will hang together to the last."[9] Despite the increase in the bounty on Dorr's head from $1,000 to $5,000, no serious attempt was made to kidnap the People's Governor during his stay in Concord.

In a much-publicized letter, Governor Hubbard refused to honor a requisition order for Dorr sent by Samuel Ward King. Hubbard noted in his August 1842 reply that "the entire theory of our system rests on the principle that all authority is to be rightful and derived from the people." Any "pretended Government in any one State not derived from this source is no government at all," argued Hubbard. He compared Dorrite ideology to "the true American doctrine" upon which rested "the superstructure of popular liberty." To say that the people have a right to alter or abolish their form of government, but not allow them to "exercise that right but at the pleasure of the Government" was, according to Hubbard, a "contradiction in terms."[10]

No male reformer took Dorr up on his offer to travel to New Hampshire. Only female allies, especially Catharine Williams and Ann Parlin, were brave enough to make the trip to New Hampshire to visit with him.[11] As Dorr noted a decade later to Mrs. Ida Russell, a devout supporter, he was appreciative of "the patriotic feelings of so many" of the female sex, "who, though exercising political power only through indirection have never been indifferent to the contest of the people for their just rights."[12] Dorr wrote a similar letter to Almira Howard thanking her for her "valuable services to the democratic cause in 1842 . . . when men were deterred by fear and expediency from openly contending for the principles which they had professed."[13]

Dorr's ideology inspired throngs of females to take an active political role. Six years before the Seneca Falls Convention in western New York, Rhode Island became the site of some of the most intense female political activism in the antebellum period. Though there was no discussion of enfranchising women at the People's Convention, Rhode Island women supported the reform effort at every turn.[14] "I have discovered that the first hailing sign was given by the women of R. Island," wrote Dorr in the summer of 1842. "You have most nobly occupied the sphere which is usually claimed by the other sex, in endeavoring to reanimate this good cause with the breath of life . . . I pray you to persevere in the good work which you have commended as suffrage women," maintained the People's Governor.[15]

While many of Dorr's followers had long lost their nerve to raise the reform torch, Parlin boldly proclaimed to a crowd of male reformers in New York City that she would "pledge" herself to "lead" an "army to death or victory." Parlin maintained that there would be soon "a movement on the part of the women," which would "move the men to action." Parlin assured the crowd that she would *"not be a silent spectator."*[16] In a letter to the editors of the newly reopened *Providence Express*, Parlin declared that she was "firm, come life or death" in terms of advocating for free suffrage and she meant to see the "matter settled."[17] When Dorr's followers were suffering in prison, Williams, Parlin, and Abby Lord attended to their needs, collecting money, food, and clothes for the men, acting as "heroines" of the day in "lady like style." Come "life or death," said Parlin, she would push forward until "victorious."[18] In a letter sent to the editors of the *Providence Express*, Protestant minister William Balch likened the Dorrite ladies to women during the Revolution. You are "engaged in a double cause feeing and clothing the bodies and encouraging the hearts of those who are struggling in the glorious strife of liberty and right."[19] According to the imprisoned Seth Luther, a suffrage lady was a "ministering angel," who attended to the Dorrite prisoners. Never one to pass up a chance to attack the bourgeois, Luther attacked the "Law and Order daughters" who supported the Charter government.[20] Dorr considered all three women to be "active politicians," dedicated to suffrage reform.[21]

As Dorr was on the run and with his followers in hiding, Rhode Island citizens awaited the outcome of yet another constitutional convention—the third in less than a year. Law and Order men, especially U.S. Senator James Simmons and Samuel Man, saw the writing on the wall. Though Dorr had failed to establish the People's Constitution, his actions and the support people gave him demonstrated that if something was not done soon to change the state's governing structure another reformer, perhaps, with more military skills than Dorr, would come to the forefront. The democratic tide could not be pushed back.

Lucinda Wilmarth, the head of the state's antislavery society, implored Abby Kelley to enlist the help once again of Frederick Douglass, who had canvassed the state against the People's Constitution six months before. Wilmarth feared that the delegates to the convention would insert a white-only clause into the constitution. "Every abolitionist I have seen is of the same opinion" in terms of the necessity of having Douglass, "who stole the hearts of the RI people," wrote Wilmarth. There "has never been a better time and so important a time here in an antislavery point of view," declared Wilmarth.[22]

Thomas Stead, a key military official, who was fully aware of black military service at the end of the rebellion, informed James Simmons that a constitution that did not include a provision for black suffrage would be voted down.[23] Brown University President Francis Wayland accurately summed up the desires of black citizens in a letter to Simmons after Dorr's forces were disbanded. Wayland forcibly argued that a white-only provision in any constitution coming out of the upcoming constitutional convention would be grossly inexpedient. "To allow native born colored persons to vote like other citizens," was what the black community wanted, said Wayland. Wayland assured Simmons that he was speaking not as an "abolitionist," but as a "Christian." In "our late troubles," African Americans "proved themselves worthy of the right of suffrage; they were to a man the friends of liberty and law and order," concluded Wayland.[24]

Despite Wayland's pleas, the delegates still went back and forth on whether "Every white male native citizen" should be "Every male native citizen." A September 19 petition from the Providence black community accurately captures the inner workings of the convention: "The undersigned . . . represent that they have noticed with concern and unqualified regret that a disposition seems to have taken place . . . to establish a difference in the suffrage qualification consequent upon color—a distinction not known to the constitution of the United States, nor to many of the free states of this Union."[25] Sentiments oscillated from those expressed by abolitionist Thomas Rowland Hazard, who invoked Rhode Island's notorious participation in the international slave trade in order to justify making recompense in the new constitution, to those who viewed the issue as pure political calculus. The "state of Rhode Island has more to answer for in regards to the slave trade than any other state in the Union," said Hazard. "What our citizens have been guilty of in regards to the poor Africans is enough of itself to call down retribution." Hazard maintained that the Law and Order Party was now presented with an opportunity to make amends for sins of the past.[26]

On the other side of the spectrum were men like Elisha R. Potter, Jr., who cared little about the state's notorious connection to slavery and the slave trade. Political calculus was all that drove Potter. The South Kingstown Democrat, who also served as delegate to the convention, offered a succinct political view of the question: "There is not so much scolding about letting the blacks vote as was expected . . . they would rather have the Negroes vote than the [damn] Irish."[27] A revealing letter Potter wrote to former governor John Brown Francis on November 14, a week before voting was to take place, shows the level of unease among key Law and Order officials about granting blacks the right to vote. "If the constitution should be adopted and the word white not be inserted, it would be the greatest misfortune that could befall us," said Potter. "I have no prejudices against the Negro myself but other people have." If the word "white" was not included, according to Potter, the "Dorrites would then give" the Law and Order constitution "the nickname of the negro constitution, which of itself would make it completely odious in the South." Potter informed Francis that "some of our side very foolishly argue in favor of the Negroes because they are conservative and go with the wealthy part of the community . . . no argument could be more unpopular with the middling and poorer classes of the white people" that they hoped to win over.[28] The Charter authorities rewarded blacks for their service as firemen and prison guards in June 1842 by allowing them to vote for delegates, but the constitution that eventually emerged out of the convention mandated a special referendum to be held with the vote on ratification.

In line with the Landholders' Constitution of February 1842, there was no reference to the sovereignty of the people. According to U.S. Senator James Simmons, to include reference to the supremacy of the people to alter their form of government would be akin to placing a powder "magazine beneath the fabric of civil society." It "left any portion of the people free to commence a revolution whenever they conceive themselves aggravated."[29] The new constitution also made no provisions for future constitutional conventions or provisions for the secret ballot—two key components contained in the People's Constitution. The constitution created a rotten-borough senate that completely disregarded population as the basis for its composition. Every town, regardless of size, was given an equal vote. In Dorr's analysis, the constitution retained "most of the unjust and odious characteristics of the old charter government" including "a landed qualification for voting."[30]

The document established three classes of voters: absolute, those who were native-born with a year's residency and owned real estate valued at $134, or had two years' residency and paid taxes on real or personal property valued at $134 or more; registry, those who had lived in the state for two years and paid a $1 registry tax; and finally, foreign-born naturalized citizens who qualified to vote or hold office only by owning $134 worth of real estate.[31] The "clear intent" of the real estate qualification was to disenfranchise Irish Catholic immigrants who were entering the state in "ever-increasing numbers."[32] Potter informed Martin Van Buren that the restrictions on the foreign-born were necessary because the state was "so small and extensively engaged in manufactures."[33]

As Rhode Island citizens prepared yet again to vote on a new frame of government, Dorr's supporters wrote to him looking for a sense of direction. Should they boycott the referendum or organize to vote down the document? If we remain in a "state of inaction, which we have ever since the 27th of June," said Charles Newell, "then will the Algerines walk proudly and triumphantly over the cause and after having adopted their Bastard Constitution it will become the bona fide law for the state."[34] Catharine Williams told Dorr that the notion of capitulating to the Charter authorities was "downright suicide."[35] Abby Lord labeled any suffrage man who considered voting for a constitution produced by the Law and Order Party a "bastard" and a "traitor."[36] Bolstered by the bravado demonstrated by women loyal to his cause, Dorr urged his flock to vote down the constitution, a document he equated with "casting a bone to a dog" in order "to perpetuate under another name the abuses and fraud of the old rotten borough system which has so long cursed the state."[37] However, most of Dorr's supporters, perhaps still fearing arrest, abstained from voting, making the ratification of the Law and Order constitution a foregone conclusion. The final tally was 7,024 to 51, with the separate referendum on black suffrage passing 3,157 to 1,004.[38]

The fact that blacks were allowed to vote on the referendum and that

the black male population of voting age numbered over 650 contributed significantly to the success of the measure. This was the only instance in antebellum history where blacks regained the franchise after having it removed
by statute. In his vast correspondence and numerous scrapbooks and note-
books, Dorr failed to acknowledge this triumph. With the adoption of the
new constitution, Dorr's hope of seeing the People's Constitution imple-
mented began to dwindle. However, the gubernatorial election in neighboring Massachusetts served to rekindle the spirits of his followers and proved
that the politics surrounding the adoption of the People's Constitution remained as potent as ever.

In his reminisces on his long career in public life, George Boutwell, former
Massachusetts governor and U.S. senator, made the connection between the
success of the Massachusetts Democracy at the polls in 1842 and the politics
surrounding the "Rhode Island Question."[39] Dorr's views on the people's
sovereignty and his aborted attempt at suffrage reform became a rallying
cry for Bay State Democrats. At the Massachusetts Democratic Convention
in September 1842, the ranks of the Democracy rallied behind Marcus Morton's candidacy for governor. Each year between 1828 and 1843, Morton
"moonlighted as the Jacksonian candidate for governor," seldom winning,
but always putting up a good fight.[40] In early November, Judge John Pitman
wrote to Joseph Story to express his fear that if Morton beat the Whig John
Davis, Dorr would be "encouraged" to raise his "flag once more on the bor-
ders" of Rhode Island. It would be a "gloomy day for Rhode Island," said
Pitman, if Morton was elected.[41]

Many prominent Massachusetts Democrats supported and took part in
the suffrage reform effort in Rhode Island from the beginning. These included Benjamin F. Hallett, a Providence newspaper editor in the 1820s,
who merged his radical *Boston Advocate* with the *Boston Post* in 1838 to create
a powerful organ for the Massachusetts Democracy; Lewis Josselyn, the editor of the *Bay State Democrat*; and Robert Rantoul, the famous author, orator, and lawyer. When Dorr went into exile in New Hampshire after his
defeat at Chepachet in June 1842, it was Josselyn's *Bay State Democrat* that
became Dorr's primary conduit for news from Rhode Island. In August,
Josselyn made a much-publicized journey to Keene, New Hampshire, to
visit with "Governor Dorr," while Rantoul lent his considerable legal talents
to incarcerated Dorrites.[42]

Dorr's attempt at reform in Rhode Island was not only a matter of personal involvement in Massachusetts, but of regular front page news in the *Boston Post* and the *Bay State Democrat* from May 1842 through January 1843. Almost daily through the summer and fall, Josselyn ran a column designed to remind readers of the "outrages" in Rhode Island and never failed to draw a direct line to associate Massachusetts Whigs with the Rhode Island Charter authorities. Headlines declared "Keep It before the People!" and "Let the People Remember." According to Josselyn, the Bay State Whigs demonstrated their "contempt of the true principles of American democracy, and the faithlessness and hypocrisy of all its late professions of friendship for the mechanics and laborers of the country."[43]

The illegal seizure of Dorrites in the Massachusetts town of Bellingham in late June 1842, the accidental shooting death of Alexander Kelby in the village of Pawtucket (the eastern half of which was then part of Massachusetts) by a member of a Rhode Island militia unit, and the investigation into the loaning of arms to Samuel Ward King constituted the political charges that Massachusetts Democrats used against their Whig opponents. The *Norfolk Democrat*, following the lead of the Boston Jacksonian press, insinuated that it was likely that the bullet that killed Kelby came from one of the arms authorized for loan by Henry Dearborn, the state's adjutant general.[44]

The main instrument of Democratic political agitation was through the use of an old Native American custom—the Rhode Island clambake. As the *Bay State Democrat* noted, "this peculiar Rhode Island festival has of late attracted much of public attention, from the fact that the suffrage party in that state have adopted it as an appropriate occasion for the meeting together and interchange of sentiments and views."[45] The Providence *Morning Courier* reminded its readers that the "true object of these clambakes was not really to help Dorr, but to help Marcus Morton."[46]

Leading many of these efforts were Rhode Island females loyal to the white male suffrage cause. While the Suffrage Association never explicitly argued for political rights, disclaiming "any right to seats in the halls of legislatures or privileges at the ballot box," women were connected with the cause from the outset.[47] Many middle-class women rationally pondered the same issues as their male counterparts and maintained a steadfast loyalty to the northern Democracy. "A Daughter of Rhode Island" urged Dorrite men to address the world and "tell them the heroes of '76 have been abused, their sufferings mocked, and the American flag dishonored while waving over the land of despotism, in this degraded State!"[48] Dorr correctly observed that the "women of the more wealthy and fashionable circles . . . coincided with their relations in denouncing the movement in RI; while it was cheered with hearty sympathies of the women of the Democratic Party."[49]

In the summer and fall of 1842, with the political vacuum created by the punitive measures enacted by the Charter authorities against those in favor of the People's Constitution, female reformers walked into the spotlight and took on roles outside of traditional gendered norms. Writing in the pages of the *Providence Express* under the pseudonym "A True Dorrite," Ann Parlin proclaimed that any woman "who thinks she has not right to speak against a government; or that man who says she has no right," was a "fool."[50] The firebrand Parlin was so dedicated to Dorr that she ruined her marriage in order to help keep the cause alive.[51] Abby Lord and Catharine Williams took it upon themselves to march right up to the executive mansion to demand the return of Dorr's personal papers from the new Rhode Island governor, conservative Democrat James Fenner. In the spring of 1842, Fenner served on King's executive council.[52] Law and Order officials had made good use of Dorr's papers, quoting letters out of context in order to concoct a story of fraud and malfeasance in the voting for the People's Constitution.

Using labels such as Ladies' Free Suffrage Association, Benevolent Association of Suffrage Ladies, Providence Ladies Dorric Circle, and the Young Women's Free Suffrage Association, women began raising money for the legal fees incurred by male Dorrites housed in Providence, Newport, and Bristol jails. On October 8, the *Providence Express* published a "Constitution of the Female Benevolent Suffrage Association." The thirteen-article document outlined the structure and mission of the group, which was to work toward universal white-male suffrage. The members used pro-Dorr newspapers to call for similar societies to constitute themselves across the state. The Suffrage women frequently sent Dorr money that they raised, medicine for his rheumatism, and news about the status of the prisoners.[53] The "good sisters," as Catharine Williams described the female Dorrites, were "as much engaged as ever, and have [worked] much toward alleviating the distress of the prisoners and the Suffrage poor."[54] Williams also updated Lydia Dorr on her son's condition and whereabouts. Concerned for Dorr's spiritual well-being, the Young Ladies Suffrage Association of Providence sent the exiled governor a pocket Bible.[55]

On August 18, 1842, over 1,000 supporters braved a torrential downpour to attend a clambake organized by Dorrite women in Somerset, Massachusetts, just a few miles from the Rhode Island border.[56] The inclement weather was not enough to drive attendees away before they could hear the keynote address. A correspondent of the *Republican Herald* noted that the rain "sharpened the appetite" rather "than dampened the spirits."[57] The stormy weather forced the organizers eventually to move the crowd to a nearby meeting house in order that Marcus Morton could address his supporters. Dwelling at length on the "tragic" demise of the People's Government, Morton proclaimed that if it were not for the interference of John Tyler and Massachusetts Governor John Davis, Dorr would have succeeded.

Morton skillfully rode the Dorr Rebellion to victory over John Davis in January 1843 after a long and protracted battle that was eventually settled by the state legislature.[58] Immediately, Morton and the Democrats in the Massachusetts Senate went after the man who had loaned arms to the Rhode Island Charter authorities. Democratic senators sent a request to Morton on January 24, 1843, to look into whether the arms loaned to Rhode Island were ever returned. In the spring of 1842, Henry Alexander Scammell Dearborn, the Massachusetts adjutant general and the son of the famous War of 1812 general, had authorized the loan of muskets and swords. In Dearborn's view, the legislature had no right to recommend his removal unless he was formally charged with a crime and court martial proceedings were initiated. At no point did he express regret for his actions in the spring of 1842. In a thirty-five-page written statement to a special House committee formed to review his conduct, Dearborn, who was also a lawyer, made clear once again his sentiments in regard to Dorr's attempt at extralegal reform. He argued that the move by the Democrats to attack his character and question his loyalty constituted a witch-hunt. It was "unprecedented in the annals of legislation and of the civil, military, and naval tribunals of justice in every civilized nation," proclaimed Dearborn.[59]

In the end, Dearborn's defense of his actions had little effect on the committee, whose report began with a stern rebuke of his conduct.[60] While the language in the report was, on the whole, guarded in its support, its sympathy for Dorr was more than apparent. The Charter government was referred to as a government by "force," while the People's Government was formed "by virtue of a constitution adopted by the people."[61] On March 3, the House recommended that Morton remove Dearborn. The Senate concurred on March 4, and Morton signed the order on March 6, 1843. While the Democrats were enjoying success in Massachusetts with their skillful use of the issues involved in the "Rhode Island Question," the same could not be said for Rhode Island Democrats.

Senator James Simmons and his conservative ally from Cumberland, Samuel Man, were able to organize the Law and Order Party into a "Rhode Island" ticket that drew from the "business interest" in the state.[62] The use of the "Rhode Island" nomenclature was instructive because it was an attempt to paint the opposition—a conglomerate of Suffrage Party members and Equal Rights Democrats—as traitors. The always colorful Elisha Potter, Jr., told his close friend John Brown Francis that the Whig-dominated "Rhode Island" ticket was headed by a group of "jackasses" in Providence that wanted to destroy the "country" Democracy, along with the Equal Rights faction.[63] A March 1843 public letter signed by the state's leading manufacturers aimed not only to win over the support of the manufacturing classes, but also the native born among the laboring class that had previously supported the Suffrage Party. The manufacturers' letter maintained that the "political strifes" of 1842 "operated to the serious injury of that large and valuable class of our fellow-citizens, who not only live, but who may hope to thrive, by the exercises of their labor and their valuable skill." The signers argued that "business will be slow to regain its customary channels . . . that skill and labor will not reap their just rewards . . . till quiet shall be restored to the state."[64] Henry Bowen Anthony's pro–Law and Order *Providence Journal* viewed the election in apocalyptic terms reminiscent of the height of rebellion. If the Democrats emerged victorious, "property would melt away in taxes" and "valuable rights would be at the mercy of demagoguism" declared the acerbic editor.[65]

The 1843 election in Rhode Island was rife with corruption. Law and Order officials used intimidation and blackmail to increase their numbers and decrease the Democratic vote count. Similar to the spring of 1842, employers threatened their workers with retaliation and landlords their tenants, if they did not vote as they were told. With the absence of a secret ballot, factory employees, of course, were told that their job would be in jeopardy if they voted Democratic. The $1 poll tax disenfranchised many poor native-born citizens, and the freehold qualification for the naturalized citizens, both provisions in the Law and Order Constitution adopted in late 1842, severely limited the Democratic voting block.[66]

The Democratic nominee was Thomas Carpenter, a leading Providence attorney who had been the party's unsuccessful candidate for governor in 1840 and 1842. Carpenter was also one of the nine lawyers who wrote the key statement of Dorrite ideology in the spring of 1842. Former Dorrites were in firm control of the Rhode Island Democracy in 1843. Conservative

Democrats such as John Brown Francis, William Sprague, and Elisha Potter, Jr., had been shut out of the convention that nominated Carpenter. All three reluctantly threw their lot in with the Law and Order faction, which was dominated by the Whigs.[67]

Dorr advised his followers to come out in full force in the election. Remarkably, Dorr was able to travel to Providence in late March. He gave a public address, after spending the night at Burrington Anthony's house and then left Providence, traveling over state lines to Pawtucket, Massachusetts.[68] However, Dorr had given his opponents a political gift with his appearance. The Law and Order press skillfully portrayed his visit as a Napoleonic return that would end in bloodshed. Law and Order fear mongering worked brilliantly because their candidate, James Fenner, defeated Carpenter by a vote of 8,990 to 7,427.[69] John Pitman labeled Fenner's victory the "finishing blow" to the Dorrites.[70]

Despondent over the news of the election and suffering from a myriad of health issues, Dorr spent his time in the summer of 1843 penning his famous "Address to the People of Rhode Island," the fullest statement of his constitutional theories. In the thirty-page address, Dorr covered the entire history of suffrage extension in Rhode Island and, of course, his own failed attempt to implement the People's Constitution.[71] At the end of the address, Dorr made it clear that his intention was to finally return to Rhode Island. Dorr had made up his mind to stand trial for treason before the same judges who had previously given their opinion against the validity of his course of action and the principles he advocated.[72]

On October 31, 1843, Dorr appeared in Providence, registered at the City Hotel, and went out to dinner. He was stopped by the police shortly thereafter at the home of William Simons, the editor of the *Republican Herald*. Dorr was kept in the Providence city jail until February 1844 when he was transported to Newport for trial. The decision to air out his theories in a court of law represented a stark turnaround for Dorr. In October 1842, Dorr informed Walter Simons that he believed the "Supreme Court of the U.S." was not "the arbiter of popular rights and sovereignty." Dorr said that he was "unwilling to submit the 'Rhode Island Question' to that tribunal, even if our opponents were willing to make up a case for that purpose." Dorr closed his letter to Simons with this admonishment: "God forbid that any Democrat should be ready to concede to any Court in this country the final decision of the question, whether the people have a right to change their form of government or not."[73]

In another letter a few weeks later, Dorr responded to a movement to bring a case before the nation's highest court. Dorr argued that he did not "see how the question of the right of the People to make a Constitution, without leave from their government, can be brought before the Supreme Court of the United States." When the Suffrage Party "allege" that the Charter government was "not republican," the U.S. Supreme Court, according to Dorr, would "reply that it is so in form and that they cannot look further than this into its alleged defects" because it constituted a political and not a legal question.[74] Ironically, this is precisely what Chief Justice Roger Taney ruled in the case of *Martin Luther v. Luther Borden* (1849). However, by 1843, Dorr had come to several important realizations.

The first was the potency of the "Rhode Island Question" in terms of political capital, something Dorr witnessed firsthand during his time in New Hampshire, and, especially, in Massachusetts, where the issues involved in the Dorr Rebellion led directly to the removal of a long-standing Whig politician. In Rhode Island, the Dorrites had lost the 1843 elections, but they had managed to take control of the Democratic Party, exiling hard-line conservatives. Moreover, Dorr's time in New Hampshire led to a friendship with Congressman Edmund Burke, who by late 1843 was putting together a strategy to bring the "Rhode Island Question" to the floor of Congress. By surrendering himself to Rhode Island authorities and turning himself into a political martyr, Dorr hoped to create another avenue for keeping the "Rhode Island Question" alive by rallying Democrats throughout the country. There is no doubt that Dorr undoubtedly went back on his ardent belief that the people's sovereignty was not a judicial question. What drove Dorr's thought process in late 1843 was political calculus. Dorr hoped that his treason trial, along with Burke's efforts in Congress, would prove to be grist for the political mill to be used by Democrats against their Whig opponents. There were numerous Democrats, however, who questioned whether or not Dorr's case would even go to trial.

The prominent New York Democrat Silas Wright, Jr., doubted that Rhode Island officials would dare try Dorr for what in his view amounted to a political offense. "I cannot suppose they will be mad enough to risk a conviction from a packed jury and prejudiced Court, for I shall look upon such a result as much more fatal to them than to you, even if your life should be taken," wrote Wright, who had recently captured the governorship of

New York. Wright concluded that treason was an exclusively national crime since the federal Constitution limited Congressional power in the entire area of treason therefore states could not possibly have the freedom to define and punish the king of crimes.[75] Aaron White, Jr., warned Dorr of the possibility that Law and Order officials might not even arrest him. White asked, "how will you escape the consequences both moral and political that the most dreaded enemy, for whose head about a year since was worth $5,000, is now allowed to walk at large in the streets un-molested—an object unworthy of apprehension." White continued, "You may do as you think best and undoubtedly you will but if I were in your place unless I was perfectly sure of being in the dungeon of the RI state prison within twenty-four hours after openly returning to Providence, I would go to Botany Bay before I would enter RI openly."[76] Many Rhode Island conservatives were embarrassed when the treason trial of the prominent suffrage reformer Franklin Cooley ended in a hung jury in December 1842. Cooley was defended by the famed Massachusetts attorney Robert Rantoul.[77] Law and Order men likely feared the prospect of Dorr winning at trial.

Others were afraid of the political fall out if Dorr *was* convicted. "If you send Mr. Dorr to the state prison like a common felon, it will only create sympathy without and within the state—the result of which I will not answer for," wrote a correspondent of the vehement anti-Dorrite Robert Hale Ives. With "one class of our citizens, Mr. Dorr is considered the advocate of the rights of the people and is suffering in their cause—such is their belief and they will act accordingly—let us disarm them if we can by patience and forbearance and whip them if they give us any more trouble."[78] Dorr was obviously banking on the fact that at least a few diehard conservatives would want to see him thrown in prison for his actions in 1842. In addition to managing his own defense during the treason trial, Dorr also helped to orchestrate a move to bring the "Rhode Island Question" before the U.S. Congress.

Ten days before Dorr was transferred from Providence to Newport for trial, Edmund Burke presented a petition from the Democratic members of the Rhode Island General Assembly. Burke informed Dorr that he was determined "to give to the country the full history of the Suffrage movement and to put in my report the true doctrines of Democracy upon the great question involved."[79] What Burke really meant was that he was preparing to write a Democratic manifesto to be used against the Whig Party in 1844. "By opposing the Suffrage movement" in Rhode Island, Henry Clay and the Whigs "have made the sovereignty of the People and the Right of Suffrage issues in the present contest," declared Burke.[80] One Democratic Congressman saw the issue as embodying nothing less than the essence of the Declaration of Independence.[81] Dorr acknowledged that "nothing" would do Martin Van Buren, "the favorite for the party nomination at this point, more good or the democracy more good than the full, faithful, earnest discussion of the whole matter in Congress." If the Whigs "sustain the Algerines, they ally themselves at once with the Tories of the Revolution, and they recommend Clay to the People as an enemy of popular sovereignty and free suffrage," declared Dorr.[82]

The resolutions Burke presented were actually ghost-written by Dorr, who challenged the right of Rhode Island Congressmen Henry Cranston and Elisha Potter, Jr., to their current seats in Congress, called for a full investigation of John Tyler's conduct in 1842, and asked Congress to utilize the Guarantee Clause to reinstate the People's Constitution.[83] The radical rhetoric of the memorial set off a contentious debate on the floor of the House of Representatives. Burke managed to get the memorial referred to a five-man committee composed of Democrats who were "not induced with any of the South Carolina heresies in relation to the sovereignty of the people." According to Burke, the southern Democracy "do not hold so absolutely to the doctrine of popular sovereignty as we do in the North."[84]

To Maryland Whig Congressman Jacob Causin, the rhetoric of the Rhode Island memorial, if assented to by the House, would only "excite the people to scenes of domestic violence."[85] Indiana Whig Caleb Blood Smith, who later served in Abraham Lincoln's administration, agreed. According to Smith if the "principles of Dorr and his infatuated followers" were deemed "correct," the "ligaments which bind us together become as feeble as ropes of sand. Every State in the Union may be divided into hundreds of independent governments."[86] Dorr's philosophy was a recipe, according to Smith, for a war between the races, especially in the states where the "colored population outnumber the whites." If by the "law of nature and the law of God, the people of one portion of the country can overturn their government, and adopt a new one, where did the gentleman [Burke] find the authority to exclude from political rights the negroes of South Carolina and Virginia?" The proslavery Smith continued: "If the Dorrites are correct in their opinions . . . [then] the government of Georgia, South Carolina, and every other slave state in this Union, is liable at any moment to be subverted whenever a majority of the people of such state, including blacks, may will its overthrow." Ignoring the history of the People's Constitution, Smith painted a picture of the horrors of "nigger" voting for his colleagues in the House. Using the opportunity to take a political swipe at the presumptive Democratic nominee Martin Van Buren, Smith absurdly linked the People's Constitution with the 1820 New York Constitution. The constitution, which Van Buren supported, allowed blacks to vote if they owned $250 of real property. However, in actuality the New York convention's actions on black voting showed that the majority of the delegates and, by extension, the majority of the state's voters, were supporters of white democracy.[87]

A few days after Burke presented the memorial, Dorr sent him a lengthy letter that detailed the history of the People's Constitution. Dorr went to great lengths to ensure that Burke knew it was designed for the "Saxon race" only. Dorr reminded Burke that the "slave was not actually a man"; he could not "partake of the sovereign power." According to Dorr, "constitutions, suffrage, bills of rights, representation, and all kindred matters" are "unmeaning sounds" to the slave. Dorr forcibly argued that the "doctrine of popular sovereignty," as it was utilized in 1842, did not in any way, shape, or form provide a recipe for a "slave insurrection." Dorr concluded with the prayerful hope that "the great doctrines of popular sovereignty and equal rights will be safe in the hearts of our democratic brotherhood and better defended by their right arms then they have been in R. Island." Dorr instructed Burke to inform the committee that he never once expressed the view "that the southern slaves" were a "part of the sovereign power in the states to which they belong." A slave was "a man in right, but not in fact," said Dorr. A slave "knows nothing of the attributes and actions of the sovereign power."[88]

The memorial was debated at length in the House of Representatives as Dorr sat in the Newport jail awaiting trial.[89] In a close vote held on March 21, 1844, Burke won a motion that empowered his committee to send for persons and papers. Benjamin Hallett collected depositions for Burke on the Rhode Island border in Pawtucket, Massachusetts, not far from where Alexander Kelby was shot.[90] Neither the Rhode Island legislature nor the executive branch cooperated with the investigation. Dorr was kept aware of the proceedings by Providence attorney Walter Burges.[91] John Quincy Adams put forth the motion calling for President Tyler to turn over "all orders and instruction to any officer of the army, any orders from the War Department reports . . . and all other correspondence of the government of the United States relating to the subject."[92] The antislavery Adams had begun to refer to Tyler in his diary as the "slave-monger," and while he disagreed with Dorr's constitutional views, he hated slavery even more.[93] Tyler complied with the request in early April. In a letter to the House of Representatives, the president denied that he had used the powers of his office to affect the outcome of the constitutional crisis in Rhode Island.[94]

The continued controversy over the "all absorbing Texas Question" eventually drew attention away from the Rhode Island memorial. According to Aaron White, the "Rhode Island Question" was merely "a puddle" in the "storm" over Texas.[95] Since the summer of 1842, President Tyler had been engaged in secret diplomacy with the Lone Star Republic to craft a treaty of annexation. Tyler put his faith in his new secretary of state, Abel P. Uphsur, a Virginia states' rights advocate, to get the job done. When Upshur died from wounds suffered from an exploding cannon onboard the *USS Princeton* in 1844, the task fell to his mentor John C. Calhoun, who saw Texas "primarily as a way of protecting (and extending) southern slavery in the face of the abolitionist onslaught" that had been waged against it for years. Calhoun "clearly, deliberately, and optimistically fanned the flames of sectional tensions."[96] Negotiators signed a treaty of annexation incorporating Texas as a territory of the United States in early April. The antislavery Democrat Benjamin Tappan's decision to hand over the treaty files to the northern press set off a firestorm of protests. Shortly afterward, on May 18, Calhoun wrote a lengthy letter to the British minister Richard Pakenham in which he accused the British of secretly trying to abolish slavery in Texas. Calhoun's rabid proslavery views were on full display as he defended slavery as a positive good and announced that the United States was annexing the vast territory in order to prevent British interference. The administration's position was now clear: annexation equaled the protection of slavery.[97]

Once the document was made public, any Democrat expecting southern support would have to give a resounding yea for annexation; if not, he was doomed. The treaty floundered in Senate when several northern Democrats voted against it. However, the Texas question sank the New Yorker Van Buren's chances of regaining the nomination at the Democratic convention in Baltimore. The former president and founder of the Democratic Party was deemed too soft on the issue, and party delegates turned to the dark horse and pro-annexationist James K. Polk of Tennessee to lead the fight against the Whig Henry Clay.[98] The Baltimore convention did not consider Dorr's resolutions on popular sovereignty, although it did adopt a resolution supporting the annexation of Texas.[99] Polk was able to secure the nomination in 1844 because he combined orthodox Democratic views on traditional party issues with a willingness to endorse the annexation of Texas and the "reoccupation" of much of the Oregon Territory. In Polk's political calculus, Texas and Oregon must join the Union, because it was America's "Manifest Destiny" to spread across the continent.[100]

Though the controversy over Texas drew attention away from the Rhode Island memorial, Edmund Burke managed to put together a 1,000-page report that promoted the people's sovereignty and attacked the Whig belief in the sanctity of law and order. Burke did not request that the House apply the federal guarantee of a republican form of government retroactively in favor of the People's Constitution so as to throw out the new state constitution as Dorr had wished.[101] Burke argued that the steps Dorr took in 1841–1842 constituted a constitutional attempt to ensure a republican form of government for Rhode Island and that the People's Constitution and the government that was organized under it in May 1842 was legitimate. However, the ratification of a new constitution in the fall of 1842 had nullified the People's Constitution. The final resolve attacked President John Tyler and his "unauthorized" attempt to interfere on the side of the "charter government."[102]

Burke's Report, as the lengthy brief quickly became known, was far from neutral. Its first printed page contained a daguerreotype of Dorr taken on May 3, 1842—the date of his inauguration. The first 90 pages are a recapitulation of Dorrite philosophy; the next 900 pages contained documents, depositions, court records, and voting lists for the People's Constitution.[103] Even though the vote on the resolutions in the report did not occur until January 1845, Burke managed to get 5,000 copies printed in June 1844.[104] The split between northern and southern Democrats on the constitutional saliency of the people's sovereignty prevented a vote on the resolutions before the approaching presidential election.

Maryland Congressmen Jacob Preston and John Causin compiled a minority report that sought to vindicate Tyler's conduct. For Causin, the "Rhode Island Question" was "one of the most important questions that could be brought before Congress—neither more nor less than a question of war or peace; and if war should result, the whole Union would be convulsed to the center."[105] The minority report maintained that after a government has been formed "the majority have no right to change or alter it, as an exercise of peaceful authority, without common consent, and that consent can only be given through" the legislature, which is "instituted by all, directs and acts for all."[106] The *Causin Report* clearly reflected southern sensitivity to the possibility of a northern majority using federal power to challenge their peculiar institution. In 1844 and 1845, abolitionists William Goodell and Lysander Spooner both promoted the Guarantee Clause as an antislavery weapon in widely read pamphlets.[107] Spooner noted that under any logical definition, "It is impossible . . . that a government, under which any considerable number of people . . . are disenfranchised and enslaved, can be a republic. A slave government is an oligarchy; and one too of the most arbitrary and criminal character." He concluded that the Guarantee Clause "is not idle verbiage. It is full of meaning. And that meaning is . . . fatal to slavery itself."[108] This view was completely unacceptable to those looking to protect and promote slavery.

Despite his best efforts, Burke was never able to get a formal vote on his massive report. A vote was taken in early January 1845 to approve an additional run of 5,000 copies of his report, but the conservative Democrat Lucius Elmer (NJ) was able to derail the vote on the more important resolutions, which Elmer deemed to be "dangerous tendency" and "principles of anarchy," with his lengthy speech in favor of the principles of law and order on January 6, 1845.[109] Despite the difficulties in Congress in getting a fair hearing on the resolutions in his massive report, Burke did manage to get resolves from the Democratic-controlled New Hampshire legislature relating to Dorr's imprisonment to the floor of the House. The fourth of five resolves proclaimed that "the doctrine of the sovereignty of the people" was of "vital importance to the stability and permanency of [the] republic." The members of the New Hampshire legislature believed that Thomas Wilson Dorr was the "chief magistrate" of Rhode Island and that he "should have been recognized" in 1842 "by the several States composing this Union, and by the United States government itself."[110]

Levi Woodbury put forth the same New Hampshire resolutions in the Senate, where they were read and summarily laid on the table with no action taken.[111] It was a different story in the House, however, where Burke was able to force a vote. So while he failed to get a vote in Congress on the seven resolutions connected with his 1,000-page report, he did manage to get a vote on whether or not the petition from the New Hampshire legislature, which more or less embodied the same principles that he advocated in his report, would be debated. Unfortunately for Burke, however, while the House voted 113 in favor with 74 opposed, the number in favor did not meet the required two-thirds majority and thus no floor debate took place. The vote fell along strict party lines, with more than 90 percent of the votes in favor stemming from the Democratic side with the opposing votes from a solid block of Whigs.[112] Once again the politics surrounding the "Rhode Island Question" made evident the political divide on the nature of the people's sovereignty. Only the ideology of territorial expansion ended up saving the Democracy from division in 1844–1845, as both northerners and southerners turned their attention to westward growth.[113]

Chapter 8

The People's Sovereignty
in the Courtroom

> My true defense is, I had a right to do as I did, and it is with great regret
> that I am debarred from my justification by the decision of the Court . . .
> My position is like that of Galileo, who was induced under the severe
> tortures of the Inquisition, to deny his theory of the rotation of the
> earth, but who, when leaving the apartments of torture, exclaimed, "still
> the earth turns."
>
> Thomas Wilson Dorr, 1844 treason trial

Dorr's treason trial, along with the trial of Peter Zenger in 1735, and the
numerous prosecutions under the Sedition Act of 1798, stands as the most
significant criminal prosecutions against serious challenges to an incumbent
regime.[1] The trial was conducted by the arch conservative Job Durfee, who
broke all rules of judicial propriety in the spring of 1842 when he used his
office as a bully pulpit. Just weeks before Dorr's trial was set to commence,
Durfee presided over the murder trial of John Gordon, an Irish immigrant
laborer accused of brutally murdering the industrialist Amasa Sprague. The
nativistic tide that influenced the restrictive suffrage clauses in the 1843 constitution had yet to recede.[2] Durfee's conduct during the Gordon murder
trial, especially his charge to the jury in which he drew a distinction between
the testimony of native-born witnesses and that of Gordon's countrymen,
made the trial a mockery of justice. Sentenced to death, John Gordon was
confined to the new state prison on the cove in Providence to await execution. Thomas Dorr would soon join him, though he would not suffer the
same unfortunate fate as John Gordon.[3]

While the prosecution was allowed to pontificate on almost any aspect
of his brief tenure as the People's Governor, Dorr was never allowed to

present his political views to Rhode Island's highest court in order to prove that his intentions were not treasonous, but rather in line with the tenets of American constitutionalism. Fully aware of the machinations of the state authorities in empanelling a biased jury, Dorr and his co-counsel George Turner did little in their cross-examination of the state's witnesses to dispute the essential facts at hand: that Dorr and his men did attempt to fire on the arsenal in Providence on May 17–18 and that he raised an army in Chepachet in late June 1842. The People's Governor said he was only trying to get "at the facts in the case." When Joseph Blake, the Attorney General, asked one witness if Dorr wished "to take possession of the State House," the witness replied that he had "reason to believe the Prisoner was for vigorous measures." Rising from his courtroom table, Dorr loudly proclaimed, "that is correct."[4]

Though he was encouraged to do so by his political allies, Dorr never challenged the constitutionality of his state-level treason trial. The "question whether there be such an offense as State Treason was secondary and comparatively unimportant," wrote Dorr. My "defense being not that treason was committed against the United States rather than against a State, but that there was no treason at all, and could be none in the discharge of the duties, to which I was called under a Constitution adopted by the majority of the whole People, in the exercise of their free and sovereign capacity," noted Dorr the following year to Secretary of the Treasury Robert Walker.[5] Neither Dorr nor Turner even raised what would have seemed to be the most obvious line of defense that the government now existing in Rhode Island under the 1843 constitution had no power to try Dorr for an alleged act of treason against a defunct government.[6]

Dorr's attempt to produce a detailed record of the votes for the People's Constitution was quickly overruled by Durfee, who said that he considered "one who rises up in opposition to the Government, and takes upon himself the authority of a Governor, to be an usurper." The only question open to interpretation was whether or not "there was an actual levying of war, and did the Defendant engage in that levying of war?" According to Durfee, the act of judging the validity of a constitution involved a function that courts were ill equipped to administer.[7] Ironically, Dorr had taken this very position in 1842 when many of his followers looked to the court system for a settlement.

On May 7, after only a few hours of deliberation, Dorr was convicted of treason by the twelve-man jury of Newporters hostile to his cause. Law and Order officials learned their lesson from the December 1842 trial of Franklin Cooley, which was held in Providence where Dorrite support remained strong. Dorr now had the honor of being the first man to commit treason against a state in U.S. history. Though one could be sentenced to death for a host of crimes in the nineteenth century, Durfee, fearing the uproar that would surely grip the state if Dorr was hanged for his crime, sentenced the People's Governor to life imprisonment in solitary confinement. George Turner quickly worked up a bill of exceptions to obtain a writ of error from the U.S. Supreme Court, but he could not act because a federal statute required written consent from the prisoner before a writ could be issued. After the guilty verdict was handed down, Turner lost access to Dorr. The motion for a bill of exceptions was summarily denied and Dorr was sent to Providence on June 27 where he was incarcerated in the new prison on the banks of the cove in the center of the city. The log book notes him simply as prisoner number 56. Dorr was placed in a cell measuring nine-by-twelve-by-nine feet, furnished with only a bunk. The lax conditions that allowed Dorr to walk in and out of his cell and receive visitors at any time of the day while he was in the town prison in Newport were no more.[8]

Released only to paint decorative hand fans in the prison workshop, Dorr spent the majority of the day confined to his cell, where his already deteriorating health began to worsen.[9] Dorr managed to keep in contact with the outside world, thanks to the efforts of an unknown female supporter who smuggled notes written on scraps of paper out of the prison and brought back messages. Lydia Dorr's unwavering love for her son helped to keep his spirits up and to endure the daily, excruciating pain that began to plague him in prison. Lydia encouraged her son to read the Bible and to find salvation in the Lord. While in prison, Dorr renewed his relationship with his Episcopal faith. He found comfort in Psalm 27, which he read on a daily basis: "When evildoers assail me, uttering slanders against me, my adversaries and foes, they shall stumble and fall. Though a host encamp against me, my heart shall not fear; though war arise against me, yet I will be confident."

Though Sullivan Dorr was greatly angered by the actions of his oldest son, he did everything in his power to secure his release. In June, Sullivan sent a petition to the General Assembly attempting to secure a pardon for his son or, at the very least, secure more comfortable accommodations. It was a waste of time. Even if Sullivan had managed to somehow persuade the Law and Order members of the legislature, his son would have refused to take an oath of allegiance to the new government in Rhode Island.[10] Dorr's uncle, Zachariah Allen, Jr., thought that his nephew should be released because he had lost his mental faculties. Allen suggested that Dorr's "unsettled state of mind," constituted clear evidence of mental derangement.[11] Despite their setback in June 1844 in the assembly, Sullivan and Lydia Dorr continued to work for their son's release, although they never claimed that he was insane. The Dorrs even went to the extraordinary length of seeking counsel from Joseph Story on how their son might petition the U.S. Supreme Court.[12] Sullivan and Lydia Dorr, however, were not the only ones working to free the People's Governor.

Within weeks of Dorr's conviction, an opportunistic New York lawyer visited Providence to seek out a group with whom he could align himself in order to initiate an appeal to the U.S. Supreme Court. Francis Treadwell, with the aid of his employer, the National Reform Association (NRA), found a sympathetic audience with Henry and Abby Lord, the heads of the newly constituted Dorr Liberation Society. In 1840, Treadwell was connected to the First Social Reform Society that authored a pamphlet urging Rhode Island reformers to call a convention if the General Assembly refused to comply. In return for Treadwell's services, the majority-female Dorr Liberation Society agreed to peddle NRA political tracts published by John Windt.[13] "Look to the time when we went from house to house with our books, to show the doubting Thomases that the case could be carried up" to the Supreme Court, wrote Treadwell to Lord in early 1845.[14]

Treadwell's goal was to appeal to the court for a writ of habeas corpus on the grounds that the Rhode Island Supreme Court had refused to admit argument on what was, in his mind, the key issue—whether treason could be committed against a state. The New York attorney believed there was a conspiracy headed by the warden of the prison and Thomas Burgess, the mayor of Providence, to prevent Dorr from signing a writ of error to the U.S. Supreme Court on this point. Treadwell was assisted by the abolitionist attorney Samuel Fessendon of Portland, Maine.[15] Dorr was furious when he heard that Treadwell was trying to take over the appeal of his conviction. He feared that Treadwell's loyalty was to the NRA and not his cause.[16]

In July 1844, the NRA resolved that "agents, representatives and lecturers" were "requested" to deliver speeches upon the "subject of the Freedom of the unappropriated public lands of the United States" and on the "subject of treason" in connection with Dorr's imprisonment.[17] The NRA was under the leadership of John Commerford and George Henry Evans, an English-born reformer and activist living in New York City and an old ally of Rhode Island labor reformer Seth Luther.[18] Access to land offered a viable alternative to the permanent dependence of the laboring classes in Evans's analysis.[19] Evans linked his doctrine to Jefferson's conception of land as the natural right of citizens. In a lengthy letter to abolitionist Gerrit Smith in August 1844 in which he tried to convince the wealthy abolitionist of the antislavery components of the NRA agenda, along with the reality of white "wage slavery," Evans used Dorr's imprisonment as a political weapon. Let the Whigs "peaceably submit to the imprisonment of Gov. Dorr, after peaceable means of liberation have failed, and they invite aggression on their rights; they *peaceably* submit to be slaves; which, it seems to me, they have no *right to do*."[20]

The *Workingman's Advocate*, the organ of the NRA, equated the suffrage cause in Rhode Island with that of the NRA's: "The cause of Dorr and Rhode Island is intimately connected with the cause in which we are engaged, a restoration of the People's Right to the soil of their birth." Ignoring the broadened suffrage provisions in the 1843 Constitution, Dorr's "oppressors" were colorfully referred to as "land-pirates." Free Suffrage was equated with "freedom of the soil."[21] The "Land-Lords of Rhode Island not only contend for the power of a majority to withhold rights from the minority; but they deny the right even of a majority to alter the power of government unless by consent of a minority!" proclaimed the *Workingman's Advocate*.[22] If the present "state of things" in Rhode Island continued, "the rich will rapidly become more wealthy and the number of the landless poor will continually augment." The "reverse would be the case if the Public Lands were made free and the right of suffrage restored."[23]

Echoing Seth Luther, Evans declared, "Let Dorr be liberated, peaceably if he can be, forcibly if he must be."[24] When asked how the "Rhode Island Question" was connected with the NRA agenda, Evans replied, "What the landed aristocracy of Rhode Island and of England were now doing to withhold the right of suffrage, the same aristocracy elsewhere would do if they could get the power."[25] While the NRA's expressed purpose was land reform, membership ranks included radical New York Locofoco Democrats, most notably "Colonel" Alexander Ming and Mike Walsh, the chairman of the Spartan Association, a ritualistic political gang and workingman's club.[26] Both Walsh and Ming supported Dorr in the spring of 1842. In the pages of his radical newspaper, the *Subterranean*, the always colorful Walsh warned Law and Order men in Providence that the "day of retribution" was "drawing near" and "unless you heed the warning" to free Dorr, "you will have none but yourselves to blame for the dreadful catastrophe which will over-take and annihilate you."[27] In 1844–1845, Evans combined his *Workingman's Advocate*, which was recently resurrected from an eight-year hiatus, with Walsh's *Subterranean*. In 1845, the two editors issued a new paper entitled *Young America*.[28] The paper helped to publicize Francis Treadwell's polemical pamphlet, *The Conspiracy to Defeat the Liberation of Gov. Dorr* (1845), which was published by John Windt of the NRA, and contained a two-page manifesto on land reform in the back.[29]

In addition to helping cultivate abolitionist allies, Dorr's imprisonment helped Evans and the NRA bridge a gap with the ongoing Anti-Rent movement in New York. Evans believed in 1845 that the "majority" of the Anti-Renters desired to "establish a system, based on the Declaration of Independence, which secures to every citizen the same right they claim for themselves, the right to land enough to live upon." The NRA and the Anti-Renters were united in their sympathy for "Rhode Islanders' struggle for liberty and right."[30] Beginning in 1839, democratic ideology led upstate New York farmers holding their lands on long-term leases to demand an end to the pre-Revolutionary rent system. Like the Dorrites, the Anti-Renters believed that popular sovereignty meant the right of the people to overthrow unjust laws or institutions that threatened the body politic—including state constitutions.[31]

The rise of the second-party system in the 1820s led to a greater clamoring for political rights in Rhode Island, while at the same time, political parties replaced landlords as the mediating agent between tenant and government. The Anti-Renters maintained that "all men" were "equal, sovereign, and independent" and that "all power" stemmed from "the people."[32] In 1847, a sick and lame Dorr dictated a memoranda to his mother in which he implored her to seek out his old friend John O'Sullivan to write a full history of the events of 1841–1842 in Rhode Island and the New York Anti-Rent War. The book "should contain an argumentative view, an investigation of the whole cause," said Dorr. "The similarity of the R.I. question in points of principle to that of N. York should be demonstrated."[33]

In order to raise funds to pay for legal counsel and defray the cost of bringing the writ of error before the Supreme Court, the Liberation Society with the help of the NRA issued "Dorr Liberation Stock." Newspaper notices for the sale of the scrip began to appear in Providence newspapers, as well as the Democratic New York press. A notice in the *Providence Gazette* read: "The friends of that persecuted and suffering men are respectfully invited to buy the stock in such sums as they may choose,—pay for it as they take it, and become vendors of it on their own accounts, for the benefit of innocence and adversity struggling with arbitrary power."[34] Dorr never sanctioned the scrip and was furious when he became aware of it. He did not want anyone profiting through the use of his name.

Dorr managed to get word to the members of the Democratic State Committee who implored the women to stop the sale of the scrip. Eventually, the controversy created a major rift within the ranks of female supporters, especially between Catharine Williams, who respected Dorr's wishes not to be released from prison if it meant swearing an oath of allegiance to the state government, and Abby Lord, who would settle for any compromise that would result in Dorr's release. "What is to become of one man, lame and rheumatic, between two parties of angry women," wrote Dorr to his mother on New Year's Day 1845.[35]

Denied access to his attorneys by the prison warden, Dorr was powerless to stop the actions of Francis Treadwell and the Liberation Society. John Harris, who was in Washington when Treadwell went before the nation's highest court, said that his oral argument was completely ineffective and almost laughable. Harris told Walter Burges that he was "obliged to hide his face" rather than watch Treadwell make a fool out of himself.[36] U.S. Supreme Court Justice John McLean held that neither the Judiciary Act of 1789 nor Article III of the Constitution granted power to a judge to issue a writ of habeas corpus to summon a state prisoner for any other reason than to be used as a witness.[37] In late 1844, George Turner and Walter Burges finally gained access to Dorr and a writ of error on the nature of state-level treason was filed with the U.S. Supreme Court.[38] This case, *Thomas W. Dorr v. Rhode Island*, lingered on the docket for years without coming up for argument. Dorr eventually requested that the case be removed from the court's docket.[39]

In the summer of 1844, Dorr's conviction was skillfully used by northern Democrats to rally support for the upcoming presidential election.[40] A letter from a Philadelphia newspaperman to the Democratic candidate James K. Polk in October 1844 is illustrative of the use of the politics surrounding Dorr's imprisonment in vetting presidential candidates. "The most exciting topic now before the public is the Rhode Island Question and the imprisonment of Gov. Dorr," wrote John Bradford to Polk. Bradford continued: "I would suggest whether it would not be well, whether in fact Justice to your-self and friends does not require that your opinion upon this deeply exciting question should not be made known . . . I would strongly advise your at-tention to the Rhode Island business."[41]

The *New England Democrat*, a Boston weekly periodical edited by Lewis Josselyn, a vocal supporter of Dorr in 1842, began to run headlines in each issue on "Governor Dorr's Sentence" and his suffering at the hands of the Charter authorities. Josselyn's paper declared that if "signers of the Decla-ration of Independence were right—if the Patriots of the Revolution were right, then were the makers and supporters of the People's Constitution of Rhode Island right."[42] On the eve of the presidential election, a crowd of over 12,000 people marched through the streets of New York with banners that read "Polk, Dallas, and the Liberation of Dorr."[43] At a gathering on Fruit Hill in the town of North Providence, banners bearing "1776, Polk, Dallas, Dorr and Liberty" hung near a large Hickory Pole.[44] Dorr was con-fident that "Polk and Dallas will receive the votes of a majority of the Elec-toral College and that popular sovereignty . . . will thus be rescued."[45]

Too sick to a attend a rally in Providence in September, Andrew Jackson apologetically informed Dorr's supporters that his health confined him to the Hermitage, his Tennessee plantation. However, Jackson took the op-portunity to repeat the sentiments that he had expressed to Francis Blair in May 1842. According to Old Hickory, Dorr had "committed no offence ex-cept that of endeavoring to supersede the royal charter by a constitution em-anating directly from the people." Jackson admitted that Dorr had "erred as to the means" he adopted for, but it was still "difficult to conceive how the severe punishment inflicted upon him can be justified."[46] In his reply to an invitation letter, Dorr's old tutor at Harvard, George Bancroft, soon to become Secretary of the Navy, condemned his student's imprisonment for "punishment of actions that were but the expressions of political opinions."[47]

In a pledge taken on board a steamboat returning to New York City from a presidential campaign rally in Providence, George Henry Evans and other members of the NRA resolved "not to give the Bankers of Rhode Is-land any further credit until Governor Dorr is liberated and the People's Constitution restored; and that we recommend to every friend of Dorr and Free Suffrage throughout the Union to refuse to take Rhode Island paper money in exchange for the products of their labor and to immediately de-mand specie for what they hold."[48] The New York editor John O'Sullivan linked Dorr's imprisonment directly to Whig aggression, and thus creating the rhetorical weapons the Democrats could use against Henry Clay: "Clay—naturally and fitly—has declared himself strongly against the popular party in the Rhode Island contest . . . we invoke our Democratic friends to draw broad and deep the line of contrast between us and our opponents on this point of vital democratic principle." The chain of events in Rhode Island "from its first stage to its last," provided "one of the best tests" ever offered of the "true character and spirit of the Whig and Democratic parties, respectively." The "heart of the Democracy," proclaimed O'Sullivan, has always been with Dorr and "the party of freedom and popular rights."[49] In addition to the *Democratic Review*, O'Sullivan used the pages of the *New York Morning News*, a paper he founded with Samuel Tilden in the summer of 1844, to promote Polk's candidacy and to blame the Whigs for Dorr's imprisonment.[50]

When the balloting was finished, Polk, the dark horse candidate, bested Henry Clay by a razor-thin margin—1,338,464 popular votes to Clay's 1,300,097. The election came down to the returns from New York: Polk had carried the state by slightly over 5,000 votes, while the Liberty Party Candidate, James Birney, who offered Dorr a position as a lecturer for the American Anti-Slavery Society in 1837, garnered 16,000 antislavery voters, which might otherwise have gone to Henry Clay.[51] "Mr. Clay's denunciation of the Dorr sympathizers exasperated the Wright and Van Buren men of [New York] in a decided manner and gave Mr. Polk the vote by which the party was saved from defeat," declared one of Dorr's correspondents. It "is my candid opinion that but for the revival of that question by Mr. [Clay] Polk would not have got the state."[52] Dorr attributed the victory, at least in part, to the influence of the "Rhode Island Question." Nearly a year after Polk's victory, Dorr noted to one correspondent that the "Rhode Island Question had an appreciable weight in the result" discussed in the "House of Representatives and in the Baltimore Convention, the People discerned this question, welcomed it, and inscribed it on their banner of victory." The state's "calamities thus became fruitful; and the democracy of the whole has gained by our losses."[53] According to Mike Walsh, the "imprisonment of Dorr was one of the most powerful agents in the election of [James] Polk" over Henry Clay.[54] Unfortunately for Dorr, Polk's victory over Clay did not mean that he would receive a presidential pardon. Young Hickory did nothing to aid Dorr other than write a private letter to a New Hampshire Democrat expressing his gratitude for his efforts to secure Dorr's release. "No incident in the course of our history has presented a more aggravated subject for consideration," said Polk "than the martyrdom of that pure and self sacrificing gentleman."[55]

By 1845, the liberation of Thomas Dorr was the major issue in Rhode Island politics. After Polk's election, James Simmons and Samuel Man—the twin pillars of the Law and Order Party—came to the realization that Dorr's imprisonment was a political liability for their Whig Party. Democrat Charles Jackson, elected governor on a "Liberation" ticket in April 1845, helped to secure Dorr's release with assistance from Simmons and Man.[56] A move was actually made several months earlier to orchestrate Dorr's release if he swore an oath of allegiance. After learning of the movement in the assembly, which was being orchestrated behind the scenes by his parents, Dorr informed Walter Burges that he could not "dishonor" himself "to regain" his "liberty."[57] Dorr wanted nothing, but unconditional liberation. Still in hiding in Connecticut, the always colorful Aaron White proclaimed that he would rather see Dorr "dead" and the city of Providence "a blazing pyre" than to see him make the "slightest submission or recantation while he has his soul left."[58] Dorr probably would have opted to forgo the fiery death, but he was determined to stick to his principles. His patience paid off.

Exactly one year after entering the state prison in Providence, Dorr was released when the General Assembly passed an act "to pardon certain offences against the sovereign power of this State and to quiet the minds of the good people thereof."[59] Female Dorrites, who had been petitioning the General Assembly for months, were at the prison to greet him when he emerged from the perimeter gates. Dorr sent out word ahead of time that he did not want a parade or a large throng of followers to greet him. The Ladies Benevolent Suffrage Association of Providence was relieved to find that the "lethargy that had for so many months weighed down the eye lids of our countrymen . . . has been shaken off and . . . the American people have awakened to a sense of their rights."[60] Rhode Island Democrats wasted no time in organizing celebrations. In reply to an invitation for a "Liberation Fete," Martin Van Buren declared that "no candid and upright mind can fail to respect and honor the modesty, fortitude and firmness under defeat and adversity" that Dorr displayed in his "conduct."[61]

His fragile health utterly ruined by his time in prison, Dorr moved back to Benefit Street so his mother could care for him. Disbarred by the General Assembly, Dorr could not resume his profitable legal career. He was at the mercy of his father for an allowance though his supporters did their best to keep his political hopes alive. On October 29, 1846, Dorr received 34 votes in the General Assembly for the post of U.S. Senator, narrowly losing to Whig industrialist John H. Clarke.[62] Unable to travel far, Dorr spent his time managing two seemingly innocuous legal disputes that stemmed from the Charter government's issuance of martial law in 1842. However, unlike the appeal of his treason conviction, the trespass suit embodied the "Rhode Island Question"—the right to alter or abolish a form of government. Dorr believed that the issues that were dear to his heart were best represented in the cases of *Martin Luther v. Luther Borden* and *Rachel Luther v. Luther Borden*. For the next several years, Dorr managed both cases from his parent's home in Providence.

In a December 1844 letter to attorney Walter Burges, Dorr proclaimed that "the *Luther* case was his case." It "presented the great point of popular sovereignty so distinctly upon the record, that the Court could not evade a decision upon it.[63] Should the "case be tried and lost," said Dorr, "another resolution will ultimately become necessary to *reestablish* the doctrines of the Declaration of Independence."[64] Though he did not want the U.S. Supreme Court to get into the game of examining the nature of republicanism as it concerned a state government, Dorr did want the Court to uphold the right of the people to alter or abolish a form of government.[65] As Dorr wrote in April 1848, the *Luther* case was a way that "the true doctrine of original and imprescritable sovereignty should be kept distinctly in the view" of the people and the "anti-republican and detestable Sophism of Sovereignty in the government . . . should be thoroughly confuted."[66]

As part of the effort to round up Suffrage Party members after Dorr fled Rhode Island for the second time in June 1842, Charter troops raided the home of Martin Luther, a Warren shoemaker and key figure in the Suffrage Party. In April 1842, Luther moderated a town meeting in Warren, which had urged support for the People's Government. In May, Luther served with Dorr in the attempted attack upon the arsenal in Providence, and he had also received votes for state and town offices under the People's Constitution. By the time troops arrived at his home, Luther had already fled to nearby Swansea, Massachusetts. The troops had to make do with harassing his elderly mother, Rachel, and ransacking his house. Since he claimed residence in Massachusetts, Luther sued for trespass in federal court. Luther Borden, an officer of a Charter militia unit, had been under orders when he entered Martin Luther's home. If the Charter government and not

Dorr's government was the legal government, then Borden was simply following orders handed down to him during a period of martial law. If Dorr's government was legally in effect at the time, then Borden was a civilian who broke into a home. Daniel Webster wrote sarcastically in his notes on the case that "treasonable force was really on the other side; and that the Supreme Court of Rhode Island made rather an important mistake—Gov. King, if anyone, should have been tried for treason, and Mr. Dorr regarded as the defender of the Constitution and laws."[67] Rachel Luther claimed personal trespass against the same defendants on the grounds that even without a change of government the invasion of her home was unauthorized because a state-wide declaration of martial law was patently illegal.[68]

In October 1842, Martin Luther filed a trespass complaint in the federal Circuit Court against the nine men who broke into his home. Luther claimed $5,000 in damages. A writ to arrest Borden and seven others who participated in the raid was issued by Chief Justice Roger Taney riding circuit on October 24, 1842. Due to the still heightened tensions in the state, Luther's case was postponed until November 1843.[69] Supreme Court Justice Joseph Story and District Judge John Pitman—both ardent anti-Dorrites—heard the case before a twelve-man jury in federal Circuit Court.

At trial Benjamin F. Hallett, counsel for Martin Luther, argued that the Charter government had become null and void after the vote on the People's Constitution in December 1841 and, therefore, Samuel Ward King possessed no power to declare martial law. Upon the conclusion of arguments, Hallett requested the lower federal court to instruct the jury that the People's Constitution had become the fundamental law of the state six months before the night the alleged trespass occurred.[70] Counsel for the defense, led by Dorr's old legal mentor John Whipple, maintained that the Charter government was the legal government in Rhode Island in 1842 despite the evidence offered by Hallett that it had somehow been superseded.[71] Whipple contended that at the time of the "pretended trespass," said Whipple, the "town of Warren was in danger of an attack from Martin Luther and his confidants."[72]

The sympathies of the two presiding judges on the Circuit Court, Story and Pitman, were unequivocally with Whipple's side of the argument. Justice Story dismissed Hallett's main contention—that the People's Government was the rightful government of Rhode Island in 1842. He also refused to allow any evidence that Hallett presented to be handed to the jury.[73] In his charge to the jury, Story maintained that Hallett's arguments were entirely without foundation and that the defendants had a rightful obligation to act as they did. However, Story's refusal to allow evidence to go before the jury was apparently done in order to facilitate an appeal to the U.S. Supreme Court.[74] The jury returned a verdict of not guilty for Luther Burden and his cohorts.

In an exchange with Hallett about the abuse that Martin Luther's mother, Rachel, suffered at the hands of the Charter authorities during the June 1842 raid, Story argued that Rhode Island "was a sovereign state and must have the right to maintain her own sovereignty" in any manner its legislature deems fit. "Should Shays's insurrection break out again in Massachusetts, or the Whiskey insurrection in Pennsylvania, can there be any doubt that each state should immediately resort to measures to suppress the disturbances, and sustain its own sovereignty?" asked Story.[75] In describing the situation in the spring of 1842, Story described a state besieged with danger "so urgent, that its legislature judged a resort to the most extraordinary means of resistance necessary and . . . declared martial law." Since the General Assembly had deemed martial law to be of a necessity at the time, courts could not look into the causes behind the statute's enactment.[76] The only question Story allowed the twelve jurors to decide in the case of *Rachel Luther v. Luther Borden* was if the defendants committed "wanton, malicious, and mischievous acts" other than those protected by the lawful declaration of martial law inside the home of Rachel Luther.[77] Only the military officers could judge the necessity of any measure. Yet, despite Story's anti-Dorrite charge, the jury failed to reach a decision in the case brought by Rachel Luther.

Before Hallett could schedule another trial, however, Story and Pitman constructed an artificial statement of division of opinion on the right of the jury to decide whether the facts proved the necessity for a blanket issuance of martial law. The Judiciary Act of 1802 allowed for Supreme Court review of Circuit Court decisions when the judges disagreed on points of law. Thus Rachel Luther's case and that of her son Martin were sent simultaneously to Washington to be heard by the U.S. Supreme Court.[78]

Nearly four years elapsed, however, before oral arguments in the *Luther* cases were heard in Washington. Absences and vacancies on the bench were responsible for the repeated delays. In 1845, Senator Levi Woodbury, who wrote numerous letters to Dorr in April 1842 praising his course of action, replaced the deceased Joseph Story. In 1847, Dorr believed at this time that there was a possibility that the Court would rule 5–4 in favor of his 1842 course of action. Dorr told George Turner and Benjamin Hallett that they could "rely" on the Democrat block of "[Levi] Woodbury, [Samuel] Nelson, [Robert] Grier and [John] Catron." With the "addition of [Peter] Daniel," said Dorr, "we have the decision in our favor." Dorr implored his two attorneys not to be afraid of Daniel Webster's "acknowledged power" in the courtroom. Dorr argued that Webster's legal prowess could not "sustain him in a cause, which . . . rests mainly on the principle, that, in this country, the sovereignty is vested in the government and not in the People." Ironically, as a young man Dorr idolized Webster, sending his portrait to numerous friends, including William Bridges Adams. You are to be "envied," said Dorr, "in your duty & privilege of assailing Mr. Webster, or any other man who shall occupy an old, exploded Tory ground like this." Nothing "should prevent you from bringing this case to final argument at the present term," instructed Dorr, who was vehemently opposed to any arrangement for an argument in writing, something that Hallett had hinted at numerous times. "I desire that our cause, in all its proportions, should be held up to the fullest scrutiny in open court; where we also wish to have exhibited the unmitigated sentiments of the Algerine Tory party, by the authority of its greatest expositor," concluded Dorr.[79]

However, sometime in mid-February 1847 the court decided to postpone arguments in order to take up other cases that had been lingering on the docket.[80] As was the case in 1844, sectional tensions created by slavery's expansion westward served to push the "Rhode Island Question" off the table. In 1846, when Democratic Congressman David Wilmot of Pennsylvania proposed an amendment to an appropriation bill requiring that slavery be prohibited in any territory acquired from the war with Mexico then under way, the nation's two major parties had begun to split along sectional lines, ushering in a new era in which slavery took a leading role in the political drama of Washington politics. Taney was not interested in throwing more fuel on the sectional fire, especially in light of recent writings by Lysander Spooner and William Goodell that highlighted the antislavery potential of the Guarantee Clause.[81] A Vermont abolitionist told Dorr that if Taney "pronounced" the People's Constitution "legal" it would be the equivalent of saying to black men "you may do as white men have done." The abolitionist was convinced that the nation's highest court was under the influence of the "Slave power."[82]

In the interim between oral argument and decision, the Court heard a case dealing with a conflict of law and conscience. *Jones v. Van Zandt* stemmed from the appeal of a conviction under the 1793 Fugitive Slave Act.

In his opinion for the Court in *Jones v. Van Zandt*, Justice Levi Woodbury affirmed the constitutionality of the 1793 statute and said the Supreme Court was bound to uphold it. Woodbury dismissed the argument from future chief justice Salmon Chase, Van Zandt's counsel, that slavery was unconstitutional by stating that the issue was a political question for each state to decide, thereby anticipating the more elaborate political question doctrine the Court would stake out two years later in the decision of *Luther v. Borden*.[83] Perhaps after reading Woodbury's opinion, Dorr came to the conclusion that the Court would most likely duck the issue in his case, for he said as much to Benjamin Hallett eight days before oral arguments were to commence.[84]

But the most important occurrence affecting the Court during the interlude was the fact that Rhode Island had replaced the 1663 Charter with a modern document. It was unlikely that the U.S. Congress or the Supreme Court would negate the 1843 Constitution and force the state to revert back to the People's Constitution. The most plausible ruling that would favor the Dorrites in some way, albeit small, would be a vindication of their cause through the condemnation of the use of martial law. Nevertheless, Dorr wrote to Hallett at the time of the oral arguments in January 1848 in order to make sure that the Boston attorney understood the "main point" of the *Luther* cases. Dorr acknowledged that his "entire justification under the People's Constitution, according to the provisions of which" he was "elected Governor of the State" would "not be entertained by the Court." Dorr wanted Hallett to argue this "great point." Dorr knew the cards were stacked against them. He was thinking in terms of the "great tribunal of public opinion."[85]

In an attempt to aid Hallett, Dorr tried to secure the assistance of Robert J. Walker, former Democratic senator from Mississippi and secretary of the treasury under Polk, and, ironically, the man who led the Democratic call for Texas annexation in early 1844 that pushed *Burke's Report* off the Congressional agenda. The slaveholder Walker refused to argue the appeal of Dorr's treason conviction and gave only a lukewarm answer as to whether or not he would argue the *Luther* cases.[86] By late 1846, with Walker still on the fence, and Silas Wright, Jr., consumed with his duties as governor of New York, Dorr turned to Nathan Clifford, Polk's attorney general, to assist Hallett. Clifford, a future Supreme Court justice, eventually agreed to get involved in the litigation in his private capacity as an attorney.[87] In an important letter to Clifford, Dorr insisted that the "main stress should not be on the minor point, that in R. Island there was no prescribed mode of proceeding to amend the government, and therefore the People here were at liberty to frame a government." As he had argued consistently for nearly a decade, "the establishment of any mode of convenience for amending a Constitution through the action of the Legislature cannot impair the general inalienable right for the People at large to make alterations in their organic laws."[88]

Hallett's oral argument lasted three days and quoted from a plethora of constitutional theorists, for which the court reporter could only construct a minor skeleton of the argument. Hallett sought to prove that a majority of the adult male citizens had approved of the People's Constitution, which had been adopted through peaceful and legal means. Moreover, the whole Dorrite agenda was in accordance with the fundamental political ideas of the American founding. Hallett's goal was to make the rebellion "respectable."[89] Hallett argued the right of a majority to oust an entrenched government as a basic exercise of its sovereignty. As Dorr did in his speech before Job Durfee read out his sentence, Hallett declared that a denial of the sanctity of the people's sovereignty represented a "condemnation of the principles of '76."[90]

Hallett refrained from demanding that the Court issue a decision using the Guarantee Clause to retroactively install the People's government. As Edmund Burke's massive report made clear, no one was denying the validity of the constitution adopted in the wake of the rebellion. Hallett's argument in defense of the Dorrite position maintained that the action of the People's Constitution replacing the unrepublican 1663 Charter was fully legitimate under the principle of the right to alter or abolish a form of government but had been superseded by subsequent actions of the people in the fall of 1842. The proper legal judgment would be to award Martin Luther $5,000 for the unwarranted trespass because the People's Constitution and not the Charter was in effect at the time martial law was invoked.

After laying out what amounted to a Revolutionary-era truism—that the right to adopt a form of government necessarily includes the right to abolish, to reform, and to alter any existing form of government—Hallett posed three questions for the Court: (1) Had the people of Rhode Island a right to adopt a constitution for themselves? (2) Were the ballots cast for the People's Constitution conclusive proof of its adoption? (3) Did the People's Constitution become the "supreme law of the State of Rhode Island" on January 13, 1842, the day the ballots were certified? "If these questions are answered in the negative," Hallett continued, "then the theory of American free government for the States is unavailable in practice."[91]

Recognizing that he was arguing in front of a court comprised of five southern justices, Hallett attempted to make clear that "the people" did not include slaves. Hallett argued that the people's sovereignty applied to all citizens, but not children, women, idiots, the mentally incompetent, or slaves. The "attempt to alarm the South on this point" was "absurd" said Hallett.[92] He reminded the Court that it was the Charter government and not Dorr's government that gave the "African race" the right to vote.[93] After reading Hallett's argument, Dorr wrote to Nathan Clifford on the ever-present subject of slavery. Dorr stated: "Our front towards opponents in the slave states is clear and well defined. The People in every state, within the limitations of the National Constitution, are competent to the making and altering of their forms of government." In conclusion, Dorr argued that "slaves were in fact not part of the sovereign body, and were in a condition of pupilage and incapacity disqualifying them from any participation in political power."[94]

The always astute Daniel Webster was well aware that the public perceived the *Luther* cases as a contest between the different brands of American constitutionalism offered by the two major parties.[95] His role as secretary of state under John Tyler afforded him with a unique vantage point on how the "Rhode Island Question" was perceived by the Whigs and Democrats, along with how it was viewed by southern politicos. Webster worked hard behind the scenes in 1842 in order to achieve a compromise. In private he expressed his displeasure with Dorr's brand of constitutionalism, but he did not make those views public. Ironically, twenty years before in the U.S. Supreme Court case of *Wilkinson v. Leland* (1829), Webster had lost to John Whipple in a case dealing with the overarching power of the Rhode Island legislature. As historian Patrick T. Conley has observed, when Webster "could not persuade" the justices that the power of the Rhode Island legislature "was excessive or un-republican, he became a convert."[96]

A few days prior to oral arguments in *Luther v. Borden*, Webster closed a case in front of the Taney Court in which he warned against the "leveling ultraisms of Anti-rentism or Agrarianism or Abolitionism."[97] Webster was referencing the New York Anti-Rent War and the growing power of the political antislavery movement. The Dorrites fit into the same mold in Webster's analysis. In notes taken in preparation for his oral argument, Webster summarized what he thought to be the essence of the argument from Dorr and his attorneys in the *Luther* cases. The People's Government was "illegal, according to all American principle, & precedent," said Webster. Moreover, "it had been declared illegal" by the Rhode Island authorities, therefore the U.S. Supreme Court could not "review acts" that had already been "stamped and marked as criminal." According to the Massachusetts statesman, Dorr was attempting to prove he was "no traitor, nor insurrectionist, but the real governor of the state at the time; that the force used by him was exercised in support of the Constitution and laws, not against them."[98]

In Webster's analysis, when the people opted for representative government during the American Revolution, they adopted a specific process for changing that form of government. Webster acknowledged this process was more difficult in Rhode Island than in other states, but nevertheless the General Assembly did possess the power to call a constitutional convention to write a new constitution. Webster's rhetorical skills were on full display in the courtroom. "Is it not obvious enough that men cannot get together and count themselves, and say they are so many hundreds and so many thousands, and judge of their own qualifications, and call themselves the people, and set up a government," declared Webster.[99]

The U.S. "Constitution does not proceed on the *ground* of revolution; it does not proceed on any *right of* revolution," said Webster. The Constitution "goes on the idea that within and under the Constitution, no new Constitution can be established without the authority of the existing government." Without pre-established laws defining the people, the American system becomes "the law of the strongest or, what is the same thing, of the most numerous for the moment, and all constitutions and all legislative rights are prostrated and disregarded," maintained Webster in language that closely resembled Henry Dorr's 1841 letter to his older brother.[100] When the people act outside of the law, even in an attempt to rectify a gross inequity, the law cannot provide a post-hoc remedy.

Webster emphasized that President John Tyler had recognized the Charter government—a course of action Webster advised him to take in 1842. The fact that the Rhode Island Supreme Court had already affirmed the supremacy of the Charter government with its *ex cathedra* opinion, along with Dorr's treason conviction in 1844, provided grounds for the U.S. Supreme Court to deny jurisdiction in the case. Finally, in order to leave no stone unturned, Webster closed with these remarks: "The government was nothing but a shadow. It was all paper and patriotism; and went out on the 4th of May, admitting itself to be, what every one must now consider it, nothing but a contemptible sham."[101]

Not wanting to have their argument become part of the upcoming presidential election, the nation's highest court withheld decision in the *Luther* cases for over a year. Dorr, however, learned of the outcome a month after oral arguments were made. Hallett informed Dorr that the Court would hold that the *Luther* cases involved "a political & local question," not amenable to judicial resolution, particularly by a federal court. According to Hallett, the judges would simply refuse to "go behind the existing Gov't & the decision of the State Courts."[102] In March, Edmund Burke confirmed that the decision "will be adverse to the people." According to Burke, Levi Woodbury was going to "take the ground that the U.S. Government has no right to interfere in the political discussions of the people of a State, and that a State Government has no right to declare martial law."[103] Even though Burke's prediction about the Court's handling of the case was accurate, Dorr was pleased that Hallett had kept "the true doctrine of original and impressionable sovereignty distinctly in the view" of their "countrymen."[104]

Taney and Woodbury were in complete agreement about the nonjudicial nature of the "Rhode Island Question." Both jurists took the same position Dorr argued in 1842—the people's sovereignty was not a question for judges to handle. This point of view was, of course, entirely consistent with Dorr's ideology. In his opinion for Court, Taney began with a statement that must have seemed like a huge *understatement* to Dorr. "This case has arisen out of the *unfortunate* political differences which agitated the people of Rhode Island in 1841 and 1842."[105] Taney did not take up Hallett's charge that the Supreme Court could not determine the issue whether a trespass was or was not committed, without first deciding which frame of government was in force in Rhode Island at the time.[106] Taney held that the power to assess either the legitimacy or the republican character of a state government rested with Congress, not the courts. Such questions, he argued, were "political" in nature and thus beyond the scope of judicial review. In his infamous opinion for the Court in *Dred Scott* (1857), Taney neglected to follow his own judicial reasoning in *Luther* and, as a result, wrote a disastrous opinion that embroiled the Court in the political controversy over slavery's expansion.

Taney found that the power to decide which constitution was valid resided in state officials, the president, and Congress; anywhere but in the federal courts. Taney declared that "certainly it is no part of the judicial function of any court of the United States to prescribe the qualification of voters in a state . . . nor has it the right to determine what political privileges the citizens of a State are entitled to."[107] The Reconstruction Amendments

would eventually change this conception of the American constitutional order but they lay two decades in the future. To the extent that the federal
Constitution addressed the situation in Rhode Island, Taney maintained that
it clearly entrusted decisions about the republican character of state governments to the Congress when that body decided whether to seat congressmen.
Moreover, in addressing situations of domestic violence, Congress had in
1795 enacted legislation that entrusted certain powers to the president.
Taney concluded that Tyler's recognition of the Charter government had
to be respected, and the Rhode Island General Assembly's declaration of
martial law was an appropriate step to secure the safety of the citizens.[108]
"The State itself must determine what degree of force the crisis demands,"
said Taney. If the "government of Rhode Island deemed the armed opposition so formidable, and so ramified throughout the State, as to require the
use of its military force and the declaration of martial law, we see no ground
upon which this court can question its authority," concluded the Chief Justice.[109]

In *Luther v. Borden*, Taney acknowledged that the evidence offered by
the defendant and the plaintiff are "not such that commonly arise in action
of trespass."[110] Taney agreed with Dorr that no one "has ever doubted the
proposition, that, according to the institutions of this country, the sovereignty in every State resides in the people of the State, and that they may
alter and change their form of government at their own pleasure."[111] The
ever-perceptive Aaron White, Jr., recognized this as soon as he read the
opinion. "This decision of the Court," wrote White "is based entirely not
on the old principles of Law and Order, but on your principle of popular
sovereignty." Dorr's view about what "could have been the result of successful force in behalf of the People's Constitution" was "certainly correct."[112]

However, the issue at hand was that Dorr had not gone far enough. As
Webster declared in his oral argument, the People's Legislature was in existence for only two days.[113] If the Supreme Court had "decided that the
charter government had no legal existence" after April 1842, Taney argued
that "the laws passed by its legislature during that time were nullities; its
taxes wrongfully collected; its salaries and compensation to its officers ille-
gally paid."[114] If the Charter government was illegitimate, then the constitution adopted in the fall of 1842 was also illegitimate. Taney was not about
to allow "one action of trespass to vindicate one disputed theory of government" in order to throw Rhode Island into chaos.[115]

In terms of the Guarantee Clause, Taney was careful to read it in conjunction with the second clause of Article IV, Section 4 dealing with domestic violence. Taney did not say a word about the definition of republican government, though he did say that to even contemplate the question would lead to "anarchy."[116] Reading the domestic insurrection provision as conferring authority on Congress and the president to protect state governments, Taney argued that the Supreme Court lacked the jurisdiction to decide upon the nature of a state's republican form of government.[117] It "was the province of a court to expound the law, not to make it," said Taney.[118] The chief justice took the view that Tyler's promise of aid to Samuel Ward King constituted recognition of the government's authority and republican character.[119] By adopting the Enforcement Acts of 1792, 1795, and 1807, Congress delegated discretionary authority to the President to act when any state requested assistance from the national government.[120] In Taney's analysis, the issue was purely a federal matter. This reasoning placed him squarely against Calhoun's interpretation of the Guarantee Clause.[121] According to Taney, the Guarantee Clause established the rule that Congress must "decide what government is established in the State before it can determine whether it is republican or not." The right to "decide," said Taney, lay with Congress, "and not in the courts."[122] The *Luther* opinion recognized that whatever rights or wrongs had been committed in Rhode Island in 1841–1842, little could be gained by giving *ex post facto* recognition to a government that had existed for a couple of days and had never been able to assert its own authority.[123]

In describing and upholding the use of martial law to put down the rebellion, Taney argued that events in Rhode Island in the spring of 1842 constituted "a state of war." The "established government," in Taney's analysis, "resorted to the rights and usages of war to maintain itself, and to overcome the *unlawful opposition*."[124] Indeed, the terms "unlawful" or "unlawfully" appeared three more times in the opinion when discussing the Dorrites, while "lawfulness" was linked to the government under Samuel Ward King, suggesting that Taney was practicing anything but judicial restraint. Taney clearly did not view the activities of the Rhode Island Suffrage Association as peaceful and legal. With this dismissal, the "Rhode Island Question" ceased to vex the federal government. Dorr would later remove the appeal of his treason conviction from the Court's docket. After reading the opinion, Dorr noted that the Supreme Court had only ruled that the *Luther* cases involved "a political and not a legal subject. The Court declined to give their opinion upon the R.I. Question for this reason. They regard the government in fact as the government in right, so far as they are concerned." Dorr never commented on Justice Levi Woodbury's dissenting opinion, which condemned the Court's reasoning in upholding the Charter government's issuance of martial law.[125] Dorr still possessed an unquestionable belief in the doctrine of the people's sovereignty after the decision in the *Luther* cases. However, the growing sectional tensions and the divisive nature of the slavery issue in national politics created great theoretical problems for Dorr's ideology in his final days.

Chapter 9

The Legacy of the People's Sovereignty

I trust our friend Gov. Dorr will be able to attend the Baltimore Convention. He has so devoted himself to the American Democracy that his name and views command much influence. He has proved his attachment to the principles of our party by greater sacrifices than any other man in the Union.

Lewis Cass to William Simons, May 28, 1852

Though he lived for a time with his younger brother Allen in the town of Cumberland, just north of Providence, by 1850 Thomas Dorr was back in his parents' home on Benefit Street. The bachelor Dorr expressed regret that he never married, however, his letters reveal a close connection to a number of women, particularly Catharine Williams, who wrote but never published a biography of her friend in the late 1850s.[1] Dorr's poor health and debilitating rheumatic flare-ups confined him to his bed for months on end, forcing him to dictate letters to his mother and to his ever-faithful friend Walter Burges. Sullivan Dorr, Jr., who also still lived in the mansion, assisted his mother in caring for his older brother. After 1850 many of his letters began with an apology for a long delay in responding. In October 1850, Williams, who had left Providence and relocated to Brooklyn, believed Dorr to be at death's door. Dorr was probably not comforted by her remark that she looked forward to the day when the two would meet in Heaven.[2]

Thomas Dorr had been sickly for most of his adult life. As a student at Harvard, he spent more time in Providence than Cambridge because he needed to be under the care of the family physician. Since his teenage years, he suffered from severe respiratory problems and stomach ailments, but an eighteenth-month stint in prison had taken a severe toll. Ironically, Dorr had led a charge to build the prison that devastated his health in the 1830s in order to end the ghastly spectacle of public executions that were drawing thousands of onlookers to Providence.[3] In 1847, Dorr was adamant that while his "physical constitution" had been greatly impaired, his enemies had not broken his "spirit" or forced a "recantation of principles" as they so desired.[4] Though sick and lame, Dorr still believed he could have some influence on the course of American politics. His first order of business, however, was to find a steady income.

Even though Dorr was released from prison in 1845, the General Assembly refused for years to restore his civil and political rights. His rights would not be restored until 1851 when the Democrats took control of the Assembly.[5] Dorr did find some solace in the fact that the so-called Dorr Democrats in the General Assembly and his uncle, Governor Philip Allen, managed to implement many of the reforms that he had advocated throughout his life, including the secret ballot, abolition of the death penalty, improvements in teacher education, and provisions for the care of the poor.[6] Not wanting to live off an allowance from his father and prevented from practicing law in the state, Dorr tried for several years to succeed in business. He wrote to old friends in New York City and Westmoreland, New Hampshire, encouraging them to invest in an idea he had to construct an iron foundry in Rhode Island. He also tried to attract business partners in a wild venture to make imitation leather.[7] In desperation, he reached out to Edmund Burke to secure a paid position as a writer or editor for the *Washington Union*.[8] Eventually, Dorr managed to secure an income as a writer for and then editor of the *Republican Herald* in Providence, a paper that was supportive of his cause a decade before.[9] He also wrote editorials extolling the virtues of the Democratic Party for William Cullen Bryant's *New York Evening Post*, a newspaper that vigorously supported Dorr's cause in 1842.[10]

Dorr spent a considerable amount of time organizing his voluminous papers and writing several autobiographical sketches that could be used as guides by future biographers. He always held out hope that either John O'Sullivan or David Dudley Field would take up the task, though neither found the time.[11] Consuming Dorr during the final years of his life was the issue of slavery's expansion westward, which appeared more and more ominous as Whigs and Democrats tried to find a solution to a seemingly intractable problem. Dorr saw the "slavery question" as a "dark cloud" descending "upon the country," filling the minds of a "large portion of the People" with "fearful forebodings of the threatening storm."[12]

The immediate source of the controversy over slavery arose from the acquisition of new lands after the Mexican War. In 1846, the Wilmot Proviso ushered in a new era in American politics where the status and future of slavery took center stage. The proviso, introduced by Pennsylvania Democratic Congressman David Wilmot as an amendment to an appropriations bill, provided that "as an express and fundamental condition to the acquisition of any territory from the Republic of Mexico by the United States . . . neither slavery nor involuntary servitude shall ever exist in any part of said territory."[13] The proviso's antecedent was hallowed, drawing directly from the antislavery language of the 1787 Northwest Ordinance. As the debate over the Wilmot Proviso commenced, party lines crumbled as every northerner, Democrat and Whig alike, supported it, while nearly all southerners opposed it.[14] Dorr was thoroughly opposed to the proviso and urged "true" Democrats to work against it.[15] Dorr argued that "non-intervention with slavery in the territories" constituted the path forward for the Democracy.[16]

In an 1850 editorial in the *Republican Herald* that would surely have left his old associates in the Rhode Island Anti-Slavery Society scratching their heads, Dorr argued that the Slave Power thesis was a vast conspiracy promoted by northern abolitionists to stir up sectional controversy. Defying the logic he used to view the American political order in the 1830s, he maintained that the 3/5 clause gave no added power to the southern states. He also went back on his stance about the power of Congress to prohibit the western expansion of slavery and to end both slavery and the slave trade in the nation's capital. "There is only one possible ground of adjustment, and that is to refer the whole subject to the People of the territories, with a total non-intervention on the part of Congress," wrote Dorr.[17] Dorr now equated party with principle and held the concept of Union over the expansive view of liberty he advocated for as a young man. He clearly regarded the Democratic Party and popular sovereignty as the only hope for the country— they were one and inseparable. This is not to say that he condoned slavery nor is it to say that he developed a deep admiration for the South. Dorr returned to a conviction he expressed in the early 1830s: the "dissolution of the Union" was "a greater evil than the continuance of slavery in this country."[18] Dorr repeated this phrase often in the late 1840s and early 1850s.

Beginning in the late 1840s, Dorr invented a new history for himself that completely left out his association with the northern abolitionist movement. He now believed that his opinions on the subject of slavery had always "coincided with those of Mr. Jefferson," though his antislavery activism in the late 1830s went far beyond anything the Sage of Monticello uttered in the post-Revolutionary period.[19] Dorr's self-conscious attempt to get right with Jefferson did disservice to his membership in the American Anti-Slavery Society and contrasted sharply with his deep-seated belief that blacks, both free and enslaved, deserved to be a part of American society. Prior to 1848, Dorr never made any of the pseudo-scientific or racist observations about the innate mental and physical inferiority of blacks that were commonplace in Jefferson's writings, especially his *Notes on the State of Virginia*. It is hard to imagine Dorr commenting on how the "Southern Slaves" were "better off and more happy than any equal number of their own race in Africa" during his time as a delegate to the annual meetings of the AASS.[20] Dorr repeated this sentiment, which he first expressed in his diary, in a lengthy letter written in 1851 stating that "the whole mass of slaves in all the Southern states" were "actually better off, better provided for, and possess a better security of life . . . than any equal number of people of their own color in Africa." Dorr now believed slavery to be a great evil perpetrated on southern whites. In racist language that was not part of his persona a decade before, he said that the "slave" was brought over to "serve" a "better race." Some "now living may see the day when the most profitable use that can be made of a negro slave *will be to give him a free passage to Africa, the country of his forefathers*." The African country was "destined" somehow "to receive a compensation for the wrongs done to it by the slave-trade," though Dorr did not offer specifics. However, Africa should take solace in knowing ex-slaves would be bringing back a "superior civilization."[21] By the 1850s, Dorr talked of slavery in terms of its degrading effect on whites and not in terms of its barbarism or the threat the institution posed to representative democracy.

Dorr, like Jefferson, was content to "leave slavery to the hands where it legally rests and which only are responsible for it; and committing it as a moral question to the workings of public sentiment in the slave states and to the Providence of God." He hoped for an "exodus of blacks to Africa," which he envisioned as working similar to the waves of Irish immigrants leaving their homeland to come to the "shores" of America. He did not specify whether this "exodus" would be conducted on a voluntary basis or if it would be forced upon those slaves who considered the United States their home by such agencies as the American Colonization Society.[22] In his analysis, slavery began "as an interest" and now had to "decline as an interest" before the South would even contemplate giving it up. If northern abolitionists continued to agitate the question, Dorr believed a "revolution" was inevitable.[23] His position on the extension of slavery was no different from the one taken by Benjamin F. Hallett in the summer of 1844, when he argued that the annexation of Texas could be viewed as an antislavery measure because it would help to diffuse the slave population within the United States and eventually lead to the triumph of free labor.[24] Both Dorr and Hallett had been ardent antislavery Democrats in the late 1830s, but by the mid-1840s both men had moved away from their earlier criticism of the Slave Power.[25]

Dorr did not perceive a change in his own ideology. He saw his ideas being adopted by a large segment of a party that supported his cause in 1842 and, therefore, his devotion to that party only grew. For Dorr and many northern Democrats slavery was a compromise that they had to live with and, therefore, abolitionism was seen as a threat to the republic's precarious political balance. As historian John Ashworth has argued, the "Democratic creed" resembled a "religious faith" and the party itself was "akin to a church."[26]

In 1842, Dorr's constituents were average working-class white males—the political backbone of the Jacksonian Democrats. Dorr never expressly embarked on his attempt to reform Rhode Island's archaic governing structure in order to free southern slaves or enfranchise free blacks, though on the latter point Dorr did do his best to ensure that blacks would be included in the People's Constitution. As the 1840s unfolded, Dorr and his allies in the northern branch of the Democratic Party were faced with a dilemma. Their constituents were largely white males concerned about "free soil" and "free labor." As Dorr noted repeatedly to his political correspondents, any attempt to end slavery, or even restrict it, would result in secession and civil war.[27] He believed that northern abolitionist "exhortations to slaveholders to abolish slavery on moral grounds" had as much "weight" as the critique of "factory labor" as "oppressing and deteriorating" to "operatives." Dorr grew increasingly disdainful of what he perceived as the moral absolutism of the abolitionists. "After slavery became unprofitable in the northern states it was abolished as a moral evil!" wrote Dorr in his diary. He believed the South would "do the like under the same circumstances."[28] Dorr sought to recast the struggle over slavery as a straightforward quarrel over interests, because such quarrels, in his analysis, were susceptible to political deal making in ways that stark confrontations between absolutes were not.

It is certainly no coincidence that Dorr's musing about slavery and his submission on some level to the mindless negrophobia of many northern Democrats occurred around the time of the Free Soil revolt. The schism within the Democratic coalition had been apparent to observers since 1844, when the rift between Van Buren and Calhoun loyalists burst into the open over the annexation of Texas. In the late 1830s, Dorr was thoroughly opposed to the extension of slavery into the southwest. That opposition had all but vanished by 1844 when the acquisition of Texas was linked with the doctrine of Manifest Destiny and the candidacy of James Polk.[29] In line with Senator Robert Walker of Mississippi, Benjamin Hallett, and John O'Sullivan, Dorr believed in the dubious theory that the annexation of Texas would actually speed the end of slavery.[30]

By the late 1840s, however, many antislavery Democrats had become disillusioned with the direction of the party and its connection to slavery's westward expansion. At the 1848 Democratic convention, New York supporters of Martin Van Buren bolted and formed their own party, nominating Martin Van Buren on a platform that excluded slavery from the territories. These so-called Barnburner Democrats could pander no longer to the Slave Power. Ominously, Alabama's William Lowndes Yancey also left the 1848 Democratic convention, but he did so on the grounds that popular sovereignty failed to fully secure slaveholders' access to the territories. The Free Soilers believed that the Democratic Party had made a Faustian deal to protect and promote slavery.

The "Conscience Whig" Charles Francis Adams, son of John Quincy Adams, was selected as the vice presidential nominee under the Free Soil banner. The Free Soil platform played down the moral evils of slavery, focusing instead on keeping the territories free for the benefit of white labor.[31] Van Buren, a Jacksonian stalwart who spent most of his life trying to suppress sectional tensions, was now leading a third-party movement that threatened to upset the delicate balance of the American political order. The fact that a former president and the son of another were willing to abandon their respective parties to run on an antislavery platform showed that opposition to slavery had spread far beyond abolitionist ranks. The 1848 Free Soil campaign became the "electoral expression" of the Wilmot Proviso.[32] Though Free Soil philosophy was right in line with the antislavery positions he staked out in the 1830s, in Dorr's mind the Free Soilers were composed of dangerous latitudinarians intent on enhancing centralized power.

Dorr informed his old friend John Greenleaf Whittier that loyalty to the Democracy and popular sovereignty was a matter of "wisdom and patriotism." In Dorr's analysis, the Free Soil Party was Whiggery in disguise. Dorr wanted nothing to do with a "3rd party which proposes other candidates and tends to lead to the overthrow of the national democracy."[33] Rejecting his previously held beliefs, Dorr reacted strongly against "abolition factionists."[34] As he noted in his diary, "which is the greater right, that of the white race, who are the vast majority, to live in prosperity under the federal Constitution, or that of the Southern negroes to insist on a nullification of the Constitution, which shall involve the white race in disunion, ruin and misery?"[35] It was because of the "strong fanatical excitement" of abolitionism that the country had "been pushed to the brink of a precipice, to the unfathomable gulf of disunion," wrote Dorr several years later as he reflected on the schism within the Democratic Party.[36]

Dorr was pleased that "a friend to the Rhode Island cause of 1842," Michigan Senator Lewis Cass, eventually received the Democratic presidential nomination in 1848.[37] Cass served as the military and civil governor of the Michigan territory from 1813 to 1831. As secretary of war under Andrew Jackson, he presided over the president's Indian removal policy. Cass also served as ambassador to France and was a leading proponent of the annexation of Texas in 1844–1845.[38] Benjamin Hallett's argument before the Taney Court in the *Luther v. Borden* case in January 1848 and John O'Sullivan's musings on the "Rhode Island Question" in the March issue of the *Democratic Review* of that year helped to revive the memory of the Dorr Rebellion in time for the Democratic convention in Baltimore.[39] Democrats also drew inspiration that year from the political revolutions that were tearing across Europe. British Chartists organized massive demonstrations in favor of political reform, the French replaced their monarchy with a republic, and the Hungarians proclaimed their independence from Austria. Dorr followed the European political revolutions, all of which eventually failed, with a close eye.[40] Suffering from a severe rheumatic attack that prevented him from descending the stairs in his parents' home, Dorr still managed to draft several resolutions on the "inherent and inalienable right of the people, in their sovereign capacity, to make and to amend their form of government" and the struggle for "political rights and equal justice."[41] His handiwork made it into the final wording of the platform.

Lewis Cass was a leading proponent of the formula Democrats had constructed in order to preserve sectional harmony on the slavery issue. Cass originally favored the Wilmot Proviso but by February 1847 he had arrived at the conclusion that it was "a firebrand thrown among us which threatens the most disastrous results."[42] Whigs feared that Cass's success in November would be a "triumph of the new school which has infused into the public mind an appetite for war, conquest, and unlimited territorial aggrandizement, to say nothing of Dorrism."[43] Though never advanced in the Jacksonian period as a solution for the problem of slavery in the western territories, popular sovereignty clearly owed much to the "legacy" of the Dorr Rebellion.[44] The version of popular sovereignty that Dorr did so much to advance in the early 1840s was more radical in terms of its emphasis on the right of the people to alter or abolish their form of government. The version of popular sovereignty that he championed at the end of the decade was still predicated on the right of the people to decide questions of government but it had lost some of its Revolutionary-era fervor. In June 1846, a group of New Hampshire Democrats led by Franklin Pierce, a close ally of Dorr in 1842, drafted a series of resolutions endorsing territorial expansion and hailing popular sovereignty as the proper method for deciding the question of slavery in the territories. Drawing from their numerous resolutions passed in favor of Dorr's brand of constitutionalism between 1842 and 1845, the Granite State Democrats made it clear that the decision to support or exclude slavery rested with the "citizens."[45] Cass built on these resolutions the following year in an influential, though artfully vague public letter that was designed to win the favor of both northern and southern Democrats. Cass and Dorr both viewed the principle of federal nonintervention in the territories and popular sovereignty as the only way the country could avoid a civil war. Thomas Hart Benton, a vocal supporter of Dorr in 1842, campaigned actively for Cass and on behalf of "harmony, union, and concession among the Democrats."[46]

In contrast to the Whig penchant for "No Territory," popular sovereignty called on Congress to leave the question of slavery to the residents.[47] Popular sovereignty used majority rule to take the slavery issue out of the hands of national politicians and move it into the hands of the people. As historian Douglas Egerton has argued, for "politicians anxious to avoid taking a public position on the explosive question of slavery expansion, popular sovereignty had the virtue of appearing to follow the revered tradition of Jeffersonian localism."[48]

In his famous December 1847 letter to Alfred O.P. Nicholson, Cass argued that congressional leadership "should be limited to the creation of popular governments and the necessary provision for their eventual admission into the Union; leaving [it] to the people inhabiting them to regulate their own internal concerns in their own way." Cass maintained that if Congress left "to the people" who would be "affected by this question, to adjust it upon their own responsibility" the libertarian tenets of democracy would be upheld.[49] Cass argued that allowing the people of each territory to decide the issue of slavery for themselves was in the tradition of the nation's founders, though he left considerable room for northerners and southerners to interpret the role of local and congressional authority in the territories. References to the Revolutionary-era doctrine of popular sovereignty did not offer any insights into the all-important question of when settlers could exercise their right to permit or legislatively prohibit slavery within a territory. When speaking before southern audiences, Cass defined popular sovereignty as operating only at the moment when a territory petitioned for entry into the Union. Up until that time, slavery would be legal. When speaking to northern audiences, Cass hinted that a territorial government could outlaw slavery if the majority willed it before statehood.[50]

In principle, popular sovereignty symbolized a weakening of the Old Democrats' proslavery rigidity. By opening up the possibility for territorial settlers to deal with the question of slavery for themselves, the ideology upheld the power of Congress to make law in this realm and flew in the face of southern rights ultras looking for a territorial slave code. As historian Yonatan Eyal has argued, providing Americans with a "chance to outlaw slavery was a large step forward from the time when Andrew Jackson's administration refused to forward abolitionist tracts through the mail."[51] After 1848, Dorr clearly believed this to be a step in the right direction. The Free Soilers had tested the bonds of Union with their "experiment" to "employ the machinery of the national government in regulating the slavery question."[52] Popular sovereignty allowed for slavery to be regulated by the people of the territories. It would not be until the events of bloody Kansas in 1855–1856 that the doctrine would be considered, as Abraham Lincoln eloquently argued, a "deceitful pretense for the benefit of slavery."[53]

Cass and the Democrats attempted to be everything to everyone in 1848. They tried to count voters in different sections of the Union by obscuring the implications of popular sovereignty on slavery in the territories. The Whigs also tried to be everything to everyone, but they were more skillful at it. The fact that they took no clear-cut position on the question of slavery's extension did not hurt, either.[54] The question of federal authority over slavery's place in the territories remained the great unresolved issue of democratic politics after Zachary Taylor, a Louisiana slaveholder, bested Cass at the polls. Van Buren captured just under 300,000 votes, and the Free Soil Party as a whole elected nine Congressmen, indicating that the sectional issues were important to a segment of the electorate.

The discovery of gold in California in 1848 began to unsettle the sectional balance even further. President Taylor made it clear that he would admit California and New Mexico into the Union as free states, bypassing the territorial stage if need be. Taylor even indicated that he would not veto the Wilmot Proviso should it resurface in Congress. Most sober, thoughtful Americans knew that their nation was at the brink of disaster. Fistfights broke out on the floor of Congress and secession and war were openly discussed.[55]

When California asked to be admitted to the Union as a free state, southern politicians opposed the measure out of fear that it would upset the delicate sectional balance. Kentucky Senator Henry Clay, a fierce opponent of Dorr in 1842, offered a plan that after months of debate led to California entering the Union as a free state and the abolition of the slave trade, but not slavery itself in Washington, D.C. The status of slavery in the remaining territories acquired from Mexico was left to the decision of the local white inhabitants. As part of the so-called Compromise of 1850, the Fugitive Slave Act of 1793 was also strengthened. Particularly offensive were the provisions that allowed a slave owner to track a slave into a free state, then either personally arrest the slave, or enlist the aid of local law enforcement officers. Under the law, the slave was brought before a local magistrate for a summary proceeding. The owner needed only to show proof of the slave's identity and proof of ownership. No defense was possible, nor was the alleged slave allowed to testify. The 1850 Fugitive Slave Law created a scenario where free blacks in the North could be falsely accused by southern bounty hunters and have no legal recourse open to them.[56]

The legal wing of the antislavery movement frequently argued that the new fugitive slave law was unconstitutional because it denied blacks life, liberty, and due process of law—exactly what Dorr believed was denied to the majority of Rhode Islanders, both white and black, in 1841–1842. In attacking Daniel Webster for his support of the revamped fugitive slave law, Whittier referred to the Massachusetts Whig politician as "Ichabod," which in Hebrew means "inglorious one." It is likely that Whittier saw the same fall from grace in his old friend Thomas Dorr, a one-time champion of political antislavery. The poet's belief in the immorality of slavery would lead him to the conviction that people should follow God's command, even if it opposed laws made by God's people. Dorr, who embraced his own higher law version of American constitutionalism in 1841–1842, now rejected this view.

In a telling example of the extent to which Dorr had become a devout party man, the former proponent of jury trials for escaped bondsmen actually argued that the new fugitive slave law was a "stronger protection against any unlawful seizure than the fugitive *ever before possessed*." The Democratic Party, said Dorr, was "honorably committed to the Compromise Platform in all its parts; and they are ready to stand or fall by it, as a measure of the duty and of safety, of Patriotism and of Peace."[57] Dorr stated the same in an August 1850 editorial, a month before the final version of the Fugitive Slave Act passed the Senate.[58] However, even after reading the final version of the law, which clearly afforded no legal protection to accused fugitives, Dorr did not change his mind.

The innovation of the Fugitive Slave Law, as Dorr surely knew, but loath to admit, was to turn the existing network of federal court commissioners into a slave-catching bureaucracy and facilitators of kidnapping.[59] Ironically, George Teomoh, a fugitive slave who had escaped from Virginia in 1853, was hired to work in the Dorr family mansion in 1854.[60] The draconian law was vilified by antislavery advocates for requiring northern states to cooperate in the return of escaped bondsmen. The Reverend Charles Woodhouse, a close associate of Dorr's during his time in Westmoreland, New Hampshire, in 1842, argued to Dorr that the act was "unchristian and unconstitutional."[61] Soon after its passage, abolitionists and antislavery advocates in the North formed vigilance committees to protect free blacks from being kidnapped. In October 1850, the prominent Boston minister Theodore Parker organized a committee to smuggle away two fugitives—William and Ellen Craft—who were in danger of being sent back to slavery in Georgia. In early 1851, a crowd of black Bostonians stormed the courthouse to rescue another fugitive named Shadrach Minkins. In April 1851, authorities were finally successful in returning a fugitive captured on the streets of Boston to slavery.[62]

During this period, Dorr railed in his diary against the "higher law men." The "consciences of the higher law men, by which they are each separately authorized to set aside valid and unrepealed laws and constitutions, seems to be like dark lanterns which shed no rays abroad."[63] In his view, "northern exhortations to slaveholders to abolish slavery on moral grounds" had about "as much weight as the exhortations of southern men would have on factory owners of the North on the ground that factory labor is oppressing and deteriorating the Northern operatives."[64] In a letter to the chairman of the Louisiana Democratic Party, Dorr attacked the "higher law" antislavery Whigs, such as former New York governor William Seward, who attempted to capture the fugitive Dorr in 1842. Dorr believed that Seward was attempting to "authorize—not a majority of the whole People—but each individual, singly, and separately, by virtue of an inward light, and only by himself, to judge, set at naught and render null and void, so far as his power will reach, the Constitution and laws of the country, and to render its institutions to anarchy and chaos."[65]

In March 1850, Seward gave a landmark speech in the Senate against extending additional political concessions to the South by arguing that there was a "higher law" than the Constitution. As James Oakes has noted, Seward's "crucial point was that the 'higher' antislavery principles of natural law were already embedded within the Constitution," most notably in the document's preamble. Dorr had argued the same in 1841–1842. Moreover, Seward articulated two points that Dorr had advocated for in the 1830s: that the inexorable tide of human history meant that slavery was on the road to extinction and that while the federal government could not directly interfere with slavery in the states where it already existed, it could and should undermine slavery in the areas where it had control.[66] Some abolitionists and Free-Soilers used Seward's logic as a justification for violating the Fugitive Slave Act. Dorr disagreed. Still harboring hatred for Seward's attempt to arrest him in 1842, Dorr wrote that Seward argues that the "majority of the whole have no right to act without legislative permission," and "in the same breath," argues that "each individual is separately a sovereign and can set aside any law."[67] Antislavery advocates firmly believed that federal officials could not be compelled to hunt down fugitive slaves and re-enslave them because slavery was only recognized by southern state law. As Charles Sumner argued in the Senate in 1852, freedom was "national"; slavery was "sectional."[68]

At the height of the fugitive slave crisis, abolitionist Gamaliel Bailey's *National Era* attempted to make a point about the supposed *unwillingness* of the Tyler administration to protect Rhode Island from rebellion, but the *willingness* to use federal resources to assist in the capture of a fugitive slave. A "rebellion breaks out in Rhode Island; that rebellion is countenanced in the first city of the Union; a great dinner is given to Dorr by the magnates of the Democratic party in the city of New York; a sword is presented to him; he is escorted to the ship that is to convey him and his fortunes to the civil war in his native State" but the federal government "folds its arms" and issues "no rebuke."[69]

The hypocrisy that Bailey perceived in terms of federal power was of no concern to Dorr. For the former People's Governor, it was all about politics and the ability to elect a Democrat to the White House in 1852. As Edmund Burke correctly noted, the "party which sustains the great compromise measures of the last Congress including the Fugitive Slave Law will in my judgment elect the next president."[70] Pennsylvania Senator James Buchanan advised Democrats throughout the country to give a strong level of "support" to the compromise measures. Buchanan believed that it was "suicidal" for Democrats to oppose the compromise legislation.[71] For Dorr, Buchanan, and Burke, the Compromise of 1850 was a natural manifestation of the party's core constitutional principles. During the long summer of debates in Congress in 1850, Dorr saw "the slavery question . . . lowering like a dark cloud upon the country." But with passage of the various acts in September, Dorr believed that the "bolt" had "been drawn from the cold; the force of the storm [had] spent itself." Secession had been averted.[72]

Dorr raged against the "negrophilists and the negromaniacs" who were upset with the Compromise. Dorr ardently believed that the 1850 measures "saved" the Union "from the greatest peril it has ever yet encountered." He declared that "constitutional laws ought to be supported and obeyed." Dorr considered "opposition" to the Compromise "opposition to the Constitution itself."[73] While he did not specify what he meant by "opposition," there could be little doubt that Dorr was referring to the fear that northerners would fail to live up to the new Fugitive Slave Law and obstruct the capture and rendition of fugitive slaves.

After Dorr's political rights were restored in 1851 by the Rhode Island General Assembly, his old friend Edmund Burke wrote to him expressing the hope that he would "take a more active part in the general politics of the country." Burke, the editor of the influential *Washington Union*, said that he hoped that "during the next presidential canvass" Dorr would visit "Washington and address the Democracy of [the] national metropolis in a mass meeting." "We all know your talents and capacities, and that you need but step into the arena of national politics to achieve a high and enviable distinction," wrote the New Hampshire Democrat.[74]

Burke believed that the 1852 campaign should be run on the issues of "Young America," which included "sympathy for the liberals of Europe and expansion of the American Republic southward and westward, and the grasping of the magnificent prow of the commerce of the Pacific."[75] Young Americans sought to promote the younger generation of leaders who could help heal the party and defeat the Whigs in 1852. In a letter to Democrats in Chicago, Dorr praised the "multiplication of association" of "younger members of the democratic party" that had popped up all over Illinois. Dorr praised the "zeal and energy of the younger" Democrats and urged them to instill vigor and a renewed vitality to the political ranks of the party.[76]

Adherents to the Young America philosophy believed in the time-honored tradition of states' rights, but also in pushing the Jacksonian coalition in new directions through the embrace of commerce, political reform, moderate tariff regulation, and expansionism.[77] However, first and foremost on their minds, as Dorr said so often in this period, was preventing "disunion."[78] Dorr encouraged all Free Soil Democrats to return to the fold in order to protect the country. If "any portion of the party have fallen into the error of attempting to accomplish under our limited national system measures which are impossible and prohibited by the letter or by the spirit of the national compact," said Dorr, "they have now the best opportunity to retrace their steps and to consent to learn . . . the just limits of the federal system." Dorr argued that the "will of the majority" could not be used to "compel the inhabitants of territories" to abolish slavery.[79]

Dorr was equally adamant that southern fire-eaters, particularly the attendees of the Nashville Convention in June 1850, should cease beating the drum of secession and disunion. A large portion of those delegates argued that the exclusion of slavery from California would destroy the equilibrium in the U.S. Senate, that the abolition of the slave trade in the nation's capital would set a precedent for a series of antislavery measures that would spell the ruin of the South, and that the institution of slavery was at the heart of southern society.[80] A second Nashville Convention met in November 1850. Delegates passed a measure asserting the constitutional right of secession. The governors of Georgia and Mississippi then called for special conventions to debate secession.[81]

The supposedly sacrosanct Compromise of 1850 was not accepted by all Democrats. "You are aware that upon the passage of the compromise measures, a large portion (perhaps a majority) of the democratic party of several southern states, and particularly of Georgia and Mississippi, became thoroughly alienated from the National Democracy . . . and proceeded to organize a sectional party under the name of 'Southern Rights,' wrote Hopkins Holsey, an editor of the *Southern Banner*. Pro-Union political coalitions were able to secure victory over secession-minded foes in 1851–1852; however, the die had been cast. Even the pro-Union resolutions passed by southern state legislatures in the wake of the compromise contained an unspoken threat of disunion. If the North did not live up to its end of the bargain by executing the provisions of the stringent Fugitive Slave Act, secession would be back on the table.[82] Dorr, a keen observer of national politics, was already aware of the threat posed by pro-secession Democrats. In a letter to a New York Democratic editor, Dorr made it clear that these southern fire-eaters were a "faction" that needed to be destroyed. True Democrats, in Dorr's analysis, were "defenders of the Constitution and the Union."[83] The man whom Dorr hoped would heal the party in 1852 was an old friend from New Hampshire, a "firm friend of the people's cause" in 1842.[84]

Former Senator Franklin Pierce earned the Democratic nomination on the forty-ninth ballot at the June 1852 convention in Baltimore. Dorr originally supported Lewis Cass for the nomination but quickly abided by the decision of the convention and threw his support to Pierce.[85] In the weeks before the Democratic convention, Pierce endorsed the Compromise of 1850. "If the compromise measures are not to be substantially and firmly maintained the plain rights secured by the constitution will be trampled in the dust," wrote Pierce in a public letter.[86]

The unexpected death of Levi Woodbury in September 1851 sent party leaders searching for another unifying figure. They eventually settled on Pierce, Woodbury's former law student. Benjamin Hallett, now chairman of the National Executive Committee, along with Edmund Burke, helped to secure Pierce's victory at the convention by ensuring that the Massachusetts delegates would switch to Pierce if Lewis Cass failed in the balloting.[87] "In my judgment if at the proper time—at the Convention—you will allow your name to be used as a compromise candidate, you stand as good a chance for the nomination as any man I can think of," wrote Burke to Pierce. "In casual conversation I have asked Southern gentlemen how you would suit the South, and they have invariably replied most favorably."[88] Alabama's William R. King was selected as vice president.

On the final day of the convention a dwindling group of delegates approved a platform that stated that the federal government had no power under the Constitution to interfere with or control the "domestic institutions of the several states." The platform warned that abolitionist efforts to persuade Congress to legislate the question of slavery would bring "alarming and dangerous consequences."[89] Pierce became the candidate of an aggressively expansionist Young America faction of the Democratic coalition.[90] Young Americans believed deeply in a romantic and aggressive nationalism, something that was anathema to Dorr in the 1830s. Pierce was not simply running for president, he was running for commander-in-chief in a period when, in the hopes of many northern and southern Democrats, a new war for territory was just around the corner.

In the summer of 1852, Pierce visited Rhode Island and stayed in the Dorr family mansion on Benefit Street. Pierce knew that Dorr's *Republican Herald* was widely circulated throughout New England.[91] Though he could not go out on the stump for his old friend, Dorr did what he could to help his cause in his paper and in a series of lengthy letters promoting Pierce's candidacy. Dorr constantly argued that everything depended on the "courage and zeal of the younger portion of the party" to work to unite the party, affirm the Compromise of 1850, and defeat the Whig candidate Winfield Scott. According to Dorr, the Compromise of 1850 "proved that while it was impossible for Congress to reach the domestic institutions of the South," the "fatal specter of abolition" threatened to destroy the "Constitution and the Union." Democrats needed to unite as one to prevent this threat. According to Dorr, the reestablishment of a "united, comprehensive, and truly national democracy" would be ably led by Franklin Pierce.[92] Dorr sent several of his letters to Thomas Ritchie's *Washington Union*, then edited by the Democrat stalwart, Andrew Jackson Donelson.[93]

Dorr was careful to custom-tailor his letters to his audience. In a missive to Democrats in Concord, Dorr, of course, drew on his connection to the Granite State and the "noble response" of Democrats there to promote Pierce, the "favorite son of New Hampshire," against Scott.[94] In a letter to Louisiana Democrats, Dorr railed against the abolitionists and their "higher law doctrines."[95] Dorr would soften his stance, however, when writing to northern Democrats whom he knew had strong antislavery convictions. In a letter to a pro-Pierce Granite Club in Lynn, Massachusetts, Dorr assured the Democratic faithful that if they rallied around the Compromise of 1850 they would "restore the ascendency of democratic principles and reunite the national democracy upon the national platform," along with laying to rest the "dangerous controversies connected with states' rights" of the Calhoun wing of the party which had "agitated the country and brought in peril the constitution and the union."[96] Dorr repeated the same in a letter to Pennsylvania Democrats, but was careful to also attack the Whig tariff policies.[97]

A vast number of Free Soilers returned to the ranks of the Democratic Party in 1852, costing the antislavery Democrat John Parker Hale, who agreed to pick up the Free Soil torch, over 100,000 votes. The Democrats' ability to rally around Pierce's candidacy prevented the outbreak of the disease of political factionalism and helped to secure for Pierce a landslide victory in the electoral college over Scott.[98] In November 1852, Pierce carried all but four states, winning the Electoral College by the impressive margin of 254 to 42. Dorr ranked Pierce's victory on par with Jefferson's victory in the election of 1800 and Jackson's reelection in 1832.[99]

With popular sovereignty serving as the policy for the remaining territories acquired from Mexico, and with the Missouri Compromise line controlling unorganized lands from Jefferson's Louisiana Purchase until 1854, there were no territories, at least for the moment, capable of generating a major crisis.[100] A personal tragedy in the Pierce family before the inauguration dashed Dorr's hope that his old friend would be able to maintain the relative political calm that followed in the wake of the Compromise of 1850. In January 1853, Pierce's son Benny was killed in a railroad accident outside of Andover, Massachusetts. "I thought of the two little boys as I last saw them at your house, so hopeful and promising to the eyes of parents & friends; of the loss of one of them, sadly consoled by the possession of the other still spared . . . and I felt that there was no power in language for an affliction like this," wrote Dorr to Pierce upon hearing the tragic news. "Be merciful unto me, O God, be merciful unto me, for my soul entrusteth in thee, yea, in the shadow of thy wings will I make my refuge until these calamities be overpast," said Dorr, quoting from the same book of Psalms, which gave him such consolation while he languished in the state prison in Providence.[101]

Though he was emotionally crushed by the tragic loss of his son, as any father would be, Pierce was not psychologically impaired, as Peter Wallner, Pierce's most thorough modern biographer, has convincingly argued. Through force of his personal charm, Pierce was able to keep a disparate cabinet together for four tumultuous years, something that had not been accomplished before.[102] In the months after his son's death, he endorsed a legislative package calling for lower tariffs, expansion of the army and navy, federal government involvement in the creation of a transcontinental railroad, and the reduction of the national debt. What Pierce lacked was a member of Congress to "propose it or lead it to fruition."[103] Pierce was selected at the Baltimore convention because of his perceived ability to unify the party. As Benjamin Hallett noted at the time, the nomination "came from Virginia and the magnanimous South, as a peace-offering of Union and brotherly concord to the North."[104] Though he was able to hold his cabinet together, Pierce failed to maintain overall party unity by dispensing patronage equally amongst all factions—satisfying none of them, and bringing complaints from all sides, thus, demonstrating how the political conditions of the times made it nearly impossible to govern. Even Pierce's friend Edmund Burke deserted him after he failed to receive the lucrative federal job he was seeking. Burke believed that Pierce had unfairly dispensed patronage to Free Soil Democrats.[105]

In terms of federal appointments, many political observers, somewhat unfairly, believed that Pierce's political appointments had been "distributed in a disproportionate abundance to those who were opposed to the compact of pacification." Even Dorr believed that there were men in Pierce's cabinet who believed in "disunion."[106] According to Hopkins Holsey, the "disciples of John Calhoun" were becoming the "lords of the ascendant" in the Democratic Party under Pierce. Holsey wrote to Dorr in 1853 informing him that radical secessionists were in control of the Democratic Party in "Virginia, Georgia, Florida, Alabama, Mississippi, and Louisiana, almost exclusively through the promotion of disloyalty to the Union." Holsey was dismayed that Pierce was turning over the reins of government to those committed to the destruction of the Union. According to Holsey, the Democratic Party as a whole was facing the prospect of being under the control of men "who attempted to dissolve the government, breathing vengeance against us for defending it, whose doctrine of secession is now established as the creed of the party for that is what they mean by the Virginia and Kentucky Resolutions and Mr. Madison's report [of 1800] thereon to be carried out in their 'obvious meaning and import.'"[107]

In December 1853, Rhode Island Democratic Congressman Thomas Davis, an Irish Protestant immigrant and the husband of Paulina Kellogg Wright, an outspoken feminist and antislavery activist, told Dorr that he believed that Pierce was weak and vacillating. The political "cross current growing" out of the status of slavery in the territories was "in conflict" with our "general freedom" and will continue to "distract the occupant of the White House with vain attempts to reconcile what is in its nature irreconcilable," wrote Davis, who served with Dorr in the Rhode Island Anti-Slavery Society and had for many years held "opinions widely at variance with the national Democratic party on the great question of American slavery."[108] In the absence of effective leadership from the White House and the breakdown of the party lines, the Whigs and Democrats moved closer together on many issues, especially the role of the federal government in promoting the economy. Illinois Senator Stephen Douglas attempted to take matters into his own hands to invigorate the Democratic faithful. His goal was to ensure that the party would retain its hold on the White House in 1856.[109]

In an attempt to prevent the controversy over the spread of slavery from derailing the Democracy's belief in westward expansion, Douglas put forth popular sovereignty as the established Democratic solution to the territorial problem and announced it explicitly as the test of Democratic constitutional principles. The true Jeffersonian way to handle things, according to Douglas, was to recognize the people of each territory "as the true source of all legitimate power in respect to their internal polity."[110] Seeing a mandate in Pierce's electoral college victory over Winfield Scott, Douglas believed he could settle the territorial question and bring the party "to new heights of personal and national glory."[111] Though Douglas made perhaps the greatest contribution of any national leader to widening the schism between the sections when he drafted the Kansas-Nebraska bill, his intention was to ensure sectional harmony by strengthening the anemic Democratic Party. As Michael Morrison rightfully notes, "popular sovereignty," as Douglas understood it, was a "homeopathic cure for a nation plagued by self-doubt and disillusion."[112] Douglas did not anticipate the act's disastrous consequences. He could see the problem of organizing the territories, but he "entirely misjudged the effects" of his solution.[113] The key provision in Douglas's act that attracted so much southern support was the explicit removal of congressional control over slavery in the territories. In the minds of many southerners, the act would help "promote a true understanding of the relationship between federal and state power, from which the South might derive incalculable benefit."[114] Moderate southern Democrats, including Howell Cobb of Georgia, believed that Douglas's act would prevent the ascendancy of a sectional antislavery party and secure protection for their section of the country.[115] However, southern ultras gave the bill only lukewarm support, looking instead for greater federal protection of private property.

Initially interested only in opening the Kansas-Nebraska Territory to settlement and starting construction of a transcontinental railroad, an idea that had been percolating in his mind since 1844, Douglas soon found that the only way to secure the necessary southern support was to repeal the Missouri Compromise ban on slavery in the territories north of the 36°30′ latitude and to divide the territory in two, with both territories potentially open to slavery. In January 1854, as chairman of the Senate Committee on the Territories, Douglas did attempt to organize the territory with the Missouri Compromise line intact. However, he quickly realized that this was a pill that southern senators would simply not swallow so he adjusted his bill, with the backing of the Pierce administration, to formally repeal the 1820 compromise.[116] For his part, Pierce knew that if he came out against the bill, he would fracture the Democratic Party beyond repair and go back on his support for the Baltimore platform of 1852, which called for support for the Compromise of 1850 and the ideology of popular sovereignty.[117]

Antislavery Democrats, including Thomas Davis, were dismayed when they learned of Douglas's plan to revoke what they considered the sacrosanct Missouri Compromise. "I think it is a daring outrage on the rights of the north to attempt by means direct or indirect to permit slavery to pass north of the 30 degrees, 30 minutes," Davis wrote to Dorr on January 14, 1854. "I had always supposed that it was settled forever and that no statesman who had the welfare of his country uppermost would seek to disturb that compromise which the north submitted to reluctantly at the time of its adoption."[118] Southerners now only needed a majority in the territory to secure the establishment of slavery in an area where it had been previously excluded.

Davis's views were in line with the "Appeal of the Independent Democrats in Congress," which was first published in the *National Era* on January 24, a day after the introduction of the final Kansas-Nebraska bill. Salmon P. Chase, who coined the slogan of the "Free Soil Party—Free Soil, Free Labor, Free Men"—outlined the differences between the Free Soil and the Popular Sovereignty wings of the Democratic Party. While Douglas argued that his bill was in line with the true tenets of Jacksonian Democracy, the Free Soilers and antislavery Democrats saw only a corrupt bargain with southern politicians. "Whatever apologies may be offered for the toleration of slavery in the States, none can be offered for its extension into Territories where it does not exist, and where that extension involves the repeal of ancient law and the violation of solemn compact," wrote Chase. He continued: "Let all protest, earnestly and emphatically, by correspondence, through the press, by memorials, by resolutions of public meetings and legislative bodies, and in whatever other mode may seem expedient, against this enormous crime."[119]

In May, Davis, in an antislavery speech equally as passionate as the one that nearly cost Massachusetts Senator Charles Sumner his life in 1856, connected Douglas's bill to the influence of the Slave Power on Pierce's administration. Pulling no punches, Davis condemned southern politicians for co-opting the pure doctrine of the people's sovereignty for proslavery ends. In Davis's mindset, the bill was "maintained by the combined power of monarchy, as represented in the executive, wielding all the patronage of government by directly rewarding those who are subservient to his dictates."[120]

The Democrats sought to drape themselves in the tried-and-true planks of the party's ideology—states' rights, strict construction, majority rule, and the sanctity of the Union. In a speech in favor of the Kansas-Nebraska Act in Nashua, New Hampshire, Benjamin Hallett reminded the citizens of the Granite State, after he took a few moments to rail against the Free Soilers and abolitionists, of the previous support they had shown for Thomas Dorr. Hallett, who was serving, thanks to Pierce, as the U.S. district attorney for Massachusetts, argued that Douglas's bill was a mere continuation of Dorr's ideology. "Did you ever hear of any greater or broader principle, as a democratic principle of government than this," proclaimed Hallett. The "people of every community within the powers given by the Constitution," wrote Hallett, "should manage their own local affairs."[121]

Many supporters still believed Douglas's measures were in line with the tenets of popular sovereignty. Since the North controlled the House of Representatives and enjoyed a small majority in the Senate, it was difficult to see why this power would not be used to prevent the spread of slavery. Burke saw the territorial government bill as in line with the same principles Dorr advocated in 1842 and those that he enshrined in his massive Congressional report in 1844.[122] Removal of the 36°30′ line was simply in keeping with the tenets of popular sovereignty. Dorr never wavered in his belief that the Douglas bill would heal sectional wounds.[123] The Young America proponents of Kansas-Nebraska were as enthusiastic about organizing the territories under the rubric of popular sovereignty, vague as it might be, as the followers of Martin Van Buren were eager to minimize the evil of the paper money system in the 1830s.[124] In 1854, the opposite result was achieved. Douglas's bill drove a wedge through the party and caused massive defections.

The eventual passage of the Kansas-Nebraska Act in May 1854 served to galvanize a sizeable number of northern Democrats, northern Whigs, and Free-Soilers against what they considered a proslavery plot, adding to the threat of disunion that Dorr feared. The spread of slavery into the territories became a subject of importance for most northerners because it threatened the free labor system they had come to hold so dear. Many northerners were coming to associate democracy with free labor and not necessarily with popular sovereignty, which did not offer a guarantee of its protection. Seventy percent of northern Democratic congressmen and senators who voted for the Kansas-Nebraska Act lost their seats in the 1854 midterm election.[125] Dorr's close friend Aaron White, Jr., a former Liberty Party supporter who returned to the Democratic fold in the late 1840s without shedding his antislavery principles, was shocked at what he perceived to be the reckless behavior of Douglas and Pierce. White told Dorr that his expectation that Pierce's election would calm "antislavery agitation" was mistaken. "Our friend Judge Douglas has been stirring up that old pot of iniquity, the slavery question, which like the Devil's essence bottled . . . is never uncovered without setting all in a quarrel," wrote White.[126]

The administration, in White's analysis, would be unable to steer a course between "Charybdis and Scylla," the mythical sea monsters in Homer's *Odyssey*, located close enough to each other that they posed an inescapable threat to passing sailors. According to White, Charybdis represented the Free Soil position and Scylla represented Douglas's territorial bill. White believed that the bill would split the Democratic Party in two, much in the same way that the "Rhode Island Question" divided the party in 1842–1844. "This slavery question is likely to assume under our present administration a more alarming aspect than it has ever before," said White. "Questions of deep interest have now become mingled with abstract questions of right and wrong and our natural sympathy for the enslaved." The "old sore is re-opened with every prospect that the relapse will be worse than the original attack."[127]

Thomas Davis maintained that the Kansas-Nebraska bill was "a victory" not of "principle but of insolent power" and that he was "irreconcilably opposed to the further encroachment of the slave power." Davis had "no respect for what the slaveholders call their rights." Davis argued that Douglas's bill would be but "the beginning of a series of measures still more daring and destructive of human freedom." Davis, however, did find a glimmer of hope in the belief that the bill would "serve to awaken the free states to a sense of their impending danger."[128] The northern response to the successful rendition of the fugitive slave Anthony Burns, just a few days after the Kansas-Nebraska Act passed the House of Representatives, was an answer to Davis's prayer.[129]

On May 24, 1854, Burns was arrested as a fugitive slave and taken to the Boston Courthouse where he was placed under heavy guard. U.S. Commissioner Edward G. Loring rejected the eloquent defense prepared by Boston's antislavery bar. U.S. District Attorney Hallett, whose son Henry served as a slave catcher in Boston during this time period, petitioned Secretary of War Jefferson Davis to call out the military in order to return Burns to slavery. "Hallett, the Dorrite, the slang-whangling radical, turned into the fiercest, and most despotic engine of power," exclaimed abolitionist and famed author Richard Henry Dana, Jr., an ideological opponent of Dorr in 1842.[130] Burns was returned to Virginia, where he was jailed for a period and then sold to a planter in North Carolina. Acting even more forcefully than John Tyler had during the 1842 Dorr Rebellion, Pierce sent marines, cavalry, a revenue cutter, and heavy artillery to Boston to ensure rendition. Dorr and other northern Democrats failed to realize that the act undermined their own credibility as a progressive political force. During Pierce's years in office, more slaves were returned by federal authorities than at any other time during the fourteen years the 1850 Fugitive Slave Act was in effect.[131] In the wake of the passage of the Kansas-Nebraska Act and the rendition of Anthony Burns, American politics underwent a profound transformation that witnessed the destruction of the Whig Party and the emergence of the Republican Party, a coalition of disenchanted Whigs, antislavery Democrats, Know-Nothings, and former Free Soilers dedicated to preventing the further extension of slavery and the return of fugitive slaves.[132]

The Kansas-Nebraska Act became the subject of Abraham Lincoln's landmark speech in October 1854 in Peoria, Illinois. As Lincoln rightfully noted, Douglas's act, while grounded in the Revolutionary-era doctrine of the right of the people to decide questions of importance for themselves, failed to detail when and by whom the decision on slavery would be made— was it to be accomplished by the territorial legislature or by several hundred settlers. Unlike Dorr and Douglas, Lincoln saw the potential introduction of slavery into western territories where it had been prohibited for three decades as a moral issue. "When the white man governs himself that is self-government; but when he governs himself, and also governs another man . . . that is despotism."[133] The juxtaposition of Lincoln's views on popular

sovereignty with the Democracy's use of the doctrine became the frame-
work for much of the public, political, and courtroom debate on the status
of slavery in the American political order from 1854 to 1860.

In 1854–1855, Democrats in the North were pummeled at the polls, losing over sixty seats in Congress. In the wake of the Kansas-Nebraska bill,
New Hampshire's John Parker Hale was triumphantly returned to the Senate where he would lead the attack against his old college classmate Franklin
Pierce. Even after proslavery Missourians cast fraudulent ballots in elections
in Kansas during 1854 and 1855, Pierce recognized the legitimacy of the re-
sulting proslavery legislature and replaced Andrew Reeder, the territorial
governor, with an openly proslavery Wilson Shannon. Settlers from the free
states soon established their own rival government in Topeka in a manner
not unlike the Dorrites in 1841–1842 and wrote a constitution that prohibited slavery (and free blacks) from the Kansas territory.[134]

In May 1856, violence erupted in Lawrence, Kansas, a free-soil stronghold. Abolitionist John Brown and several of his sons sought revenge for
the "sack of Lawrence." Brown and his boys massacred five proslavery settlers, two of whom were previously slave-catchers, near Pottawatomie
Creek. Eventually, 200 people lost their lives in what became known as
Bleeding Kansas, completely discrediting Douglas's policy of popular sovereignty as a cure for sectional ills. Three years later, Brown would become
the second man convicted of treason against a state after he led an abortive
raid on the federal arsenal at Harpers Ferry, Virginia. Unlike Dorr, however,
Brown was executed.[135]

During the controversy over the drafting of a constitution in the Kansas
territory, the antislavery John Parker Hale took to the floor of the Senate to
protest the interference of proslavery stalwarts, especially President Pierce.
In his speech, Hale went into a lengthy diatribe about Pierce's past support
for Thomas Dorr. Hale quoted in full from an 1842 New Hampshire state
legislature resolve that condemned President John Tyler for his support of
the Rhode Island Charter authorities. Hale then rewrote the resolution, sub-
stituting "Pierce" for "Tyler," in order to capture the scene in Kansas:

> That Franklin Pierce, the acting President of the United States, in
> interfering with, and assuming to decide, by the arm of the military
> power of the federal Government, the question of Slavery pending
> between the people and the Pro-Slavery party of Kansas thereby for a
> time prostrating the cause of free suffrage and paralyzing the efforts

of its friends in that Territory has been guilty of a flagrant usurpation of constitutional power.[136]

Hale clearly recognized the hypocrisy of northern Democrats who were willing to support Dorr's conception of the people's sovereignty in 1842 and the condemnation of presidential interference, but not in 1856, if it meant stopping the encroachment of slavery in Kansas. As Horace Greeley's *New York Tribune* declared, "it was all very well for the Providence Plantationers to make a Constitution for themselves. That was Popular Sovereignty vindicated. But it is all very ill for the people of Kansas to do the same thing. That is treason."[137]

Benjamin Hallett's willingness to distort history knew no bounds. In a speech in Keene, New Hampshire, in July 1856, he argued that the Dorrites immediately *backed down* in April 1842 once it was clear that President Tyler would support the Charter authorities if he deemed it necessary.[138] Hallett's attempt to prevent the events of 1842 in Rhode Island from being used as justification for the stance taken by free-soil settlers in Kansas was self-serving and pathetic even for his normally low standards. Hallett condemned those who compared the free-soil Topeka Constitution with the People's Constitution.

Stephen Douglas's attempt to use popular sovereignty as the panacea for sectional tensions ended about as well as Dorr's invocation of the theme in 1842. Though the Democratic Party united in 1856 under a platform written by Hallett, antislavery Democrats fled the party and joined the nascent Republican coalition. As historian Allan Nevins noted, Hallett and Stephen Douglas "had converted more men to intransigent freesoil doctrine in two months than [William Lloyd] Garrison and [Wendell] Phillips had converted to abolitionism in twenty years."[139] The 1856 Cincinnati platform endorsed the southern version of popular sovereignty that denied territorial residents the right to settle the question of slavery until they reached the stage of drafting a constitution.[140] However, even this concession was not enough to appease ardent slavocrats. As Mississippi Senator Albert Gallatin Brown observed in 1858, if the "doctrine of popular sovereignty is to prevail, law or no law, then Dorr was right." Brown said he believed Dorr to be "very wrong." He did not want to see Dorr's ideology used to support the antislavery forces in Kansas. Brown said he had no faith in "popular sovereignty" to cure sectional ills.[141] Instead, Brown put his faith in Chief Justice Roger Taney, who in March 1857 in the case of *Dred Scott v. Sanford* defined popular sovereignty as the right of the people in a territory to determine the status of slavery only when they drafted a constitution asking for admission to the Union. Territorial legislatures therefore could not prohibit slavery or restrict the right of a person to hold slaves as property.[142] The coming of the Civil War was caused by the clash between the competing and mutually exclusive visions of popular sovereignty articulated by various elements within the Democratic Party and the principle of federal exclusion of slavery in the territories that the Republican Party championed.

Coda

Never chosen by direct popular vote for any national office, Thomas Wilson Dorr became a Democratic martyr in 1844, helping James K. Polk defeat the perennial Whig Party candidate Henry Clay in a transformative presidential election. Polk's triumph over Clay, however, set in motion a chain of events that would nearly destroy the country a decade and a half later. If Dorr had been given to self-criticism, the Mexican-American War and the controversy over the 1854 Kansas-Nebraska Act might have led him to contemplate his role in infusing popular sovereignty into antebellum political ideology. In the late 1840s and early 1850s, Dorr faced a major moral dilemma: to have his principles vindicated was to risk the destruction of the country he so deeply loved; to fail was akin to heaping further disgrace on his name. Perhaps it was best that he did not live long enough to see the rift that would become a chasm within the Democratic Party in 1860.[1]

Dorr had never displayed great capacity for introspection. Even in the 1830s, Dorr was talking of what a young generation of Americans could do to improve their country. He felt the same in the 1850s, looking for a new generation to solve the nation's problems. In his version of events, he bore no responsibility for the troubles of the late 1850s, other than articulating a vision of the legacy of the American Revolution. Dorr was unable to turn against the party who had supported him in 1842. Dorr saw Stephen Douglas's Kansas-Nebraska Act as embodying the principles he had promoted in earnest throughout his life, regardless of the fact that it opened territory that had been previously closed to slaveholders. Dorr found no solace in the fact that Douglas's bill provided the political setting for a more morally engaged Abraham Lincoln to emerge onto the American political scene. Lincoln would become popular sovereignty's greatest foe.

The gap in the vast Dorr correspondence files at Brown University indicates that the People's Governor was too sick to write in November and

December 1854. One pictures his loving mother, Lydia, attending to her son's needs in the small upstairs bedroom in the family mansion in which he was raised. The last letter he received was from a friend in Cambridge, Massachusetts, wishing him a merry Christmas and sharing some lines of poetry she wrote for a local newspaper. Sarah Jacobs asked Dorr to hold on a little longer so she could see him one more time.[2] It was not to be. Thomas Wilson Dorr succumbed to his long battle with debilitating health issues on December 27, 1854.

One can only wonder at Dorr's final thoughts. Perhaps he went through his papers in order to make them accessible to his friends and family. We will never know if he thoroughly reviewed his correspondence from the height of the Rhode Island constitutional crisis in 1842, but one letter to Dorr from Aaron White, Jr., speaks volumes concerning the fate not only of the people's sovereignty, but also of the future of freedom in America. In what is certainly prophetic prose, White noted that President John Tyler's support for the Charter government in 1842 gave opponents of slavery a way of attacking the institution. White longed for the day when James Birney, the Liberty Party candidate for president in 1840 and 1844, would capture the White House and use the power of the federal government to "cram Emancipating Constitutions down the throats" of the white Southerners by way of military necessity. White argued that "if President Tyler under pretence of suppressing domestic violence can interfere in behalf of a minority to guarantee an Aristocratic Constitution, a fortiori, may President Birney interfere to guarantee a Republican Constitution."[3] Eventually, Lincoln would do exactly what White hoped for by using executive power to end slavery.

In perhaps one of the greatest ironies of the long saga of the Dorr Rebellion and the ideology of popular sovereignty in antebellum America, Maryland Democrat Reverdy Johnson drew from an understanding of wartime powers as expressed in *Luther v. Borden* (1849) to justify Lincoln's suspension of habeas corpus in 1861. Johnson argued that Chief Justice Roger Taney's opinion in the *Luther* case provided justification for strong presidential action in times of national crisis. Johnson, along with Lincoln's attorney general, Edward Bates, cited Taney's endorsement of Tyler's actions in 1842 in a memorandum as precedent for the power of the president in times of national crisis.[4] A few years later, during the period known as Reconstruction, Congress utilized Taney's opinion in *Luther v. Borden* to justify the use of broad powers to enforce Article IV's promise of republican

government when dealing with the readmittance of southern state governments.[5]

In her 1844 history of the Dorr Rebellion, Thomas Dorr's friend Frances
Whipple Greene selected the title *Might and Right* to signify what she
deemed to be the arbitrary power of the Charter authorities over the weaker
Rhode Island Suffrage Association. In that case the "might" of the Charter
forces enabled them to crush the righteous cause of the Suffrage Party.[6] In
his pivotal speech at Cooper Union in New York City in 1860, Lincoln also
spoke about right and might. "Let us have faith that right makes might, and
in that faith, let us, to the end, dare to do our duty as we understand it," proclaimed Lincoln in the speech that, as Harold Holzer persuasively argues,
made him president.[7] Lincoln believed that the righteousness of the Republican Party's pledge to stop the spread of slavery would eventually translate
into the might to end the institution everywhere. Lincoln was committed to
banning slavery from the territories, abolishing the institution in Washington, D.C., and prohibiting the admission of new slave states—all things that
Thomas Dorr called for in the 1830s. Lincoln effectively attacked the
morally bankrupt policy of popular sovereignty not in terms of its effects,
but the principle itself.[8] For Lincoln, democracy included a moral component that was at odds with the ideal of the people's sovereignty. Governing
others without their consent was not something that could be covered by
the concept of self-government. It would take the loss of more than 600,000
American lives to settle this crisis of democracy.

Notes

Introduction

1. Thomas Jenckes to Thomas Burgess, April 30, 1842. Correspondence of Providence Mayor Thomas M. Burgess, Providence City Archives.

2. Joseph W. Sullivan, "Reconstructing the Olney's Lane Riot: Another Look at Race and Class in Jacksonian Rhode Island," *Rhode Island History* 65 (Summer 2007): 54. See also John A. C. Randall, "Snow Town Riot Eyewitness Account," Item #70, http://library.brown.edu/omeka/exhibits/show/africanamericanprovidence/SnowTown/item/70.

3. See Samuel Ames to King, April 4, 1842. Samuel Ward King Papers, misc. manuscripts (9001-K), Rhode Island Historical Society (RIHS).

4. Charles Potter to James Simmons, May 19, 1842. James Fowler Simmons Papers (General Correspondence, Box 15), Library of Congress (LofC). Hereafter JFS Papers. See also William Bailey to Jane Keeley, May 17 and June 14, 1842. William M. Bailey Papers, misc. manuscripts (9001-B), RIHS, and Diary of Edward L. Peckham (May 17, 1842). Dorr Rebellion manuscripts (reel C), John Hay Library (JHL), Brown University.

5. *Albany Evening Journal,* May 25, 1842. On Shays's Rebellion see Leonard Richards, *Shays's Rebellion: The American Revolution's Final Battle* (Philadelphia: University of Pennsylvania Press, 2003).

6. *Daily National Intelligencer,* December 29, 1854.

7. Diary, 1845–1850, 6, Thomas Wilson Dorr Papers, JHL. Hereafter TWD Papers. For an insightful and learned history of the First Baptist Church in Providence, see J. Stanley Lemons, *FIRST: First Baptist Church in America* (Providence, RI: Charitable Baptist Society, 2001).

8. Quoted in Mark S. Schantz, *Piety in Providence: Class Dimensions of Religious Experience in Antebellum Rhode Island* (Ithaca, NY: Cornell University Press, 2000), 204.

9. Scott Molloy, *Irish Titan, Irish Toilers: Joseph Banigan and Nineteenth-Century New England Labor* (Lebanon, NH: University of New England Press, 2008), 33–34.

10. See, for example, William Brayton to John Brown Francis, March 15, 1842, and Christopher Allen to John Brown Francis, March 25, 1842. Henry A.L. Brown Deposit, MSS 1031 (Box 7, folders 101 and 102), RIHS. See also Ronald P. Formisano, *For the People: American Populist Movements from the Revolution to the 1850s* (Chapel Hill: University of North Carolina Press, 2007), 163.

11. *The Subterranean United with the Workingman's Advocate*, December 14, 1844.

12. TWD to Kendall, September 24, 1840, and TWD to Jesse Calder, May 4, 1841. Rider Collection, Dorr Correspondence (Box 3, folders 9 and 12), JHL. Hereafter RCDC. See also Peter Coleman, *The Transformation of Rhode Island* (Providence, RI: Brown University Press, 1963), 270.

13. Patrick T. Conley, *Democracy in Decline: Rhode Island's Constitutional Development, 1776–1841* (Providence: Rhode Island Historical Society Publications, 1977).

14. ERP to Thomas M. Potter, April 28, 1842. Thomas Mawney Potter Papers, MSS 629, subgroup 4, RIHS. For more on Potter, see Patrick T. Conley, *The Makers of Modern Rhode Island* (Charleston, SC: History Press, 2012), 70–74.

15. Diary of John Park (April 11 and May 2, 1842), 429, 433. Boston Public Library, manuscripts division.

16. Allan Nevins, ed., *Diary of Philip Hone, 1838–1851*, 2 vols. (New York: Dodd, Mead, and Co., 1927), 2:597.

17. William Bailey to Jane Keeley, May 17 and June 14, 1842. William M. Bailey Papers, RIHS.

18. Diary of Levi Lincoln Newton (April 22, 1842). Newton Family Papers, American Antiquarian Society (AAS).

19. *Southern Patriot*, May 21, 1842.

20. *Democratic Republican New Era*, May 7, 1842.

21. Ibid., August 31, 1839.

22. Ibid., September 7 and 10, 1839.

23. See Dorr's "DeLocofocis" (1839) in the TWD Papers (Box 2, folder 21), JHL. On radical New York Democrats, see Sean Wilentz's classic, *Chants Democratic: New York City and the Rise of the American Working Class, 1788–1850* (New York: Oxford University Press, 1984), 299–359.

24. Diary of Aurilla Moffitt (May 16, 1842). Old Colony Historical Society, Taunton, Massachusetts.

25. Dorr even went so far as to try to plant saplings taken from Napoleon's tomb at his Providence home. See James Mix to TWD, July 3, 1834. RCDC (Box 1, folder 21), JHL.

26. See "Resolutions for Political Action," TWD Papers (Box 2, folder 15), JHL.

27. Historians Christian G. Fritz and Ronald P. Formisano both advance this argument in recent monographs. See Fritz, *American Sovereigns: The People and America's Constitutional Tradition before the Civil War* (New York: Cambridge University Press, 2008), 246–277, and Formisano, *For the People:* 159–176. For discussion of

these two important works, see Erik J. Chaput, "'The Rhode Island Question': The Career of a Debate," *Rhode Island History* 68 (Summer/Fall, 2010): 47–77. Arguments focusing on the collective sovereign were part and parcel of conflicts in the post-Revolutionary period ranging from Shays's Rebellion of 1786 in Massachusetts to the Whiskey Rebellion of 1794 and Fries's Rebellion of 1799 in Pennsylvania, to Dorr's Rebellion of 1842 in Rhode Island. In all of these cases, the "rebellion" label was given by victors. See James Roger Sharp, *American Politics in the Early Republic: The New Nation in Crisis* (New Haven, CT: Yale University Press, 1993), 95–98, 209–210, 320. See also Ronald Formisano, "Rhode Island and the People's Sovereignty, 1776–1843," in Patrick T. Conley, ed., *Constitution Day: Reflections by Respected Scholars* (Providence: Rhode Island Publications Society, 2010), 186–210, and Robert E. Shalhope, *The Baltimore Bank Riot: Political Upheaval in Antebellum Maryland* (Urbana: University of Illinois Press, 2009), 6–10. Witnesses to the events of 1842 in Rhode Island made the connection to past revolutionary movements. See, for example, Francis Bowen, *The Recent Contest in Rhode Island* (Boston, 1844), 65–66.

28. TWD to Daniel Delanau, July 2, 1851. RCDC (Box 13, folder 9). See also Alexander Hill Everett to TWD, November 1, 1841. RCDC (Box 3, folder 16), JHL.

29. The letter is addressed to Connecticut Governor Chauncey Cleveland and is dated July 18, 1842. Private Collection of Russell J. DeSimone.

30. See Ronald P. Formisano, "The Role of Women in the Dorr Rebellion," *Rhode Island History* 51 (August 1993): 89–104.

31. See Ronald J. Zboray and Mary S. Zboray, *Voices without Votes: Women and Politics in Antebellum New England* (Hanover, NH: University Press of New England, 2010), 112–130.

32. Alfred F. Young, Gary B. Nash, and Ray Raphael, eds., *Revolutionary Founders: Rebels, Radicals, and Reformers in the Making of a Nation* (New York: Alfred A. Knopf, 2011), 6.

33. Christian G. Fritz, "Alternate Visions of American Constitutionalism: Popular Sovereignty and the Early American Constitutional Debate," *Hastings Constitutional Law Quarterly* 24 (1996–1997): 356.

34. John Bassett Moore (ed.), *The Works of James Buchanan*, 12 vols. (Philadelphia, 1908), 3:146. See also Elisha Potter, Jr., to John Brown Francis, April 17, 1842. Henry A.L. Brown Deposit (Box 7, folder 102), RIHS. "When Michigan was admitted into the Union, the assent of the state to some conditions imposed by Congress was given by an irregular convention called in the same way the People's Convention was," wrote Potter.

35. Jacob Harvey to William Seward, May 18, 1842. William Henry Seward Papers, University of Rochester.

36. *Journal of the Convention Assembled to Frame a Constitution for the State of Rhode Island, at Newport, Sept. 12, 1842* (Providence, 1842), 29. Rhode Island State Archives (RISA).

37. Ives to John Brown Francis, April 6, 1842. Henry A. L. Brown Deposit (Box 7, folder 102), RIHS.

38. Bailey to Jane Keeley, June 14, 1842. William M. Bailey Papers, RIHS.

39. Quoted in *New England Democrat*, April 4, 1844. See also Charles Jewett, *The Close of the Late Rebellion in Rhode Island* (Providence, 1842), 15.

40. Almon D. Hodges, Jr., ed., *Almon Danforth Hodges and His Neighbors: An Autobiographical Sketch of a Typical Old New Englander* (Boston: privately printed, 1909), 186.

41. Zachariah Allen, "An Account of the Rebellion, 1842," 111. Zachariah Allen Papers, MSS 254 (Box 3), RIHS. See also Edward Carrington to James Simmons, May 18, 1842. JFS Papers (General Correspondence, Box 15), LofC.

42. Howard R. Ernst, "A Call to Arms: Thomas Wilson Dorr's Forceful Effort to Implement the People's Constitution," *Rhode Island History* 66, no. 3 (Fall 2008): 68–69.

43. *Providence Journal*, May 26, 1842.

44. Obituary of Sullivan Dorr, Jr., in the Dorr Family Scrapbook, vol. 8, 57. RIHS.

45. George Howland to TWD, October 24, 1852. RCDC (Box 13 folder 26), JHL.

46. Samuel F. Man to James F. Simmons, May 23, 1842. JFS Paper (General Correspondence, Box 15), LofC.

47. *New York Express*, May 18, 1842.

48. *National Anti-Slavery Standard*, June 23, 1842.

49. *Emancipator and Free American*, May 12, 1842. See also the June 2, 1842, issue for a summary of the "abolitionist" plot as well as F. H. Richmond to James Simmons, May 7, 1842. JFS Papers (General Correspondence, Box 15), LofC.

50. See William M. Wiecek, *The Sources of Antislavery Constitutionalism, 1760–1848* (Ithaca, NY: Cornell University Press, 1977), 269–270. See also Wiecek, *The Guarantee Clause of the U.S. Constitution* (Ithaca, NY: Cornell University Press, 1972).

51. Mark Tucker, *A Discourse Preached on Thanksgiving Day, July 21, 1842* (Providence, 1842), 14.

52. Jonathan Earle, *Jacksonian Antislavery and the Politics of Free Soil, 1824–1854* (Chapel Hill: University of North Carolina Press, 2004).

53. Susan Sisson to Abby Kelley, March 15, 1842. Abby Kelley Foster Papers, AAS.

54. *Emancipator and Free American*, June 30, 1842.

55. *Philanthropist*, July 23, 1842. Private Collection of Russell DeSimone.

56. See John Ashworth's often overlooked work, *Agrarians and Aristocrats: Party Political Ideology in the United States, 1837–1846* (London: Cambridge University Press, 1987), 230–235. Testifying to the significance of the Dorr Rebellion is the startling fact that there are over two hundred known broadsides and scores of political pamphlets related to the event. See Russell J. DeSimone and Daniel Schofield,

The Broadsides of the Dorr Rebellion (Providence: Rhode Island Supreme Court Historical Society, 1992). For a list of pamphlets see Conley, *Democracy in Decline*, 384–391.

57. Sean Wilentz, *The Rise of American Democracy: Jefferson to Lincoln* (New York, W.W. Norton, 2005), 543. See also Harold M. Hyman and William M. Wiecek, *Equal Justice under Law: Constitutional Development, 1835–1875* (New York: Harper and Row, 1982), 3.

58. Quoted in Robert D. Sampson, *John L. O'Sullivan and His Times* (Kent, OH: Kent State University Press, 2003), 126.

59. TWD to Seth Salisbury, December 11, 1852. RCDC (Box 13, folder 28), JHL.

60. Hopkins Holsey to TWD, July 2, 1853. RCDC (Box 14, folder 24), JHL. Issues of slavery and race are completely ignored in Arthur May Mowry, *The Dorr War: The Constitutional Struggle in Rhode Island* (1901; New York: Chelsea House Publishers, 1970). Despite unduly harsh reviews that incorrectly painted the book as simply a New Left political manifesto, Marvin Gettleman's *The Dorr Rebellion: A Study in American Radicalism, 1833–1849* (New York: Random House, 1973), moves beyond Mowry in terms of both accuracy and detail. However, Gettleman's focus on the question of Dorr's radicalism prevented him from probing further, especially into the areas of slavery, race, and gender. George M. Dennison in his *The Dorr War: Republicanism on Trial, 1831–1861* (Lexington: University of Kentucky Press, 1976), concentrates on the Revolutionary-era political and constitutional theories of the Dorrites, often at the expense of the actual details of the events of 1841–1844. While there is no doubt that the underlying ideology of the Dorrites can be traced back to the American Revolution, their battle was waged in a much different era. It was an era in American history when abolitionism, the westward expansion of slavery, and sectional tensions were beginning to surface in dangerous and unsettling ways.

Chapter 1: Beginnings

1. TWD, "Memoranda of August 16, 1847." TWD Papers (Box 3, folder 6). See also TWD Diary, June 29, 1847. TWD Papers (Box 3), JHL.

2. TWD, "Memoranda of August 16, 1847." TWD Papers (Box 3, folder 6), JHL.

3. Edward L. Widmer, *Young America: The Flowering of Democracy in New York City* (New York: Oxford University Press, 1999), 53, 21. See also Yonatan Eyal, *The Young America Movement and the Transformation of the Democratic Party, 1828–1861* (New York: Cambridge University Press, 2007), 3.

4. Quoted in Widmer, *Young America*, 56.

5. See TWD to O'Sullivan, October 24, 1852, and O'Sullivan to TWD, November 18, 1853. RCDC (Box 14, folder 29), JHL.

6. TWD, "Memoranda of August 1, 1845." TWD Papers (Box 3, folder 4), JHL. A superficial biography of Dorr was published in Boston in 1859. See Daniel King, *The Life and Times of Thomas Wilson Dorr*.

7. See John O'Sullivan, "Thomas Wilson Dorr," *Democratic Review* (August 1842): 201–205.

8. Quoted in Robert Sampson, *John L. O'Sullivan and His Times* (Kent, OH: Kent State University Press, 2003), 200–201.

9. David Hackett Fischer, *Paul Revere's Ride* (New York: Oxford University Press, 1995), 388, and James Kirker, *Adventures to China: Americans in the Southern Oceans, 1796–1816* (New York: Oxford University Press, 1970), 57.

10. See Howard Corning, "Sullivan Dorr, China Trader," *Rhode Island History* (July 1944): 75–90, and Corning, ed., "Letters of Sullivan Dorr," *Proceedings of the Massachusetts Historical Society* (October 1941–May 1944): 178–364.

11. Diary, December 31, 1847. TWD Papers, JHL.

12. TWD, "Memoranda of August 1, 1845." TWD Papers (Box 3, folder 4). See also TWD Papers (Box 2 folder 18), JHL.

13. Sullivan Dorr to Lydia Dorr, August 10, 1805. Edward Carrington Papers, MSS 333, (Box 138), RIHS.

14. See TWD Papers (Box 2, folder 18), JHL.

15. The seven Dorr children: Thomas (1805–1854); Allen (1808–1889); Ann Allen (1810–1884); Mary Throop (1811–1869); Sullivan, Jr. (1813–1884); Candace (1815–1886); Henry Crawford (1820–1897).

16. On the Dorr family mansion, see Ann E. Brown, *Painted Rooms of Rhode Island: Colonial and Federal* (Monroe, CT: The Connecticut Press, 2012), 120–126.

17. See Peter Coleman, *The Transformation of Rhode Island, 1790–1860* (Providence, RI: Brown University Press, 1963), and Patrick T. Conley, *Democracy in Decline: Rhode Island's Constitutional Development, 1776–1841* (Providence: Rhode Island Historical Society Publications, 1977), 144–160. See also the invaluable collection of essays edited by the staff at the Worcester Historical Museum, *Landscape of Industry: An Industrial History of the Blackstone Valley* (Lebanon, NH: University Press of New England, 2009).

18. For an informative illustrated history of the city, see Patrick T. Conley and Paul Campbell, *Providence: A Pictorial History* (Norfolk, VA: Donning, 1986).

19. Stewart Schneider, "Railroad Development in Nineteenth Century Rhode Island," *Rhode Island History* 61 (Summer 2003): 37–48.

20. *Cincinnati Daily Enquirer*, May 17, 1842. See also Coleman, *The Transformation of Rhode Island*, 218–228.

21. John Wood Sweet, *Bodies Politics: Negotiating Race in the American North, 1730–1840* (Philadelphia: University of Pennsylvania Press, 2003), 356–360.

22. See Richard E. Greenwood, "Zachariah Allen and the Architecture of Industrial Paternalism," *Rhode Island History* 46 (1988): 117–135.

23. James McLachlan, *American Boarding Schools: A Historical Study* (New York: Charles Scribner's Sons, 1970), 42.

24. Frank Cunningham, *Familiar Sketches of Phillips Exeter Academy* (Exeter, NH: 1883), 254, and *Catalogue of the Golden Branch* (Exeter, NH: 1850). The numerous letters from Allen Dorr to Thomas Dorr in the RCDC (Box 1, folders 3–6) constitute a treasure trove of material for those interested in early American education.

25. Gordon S. Wood, *Empire of Liberty: A History of the Early Republic, 1789–1815* (New York: Oxford University Press, 2009), 24.

26. Benjamin Abbot to Sullivan Dorr, July 12, 1818. Sullivan Dorr Papers, MSS 390, RIHS.

27. David B. Tyack, *George Ticknor and the Boston Brahmins* (Cambridge, MA: Harvard University Press, 1967), 92–93.

28. Samuel Eliot Morison, "The Great Rebellion at Harvard College," *Transactions of the Colonial Society of Massachusetts* 27 (1928): 54–113.

29. Samuel Eliot Morison, *Three Centuries at Harvard, 1636–1936* (Cambridge, MA: Harvard University Press, 1936), 230–231.

30. Jason Whitman to TWD, June 24, 1821. RCDC (Box 1, folder 3), JHL.

31. Samuel Dorr to TWD, March 17, 1820. RCDC (Box 1, folder 2), JHL.

32. George Bancroft to Samuel Eliot, April 2, 1823. George Bancroft Papers, Massachusetts Historical Society Library.

33. After Bancroft left Harvard to help found the Round Hill School in the Connecticut River Valley in western Massachusetts in 1823, Dorr convinced his parents to send Sullivan, Jr., to the new school. TWD to Sullivan Dorr, Jr., July 4, 1825. Private Collection of Russell J. DeSimone.

34. Diary of Pickering Dodge in Morison, "The Great Rebellion," 72.

35. Ibid., 70.

36. Ibid., 72.

37. Ibid., 74. See also Ted Widmer, "Brief Life of a Harvard Demagogue, 1805–1854: Thomas Wilson Dorr," *Harvard Magazine* 93, no. 3 (1991): 3.

38. Dorr's thesis, "Calculation and Projection of a Lunar Eclipse in 1825," is on file at the Harvard University Archives. See http://oasis.lib.harvard.edu/oasis/deliver/~hua17004 (accessed July 29, 2011).

39. Harvard Faculty Records quoted in Morison, "The Great Rebellion," 80, note 1.

40. See Allen Dorr to TWD, July 21, 1821; Robinson to TWD, July 29, 1821. RCDC (Box 1, folder 4); and Robinson to TWD, May 13, 1851. RCDC (Box 13, folder 6), JHL. See also *The Golden Branch Society of Phillips Exeter Academy* (Exeter, NH, 1850), 6–8.

41. Diary of Pickering Dodge in Morison, "The Great Rebellion," 80–81.

42. Ibid., 83.

43. Ibid., 86.

44. See Sidney S. Rider Papers (Box 6, folder 17), JHL. Hereafter cited as SSR Papers. See also *Providence Gazette*, September 9, 1823, and *Essex Register*, August, 28, 1823.

45. Compare Dorr's experience with that of Charles Sumner. See David Donald, *Charles Sumner and the Coming of the Civil War* (New York: Alfred A. Knopf, 1960), 12–15.

46. Usher Parson to James Blunt, January 25, 1824. RCDC (Box 1, folder 9). See also Dorr's draft letter to the judges of the Supreme Court of New York, May 16, 1831. RCDC (Box 1, folder 14), JHL.

47. Unfortunately, the James Kent Papers at the Library of Congress do not shed any light on Thomas Dorr or the Dorr Rebellion.

48. TWD to Whipple, May 16, 1831, and TWD to Whipple, May 27, 1831. RCDC (Box 1, folders 14 and 15), JHL.

49. TWD to Thomas Tappan, January 4, 1828. RCDC (Box 12, folder 1), JHL.

50. See the memoranda in RCDC (Box 1, folder 13), JHL.

51. On Dorr's health, see TWD to Lydia Dorr, August 24, 1830. RCDC (Box 1, folder 14) JHL.

52. For Dorr's whereabouts, see TWD Papers (Box 3, folder 27) and RCDC (Box 1, folder 13), JHL; for Lincoln's whereabouts, see Eric Foner, *The Fiery Trial: Abraham Lincoln and American Slavery* (New York: W. W. Norton, 2010), 9–10.

53. Joanne Pope Melish, *Disowning Slavery: Gradual Emancipation and "Race" in New England, 1780–1860* (Ithaca, NY: Cornell University Press, 1998), 74.

54. Dorr seemed to have had a close relationship with Lippitt because he agreed to serve as a witness to her will. See Cherry Fletcher Bamberg, "Dorcas Lippitt of Providence, Rhode Island, and Her Descendants," *New England Historical and Genealogical Magazine*, 162 (January 2008): 162.

55. See Charles Hoffman and Tess Hoffman, *North By South: The Two Lives of Richard James Arnold* (Athens: University of Georgia Press, 1988), xiii, 2.

56. Ibid., 7. On Rhode Island slave trade, see Jay Coughtry, *The Notorious Triangle: Rhode Island and the African Slave Trade, 1700–1807* (Philadelphia: Temple University Press, 1981), and J. Stanley Lemons, "Rhode Island and the Slave Trade," *Rhode Island History* 60 (November 2002): 94–104.

57. See RCDC (Box 14, folder 1), JHL.

58. See, for example, TWD to Sullivan Dorr, October 2, 1830. TWD Papers (Box 1, folder 10), JHL.

59. Henry Dorr to TWD, May 28, 1841. RCDC (Box 3, folder 13), JHL.

60. On Field, see Widmer, *Young America*, 155–184.

61. TWD to William B. Adams, May 30, 1831. SSR Papers (Box 3, folder 22), JHL. Dorr's thinking was very much in line with that of Alexander Hill Everett. See the "Prospect of Reform in Europe," in the *North American Review* (July 1831): 154–191.

62. Adams to TWD, July 5, 1831. Private Collection of Frank Mauran III. This and subsequent material from this collection is quoted with permission.

63. TWD to Lydia Dorr, August 30, 1830. RCDC (Box 1, folder 14), JHL.

64. TWD to Adams, May 30, 1831. SSR Papers (Box 3, folder 22), JHL.

65. For more on this, see Raymond Lavertue, "The People's Governor: Thomas Wilson Dorr and the Politics of Sacrifice, 1834–1843" (Ph.D. diss., St. Catherine's College, Oxford University, 2013), ch. 2.

66. See the undated draft letter (most likely between February 17, 1829, and December, 20, 1830) from TWD to Adams in RCDC (Box 1, folder 13), JHL, and Adams to TWD, July 5, 1831. Private Collection of Frank Mauran III.

67. See Maurice Baxter, *One and Inseparable: Daniel Webster and the Union* (Cambridge, MA: Harvard University Press, 1984), 180–190.

68. See Jason Evan Camlot, "Character of the Periodical Press: John Stuart Mill and Junius Redivivus in the 1830s," *Victorian Periodicals Review* 32, no. 2 (Summer 1999): 166–176.

69. William Bridges Adams, *The Political Unionist's Catechism: A Manual of Political Instruction*, 2nd ed. (1833), 39.

70. William Bridges Adams, *The Rights of Morality: An Essay on the Present State of Society, Moral, Political, and Physical, in England* (1832), 81.

71. TWD to Adams, November 7, 1831. RCDC (Box 1, folder 15), JHL.

72. Adams to TWD, July 5, 1831. Private Collection of Frank Mauran III.

73. TWD to Adams, May 28, 1832. RCDC (Box 1, folder 16), JHL.

74. Adams to TWD, July 5, 1831. Private Collection of Frank Mauran III. Quoted with permission.

75. TWD to Adams, November 7, 1831. RCDC (Box 1, folder 15), JHL.

76. TWD to Adams, May 30, 1831. SSR Papers (Box 3, folder 22), JHL.

77. Ibid.

78. Fox to TWD, October 12, 1832. RCDC (Box 1, folder 15), JHL.

79. Mark S. Schantz, *Awaiting the Heavenly Country: The Civil War and America's Culture of Death* (Ithaca, NY: Cornell University Press, 2008), 16.

Chapter 2: Jacksonian Dissident

1. Charles Hoffman and Tess Hoffman, *North and South: The Two Lives of Richard James Arnold* (Athens: University of Georgia Press, 1988), 88–89. See also Joseph Sullivan, "Reconstructing the Olney's Lane Riot," *Rhode Island History* 65 (Summer 2007): 49–60, and Howard P. Chudacoff and Theodore C. Hirt, "Social Turmoil and Governmental Reform in Providence, 1820–1832," *Rhode Island History* 31 (Winter 1971): 24–30.

2. Henry Dorr to TWD, February 26, 1831. Edward Carrington Papers, MSS 333 (Box 138), RIHS.

3. Ann Dorr to TWD, November 12, 1829. RCDC (Box 1, folder 13), JHL. See also Patrick T. Conley, "Tom Dorr: Up Close and Personal," in Patrick T. Conley, *People, Places, Laws and Lore of the Ocean State: A Rhode Island Historical Sampler* (Providence, RI: Rhode Island Publications Society, 2012), 9–11.

4. *Report of the Examination of David Gibbs, Fanny Leach and Eliza P. Burdick for the Alleged Murder of Sally Burdick at Coventry, R.I. on the 18th Feb. 1833* (Hartford, CT, 1833), 11.

5. Jonah Titus to William Simons, February 28, 1833. Jonah Titus Papers, JHL.

6. Dorr used the pen name of "Aristides" in *Political Frauds Exposed* (1838), a hard-hitting political pamphlet about corruption in the Rhode Island Whig Party.

7. David Kasserman, *Fall River Outrage: Life, Murder and Justice in Early Industrial New England* (Philadelphia: University of Pennsylvania Press, 1986). See also Patrick T. Conley, "*State of Rhode Island v. Reverend Ephraim K. Avery* (1833): The Legal and Geographical Setting," in Patrick T. Conley, ed. *Rhode Island in Rhetoric and Reflection* (Providence, RI: Rhode Island Publications Society, 2002), 215–222.

8. Quoted in Stephen Chambers, "'Neither Justice nor Mercy': Public and Private Executions in Rhode Island, 1832–1833," *New England Quarterly* 82 (September 2009): 436.

9. See Erik J. Chaput and Raymond J. Lavertue, "'The Instigation of the Devil': Sex, Lust, and Murder in Nineteenth-Century Rhode Island" (talk delivered at the Providence Athenaeum, November 23, 2012).

10. See the records for the Providence City Council (June 1833). Providence City Archives. See also William Tillinghast to Martin Van Buren, May 31, 1833. Martin Van Buren Papers, LofC.

11. Seth Luther, *An Address Delivered before the Mechanics and Working-Men of the City of Brooklyn, July 4, 1836* (Brooklyn, 1836). See the informative entry on Luther in Patrick T. Conley, *The Makers of Modern Rhode Island* (Charleston, SC: History Press, 2012), 154–159, and Scott Molloy, Carl Gersuny, and Robert Macieski, eds., *Peaceably If We Can, Forcibly If We Must! Writings by and about Seth Luther* (Providence, RI: Rhode Island Labor History Society, 1998).

12. Seth Luther, *An Address on the Right of Free Suffrage* (Providence, 1833), 24, 25.

13. Contrary to the national trend of the Jacksonian Democratic Party, large numbers of Rhode Island Democrats continued to affirm their support for the yeomen farmer and opposed large-scale political reform that would enfranchise propertyless workers. See Edward F. Sweet, "The Origins of the Democratic Party in Rhode Island, 1824–1836" (Ph.D. diss., Fordham University, 1971). See also Patrick T. Conley, *Democracy in Decline: Rhode Island's Constitutional Development, 1776–1841* (Providence: Rhode Island Historical Society Publications, 1977), 243–245.

14. For a ringing defense of the freehold in the antebellum period, see Elisha Potter, Jr., to Dutee Pearce, December 20, 1841. Elisha R. Potter Jr. Papers, MSS 629, subgroup 3 (Box 1, folder 6), RIHS. Hereafter cited as ERP Papers.

15. Henry C. Dorr to TWD, January [no date], 1842. RCDC (Box 3, folder 16), JHL.

16. See Marvin Gettleman, *The Dorr Rebellion: A Study in American Radicalism,*

1833–1849 (New York: Random House, 1973), 21. See also Marvin Gettleman and Noel Conlon, eds., "Responses to the Rhode Island Workingmen's Reform Agitation of 1833," *Rhode Island History* 28 (August 1969): 75–94.

17. See the papers relating to the Constitutional Party, 1834–1837, in the Dorr Rebellion manuscripts (Reel B), JHL. See also Dorr's correspondence with Smithfield physician Metcalf Marsh at the North Smithfield Heritage Society. The most detailed discussion of the Constitutional Party is Patrick T. Conley, *Democracy in Decline*, 254–278.

18. Christopher Robinson to Metcalf Marsh, December 16, 1833. Metcalf Marsh Papers, North Smithfield Heritage Association.

19. The address is reprinted in Edmund Burke, *Interference of the Executive in the Affairs of Rhode Island*, 29th Cong., 1st sess., 1844, House Report No. 546, 151–185; quotes at 156. Hereafter cited as *Burke's Report*.

20. *Burke's Report*, 160, 164, 176.

21. Deborah Van Broekhoven, *The Devotion of These Women: Rhode Island in the Antislavery Network* (Amherst: University of Massachusetts Press, 2002), 27, 36, and 158.

22. Conley, *Democracy in Decline*, 287.

23. See Dorr's verso annotation on Phillip Stiness to TWD, November 8, 1838. RCDC (Box 2, folder 24), JHL.

24. *Providence Journal*, February 5, 1834.

25. On "New School Whigs," see Sean Wilentz, *The Rise of American Democracy: Jefferson to Lincoln* (New York: W. W. Norton, 2005), 483.

26. *Rhode-Island Republican*, January 21, 1835. See also Dorr's reform agenda in TWD Papers (Box 2, folder, 15), JHL.

27. See "A Dissertation on the Public Utility of Education and the Best Means of Extending the Rudiments to All" in the SSR Papers (Box 6, folder 13), JHL.

28. *Morning Courier*, December 30, 1836, quoted in Patrick T. Conley, "Thomas Wilson Dorr: Neglected Educational Reformer," in Patrick T. Conley, ed., *Rhode Island in Rhetoric and Reflection* (Providence: Rhode Island Publications Society, 2002), 122.

29. See the recently discovered annual reports of the Providence School Committee in the Providence City Archives.

30. TWD to Metcalf Marsh, January 14, 1837. Metcalf Marsh Papers, North Smithfield Heritage Association. Contrary to historian Daniel Walker Howe's assertion, Dorr left the party of his own accord after developing a Jacksonian hard-money policy at odds with Whig orthodoxy. Howe, *What Hath God Wrought: The Transformation of America, 1815–1848* (New York: Oxford University Press, 2007), 600.

31. TWD, "Memoranda," August 1, 1845. TWD Papers (Box 3, folder 4), JHL.

32. Ibid. See also TWD to George Curtis, August 5, 1839. RCDC (Box 2, folder 26), JHL. For Dorr's report on the solvency of Rhode Island banks, see *Providence Journal*, July 4, 1836.

33. *Rhode Island Schedules*, January 1837, 89–92. Rhode Island State Archives. Hereafter cited as RISA.

34. *Rhode Island Schedules*, June 1836, 62–70. RISA. See also *Rhode Island Republican*, July 6, 1836.

35. John B. Rae, "Rhode Island Pioneers in the Regulation of Banking," *Rhode Island History* 2 (October 1842): 108–109, and John J. Wallis, "The Constitutions, Corporations, and Corruption: American States and Constitutional Change, 1842 to 1852," *Journal of Economic History* 65 (March 2005): 217.

36. Conley, *Democracy in Decline*, 279.

37. *Rhode Island Schedules*, January 1837, "Report of Bank Commissioners," 89–92, RISA.

38. *Rhode Island Schedules*, January 1837, 5, RISA.

39. *Rhode Island Schedules*, June 1837, 42–43, RISA, and *Rhode Island Republican*, June 28, 1837.

40. B. Michael Zuckerman, "The Political Economy of Industrial Rhode Island, 1790–1860" (Ph.D. diss., Brown University, 1981), 254.

41. Sean Wilentz, "Slavery, Antislavery, and Jacksonian Democracy," in Melvyn Stokes and Stephen Conway, eds., *The Market Revolution in America: Social, Political, and Religious Expressions, 1800–1880* (Charlottesville: University Press of Virginia, 1996), 202–223.

42. *Newport Mercury*, January 30, 1836, *Liberator*, February 27, 1836, and July 2, 1836. See also *Friend of Man*, July 7, 1836. See also Van Broekhoven, *The Devotion of These Women*, 22.

43. *Liberator*, February 6, 1836. See also Van Broekhoven, *The Devotion of These Women*, 18.

44. *Newport Mercury*, June 4, 1836, and *Liberator*, July 2, 1836. See also William Lloyd Garrison to Isaac Knapp, June 22, 1836, in Louis Ruchamese, ed., *A House Dividing against Itself* (Cambridge, MA: Harvard University Press, 1971), 131–132.

45. Broadside, "To the People of R. Island" (1836). Providence Athenaeum Collection.

46. *Newport Mercury*, June 25, 1836.

47. Peter A. Wallner, *Franklin Pierce: New Hampshire's Favorite Son* (Concord, NH: Plaidswede Publishing 2004), 61–63.

48. William Bridges Adams, *The Producing Man's Companion: An Essay on the Present State of Society* (1833), 86.

49. See Dorr's notes on the federal Constitution in TWD Papers (Box 2, folder 16), JHL.

50. In this way, Dorr's views closely mirrored those of the Jacksonian antislavery leader William Leggett. See Sean Wilentz, "The Conversion of William Leggett," in John Patrick Diggins, ed., *The Liberal Persuasion: Arthur Schlesinger Jr. and the Challenge of the American Past* (Princeton, NJ: Princeton University Press, 1997), 94–98.

51. Daniel Feller, "A Brother in Arms: Benjamin Tappan and the Antislavery Democracy," *Journal of American History* 88 (June 2001): 56.

52. Carol Faulkner, *Lucretia Mott's Heresy: Abolition and Women's Rights in Nineteenth-Century America* (Philadelphia: University of Pennsylvania Press, 2011), 62.

53. See the files on the Kent County Female Anti-Slavery Society in misc. manuscripts (9001-k), RIHS.

54. Angelina Grimké to Abby Kelley, April 15, 1837. Abby Kelly Foster Papers, AAS.

55. See the entry on Arnold Buffum and Elizabeth Buffum Chace in Conley, *The Makers of Modern Rhode Island*, 169–171. See also Elizabeth C. Stevens, *Elizabeth Buffum Chace and Lillie Chace Wyman: A Century of Abolitionist, Suffragist and Workers' Rights Activism* (Jefferson, NC: McFarland Press, 2003).

56. See John L. Myers, "Antislavery Agencies in Rhode Island, 1832–1835," *Rhode Island History* 29 (Summer/Fall, 1970): 93, and Myers, "Antislavery Agencies in Rhode Island, 1835–1837," *Rhode Island History* 30 (Winter 1971): 21–24. See also Seth Rockman, "Slavery and Abolition along the Blackstone," in *Landscape of Industry: An Industrial History of the Blackstone Valley* (Hanover, NH: University of New England Press, 2009), 119, and Oliver Johnson to Lewis Tappan, March 22, 1837, Lewis Tappan Papers (reel 2), LofC.

57. Van Broekhoven, *The Devotion of These Women*, 26.

58. See *Liberator*, April 15, 1835, and John S. Gilkeson, Jr., *Middle-Class Providence, 1820–1940* (Princeton, NJ: Princeton University Press, 1986), 38. Gilkeson incorrectly notes that Paulina Wright Davis was involved in these organizations. She did not come to Rhode Island until 1849.

59. *Providence Journal*, January 27, 1834. See also "Notes on Meeting of Colonization Society," TWD Papers (Box 2, folder 15), JHL and *Remarks on the American Colonization Society* (Providence, 1834), 11. SSR Papers (Box 8), JHL.

60. See Douglas R. Egerton, *Charles Fenton Mercer and the Trial of National Conservatism* (Jackson: University Press of Mississippi, 1989), 105–112. See also Egerton, "'Its Origin Is Not a Little Curious': A New Look at the American Colonization Society," *Journal of the Early Republic* 5 (Winter 1985): 463–480.

61. TWD's notes on Anti-Slavery (1834) in TWD Papers (Box 2, folder 15), JHL.

62. Ibid.

63. Eric Foner, *Free Soil, Free Labor, Free Men: The Ideology of the Republican Party before the Civil War* (New York: Oxford University Press, 1970), 87.

64. See Phillips to TWD, May 11, 1839, and TWD to Phillips, May 13, 1839. RCDC (Box 2, folder 25), JHL.

65. In January 1838, Dorr put forth a motion to require Rhode Island representatives in Congress to push for the abolishment of slavery and the slave trade in Washington, D.C. The motion, which Dorr labeled "right and just," failed by a vote of 47–7. Richard Randolph led the charge against the motion. See Dorr's political scrapbook, p.18, JHL.

66. John Quincy Adams to Lewis Tappan, April 29, 1837, and April 7, 1838. Lewis Tappan Papers (reel 2), LofC.

67. William M. Wiecek, *The Sources of Antislavery Constitutionalism, 1760–1848* (Ithaca, NY: Cornell University Press, 1977), 189–190.

68. Ibid., 204. For more on the politics surrounding abolition in the District of Columbia, see Donald E. Fehrenbacher, *The Slaveholding Republic: An Account of the United States Government's Relation to Slavery* (New York: Oxford University Press, 2001), 72–88.

69. TWD to William Chace, July 25, 1837. RCDC (Box 2, folder 20), JHL. Dorr's remarks were printed in *Liberator*, August 11, 1837.

70. Ibid.

71. TWD to Edmund Quincy, September 29, 1838. RCDC (Box 2, folder 23), JHL. Emphasis added. See also *Friend of Man*, October 24, 1838, and Edmund Quincy's Diary in the Quincy, Wendell, Holmes, and Upham Papers. Massachusetts Historical Society Library.

72. TWD to William Chace, July 25, 1837. RCDC (Box 2, folder 20), JHL.

73. On Morton, see Jonathan Earle, "Marcus Morton and the Dilemma of Jacksonian Antislavery in Massachusetts, 1817–1849," *Massachusetts Historical Review* 4 (2002): 61–87, esp. 74.

74. See TWD to Quincy, September 29, 1838. RCDC (Box 2, folder 23), JHL. Dorr's letter to Quincy was republished in *Liberator*, October 12, 1838. Dorr knew Quincy from his time at Harvard and he had likely attended Quincy's July 4 lecture in Providence a few months before.

75. Howe, *What Hath God Wrought*, 559–661. See also Joel Silbey, *Storm over Texas: The Annexation Controversy and the Coming of the Civil War* (New York: Oxford University Press, 2005).

76. See TWD notes on the nature of republicanism in SSR Papers (Box 6, folder 19), JHL.

77. TWD to William Chace, July 25, 1837. RCDC (Box 2, folder 20), JHL.

78. Quoted in Gary May, *John Tyler* (New York: Times Books, 2008), 97.

79. Leonard L. Richards, *The Life and Times of Congressman John Quincy Adams* (New York: Oxford University Press, 1986), 160, and Richards, *The Slave Power: The Free North and Southern Domination, 1780–1860* (Baton Rouge: Louisiana State University Press, 2000), 141.

80. Quoted in Elizabeth Varon, *Disunion! The Coming of the American Civil War, 1789–1859* (Chapel Hill: University of North Carolina Press, 2008), 95. See also Faulkner, *Lucretia Mott's Heresy*, 64–65.

81. Wiecek, *The Sources of Antislavery Constitutionalism*, 16, 167–169.

82. *Providence Journal*, June 11, 1842.

83. Dorr to James Birney, December 26, 1837. RCDC (Box 2, folder 22), JHL.

84. See Manuscript Memorandum (*Back v. Miss Grimké*), December 22, 1838 in Dwight L. Dumond, ed., *Letters of James G. Birney, 1831–1857*, vol. 1 (New York: Appleton-Century, 1938), 478–479. See also the *Fifth Annual Report of the Executive*

Committee of the American Antislavery Society (New York, 1838), 4, 12. Samuel J. May Anti-Slavery Collection. Cornell University. I thank Raymond J. Lavertue for alerting me to this important source.

85. Clipping dated November 14, 1837, in the Papers of Lewis Tappan (reel 1), LofC.

86. Daniel Feller, *The Jacksonian Promise: America, 1815–1840* (Baltimore, MD: Johns Hopkins University Press, 1995), 113.

87. Roger G. Walters, *American Reformers, 1815–1840* (New York: Hill and Wang, 1978), 80.

88. *Fifth Annual Report of the Executive Committee of the American Anti-Slavery Society* (1838), 17. Samuel J. May Anti-Slavery Collection. Cornell University.

89. See *Herald of Freedom*, August 19, 1837, and August 24, 1839. *Liberator*, August 16, 1839, and *Friend of Man*, September 11, 1839.

90. *Rhode-Island Republican*, November 6, 1839.

91. *Liberator*, August 16 and 23, 1839. See also *Herald of Freedom*, August 10, 1839.

92. Quoted in Richards, *The Slave Power*, 23. See also Jonathan Earle, *Jacksonian Antislavery and the Politics of Free Soil, 1848–1854* (Chapel Hill: University of North Carolina Press, 2004), 37–44, and Foner, *Free Soil, Free Labor, Free Men*, 90–92.

93. On Hale, see Richard H. Sewell, *John P. Hale and the Politics of Abolition* (Cambridge, MA: Harvard University Press, 1965).

94. See Dorr's notes on the results dated August 27, 1839. TWD Papers (Box 2, folder 21), LofC. See also *Rhode-Island Republican*, July 24, 1839, and *Emancipator and Free American*, November 21, 1839.

95. See TWD's August 1847 Memoranda in the TWD Papers (Box 3, folder 6), LofC. See also *Liberator*, April 26, 1839.

96. See *Liberator*, March 22, 1839, discussing the efforts of an executive committee that included Dorr, Whittier, Lewis Tappan, and Joshua Leavitt.

97. See Barstow's letters to the editors of the *Emancipator and Free American*, June 9, 1842, and July 21, 1842. The letters were written in response to William Goodell's *Lessons of a Single Day* (1842) pamphlet and his June 30, 1842, editorial in the *Emancipator and Free American*.

98. TWD Papers (Box 2, folder 21), JHL. See also "Reports of the Select Committee to Whom were Referred the Resolutions of Mr. Wells of Hopkinton" (January 1839 session), RISA.

99. See "Notes on U.S. Constitution" TWD Papers (Box 2, folder 15), JHL. See also James Oakes, *Freedom National: The Destruction of Slavery in the United States, 1861–1865* (New York: W. W. Norton, 2012), 7.

100. Wiecek, *The Guarantee Clause of the United States Constitution* (Ithaca, NY: Cornell University Press, 1972), 156–157.

101. Wilentz, "The Conversion of William Leggett," 98.

102. See Dorr notes in TWD Papers (Box 2, folder 20). See also John Ames to Dorr June 7, 1838. RCDC (Box 2, folder 23), JHL.

103. TWD to Lydia Dorr, November 1, 1844. TWD Papers (Box 1, folder 1), JHL.

104. See Van Broekhoven, *The Devotion of These Women*, 227–232.

105. Faulkner, *Lucretia Mott's Heresy*, 81; see also Dorothy Sterling, *Ahead of Her Time: Abby Kelley and the Politics of Antislavery* (New York: W. W. Norton, 1991), 104–106.

106. See Bruce Laurie, *Beyond Garrison: Antislavery and Social Reform* (New York: Cambridge University Press, 2005), 10. See also Reinhard O. Johnson, *The Liberty Party, 1840–1848: Antislavery Third-Party Politics in the United States* (Baton Rouge: Louisiana State University Press, 2009).

107. Wilentz, *The Rise of American Democracy*, 499–500.

108. Arthur M. Schlesinger, Jr., *The Age of Jackson* (Boston: Little, Brown, 1945), 411.

109. TWD to Robert Rantoul, January 6, 1840. RCDC (Box 3, folder 2). See also TWD to Rantoul, February 1, 1840. RCDC (Box 3, folder 4), JHL.

110. Merle E. Curti, "Robert Rantoul, Jr., the Reformer in Politics," *New England Quarterly* 5 (April 1932): 274–276.

111. *Bay State Democrat*, March 4, 1840.

112. Francis to Potter, August 27, 1837, December 22, 1837. ERP Papers (Box 1, folder 2), RIHS.

113. Feller, "A Brother in Arms," 64.

114. TWD to Kendall, September 24, 1840. RCDC (Box 3, folder 9), JHL. On Kendall, see Donald B. Cole, *A Jackson Man: Amos Kendall and the Rise of American Democracy* (Baton Rouge: Louisiana State University Press, 2004).

115. On Van Buren and the *Amistad* affair, see Howe, *What Hath God Wrought*, 521–522.

Chapter 3: The Abolitionists and the People's Constitution

1. See Alasdair Roberts, *America's First Great Depression: Economic Crisis and Political Disorder after the Panic of 1837* (Ithaca, NY: Cornell University Press, 2012), 18–49, and Daniel Walker Howe, *What Hath God Wrought: The Transformation of America, 1815–1849* (New York: Oxford University Press, 2007), 504–506.

2. Donald B. Cole, *Martin Van Buren and the American Political System* (Princeton, NJ: Princeton University Press, 1984), 349.

3. Diary of John Park (March 15, 1842), 425, Boston Public Library, special collections.

4. Harry L. Watson, *Liberty and Power: The Politics of Jacksonian America* (New York: Hill and Wang, 1990), 212.

5. See Sean Wilentz, *The Rise of American Democracy: Jefferson to Lincoln* (New York: W. W. Norton, 2005), 495–508.

6. Ronald P. Formisano, *For the People: American Populist Movements from the*

Revolution to the 1850s (Chapel Hill: University of North Carolina Press, 2007), 150–152.

7. Ted Widmer, *Martin Van Buren* (New York: Time Books, 2005), 136–137.

8. Francis to TWD, March 4, 1840. RCDC (Box 3, folder 6), JHL.

9. Formisano, *For the People*, 152.

10. Quoted in Elizabeth Varon, *Disunion! The Coming of the American Civil War, 1789–1859* (Chapel Hill: University of North Carolina Press, 2008), 143.

11. Quoted in Patrick T. Conley, *Democracy in Decline: Rhode Island's Constitutional Development, 1776–1840* (Providence: Rhode Island Historical Society Publications, 1977), 297–298, note 17.

12. *Political Plaindealer*, March 25, 1837.

13. *Address to the People of Rhode Island Who Are Denied the Right of Suffrage* (New York, January 1840), 7–8. See also Joshua Greenberg, "The Panic of 1837 as an Opportunity for Radical Economic Ideas," 8. Accessed online at http://www .librarycompany.org/economics/2007conference/greenberg.pdf.

14. Ibid., 1–2.

15. Frances Whipple Greene, *Might and Right* (Providence, 1844), 71–72.

16. Quoted in ibid., 75. Greene reprinted the entire preamble. See pp. 72–75.

17. Samuel Man to James Simmons, September 5, 1841: "This suffrage business is nothing more nor less than a move to divide the Whigs." James Fowler Simmons Collection (Microfilm), LofC.

18. John Brown was not related to the prominent Brown family of the east side of Providence.

19. *New Age and Constitutional Advocate*, November 20, 1840.

20. Ibid., December 25, 1840.

21. *Liberator*, November 19, 1836.

22. Goodell, *The Rights and the Wrongs of Rhode Island* (New York, 1842), 27.

23. *Herald of Freedom*, November 26, 1841.

24. Eric Foner, *Politics and Ideology in the Age of the Civil War* (New York: Oxford University Press, 1980), 68–69.

25. *Friend of Man*, January 12, 1841.

26. *Emancipator and Free American*, June 30, 1842. See also June 9, 1842, and August 11, 1842.

27. William Goodell, *Lessons of a Single Day* (Pawtucket, 1842), 6–7. On the Slave Power see *Friend of Man*, September 2, 9, 30, 1840.

28. Wiecek, *The Guarantee Clause of the U.S. Constitution* (Ithaca, NY: Cornell University Press 1972), 161.

29. Henry Dorr to TWD, June 17, 1841. RCDC (Box 3, folder 13), JHL.

30. TWD to Elisha R. Potter, Jr., July 16, 1840. ERP Papers (Box 1, folder 6), MSS 629, subgroup 3, RIHS. See also Dorr's political scrapbook, p. 113, JHL.

31. See William Nesbet Chambers, "The Election of 1840," in Arthur Schlesinger, Jr., ed., *The History of American Presidential Elections, 1798–2008*, 4 vols. (New York, 2011), 1:290.

32. For a detailed discussion of the 1824 and 1834 constitutional conventions, see Conley, *Democracy in Decline*, 184–213, 255–268.

33. Edmund Burke, *Interference of the Executive in the Affairs of Rhode Island*, 29th Cong., 1st sess., 1844, House Report No. 546, 404. Hereafter cited as *Burke's Report*.

34. *New Age and Constitutional Advocate*, April 23, 1841. See also the Diary of Aurilla Moffitt (April 17, 1841). Old Colony Historical Society. For an informative discussion of the rallies, see Mark S. Schantz, *Piety in Providence: Class Dimensions of Religious Experience in Antebellum Rhode Island* (Ithaca, NY: Cornell University Press, 2000), 200–205, and John B. Rae, "The Great Suffrage Parade," *Rhode Island History* 1 (July 1942): 91.

35. TWD to Jesse Calder, May 4, 1841. RCDC (Box 3, folder 12), JHL.

36. Burges to Jesse Calder, May 4, 1841. TWD Papers (Box 1, folder 7), JHL.

37. *Republican Herald*, November 14, 1841. William Goodell selected "The Democracy of Christianity" as the title for his 1849 exploration of the connections between democratic government and the Christian faith.

38. William S. Balch, *Popular Liberty and Equal Rights: An Oration Delivered before the Convention of the Rhode Island Suffrage Association, July 5, 1841* (Providence, 1841), 18.

39. See Dorr's draft Resolutions for the Mass Convention at the Dexter Training Ground in Providence, July 5, 1841. TWD Papers (Box 2, folder 23), JHL.

40. *New Age and Constitutional Advocate*, July 16 and July 23, 1841.

41. *Providence Journal*, August 28, 1841.

42. *New Age and Constitutional Advocate*, August 26, 1841.

43. John Wood Sweet, *Bodies Politic: Negotiating Race in the American North, 1730–1830* (Philadelphia: University of Pennsylvania Press, 2003), 364–365.

44. John S. Gilkeson, Jr., *Middle-Class Providence, 1820–1940* (Princeton, N.J.: Princeton University Press, 1986), 19–20, and Mark S. Schantz, *Piety in Providence*, 101.

45. See *Rhode Island Digest*, 1822, "An Act Regulating the Manner of Admitting Freemen and Directing the Method of Electing Officers of the State," 89–90, RISA. See also Christopher Malone, *Between Freedom and Bondage: Race, Party, and Voting Rights in the Antebellum North* (New York: Routledge Press, 2008), 123–129.

46. Patrick Rael, "The Market Revolution and Market Values in Antebellum Black Protest Thought," in Rael, ed., *African-American Activism before the Civil War* (New York: Routledge Press, 2008), 276 and 279.

47. Sweet, *Bodies Politic*, 355.

48. See Petition of the Colored People for the Relief Against Taxation, January 11, 1831. Failed Petitions folder, RISA.

49. See the records for the Providence City Council (June 1833), Providence City Archives.

50. Petition of the Colored People for the Relief against Taxation, January 11, 1831.

51. *Acts and Resolves of the General Assembly*, 1841–1842, pp. 36–37, RISA.

52. *New Age and Constitutional Advocate*, February 19, 1841. See also *Rhode Island Schedules* (January session 1841), 82, and *Report of the Committee on the Subject of the General Assembly on the Subject of the Constitution March 1842* (Providence, 1842), 4–5, RISA.

53. Petition from Ichabod Northup, James Hazard, and others, June 23, 1841. Petitions Failed/Withdrawn, June 1841 Session, RISA.

54. Robert J. Cottrol, *Afro-Yankees: Providence's Black Community in the Antebellum Era* (Westport, CT: Greenwood Press, 1982), 71.

55. *Providence Journal*, August 30, 1841.

56. *New Age and Constitutional Advocate*, August 20, 1841. See also Gabriel Loiacono, "Poverty and Citizenship in Nineteenth Century Rhode Island" (Ph.D. diss., Brandeis University, 2008), 200–205.

57. *Providence Journal*, September 30, 1841.

58. *Providence Journal*, September 15, 1841. On the authorship of the "Town Borne" essays, see C. Peter McGrath, "Samuel Ames: The Great Chief Justice of Rhode Island," in Patrick T. Conley, ed., *Liberty and Justice: A History of Law and Lawyers in Rhode Island, 1636–1998* (Providence: Rhode Island Publications Society, 1998), 306.

59. *Providence Journal*, September 15, 1841.

60. Ibid., September 30, 1841.

61. John O'Sullivan to TWD, August 9, 1841. RCDC (Box 3, folder 14), JHL.

62. *Burke's Report*, 111–113. Abolitionist protests against the People's Constitution were inserted in *Burke's Report* not for the purpose of compiling an accurate historical record, but in order to disavow any connection with abolitionism.

63. *National Anti-Slavery Standard*, September 30, 1841. On Child, see Carolyn L. Karcher, *The First Woman in the Republic: A Cultural Biography of Lydia Maria Child* (Durham, NC: Duke University Press, 1994).

64. *Republican Herald*, October 13, 1841. See also Wilson J. Moses, *Alexander Crummell: A Study of Civilization and Discontent* (Amherst: University of Massachusetts Press, 1989), 35.

65. *Burke's Report*, 113.

66. *Republican Herald*, October 13, 1841.

67. *New Age and Constitutional Advocate*, October 22, 1841.

68. *Providence Journal*, October 11, 1841.

69. Ibid., October 9, 1841.

70. Nicholas Wood, "'A Sacrifice on the Altar of Slavery': Doughface Politics and Black Disenfranchisement in Pennsylvania, 1837–1838," *Journal of the Early Republic* 31 (Spring 2011): 85–86.

71. *New Age and Constitutional Advocate*, October 22, 1841.

72. See the Dorr Rebellion manuscripts (reel A), JHL.

73. Pearce was attorney general during the 1824 Hard Scrabble riot. He failed in his attempt to prosecute the rioters.

74. *Providence Journal*, October 11, 1841.

75. Ibid., October 9, 1841.

76. *New Age and Constitutional Advocate*, October 22, 1841, *Providence Journal*, October 11, 1841, and *National Anti-Slavery Standard*, October 21, 1841.

77. The convention adjourned on October 9 and resumed again on November 16. See *New Age and Constitutional Advocate*, November 5, 1841. A draft of the People's Constitution ran in *New Age* on October 15.

78. *Providence Journal*, October 9, 1841.

79. *National Anti-Slavery Standard*, October 21, 1841.

80. Quoted in Sarah C. O'Dowd, *A Rhode Island Original: Frances Harriet Whipple Green McDougall* (Hanover, NH: University Press of New England, 2004), 74–75. See also Patrick T. Conley, *The Makers of Modern Rhode Island* (Charleston, SC: History Press, 2012), 139–142.

81. *National Anti-Slavery Standard*, November 4, 1841.

82. *Liberator*, October 29, 1841.

83. Bruce Laurie, *Beyond Garrison: Antislavery and Social Reform* (New York: Cambridge University Press, 2005), 5.

84. Goodell, *Lessons of a Single Day*, 6–7.

85. Goodell, *The Rights and Wrongs of Rhode Island*, 4–5.

86. Eric Foner, *Give Me Liberty!* (New York: W. W. Norton, 2010), 454.

87. Henry Louis Gates, Jr., ed., *Douglass: Autobiographies* (Washington, DC: Library of America, 1994), 667.

88. Bruce Dorsey, *Reforming Men and Women: Gender in the Antebellum City* (Ithaca, NY: Cornell University Press, 2002), 153.

89. Abby Kelley to William Lloyd Garrison, September 30, 1841. Boston Public Library, manuscript division. MS.A.1.2.12.pt.1. See also Carol Faulkner, *Lucretia Mott's Heresy: Abolition and Women's Rights in Nineteenth-Century America* (Philadelphia: University of Pennsylvania Press, 2011), 125–126.

90. Jane Pease, "The Freshness of Fanaticism: Abby Kelley Foster: An Essay in Reform" (Ph.D. diss., University of Rochester, 1969), 37.

91. Susan Sisson to Abby Kelley, August 9, 1841. Abby Kelley Foster Papers, AAS. See also Abby Kelley to George Benson, September 13, 1841. Boston Public Library, special collections. MS.A.1.12.pt.1.107.

92. Asa Fairbanks to Abby Kelley, October 11, 1841. See also Mrs. French to Abby Kelley, October 1, 1841, Abby Kelley Foster Papers, AAS.

93. Abby Kelley to William Lloyd Garrison, September 30, 1841. Boston Public Library.

94. *National Anti-Slavery Standard*, November 4, 1841.

95. Sarah (Pratt?) to Abby Kelley, November 15, 1841. Abby Kelley Foster Papers, AAS. For a general discussion, see John R. McKivigan, *The War against Proslavery Religion: Abolitionism and Northern Churches, 1835–1865* (Ithaca, NY: Cornell University Press, 1984).

96. Stephen Foster to Kelley, January 9, 1842. Abby Kelley Foster Papers, Worcester Historical Society.

97. Everett to TWD, November 1, 1841. RCDC (Box 3, folder 16), JHL.

98. See Leonard L. Richards, *The Life and Times of Congressman John Quincy Adams* (New York: Oxford University Press, 1986), 162.

99. TWD to JQA, October 22, 1841. RCDC (Box 3, folder 15), JHL.

100. In November 1842, Adams gave a lecture at the Franklin Lyceum in Providence in which he waged a thinly veiled attack on Dorr's ideology. Adams, *The Social Compact Exemplified in the Constitution of Commonwealth of Massachusetts* (Providence, 1842), 18.

101. Jackson to Blair, May 23, 1842, in John Spencer Bassett, ed., *Correspondence of Andrew Jackson* (Washington, DC: Carnegie Institution, 1933), 6:153.

102. See the roll call of members in ERP Papers (Box 4, folder 3), RIHS.

103. See the Report of the Committee on the Declaration of Rights and Principles, November 5, 1841. Constitutional Convention 1841–1842 (Box 1, folder 1), RISA.

104. Henry Dorr to TWD, October 25, 1841. RCDC (Box 3, folder 16), JHL.

105. See Dorr's Notes on the Proceedings of the Committee on Electors and Suffrage, November 3, 1841. TWD Papers (Box 2, folder 23), JHL. See also the *Official Record of the Constitutional Convention of 1841* (Box 1, folder 14), RISA.

106. *Providence Journal*, November 15, 1841.

107. See the broadside "Trouble in the Spartan Ranks" (1843), AAS.

108. "Memorial of the Colored Citizens of Rhode Island" (signed Thomas Howland, Ichabod Northup, James Hazard, James Grimes), November 4, 1841. Constitutional Convention, 1841–1842 (Box 1, folder 6), RISA.

109. See Evelyn Savidge Sterne, *Ballots and Bibles: Ethnic Politics and the Catholic Church in Providence* (Ithaca, NY: Cornell University Press, 2004), 14.

110. See, for example, *Providence Journal*, August 16, 1838, and *Providence Journal*, December 24, 1841. On Anthony see Patrick T. Conley, "Henry Bowen Anthony," in Patrick T. Conley, ed., *Rhode Island in Rhetoric and Reflection* (Providence: Rhode Island Publications Society, 2002), 405–406.

111. Article on the Elective Franchise, November 6, 1841. Constitutional Convention 1841–1842 (Box 1, folder 2), RISA.

112. *Draft of Constitution of the State of Rhode Island and Providence Plantations . . . November 1841* (Providence, 1841), RISA.

113. *Liberator*, August 26, 1842.

114. Ibid., November 19, 1841.

115. William Lloyd Garrison to Edmund Quincy, November 9, 1841, in Walter Merrill, ed., *Letters of William Lloyd Garrison: No Union with Slaveholders* (Cambridge, MA: Harvard University Press, 1974), 3:28.

116. *Herald of Freedom*, November 26, 1841. See also *National Anti-Slavery Standard*, November 4 and 25, 1841.

117. The text of the speech appears in the *National Anti-Slavery Standard*, December 23, 1841.

118. *Herald of Freedom*, December 3, 1841.

119. *Liberator*, July 1, 1842.

120. John Blassingame, ed., *The Frederick Douglass Papers, 1841–1846* (New Haven, CT: Yale University Press, 1979), xxix.

121. Quoted in ibid., xlii.

122. *Herald of Freedom*, December 3, 1841.

123. Kathryn Grover, *The Fugitive's Gibraltar: Escaping Slaves and Abolitionism in New Bedford, Massachusetts* (Amherst: University of Massachusetts Press, 2001), 169.

124. *Liberator*, January 21, 1842.

125. Gregory P. Lampe, *Frederick Douglass: Freedom's Voice, 1818–1845* (East Lansing: Michigan State University Press, 1998), 82, 87–88. Though no transcriptions of his speeches have survived, Douglass drew from his powerful indictment of northern racism expressed in his November 4 speech in Hingham, Massachusetts. Blassingame, ed., *The Papers of Frederick Douglass*, 9–13.

126. *National Anti-Slavery Standard*, December 23, 1841.

127. Quoted in Lampe, *Frederick Douglass*, 84.

128. *National Anti-Slavery Standard*, December 23, 1841.

129. *New Age and Constitutional Advocate*, November 19, 1841.

130. *Herald of Freedom*, December 3, 1841.

131. *New Age and Constitutional Advocate*, November 19, 1841.

132. *Liberator*, December 10, 1841.

133. *New Age and Constitutional Advocate*, November 19, 1841, and Goodell, *The Rights and Wrongs of Rhode Island*, 22. Article XIV, section 22: "The General Assembly shall, at their first session, after the adoption of this Constitution, propose to the electors the question, whether the word 'white,' in the first line of the first section of Article II of the Constitution, shall be stricken out. The question shall be voted upon at the succeeding annual election; and if a majority of the electors voting, shall vote to strike out the word aforesaid, it shall be stricken from the Constitution; otherwise, not."

134. *Liberator*, December 10, 1841.

135. *National Anti-Slavery Standard*, December 23, 1841.

136. Dorr to Samuel Allen, December 13, 1841. RCDC (Box 3, folder 17), JHL.

137. *New Age and Constitutional Advocate*, December 24, 1841.

138. Ibid., November 19, 1841, and December 25, 1841. Dorr's closing remarks are also reprinted in *Burke's Report*, 851–864.

139. *Burke's Report*, 864.

140. Wood, "A Sacrifice on the Altar of Freedom," 96.

141. Louis Lapham to TWD, April 16, 1842. RCDC (Box 4, folder 6), JHL.

142. Susan Sisson to Abby Kelley, March 15, 1842. Abby Kelley Foster Papers, AAS.

143. ERP to Pearce, December 20, 1841. ERP Papers (Box 1, folder 6), RIHS. See also ERP to Thomas M. Potter, November 22, 1841. Thomas Mawney Potter Papers, MSS 629, subgroup 4, RIHS.

144. ERP to Pearce, December 20, 1841. ERP Papers (Box 1, folder 6), RIHS. See also *National Intelligencer*, May 21, 1842.

145. ERP to John Brown Francis, January 1, 1842. Henry A. L. Brown Deposit, MSS 1031, (Box 7, folder 100), RIHS. See also Christopher Allen to JBF, September 24, 1841 (Box 7, folder 99).

146. Francis to ERP, January 3, 1842. ERP Papers (Box 1, folder 7), RIHS.

147. See Henry Dorr to TWD, October 25, 1841. RCDC (Box 3, folder 16), JHL.

148. Henry Dorr to TWD, January, n.d., 1842. RCDC (Box 3, folder 16), JHL.

Chapter 4: Peacefully If We Can, Forcibly If We Must

1. *New Age*, December 17, 1841. See also Erik J. Chaput and Russell J. DeSimone, "Strange Bedfellows: The Politics of Race in Antebellum Rhode Island," *Common-Place* 10, no. 2 (January 2010); http://www.common-place.org/vol-10/no-02/chaput-desimone/.

2. See William Goodell, *The Rights and Wrongs of Rhode Island* (New York, 1842).

3. *National Anti-Slavery Standard*, December 23, 1841.

4. Ibid., October 21, 1841.

5. *The Suffrage Examiner*, December, nd, 1841.

6. Ibid.

7. *National Anti-Slavery Standard*, November 25, 1841.

8. *Providence Journal*, December 15, 1841.

9. *Herald of Freedom*, January 14, 1842.

10. Stacy Robertson, *Parker Pillsbury: Radical Abolitionist, Male Feminist* (Ithaca, NY: Cornell University Press, 2000), 110.

11. *Liberator*, December 10, 1841, Liberator, December 24, 1841, *National Anti-Slavery Standard*, November 25 and December 16, 1841. See also Gregory P. Lampe, *Frederick Douglass: Freedom's Voice, 1818–1845* (East Lansing: Michigan State University Press, 1998), 84–88.

12. See Abby Kelley's comments about Rhode Island's participation in the international slave trade in *National Anti-Slavery Standard*, November 4, 1841.

13. *National Anti-Slavery Standard*, December 30, 1841.

14. Ibid., December 23, 1841. See also Edmund Burke, *Interference of the Executive in the Affairs of Rhode Island*, 29th Cong., 1st sess., 1844, House Report No. 546, 116. Hereafter cited as *Burke's Report*.

15. *National Anti-Slavery Standard*, December 23, 1841. For the *New Age*'s attack on the abolitionists, see December 10, 1841.

16. Henry Louis Gates, Jr., ed., *Douglass: Autobiographies* (Washington, DC: Library of America, 1994), 666.

17. *National Anti-Slavery Standard*, January 6, 1842.

18. John Blassingame, ed., *The Frederick Douglass Papers, 1841–1846* (New Haven, CT: Yale University Press, 1979), xlvi.

19. Quoted in Dorothy Sterling, *Ahead of Her Time: Abby Kelley and the Politics of Antislavery* (New York: W. W. Norton, 1994), 141.

20. *National Anti-Slavery Standard*, January 13, 1842, and *Liberator*, January 21, 1842.

21. Dutee Pearce to John Brown Francis, January 5, 1842. Dorr War microfilm (F.83.4 G48), RIHS. For Abby Kelley's version of events, see *Liberator*, January 21, 1842.

22. *National Anti-Slavery Standard*, January 13, 1842, and *Liberator*, January 21, 1842.

23. *Liberator*, January 14, 1842. On the *Creole* revolt, see Edward Crapol, *John Tyler: The Accidental President* (Chapel Hill: University of North Carolina Press, 2006), 95–103, and James Oakes, *Freedom National: The Destruction of Slavery in the United States, 1861–1865* (New York: W. W. Norton, 2012), 22–25.

24. Ibid., August 19, 1842.

25. Ibid., June 17, 1842, quoting the *Madisonian*.

26. *Burke's Report*, 205.

27. ERP to John Brown Francis, January 1, 1842. Henry A.L. Brown Deposit, MSS 1031, (Box 7, folder 100), RIHS.

28. TWD to Pearce, December 13, 1841. RCDC (Box 3, folder 17), JHL.

29. Pearce to TWD, November 21, 1841. RCDC (Box 3, 16), JHL.

30. TWD to William Simons, December 20, 1842. RCDC (Box 5, folder 25), JHL.

31. TWD to Levi Woodbury, April 5, 1842. TWD Papers (Box 1, folder 11), JHL. See also Patrick T. Conley, *Democracy in Decline: Rhode Island's Constitutional Development, 1776–1841* (Providence: Rhode Island Historical Society, 1977), 315.

32. *New Age and Constitutional Advocate*, January 14, 1841.

33. John Pitman to Joseph Story, January 26, 1842. Pitman-Story Correspondence, William Clements Library (WCL).

34. TWD to Dutee Pearce, January 17, 1842. Thomas Wilson Dorr Collection, Vault A, Box 38, folder 6, Newport Historical Society (NHS).

35. The resolutions eventually passed on January 28. See *Providence Journal*, January 29, 1842.

36. John Pitman to Joseph Story, January 26, 1842. Pitman-Story Correspondence, WCL.

37. See TWD's draft of January 28, 1842, resolutions in the TWD Papers (Box 3, folder 1), JHL.

38. Conley, *Democracy in Decline*, 316.

39. See TWD's draft of the proposal to adjourn in the TWD Papers (Box 3, folder 1), JHL.

40. Thomas Hazard to Samuel F. Man, November 4, 1841, in *Private Letters from Prominent RI Men to Samuel F. Man Relating to the Political Affairs of Rhode Island during the Political Troubles of 1842*, JHL.

41. See the changes to the election law in the *Journal of the House* (February 5, 1842), RISA.

42. Zachariah Allen to Richard James Arnold, March 2, 1842. Richard James Arnold Papers, MSS 32, RIHS.

43. King to James Simmons, February 11, 1842. Dorr War microfilm (F.83.4 G48), RIHS.

44. Goodell, *The Rights and Wrongs of Rhode Island*, 34–36.

45. Conley, *Democracy in Decline*, 326.

46. Diary of Levi Lincoln Newton (May 19, 1842), Newton Family Papers, AAS. See also the Diary of John Park (April 13, 1842), 429–430, Boston Public Library, special collections, and John Brown Francis to Elisha R. Potter, Jr., January 3, 1842, and Francis to ERP, March 25, 1842. ERP Papers (Box 1, folder 7), RIHS.

47. Ives to Francis, April 8, 1942. Henry A. L. Brown Deposit (Box 7, folder 102), RIHS.

48. Dearborn to Thomas Stead, September 8, 1842, in Henry Dearborn, *Writings on Many Subjects*, vol. 2. New York Public Library, manuscripts division.

49. Anna Herroshoff to Charles Herroshoff, May 20, 1842, in *New England Women and Their Families, 18th and 19th Century Series* (reel 21), and William Bailey to Jane Keeley, June 14, 1842, William M. Bailey Papers, misc., manuscripts (9001-B), RIHS.

50. Francis Wayland, *A Discourse Delivered in the First Baptist Church* (Providence, 1842), 18.

51. Mark Tucker, *A Discourse Preached on Thanksgiving Day, July 21, 1842* (Providence, 1842), 11. Tucker served on the Providence School Committee from 1839 to 1841.

52. Mark S. Schantz, *Piety in Providence: Class Dimensions of Religious Experience in Antebellum Rhode Island* (Ithaca, NY: Cornell University Press, 2000), 162, 122–123, 198.

53. TWD Diary, 1844–1849, 6. TWD Papers (Box 3), JHL.

54. Hazard to Randolph, May 10, 1842. Joseph Peace Hazard Papers, MSS 483, subgroup 13 (Box 1, folder 3), RIHS.

55. See the broadside circular (Providence, RI), March 4, 1842. AAS.

56. TWD to Pearce, March 18, 1842. Thomas Wilson Dorr Collection, Vault A, Box 38, folder 6, NHS.

57. Joshua Rathburn to TWD, March 25, 1842. RCDC (Box 4, folder 4), JHL.

58. Conley, "Politics, Prejudice, Patriotism and Perseverance: Rhode Island's Catholic Irish Confront the Civil War," in Frank Williams, ed., *The Rhode Island Homefront in the Civil War Era* (forthcoming). For a succinct overview of nativism

in the antebellum period, see David H. Bennett, *The Party of Fear: The American Far Right from Nativism to the Militia Movement* (New York: Vintage, 1995), 35–47.

59. Joshua Rathburn to TWD, March 25, 1842. RCDC (Box 4, folder 4), JHL. See also Samuel Man to James Simmons, April 2, 1842. JFS Papers (General Correspondence, Box 15), LofC.

60. "Native American Citizens! Read and Take Warning!" (March, 1842), reprinted in Conley, *Democracy in Decline*, 308.

61. Diary of Aurilla Moffitt (March 24, 1842), Old Colony Historical Society. See also Ronald Zboray and Mary Zboray, *Voices without Votes: Women and Politics in Antebellum New England* (Hanover, NH: University Press of New England, 2010), 115–118.

62. Quoted in Patrick T. Conley, *The Dorr Rebellion: Rhode Island's Crisis in Constitutional Government* (Providence: Rhode Island Bicentennial Commission, 1976), 8.

63. Dutee Pearce to TWD, March 6, 1842. RCDC (Box 4, folder). On *Prigg*, see Paul Finkelman, "Story Telling on the Supreme Court: *Prigg v. Pennsylvania* and Justice Joseph Story's Judicial Nationalism," *Supreme Court Review* (1995): 247–294.

64. *Providence Journal*, March 12, 1842. See also Conley, *Democracy in Decline*, 317–318.

65. Francis to ERP, March 25, 1842. ERP Papers (Box 1, folder 7), RIHS.

66. Pitman to ERP, March 4, 1842. ERP Papers (Box 1, folder 7), RIHS. See Pitman, *To the General Assembly of Rhode Island* (Providence, 1842).

67. *Providence Journal*, January 21–22, 1842.

68. Story to Pitman, February 10, 1842, in Walter Story, ed., *Life and Letters of Joseph Story*, 2 vols. (Boston: Charles C. Little & James Brown, 1851), 2:416.

69. Durfee to ERP, March 13, 1842. ERP Papers (Box 1, folder 7), RIHS.

70. *Chief Justice Job Durfee's March 1842 Charge to the Bristol Grand Jury* (Providence, 1842), 3, 15.

71. Joshua Rathburn to TWD, March 4, 1842. RCDC (Box 4, folder 4), JHL.

72. See Thomas P. Slaughter, "'The King of Crimes': Early American Treason Law, 1787–1860," in Ronald Hoffman and Peter J. Albert, eds., *Launching the "Extended Republic": The Federalist Era* (Charlottesville: University Press of Virginia, 1996), 54–135.

73. See Draft of "Nine Lawyers' Opinion," p. 8, in TWD Papers (Box 3, folder 1). For the final version see *Providence Express*, March 16, 1842. For Dorr's comments on the "Nine Lawyers' Opinion," see his letter to Dutee Pearce, March 15, 1842. Thomas Wilson Dorr Collection, Vault A, Box 38, folder, NHS.

74. Draft of "Nine Lawyers' Opinion," p. 1.

75. Accessed online at the Avalon Project at the Yale Law School: http://avalon.law.yale.edu/18th_century/washing.asp (accessed January 2, 2012).

76. TWD to Dutee Pearce, March 18, 1842. Thomas Wilson Dorr Collection, Vault A, Box 38, folder 6, NHS.

77. TWD to Dutee Pearce, March 15, 1842. Private Collection of Richard Slaney.

78. TWD to Dutee Pearce, March 23, 1842. Thomas Wilson Dorr Collection, Vault A, Box 38, folder 6, NHS.

79. John Pitman to Joseph Story, March 30, 1842. Pitman-Story correspondence, WCL.

80. TWD to Dutee Pearce, March 23, 1842. Thomas Wilson Dorr Collection, Vault A, Box 38, folder 6, NHS.

81. *New Age and Constitutional Advocate* (semi-weekly), March 22, 1842.

82. See *Report of the Committee on the Action of the General Assembly on the Subject of the Constitution*, March Session (Providence, 1842), 11, RISA.

83. See the partial letter from a man claiming to have been selected to run as the secretary of state under the People's Constitution to Dorr, April 2, 1842. RCDC (Box 4, folder 4), JHL.

84. James Mason Clark to Samuel Ames to April 4, 1842; King to Ames, April 9, 1842; and Raymond Sea to Samuel Ames, May 26, 1842. Quartermaster General files (1842), RISA and Samuel Ward King to Elisha Dyer, April 9, 1842. Adjutant General Correspondence (1842), RISA.

85. See the printed orders April 5, 1842, issued by Samuel W. King and Elisha Dyer, Jr.; Adjutant General Report, April 25, 1842; Josiah Martin to Elisha Dyer, Jr., April 6, 1842; Westcott Handy to Samuel Ward King, April 6, 1842. See also George Nightingale to Elisha Dyer, Jr., April 16, 1842. All items are in the Adjutant General files (1842) at the RISA.

86. TWD to Woodbury, April 11, 1842. Levi Woodbury Papers, LofC.

87. TWD to Dutee Pearce, April 4, 1842. Thomas Wilson Dorr Collection, Vault A, Box 38, folder 6, NHS.

88. Sullivan and Lydia Dorr to TWD, April 8, 1842. RCDC (Box 4, folder 5), JHL.

89. King to John Tyler, April 4, 1842, reprinted in James David Richardson, ed., *A Compilation of the Messages and Papers of the Presidents, 1789–1908*, 20 vols. (Washington, DC: Bureau of National Literature and Art, 1908), 4:286.

90. TWD to Dutee Pearce, April 7, 1842. SSR Papers (Box 6, folder 21), JHL.

91. Charles Wiltse, *John C. Calhoun: Sectionalist, 1840–1850* (New York: Bobbs-Merrill, 1951), 80–82.

92. It seems strange that biographers of John Tyler could omit mention of the Dorr Rebellion, but somehow Edward Crapol and Dan Monroe manage to do just that. See Crapol, *John Tyler: The Accidental President* (Chapel Hill: University of North Carolina Press, 2006), and Monroe, *The Republican Vision of John Tyler* (College Station: Texas A&M University Press, 2003).

93. TWD to Levi Woodbury, April 5, 1842. TWD Papers (Box 1, folder 11), JHL. See also TWD to Woodbury, April 7 and 11, 1842. Levi Woodbury Papers, LofC.

94. Charles Francis Adams, ed., *The Memoirs of John Quincy Adams, Comprising Portions of His Diary from 1795 to 1848*, 12 vols. (Philadelphia, 1877), 11:129. See also James Simmons to Samuel Man, April 19, 1842, in *Private Letters from Prominent RI Men to Samuel F. Man*.

95. John Brown to TWD, April 10, 1842. See also William Allen to TWD, April 15, 1842. RCDC (Box 4, folders 5 and 6), JHL. For more on Allen see Jean H. Baker, *Affairs of Party: The Political Culture of Northern Democrats in the Mid-Nineteenth Century* (New York: Fordham University Press, 1983), 42–45.

96. *Providence Express*, April 12, 1842, and *Bay State Democrat*, April 13, 1842. See also Wright to TWD, April 16, 1842. RCDC (Box 4, folder 6), JHL.

97. William M. Wiecek, "Popular Sovereignty in the TWD War—Conservative Counterblast," *Rhode Island History* 32 (May 1973): 47.

98. See Michael F. Holt, *The Rise and Fall of the American Whig Party: Jacksonian Politics and the Onset of the Civil War* (New York: Oxford University Press, 1999), 170–175.

99. *Boston Post*, April 15, 1842.

100. William M. Wiecek, *The Guarantee Clause of the U.S. Constitution* (Ithaca, NY: Cornell University Press, 1972), 78–9, 85–86.

101. *Southern Patriot*, May 3, 1842. This view was echoed in the *Richmond Enquirer*, May 6 and 17, 1842, and the *Charleston Mercury*, May 20, 1842. Oakes, *Freedom National*, 36–39.

102. *Richmond Enquirer*, May 6, 1842.

103. *Emancipator and Free American*, June 2, 1842.

104. King to Tyler, April 4, 1842. Reprinted in Richardson, ed., *A Compilation of the Messages and Papers of the Presidents, 1789–1908*, 286.

105. Ibid., 287.

106. See the "Statement of Facts" drafted by Whipple, Francis, and Potter in *Burke's Report*, 669–672.

107. JBF to Elizabeth Francis, April 10, 1842. Henry A. L. Brown Deposit (Box 7, folder 102), RIHS.

108. Whipple to Tyler, April 11, 1842. Quoted in Richardson, ed., *A Compilation of the Messages and Papers of the Presidents, 1789–1908*, 288.

109. Ibid., 288–290.

110. See Tyler to King, April 11, 1842, in Richardson, ed., *A Compilation of the Messages and Papers of the Presidents, 1789–1908*, 290–291. See also Wiecek, *Guarantee Clause*, 81–84, and Robert J. Morgan, *A Whig Embattled: The Presidency under John Tyler* (New York: Archon Books, 1974), 99.

111. Lyon Gardiner Tyler, ed., *The Letters and Times of the Tylers*, 20 vols. (Richmond, VA, 1885), 2:194.

112. Quotes taken from "Governor Dorr's Address to the People of Rhode Island" (August 1843) in *Burke's Report*, 739. For remarks against Tyler in the spring of 1842, see TWD to Levi Woodbury, April 13, 1842. RCDC (Box 4, folder 5).

113. Dexter Randall, *Democracy Vindicated and Dorrism Unveiled* (Providence, 1846), 21. See also *Burke's Report*, 740–741.

114. TWD to James Buchanan, April 23, 1842. James Buchanan Papers (reel 7), Historical Society of Pennsylvania.

115. Joseph Story to Daniel Webster, April 26, 1842. Daniel Webster Papers, New Hampshire Historical Society.

116. John Pitman to Joseph Story, March 30, 1842. Pitman-Story Correspondence, WCL.

117. Joseph Story to Daniel Webster, April 26, 1842. Daniel Webster Papers, New Hampshire Historical Society.

118. John Davis to Henry A. S. Dearborn, May 8, 1842. See Henry A. S. Dearborn, ed., *Writings on Many Subjects by H. A. S. Dearborn*, vol. 2 (1846). Manuscripts Division. New York Public Library.

119. *Burke's Report*, 700.

120. ERP to Thomas M. Potter, May 3, 1842. Thomas Mawney Potter Papers, RIHS.

121. *Cincinnati Daily Enquirer*, May 9, 1842.

122. TWD to William Allen, April 14, 1842. RCDC (Box 4, folder 5), JHL.

123. TWD to Levi Woodbury, April 13, 1842. Levi Woodbury Papers, LofC. A draft of this letter is in the RCDC (Box 4, folder 5), JHL. See also TWD to James Buchanan, April 13, 1842. Buchanan Papers (reel 7), Historical Society of Pennsylvania.

124. William Allen to TWD, April 15, 1842. RCDC (Box 4, folder 6), JHL. See also Patrick T. Conley, "No Tempest in the Teapot: The Dorr Rebellion," *Rhode Island History* 50 (August 1992): 67–100.

125. TWD to Dutee Pearce, April 15, 1842. Thomas Wilson Dorr Collection, Vault A, Box 38, folder 6, NHS.

126. Woodbury to TWD, April 15, 1842. RCDC (Box 4, folder 6), LofC. See also Dorr to Woodbury, April 19, 1842. Levi Woodbury Papers, LofC.

127. Benton to TWD, April 16, 1842. RCDC (Box 4, folder 6), JHL.

128. Woodbury to TWD, April 15, 1842. RCDC (Box 4, folder 6), JHL.

129. Benton to TWD, April 16, 1842. RCDC (Box 4, folder 6), JHL.

130. Silas Wright to TWD, April 16, 1842. RCDC (Box 4, folder 6), JHL. Wright promised all necessary aid to lawmen in suppressing the Anti-Renters. Reeve Huston, *Land and Freedom: Rural Society, Popular Protest, and Party Politics in Antebellum New York* (New York: Oxford University Press, 2000), 147. While northern Democrats generally looked with favor on Dorr's ideology, New York Democrats (the majority of the landlords) were skeptical of the anti-rent agenda insisting that the relation of landlord to tenant was a private, contractual issue. See Huston, *Land and Freedom*, 100–102.

131. Conley, *Democracy in Decline*, 326–327.

132. Silas Wright to TWD, April 25, 1842. RCDC (Box 4, folder 7), JHL and William Sprague to John Brown Francis, April 24, 1842. Henry A. L. Brown Deposit (Box 7, folder 102), RIHS. See also *Senate Journal* (April 18, 1842) and *Congressional Globe* (27th Cong., 2nd sess., 1842), 430–432, 438, 446.

133. Silas Wright to TWD, April 16, 1842. RCDC (Box 4, folder 6), JHL. For

Wright's connection to Calhoun, see Wright to Van Buren, April 2, 1842. Martin Van Buren Papers, LofC.

134. Diary of John Park (April 11–30, 1842), 429–431. Boston Public Library, special collections.

135. See the summons for Dorr to appear before a magistrate in the "Thomas Wilson Dorr, 1842" folder in the Albert C. Greene Papers (Box 15, folder 78), MSS 452, RIHS.

136. Ives to John Brown Francis, April 11, 1842. Henry A. L. Brown Deposit (Box 7, folder 102), RIHS.

Chapter 5: The Arsenal

1. The warrant for his arrest (May 9, 1842) is at the Providence City Archives.

2. John Brown Francis to Elisha R. Potter, Jr., May 11, 1842. ERP Papers, MSS 629, subgroup 3, (Box 4, folder 7), RIHS.

3. Susan Sisson to Abby Kelley, March 15, 1842. Abby Kelley Foster Papers, AAS.

4. B. M. Potter to Thomas Potter, April 28, 1842. Thomas Mawney Potter Papers, MSS 629, sub group 4, RIHS.

5. James Mason Clark to Samuel Ames to April 4, 1842. Quarter-Master General Correspondence, RISA.

6. Diary of Aurilla Moffitt (May 3, 1842), Old Colony Historical Society, and Diary of John Park (May 2–3, 1842), p. 433, Boston Public Library, special collections.

7. Thomas Jenckes to Thomas Burgess, April 30, 1842. Correspondence of Providence Mayor Thomas Burgess, Providence City Archives.

8. Rhoda Newcomb to Charles Newcomb, May 3, 1842. Charles Newcomb Papers (Box 3), JHL. For more on the inaugural, see the Diary of Hiram Hill (May 3 and 4, 1842; microfilm, CS71.H64), RIHS.

9. Zachariah Allen, Jr., "The Dorr Rebellion," unpublished manuscript, p. 89, MSS 254, (Box 3), RIHS.

10. For mention of the troops, see Elisha Potter, Jr., to Thomas M. Potter, May 3, 1842. Thomas Mawney Potter Papers, RIHS.

11. See Joshua Spooner to George Ader, May 3, 1842. Joshua Spooner Papers, MSS 732, RIHS. Edward Carrington to James Simmons, May 3, 1842, JFS Papers (General Correspondence, Box 15), LofC.

12. Diary of John Park (May 3, 1842), p. 433. Boston Public Library, special collections.

13. TWD to William Simons, August 7, 1842. SSR Papers (Box 3), JHL.

14. TWD to Albert Tracy, August 25, 1845. Albert Tracy Papers, New York Public Library, special collections.

15. Quoted in Patrick T. Conley, *Democracy in Decline: Rhode Island's Constitu-*

tional Development, 1776–1841 (Providence: Rhode Island Historical Society Publications, 1977), 329.

16. Ronald P. Formisano, *For the People: American Populist Movements from the Revolution to the 1850s* (Chapel Hill: University of North Carolina Press, 2008), 168 and 280, note 43.

17. Sprague to John Brown Francis, June 12, 1842. Henry A. L. Brown Deposit, MSS 1031, (Box 7, folder 104), RIHS. See also Christopher Allen to John Brown Francis, March 25, 1842, Henry A. L. Brown Deposit (Box 7, folder 103), RIHS.

18. See Patrick T. Conley, *The Makers of Modern Rhode Island* (Charleston, SC: History Press, 2012), 64–68.

19. John Harris to TWD, May 30, 1842. RCDC (Box 4, folder 12), JHL.

20. Emily Aplin to Joseph Carpenter, November 2, 1842, quoted in John D. Tew, "Echoes from the Dorr Rebellion: The 1842 Aplin/Carpenter Correspondence," *American Ancestors* 12 (Fall 2011), 39.

21 Walter Burges to TWD, May 9, 1842. RCDC (Box 4, folder 10), JHL.

22. David Parmenter to TWD, May 30 and June 7, 1842. See also William Miller to TWD, June 15, 1842. RCDC (Box 4, folders 16, 17, and 19), JHL.

23. See "Foreign Voters!!" broadside (1842), Harris Collection of Broadsides, JHL. See also Samuel Man to James Simmons, May 13, 1842, JFS Papers (General Correspondence, Box 15), LofC.

24. ERP to Francis, May 1, 1842. Henry A. L. Brown Deposit (Box 7, folder 103), RIHS.

25. Francis to ERP, May 3, 1842. ERP Papers, (Box 1, folder 7), RIHS. See also Evelyn Sterne, *Ballots and Bibles: Ethnic Politics and the Catholic Church in Providence* (Ithaca, NY: Cornell University Press, 2003), 22–24.

26. Mark S. Schantz, *Piety in Providence: Class Dimensions of Religious Experience in Antebellum Rhode Island* (Ithaca, NY: Cornell University Press, 2000), 168. See also Robert W. Hayman, *Catholicism in Rhode Island and the Diocese of Providence, 1780–1886* (Providence, RI: Diocese of Providence Press, 1982), 46, and Patrick T. Conley and Matthew Smith, *Catholicism in Rhode Island: The Formative Era* (Providence, RI: Diocese of Providence Press, 1976), 44–48.

27. Erik J. Chaput, "Reform and Reaction: Populism in Early America," *Common-Place* 9, no. 2 (January 2009); http://www.common-place.org/vol-09/no-02/reviews/chaput.shtml.

28. ERP to Francis, May 1, 1842. Henry A. L. Brown Deposit, RIHS. On the population figure, see Conley and Smith, *Catholicism in Rhode Island*, 24, 57.

29. James David Richardson, ed., *A Compilation of the Messages and Papers of the Presidents, 1789–1897*, 20 vols. (Washington, DC: Bureau of National Literature and Art, 1897), 4:405.

30. See Henry A. S. Dearborn to John Davis, May 8, 1842, in Henry Dearborn, ed., *Writings on Many Subjects by H. A. S. Dearborn*, vol. 2. (1846). New York Public Library, manuscript division.

31. See Zachariah Allen, Jr., "The Dorr Rebellion," unpublished manuscript, pp. 143–145, RIHS. See also the Quartermaster General Correspondence (April-June 1842), RISA.

32. Spooner to George Ader, May 5, 1852, Joshua Spooner Papers, RIHS.

33. Edmund Burke, *Interference of the Executive in the Affairs of Rhode Island*, 29th Cong., 1st sess., 1844, House Report No. 546, 726. Hereafter cited as *Burke's Report*.

34. Ibid., 461. The complete files of the People's Legislature are in *Burke's Report*, 447–469.

35. See Joshua Spooner to George Ader, May 9, 1842, Joshua Spooner Papers, RIHS.

36. John Harris to TWD, May 9, 1842. RCDC (Box 4, folder 10), LofC.

37. Walter S. Burges to TWD, May 5, 1842. TWD Papers (Box 1, folder 7), JHL.

38. TWD to Bradford Allen, May 8, 1842. RCDC (Box 4, folder 9), JHL. Bradford Allen was not related to Lydia (Allen) Dorr.

39. See Dorr's political scrapbook, p. 18, JHL.

40. ERP, "Memorandum on the Dorr Rebellion." ERP Papers (Box 4, folder 4), RIHS. See also ERP to John Brown Francis, May 14, 1842. Dorr War microfilm (F83.4 G48), RIHS.

41. *Providence Daily Express*, May 30, 1842.

42. ERP to John Brown Francis, May 14, 1842. Dorr War microfilm, RIHS.

43. William Watson to Simmons, April 23, 1842. JFS Papers (General Correspondence, Box 15), LofC.

44. Man to James Simmons, May 27, 1842. JFS Papers (General Correspondence, Box 15), LofC.

45. Elisha R. Potter, Jr., *Speech of Mr. Potter of Rhode Island* (Washington, DC: Globe Office, 1844), 8.

46. ERP, "Memorandum on the TWD Rebellion." ERP Papers (Box 4, folder 4), RIHS.

47. Calhoun to John Mathews, May 22, 1842, in Clyde N. Wilson, ed., *The Papers of John Calhoun*, 28 vols. (Columbia: University of South Carolina Press, 1984), 16:267.

48. TWD to Burges, May 12, 1842. RCDC (Box 4, folder 11), RIHS.

49. William Goodell, *The Rights and Wrongs of Rhode Island* (New York, 1842), 16.

50. Dixon Lewis to Richard Cralle, May 30, 1842, in Wilson, ed., *The Papers of John C. Calhoun*, 16:263.

51. Quoted in Irving Bartlett, *John Calhoun* (New York: W. W. Norton, 1993), 304. See also Wilson, ed., *The Papers of John C. Calhoun*, 16:xviii.

52. See Robert DeGroff Buckley, Jr., "Robert Rantoul, Jr., 1805–1852: Politics and Reform in Antebellum Massachusetts" (Ph.D. diss., Princeton University, 1971), 301–306. See also I. O. Barnes to Levi Woodbury, February 28, May 2, May

9, May 21, 1842, and Joseph Scoville to Woodbury, June 17, 1842. Levi Woodbury Papers.

53. Charles Sellers, *James K. Polk: Continentalist, 1843–1846* (Princeton, NJ: Princeton University Press, 1966), 25. See also Michael A. Bernstein, "Northern Labor Finds a Southern Champion: A Note on the Radical Democracy, 1833–1849," in Conrad E. Wright and William Pencak, eds., *New York and the Rise of American Capitalism: Economic Development and the Social and Political History of an American State 1780–1870* (New York: New York Historical Society Publications, 1989), 147–168.

54. ERP to John Brown Francis, May 14, 1842. Dorr War microfilm, RIHS.

55. John Calhoun to William Smith, July 3, 1843, in Wilson, ed., *The Papers of John C. Calhoun*, 17:278. See also John R. Vile's learned article, "John C. Calhoun on the Guarantee Clause," *South Carolina Law Review* 40 (1989): 667–680.

56. Quoted in John Ashworth, *Agrarians and Aristocrats: Party Political Ideology in the United States, 1837–1846* (London: Cambridge University Press, 1987), 244.

57. Edward P. Crapol, *John Tyler: The Accidental President* (Chapel Hill: University of North Carolina Press, 2006), 77.

58. Wilson, ed., *The Papers of John C. Calhoun*, 17:277.

59. Ibid., 277.

60. William M. Wiecek, *The Sources of Antislavery Constitutionalism, 1760–1848* (Ithaca, NY: Cornell University Press, 1977), 122.

61. Preston quoted in F. H. Richmond to James Simmons, May 7, 1842. JFS Papers (General Correspondence, Box 15), LofC.

62. Dixon Lewis to Richard Cralle, May 30, 1842, in Wilson, ed., *The Papers of John C. Calhoun*, 16:263.

63. William Smith to James Buchanan, June 3, 1843. See also Smith to Buchanan, June 28, 1843. James Buchanan Papers (reel 7 and 45), Historical Society of Pennsylvania.

64. Smith to George Bancroft, February 10, 1843. George Bancroft Papers, Massachusetts Historical Society.

65. Ibid.

66. Smith to Martin Van Buren, February 10, 1843. Martin Van Buren Papers, LofC; Smith to James Buchanan, February 10, 1843. James Buchanan Papers (reel 7), Historical Society of Pennsylvania. Smith's letter to John Calhoun has not survived, but Calhoun incorporated the questions into his reply to Smith on July 3, 1843. See Wilson, ed., *The Papers of John C. Calhoun*, 17:270–291.

67. Buchanan's letter to Smith has not survived, but Smith quoted them in a letter to John C. Calhoun on June 28, 1843. See Wilson, ed., *The Papers of John C. Calhoun*, 17:260–261.

68. The Virginia Declaration of Rights (June 12, 1776). Accessed online at http://oll.libertyfund.org. January 2, 2012.

69. Martin Van Buren to Smith, July, nd, 1843. Martin Van Buren Papers, LofC.

70. Wright to Van Buren, June 19, 1843. Martin Van Buren Papers, LofC.

71. John Calhoun to Smith, July 3, 1843, in Wilson, ed., *The Papers of John C. Calhoun*, 17:284.

72. Ibid.

73. Ibid., 277.

74. Ibid., 286.

75. Harold Hyman and William M. Wiecek, *Equal Justice under Law: Constitutional Development, 1835–1875* (New York: Harper and Row, 1982), 388–397.

76. William M. Wiecek, *The Guarantee Clause of the U.S. Constitution* (Ithaca, NY: Cornell University Press, 1972), 133.

77. Robert Hunter to Calhoun, September 12, 1843, in Wilson, ed., *The Papers of John C. Calhoun*, 17:433.

78. Rhett to Calhoun, July 22, 1843, in Wilson, ed., *The Papers of John C. Calhoun*, 17:312.

79. Robert Hunter to Calhoun, September 30, 1843, in Wilson, ed., *The Papers of John C. Calhoun*, 17:474.

80. Hunter to Calhoun, October 24, 1843, in Wilson, ed., *The Papers of John C. Calhoun*, 17:521.

81. Smith to James Buchanan, June 28, 1843. James Buchanan Papers (reel 45), Historical Society of Pennsylvania.

82. John Brown Francis to ERP, May 23, 1842. ERP Papers (Box 1, folder 7), RIHS. See also ERP to John Brown Francis, May 14, 1842. Dorr War microfilm, RIHS.

83. Webster to Whipple, May 9, 1842. Daniel Webster Papers, New Hampshire Historical Society.

84. TWD to Aaron White, May 12, 1842. RCDC (Box 4, folder 11), JHL.

85. Brownson to TWD, May 14, 1842. RCDC (Box 4, folder 12), JHL.

86. Potter to Tyler, May 15, 1842, and June 2, 1842. ERP Papers (Box 1, folder 7), RIHS.

87. TWD to Chauncey Cleveland, May 13, 1842. RCDC (Box 4, folder 11), JHL. Dorr sent the same letter to Maine Governor John Fairfield on May 17. The letter is in the Maine State Archives.

88. *New York Evening Post*, May 14; *New York Tribune*, May 26, 1842; *New York Express*, May 27, 1842; *Providence Journal*, May 18 and 26, 1842; *Providence Daily Express*, May 13 and May 26, 1842.

89. White to TWD, May 13, 1842. RCDC (Box 4, folder 12), JHL.

90. *Providence Daily Express*, May 27, 1842.

91. Tyler to King, May 9, 1842, in Richardson, ed., *A Compilation of the Messages and Papers of the Presidents, 1789–1908*, 294. See also King to Tyler, May 12, 1842, in ibid., 295.

92. Diary of Levi Lincoln Newton (April 22, 1842), Newton Family Papers, AAS.

93. *New York Tribune*, May 26, 1842.

94. Man to Simmons, May 16, 1842. JFS Papers (General Correspondence, Box 15), LofC.

95. TWD to Bradford Allen, May 8, 1842. RCDC (Box 4, folder 9), JHL.

96. Allan Nevins, ed., *Diary of Philip Hone, 1838–1851* (New York: Dodd, Mead, and Co., 1927), 603 (May 18, 1842). See also *Albany Evening Journal*, May 18, 1842.

97. Rallies were held on April 27 and May 17. See *Democratic Republican New Era*, April 29, 1842, and *New York Tribune*, May 18, 1842, and *Hartford Courant*, May 21, 1842. See also Frederick Seward, ed., *William H. Seward: An Autobiography from 1801–1834 with a Memoir of His Life and a Selection of His Letters from 1831–1846* (New York, 1891), 602.

98. I thank Russell DeSimone for letting me read the rare published pamphlet of Moore's July 4, 1843, oration to New York City mechanics and workingmen.

99. *New York Herald*, May 18, 1842.

100. Nevins, ed., *Diary of Philip Hone, 1838–1851*, 598 (April 27, 1842).

101. Sean Wilentz, *Chants Democratic: New York City and the Rise of the American Working Class, 1788–1850* (New York: Oxford University Press, 1984), 327–328.

102. Sean Wilentz, *The Rise of American Democracy: From Jefferson to Lincoln* (New York: W. W. Norton, 2005), 533.

103. Potter to James F. Simmons, May 18, 1842. JFS Papers (General Correspondence, Box 15), LofC.

104. Dorr to Aaron White, Jr., May 12, 1842. RCDC (Box 4, folder 10), JHL.

105. *New York Express*, May 17, 1842, and *Niles' Weekly Register*, May 21, 1842. See also Ming and Crasto to TWD, May 13, 1842. RCDC (Box 4, folder 12), JHL.

106. Henry Storms to Seward, May 17, 1842. William Henry Seward Papers, University of Rochester.

107. Providence *Daily Express*, May 13, 1842.

108. See the Diary of Hiram Hill (May 15 and 16, 1842), RIHS.

109. Charles Coffin Jewett, *The Close of the Late Rebellion in Rhode Island* (Providence, RI: B. Cranston & Co., 1842), 3–4.

110. Man to Simmons, May 16, 1842. JFS Papers (General Correspondence, Box 15), LofC.

111. Diary of Aurilla Moffitt (May 16, 1842), Old Colony Historical Society.

112. *Providence Journal*, May 17, 1842.

113. Man to Simmons, May 16, 1842. JFS Papers (General Correspondence, Box 15), LofC. *Charleston Mercury*, May 23, 1842.

114. *Journal of the Senate of Connecticut* (May 9, 1842), 332, and Connecticut *Executive Council Journal*, vol. 6, p. 129.

115. See, for example, Rhoda Newcomb to Charles Newcomb, May 22, 1842. Charles Newcomb Papers (Box 3).

116. Almon D. Hodges, ed., *Almon Danforth Hodges and His Neighbors: An Autobiographical Sketch of a Typical Old New Englander* (Boston, 1909), 186.

117. See the Testimony of George W. Bennett (1842) in the quarter-master general files at the RISA.

118. Joshua Spooner to George Ader, May 17, 1842, Joshua Spooner Papers, RIHS.

119. William Bailey to Jane Keeley, May 17, 1842, William M. Bailey Papers, misc., manuscripts (9001-B), RIHS.

120. *Democratic Republican New Era*, May 28, 1842.

121. Burgess to James Fenner, May 18, 1842. Executive Department Correspondence, RISA.

122. Diary of Edward Peckham (May 17, 1842), Dorr Rebellion manuscripts (reel C), JHL. For more on Peckham, see Patrick T. Conley and Paul Campbell, *Providence: A Pictorial History* (Norfolk, VA: Donning, 1982), 53.

123. William Bailey to Jane Keeley, May 17, 1842, William M. Bailey Papers, RIHS.

124. Walter Simmons to James Simmons, May 17, 1842. JFS Papers (Family Correspondence, Box 2), LofC.

125. Edward Carrington to James Simmons, May 18, 1842. JFS Papers (General Correspondence, Box 15), LofC. See also Diary of Levi Lincoln Newton (May 18, 1842), Newton Family Papers, AAS; Joshua Spooner to George Ader, May 18, 1842, RIHS; Bailey to Keeley, May 18, 1842, William M. Bailey Papers, RIHS; and regimental history of the First Light Infantry compiled by Frederic Hayes in 1877, Records of the First Light Infantry, MSS 673, RIHS.

126. Diary of Edward Peckham (May 17, 1842), JHL.

127. Joshua Spooner to George Ader, May 21, 1842, Joshua Spooner Papers, RIHS.

128. Samuel Man to James Simmons, May 18, 1842. JFS Papers (General Correspondence, box 15), JHL.

129. *Providence Journal*, May 26, 1842. See also Howard R. Ernst, "A Call to Arms: Thomas Wilson Dorr's Forceful Effort to Implement the People's Constitution," *Rhode Island History* 66, no. 3 (Summer 2008): 67.

130. Joshua Spooner to George Ader, May 18, 1842, Joshua Spooner Papers, RIHS.

131. Diary of Henry Hodges. Private Collection of Russell J. DeSimone. See also Francis Bowen, *The Recent Contest in Rhode Island* (Boston, 1844), 36.

132. Jewett, *The Close of the Late Rebellion in Rhode Island*, 5–6.

133. Diary of Edward Peckham (May 17, 1842), JHL. See also the "History of the First Light Infantry Company," Records of the First Light Infantry, Joshua Spooner to George Ader, May 18, 1842, Joshua Spooner Papers and the Diary of Hiram Hill (May 18, 1842), RIHS.

134. William Bailey to Jane Keeley, May 18, 1842, William M. Bailey Papers, RIHS. See also Diary of Edward Peckham (May 17, 1842), JHL. See also *Democratic Republican New Era*, May 28, 1842.

135. Susan Graham, "'Call Me a Female Politician, I Glory in the Name':

Women Dorrites and Rhode Island's 1842 Suffrage Crisis" (Ph.D. diss., University of Minnesota, 2006), 265.

136. Diary of Hiram Hill (May 18, 1842), RIHS.

137. TWD reflected on the failed arsenal attack in his May 21, 1842, proclamation. See *New York Tribune*, May 28, 1842. See also Ann Parlin to TWD, September 4, 1842. RCDC (Box 5, folder 3), JHL.

138. J. W. Burke to J. Walters, May 20, 1842. Elijah Williams Family Papers, MSS 34, (Box 3), RIHS. Rhoda Newcomb to Charles Newcomb, May 22, 1842. Charles Newcomb Papers (Box 3), JHL.

139. Quoted in Conley, *Democracy in Decline*, 357.

140. Dorr to William Simons, August 7, 1842. SSR Papers (Box 3), JHL. See also Dorr to Willard, Low, and Miller, June 25, 1842. Gilder Lehrman Collection.

141. J. F. Chamberlain to A. J. McCall, May 23, 1842. James McCall Papers, Cornell University Library.

142. Samuel Wales to Dorr, May 18, 1842 (Box 4, folder 14) and Aaron White to Dorr, May 25, 1842, RCDC (Box 4, folder 15), JHL.

Chapter 6: An Abolitionist Plot

1. Quotes taken from Anna Herreshoff to Charles Herreshoff, May [27?], 1842. *New England Women and Their Families, 18th and 19th Century*, Series C (reel 21), RIHS.

2. Diary of Aurilla Moffitt (May 18, 1842). Old Colony Historical Society.

3. Anna Herreshoff to Charles Herreshoff, May [27?], 1842. *New England Women and Their Families, 18th and 19th Century*, Series C (reel 21), RIHS.

4. Harriet Bailey to Jane Keeley, June 24, 1842. William M. Bailey Papers, misc., manuscripts (9001-B), RIHS. See also Ronald Formisano, "The Role of Women in the Dorr Rebellion," *Rhode Island History* 51 (August 1993): 92.

5. Quotes taken from Charles Herreshoff to Julia Herreshoff, May 31, 1842. *New England Women and Their Families, 18th and 19th Century*, Series C (reel 23), RIHS. See also Francis Wayland, *The Affairs of Rhode Island* (Boston, 1842), 28.

6. Watson to Simmons, May 19, 1842. JFS Papers (General Correspondence, Box 15), LofC.

7. Wayland, *The Affairs of Rhode Island*, 9, 20–21, 7, 27.

8. Mark S. Schantz, *Piety in Providence: Class Dimensions of Religious Experience in Antebellum Rhode Island* (Ithaca, NY: Cornell University Press, 2000), 198. Within the Baptist ranks, however, there were those who sided with Dorr, including James McKenzie, the pastor of the Roger Williams Baptist Church. See the James A. McKenzie Papers, MSS 547, RIHS.

9. William Adams to sons, June 17, 1842. Adams Family Papers, MSS 909, RIHS. For a biographical sketch of Adams see *Liberator*, October 16, 1840.

10. Diary of Aurilla Moffitt (June 18, 1842). Old Colony Historical Society.

11. Backus to White, May 30, 1842. James W. C. Ely Family Papers, MSS 889, RIHS. See also Mary Greene to Albert C. Greene, May 30, 1842. Albert C. Greene Papers, MSS 452 (Box 3, folder 7), RIHS. See also Diary of Hiram Hill (June 26, 1842) (microfilm CS71.H647), RIHS.

12. Harriet Bailey to Jane Keeley, June 14, 1842. William M. Bailey Papers, RIHS.

13. *Providence Express*, May 25, 1842, and *Providence Journal*, May 26, 1842. See also Walter Simmons to James Simmons, May 19, 1842. JFS Papers (Family Correspondence, Box 2), LofC.

14. *Providence Journal*, June 7, 1842.

15. Samuel Man to James F. Simmons, May 22, 1842. JFS Papers (General correspondence, box 15), LofC.

16. Diary of Aurilla Moffitt (May 20, 1842). Old Colony Historical Society.

17. Mary Greene to Albert Greene, May 30, 1842. Albert C. Greene Papers (Box 3, folder 7), RIHS.

18. Man to James F. Simmons, May 22, 1842. JFS Papers (General Correspondence, Box 15), LofC.

19. *Democratic Republican New Era*, May 28, 1842. Samuel Man to James Simmons, May 22, 1842, JFS Papers (General Correspondence, Box 15), Walter Simmons to James Simmons, May 21, 1842. JFS Papers (Family Correspondence, Box 2), LofC.

20. TWD to Aaron White, May 27, 1842. RCDC (Box 4, folder 15), JHL.

21. Peter Adams, *The Bowery Boys: Street Corner Radicals and the Politics of Rebellion* (Westport, CT: Praeger Press, 2005), 58. For the $1,000 reward for TWD, see Samuel Man to James Simmons, June 9, 1842. JFS Papers (General Correspondence, Box 15), LofC.

22. TWD to Henry D'Wolf, May 19, 1842. RCDC (Box 4, folder 14), JHL.

23. *National Anti-Slavery Standard*, May 19, 1842. See also the Diary of Edmund Quincy in the Quincy, Wendell, Holmes, and Upham Papers (reel 9), Massachusetts Historical Society.

24. W. Caleb McDaniel, "Repealing Unions: American Abolitionists, Irish Repeal, and the Origins of Garrisonian Disunionism," *Journal of the Early Republic* 28 (Summer 2008): 252.

25. As quoted in ibid., 251.

26. *Liberator*, April 29, 1842.

27. Ibid., May 13, 1842.

28. Daniel Feller, *The Jacksonian Promise: America, 1815–1840* (Baltimore: Johns Hopkins University Press, 1995), 113.

29. See issues on May 24, 25, and 26, 1842.

30. *Madisonian*, May 21, 1842, and *Boston Post*, May 24, 1842.

31. Samuel Man to James Simmons, May 27, 1842. JFS Papers (General Correspondence, Box 15), LofC.

32. For discussions of the *Creole* revolt, see *Herald of Freedom*, January 4, 1842,

and Stephen Foster to Abby Kelley, January 9, 1842. Abby Kelley Foster Papers, Worcester Historical Society.

33. James Oakes, *Freedom National: The Destruction of Slavery in the United States, 1861–1865* (New York: W. W. Norton, 2012), 25.

34. *Madisonian*, May 21, 1842.

35. *Providence Express*, May 27, 1842.

36. Quotes from Henry Clay, "Speech in Lexington, Kentucky," June 9, 1842, in Robert Seager, ed., *The Papers of Henry Clay*, 10 vols. (Lexington: University Press of Kentucky, 1988), 9:715, and Clay to John Brown Francis, March 31, 1844, in Melba Porter Hay, ed., *The Papers of Henry Clay*, 10 vols. (Lexington: University Press of Kentucky, 1991), 9:23. See also Gerald Leonard, *The Invention of Party Politics: Federalism, Popular Sovereignty, and Constitutional Development in Jacksonian Illinois* (Chapel Hill: University of North Carolina Press, 2002), 247–248.

37. "Speech in Richmond, Indiana," October 1, 1842, in Seager, ed., *The Papers of Henry Clay*, 9:780.

38. "Speech in Raleigh, North Carolina," April 13, 1844, in Hay, ed., *The Papers of Henry Clay*, 10:24.

39. For Vesey's plans to attack the arsenal, see Douglas R. Egerton, *He Shall Go Out Free: The Lives of Denmark Vesey* (Lanham, MD: Rowman and Littlefield, 2004), 142.

40. William Graham to Paul Cameron, May 20, 1842, in J. G. de Roulhac Hamilton, ed., *The Papers of William Alexander Graham* (Raleigh, NC: State Department of Archives, 1959), 313.

41. *Journal of the Senate* (April 18, 1842), 300. See also James Simmons to Samuel Man, April 18, 1842, in *Private Letters from James F. Simmons to Samuel Man*, JHL.

42. *Congressional Globe* (May 17, 1842), 506–507. See also Ambrose Dudley Mann to Daniel Webster, May 25, 1842. Daniel Webster Papers, New Hampshire Historical Society.

43. *Journal of the Senate* (May 18, 1842), 350.

44. *Democratic Republican New Era*, May 28, 1842.

45. Quotes from Dorr's "Notes on the State of the People's Constitution." Gilder Lehrman Collection, New York Historical Society. The notes are undated but the document was designed to be published as an editorial in the *Providence Daily Express*. It presumably was intercepted because it was never published.

46. Charles Wiltse, *John C. Calhoun: Sectionalist, 1840–1850* (New York: Russell & Russell, 1968), 80. On Slamm's connection to Calhoun, see Charles Sellers, *James K. Polk: Continentalist, 1843–1846* (Princeton, NJ: Princeton University Press, 1966), 25–26.

47. *Democratic Republican New Era*, May 26, 1842. For a response to this editorial, see Dixon H. Lewis to Joseph Scoville, May 30, 1842, in Clyde N. Wilson, ed., *The Papers of John Calhoun*, 28 vols. (Columbia: University of South Carolina Press, 1984), 16:265–267. See also Calhoun to John Mathews, May 22, 1842, in ibid., 256.

48. John Brown Francis to Elisha Potter, Jr., May 23, 1842. ERP Papers, MSS 629, subgroup 3, (Box 4, folder 7) and *Congressional Globe* (May 17, 1842), 507.

49. "Resolutions Prepared to be Offered Had the Rhode Island Controversy Been Brought Up for Discussion," in Wilson, ed., *The Papers of John C. Calhoun*, 16:270. See also Simmons to Man, May 18, 1842, in *Private Letters from James F. Simmons to Samuel Man*.

50. Ibid., 92.

51. See, for example, *Democratic Republican New Era*, May 26, 1842, and *New York Herald*, May 19, 1842. See also Sean Wilentz, *The Rise of American Democracy: Jefferson to Lincoln* (New York: W. W. Norton, 2005), 539.

52. White to TWD, May 29, 1842. RCDC (Box 4, folder 16), JHL.

53. Walter Simmons to James Simmons, June 6, 1842. JFS Papers (Family Correspondence, Box 2), LofC.

54. Carrington to James Simmons, June 4, 1842. JFS Papers (General Correspondence, Box 15), LofC.

55. Walter Simmons to James Simmons, May 23, 1842. JFS Papers (Family Correspondence, Box 2), LofC.

56. Samuel Man to James Simmons, May 22, 1842. JFS Papers (General Correspondence, Box 15), LofC.

57. TWD to Aaron White, May 27, 1842. RCDC (Box 4, folder 15), JHL.

58. William Bailey to Jane Keeley, June 14, 1842. William M. Bailey Papers, RIHS.

59. A copy of Davis's warrant for TWD is in the SSR Papers (Box 3), JHL.

60. King to Tyler, May 25, 1842, in James David Richardson, ed., *A Compilation of the Messages and Papers of the Presidents, 1789–1897*, 10 vols. (Washington, 1897), 4:298.

61. "President's Instructions, May 28, 1842," in Richardson, ed., *A Compilation of Messages and Papers of the Presidents, 1798–1908*, 4:299–300. Tyler also instructed Webster to employ an agent to go to Rhode Island and report back as soon as possible. See Tyler to Webster, May 27, 1842, in Harold D. Moser, ed., *The Papers of Daniel Webster* (Hanover, NH: University Press of New England, 1982), 5:214.

62. See ERP to Tyler, June 2, 1842. ERP Papers, MSS 629, subgroup 3 (Box 1, folder 7), RIHS.

63. Joseph Story, *Charge by Story on the Law of Treason, to Grand Jury of the Circuit Court of the United States Holden at Newport on June 15, 1842* (Providence, R.I.: H.H. Brown, 1842).

64. George M. Dennison, "Thomas Wilson TWD: Counsel of Record in *Luther v. Borden*," *St. Louis University Law Journal* 15 (1970–1971): 402–403.

65. The petitions are also preserved at the RISA.

66. Potter to Tyler, July 6, 1842. ERP Papers (Box 1, folder 7), RIHS.

67. Francis to Potter, June 14, 1842. ERP Papers (Box 1, folder 7), RIHS.

68. Potter to Tyler, June 10, 1842. ERP Papers (Box 1, folder 7), RIHS. See also

Rhoda Newcomb to Charles Newcomb, June 25, 1842. Charles Newcomb Papers (Box 3), JHL.

69. See draft note (undated) in RCDC (Box 4, folder 18), JHL.

70. Joanne Pope Melish, ed., *The Life of William J. Brown of Providence, R.I., with Personal Recollections of Incidents in Rhode Island* (Hanover, NH: University of New England Press, 2006), xxxiii.

71. TWD to Willard, Low, and Miller, June 25, 1842. Gilder Lehrman Collection, New York Historical Society.

72. TWD to Gen. Sprague, Col. D'Wolf, and Col. Aldrich, June 6, 1842. RCDC (Box 4, folder 17), JHL.

73. Samuel Ward King to Samuel Ames, May 31 and June 6, 1842. Quartermaster General Correspondence, RISA.

74. Bankhead to Spencer, June 23, 1842, in Richardson, ed., *A Compilation of Messages and Papers of the Presidents, 1798–1908*, 4:304, and John Spencer to John Clark, June 3, 1842. Edward Carrington Papers, MSS 333 (Box 243), RIHS.

75. Tyler to King, June 25, 1842, in Richardson, ed., *A Compilation of Messages and Papers of the Presidents, 1798–1908*, 4:303.

76. Ibid., 304–305.

77. Robert Seager, *And Tyler Too: A Biography of John and Julia Gardiner Tyler* (New York: McGraw-Hill Book Company, 1963), 285.

78. Edmund Burke, *Interference of the Executive in the Affairs of Rhode Island*, 29th Cong., 1st sess., 1844, House Report No. 546, 903–905. Hereafter cited as *Burke's Report*.

79. See the article in the *Southern Patriot*, July 7, 1842, praising Tyler's course of action.

80. William H. Seward and Frederick W. Seward, eds., *William H. Seward: An Autobiography from 1801–1834 with a Memoir of His Life and a Selection of His Letters, 1831–1846* (New York, 1891), 603. See also Harriet Weed, ed., *Life of Thurlow Weed* (New York, 1883), 530, and the coverage in Weed's *Albany Evening Journal*, June 27–July 4, 1842.

81. For an informative overview of Chepachet and the Dorr Rebellion, see the essays by Clifford W. Brown, Jr., on the website for the Chepachet Freewill Baptist Church: http://www.chepachetfreewill.org/dorrrebellion1.htm.

82. General Orders, June 25, 1842, and TWD to Willard, Low, and Miller, June 25, 1842. Gilder Lehrman Collection, New York Historical Society.

83. Ester Smith to Mrs. Noah Blanding, June 26, 1842. Private Collection of Russell J. DeSimone.

84. Walter Simmons to James Simmons, June 23, 1842. JFS Papers (Family Correspondence, Box 2), LofC.

85. TWD to William Simons, August 7, 1842. SSR Papers (Box 3), JHL. For a detailed breakdown of the men at Chepachet, see Russell J. DeSimone, *Rhode Island's Rebellion: Dorrite Prisoners of War* (Middletown, RI: Bartlett Press, 2009), RIHS.

86. James Fenimore Cooper to William P. Barton, June 30, 1842. Boston Public Library, special collections. MS.G.51.7.2 (7).

87. *New York Evening Post*, June 29, 1842.

88. John Harris to TWD, June 12, 1842, and Aaron White to TWD, June 12, 1842. RCDC (Box 4, folder 18), JHL.

89. Walter Simmons to James Simmons, June 23, 1842. JFS Papers (Family Correspondence, Box 2), J. Sprague to Simmons, June 23, 1842 (General Correspondence, Box 15), LofC.

90. Louisa Park Hall to John Park, June 24, 1842. Note: John Park copied his daughter Louisa's letter into his diary on June 26. See pp. 442–446. Boston Public Library, special collections.

91. William Bailey to Jane Keeley, June 25, 1842. William M. Bailey Papers, RIHS.

92. General Order, June 25, 1842. Gilder Lehrman Collection, New York Historical Society.

93. J. Sprague to James Simmons, June 23, 1842. JFS Papers (General Correspondence, Box 15), LofC.

94. Anthony to Simmons, June 23, 1842. JFS Papers (General Correspondence, Box 15), LofC.

95. Walter Simmons to James Simmons, June 22, 1842. JFS Papers (Family Correspondence, Box 2), LofC.

96. Louisa Park to John Park, June 24, 1842. Diary of John Park (June 26, 1842), pp. 442–444, Boston Public Library, special collections.

97. Andrew Warshauer, *Andrew Jackson and the Politics of Martial Law* (Knoxville: University of Tennessee Press, 2007), 148–149.

98. See S. C. Newman Journal (1842), Misc. manuscripts (9001-N), RIHS.

99. Christopher Allen to John Brown Francis, August 1, 1842. Henry A.L. Brown Deposit, MSS 1031, (Box 7, folder 104), RIHS.

100. Patrick T. Conley, "Thomas Wilson Dorr: Neglected Educational Reformer," in Conley, ed., *Rhode Island in Rhetoric and Reflection* (Providence: Rhode Island Publications Society, 2002), 124.

101. William Miller to TWD, June 15, 1842, and Jediah Sprague to TWD, June 15, 1842. RCDC (Box 4, folder 19), JHL.

102. *New York Express*, June 29, 1842.

103. Diary of Aurilla Moffitt, June 26, 1842. Old Colony Historical Society.

104. Executive Department order signed by Samuel Ward King, June 28, 1842. Executive Department Correspondence, RISA.

105. See "The Account of William M. Rodman" edited by Jane Lancaster in "The Battle of Chepachet: An Eyewitness Account," *Rhode Island History* 64 (Summer 2004): 19.

106. Ibid.

107. Dorr mentions his meeting with his father, whom he says he had not communicated with since April, in a letter to William Simons dated August 7, 1842.

SSR Papers (Box 3), JHL. See also Aaron White, Jr., to TWD, June 26, 1842. RCDC (Box 4, folder 18), JHL. For Pearce's visit see *Burke's Report*, 898. *Providence Journal*, July 6, 1842.

108. TWD to Burges, June 27, 1842. RCDC (Box 4, folder 18), JHL.

109. See Arthur May Mowry, *The Dorr War: Constitutional Struggle in Rhode Island* (New York: Preston and Rounds, 1901), 216–217.

110. Tyler to Spencer, June 29, 1842, in Richardson ed., *A Compilation of Messages and Papers of the Presidents, 1798–1908*, 4:307.

111. For Dorr's description of the dismemberment of the camp at Chepachet, see Dorr to William Simons, August 7, 1842. SSR Papers (Box 3), JHL.

112. See Zachariah Allen, "An Account of the Rebellion, 1842," 139–140, RIHS.

113. Diary of Edward Peckham (June 28, 1842), Dorr Rebellion manuscripts (reel C), JHL.

114. John Wilson to Alexander H. Stevens, June 27, 1842. Alexander H. Stevens Papers. David M. Rubenstein Rare Book and Manuscript Library, Duke University.

115. Allan Nevins, ed., *The Diary of George Templeton Strong: A Young Man in New York, 1835–1849* (New York: Macmillan, 1952), 184.

116. Diary of Edward Peckham (June 27, 1842), JHL. See the testimony transcribed in DeSimone, *Rhode Island's Rebellion*. Some of the arrests were so arbitrary that John Quincy Adams agreed to serve as defense council, most notably for Dutee Pearce. See the September 1842 correspondence between Adams in Pearce in the John Quincy Adams letter book at the Massachusetts Historical Society. See also Erik J. Chaput, "'Let the People Remember!': Rhode Island's Dorr Rebellion and Massachusetts Politics 1842–1843," *Historical Journal of Massachusetts* 39 (Summer 2011), 100–130.

117. Diary of Edward Peckham (June 29, 1842), JHL.

118.. See Russell J. DeSimone and Erik J. Chaput, "Strange Bedfellows: The Politics of Race in Antebellum Rhode Island," *Common-Place* 10, no. 2 (January 2010); http://www.common-place.org/vol-10/no-02/chaput-desimone/. See also *Burke's Report*, 79 and 319.

119. Louisa Park Hall to John Park, June 24, 1842, in Diary of John Park (June 26, 1842), p. 442. Boston Public Library, special collections.

120. *Emancipator and Free American*, August 11, 1842.

121. Melish, ed., *The Life of William J. Brown of Providence, RI*, 96.

122. *Providence Journal*, June 28, 1842.

123. See the Nicholas Powers to TWD, September 18, 1842. Power-Whitman Papers, MSS 631, (Folder 28), RIHS.

124. Quoted in Schantz, *Piety in Providence*, 222.

125. See Daniel Webster's notes for *Luther v. Borden* (1849) in Henry J. Raymond Papers, New York Public Library, Manuscripts Division.

126. Williams to TWD, September 6, 1842. RCDC (Box 5, folder 5). See also See Ronald Formisano's tour-de-force article, "The Role of Women in the Dorr Rebellion," and Susan Graham, "'Call Me a Female Politician, I Glory in the

Name': Women Dorrites and Rhode Island's 1842 Suffrage Crisis" (Ph.D. diss., University of Minnesota, 2006), 235–238.

127. Catherine R. Williams, "Recollections of the Life and Conversations of Thomas W. Dorr," 19, JHL.

128. TWD to Lydia Dorr, November 12, 1844. TWD Papers (Box 1, folder 12), JHL.

129. Samuel Whipple to TWD, September 6, 1842. RCDC (Box 5, folder 4), JHL.

130. See Ronald J. Zboray and Mary S. Zboray, "Whig Women, Politics, and Culture in the Campaign of 1840: Three Perspectives from Massachusetts," *Journal of the Early Republic* 17 (Summer 1997): 281. The Dorrite women were nearly all aligned with the Democratic Party.

131. TWD to Albert Tracy, August 25, 1842. New York Public Library, Manuscripts division.

132. A copy of the grand jury indictment is in the Albert C. Greene Papers (Box 15, folder 78), RIHS.

133. See petition from F. L. Beckford to Thomas Burgess, September 4, 1842. Correspondence of Providence Mayor Thomas M. Burgess, Providence City Archives.

Chapter 7: Grist for the Political Mill

1. TWD to William Simons, August 7, 1842. SSR Papers (Box 3), JHL. See also TWD to William Simons, September 26, 1842. RCDC (Box 5, folder 9), JHL. Dorr built upon these lengthy letters to Simons in his August 1843 address to the citizens of Rhode Island. His address is the fullest explanation of his ideology and motivations, and, of course, his understanding of the events of 1842. See Edmund Burke, *Interference of the Executive in the Affairs of Rhode Island*, 29th Cong., 1st sess., 1844, House Report No. 546, 731–770. Hereafter cited as *Burke's Report*.

2. 1842 Inaugural address of Charles Paine, Vermont State Archives.

3. For more a detailed discussion of Dorr's time in New Hampshire see Erik J. Chaput, "A Governor in Exile: New Hampshire and the 'Rhode Island Question,'" *Historical New Hampshire* 66 (Winter 2012–2013): 91–119.

4. Sarah H. Buffum to TWD, February 20, 1843. RCDC (Box 6, folder 7), JHL.

5. William Balch to TWD, October 13, 1842. RCDC (Box 5, folder 12), JHL.

6. TWD to William Simons, August 7, 1842. SSR Papers (Box 3), JHL.

7. Lex Renda, *Running on the Record: Civil War-Era Politics in New Hampshire* (Charlottesville: University of Virginia Press, 1997), 20.

8. Peter Wallner's recent two-volume biography of the fourteenth president is learned and comprehensive: See *Franklin Pierce: New Hampshire's Favorite Son* (Concord, NH: Plaidswede Publishing, 2004) and *Franklin Pierce: Martyr for the Union* (Concord, NH: Plaidswede Publishing, 2008).

9. *Dover Enquirer*, August 25, 1842.

10. Hubbard to King, August 15, 1842. *New Hampshire Executive Council Records* (1840–1846), 8:205, 206, 208. New Hampshire State Archives. See also the published pamphlet, *The Letters of Hon. C. F. Cleveland and Henry Hubbard, and Marcus Morton to Samuel Ward King, Refusing to Deliver Up Thomas Wilson Dorr* (Fall River, 1842).

11. On Williams, see Susan Graham, "'A Warm Politician and Devotedly Attached to the Democratic Party': Catharine Read Williams, Politics, and Literature in Antebellum America," *Journal of the Early Republic* 30 (Summer 2010): 253–278. See also Patrick T. Conley, *The Makers of Modern Rhode Island* (Charleston, SC: History Press, 2012), 136–139. On Parlin, see Russell J. DeSimone, *Rhode Island's Rebellion: Lewis and Ann Parlin* (Middletown, RI: Bartlett Press, 2009), RIHS.

12. TWD to Russell, June 21, 1851. RCDC (Box 13, folder 8), JHL.

13. TWD to Howard, May 2, 1853. RCDC (Box 14, folder 20), JHL.

14. See Susan Graham, "'Call Me a Female Politician, I Glory in the Name': Women Dorrites and Rhode Island's 1842 Suffrage Crisis" (Ph.D. diss., University of Minnesota, 2006).

15. TWD to the Suffrage Ladies of Providence, August 24, 1842. RCDC (Box 4, folder 26), JHL.

16. Parlin to TWD, November 6, 1842. RCDC (Box 5, folder 17), JHL (emphasis added).

17. *Providence Express*, September 17, 1842.

18. Parlin to TWD, September 4, 1842. RCDC (Box 5, folder 3), JHL.

19. *Providence Express*, October 1, 1842.

20. See Seth Luther's published poem to Female Dorrites, *The Garland of Gratitude: Respectfully Dedicated to the Constitutional Suffrage Ladies of Rhode Island* (Providence, 1842). Languishing in prison in November 1842, Luther wrote to Dorr to express his support for "the great principle of the sovereignty of the people." See Luther to TWD, November 2, 1842. RCDC (Box 5, folder 2), JHL. See also Carl Gersuny, "Seth Luther—The Road from Chepachet," *Rhode Island History* 33 (May 1974): 47–55.

21. See verso note on TWD to William Simons, September 26, 1842. RCDC (Box 5, folder 9), JHL.

22. Wilmarth to Kelley, July 11, 1842. Abby Kelly Foster Papers, AAS.

23. Thomas Stead to James Simmons, September 19, 1842. JFS Papers (General Correspondence, Box 16), LofC.

24. Francis Wayland to James Simmons, September 21, 1842. JFS Papers (General Correspondence, Box 16), LofC.

25. *Records of the States of the United States* (Rhode Island), microfilm reel 1, section C, Constitutional Records, LofC. Another petition from Providence's black community was submitted on September 20.

26. Thomas Hazard to Samuel Man, November 14, 1842, in *Private Letters from Prominent RI Men to Samuel F. Man*, JHL.

27. Potter to Francis, July 22, 1842. Henry A. L. Brown Deposit, MSS 1031 (Box 7, folder 104), RIHS.

28. Potter to Francis, November 14, 1842. Henry A. L. Brown Deposit (Box 7, folder 106), RIHS.

29. See *Journal of the Convention, September 1842* (Providence, 1842), 29–30, RISA.

30. TWD to William Simons, November 12, 1842. RCDC (Box 5, folder 18), JHL.

31. For an informative overview of the differences between the 1843 constitution and the People's Constitution, see Patrick T. Conley, *Rhode Island in Rhetoric and Reflection: Public Addresses and Essays by Patrick T. Conley* (Providence: Rhode Island Publications Society, 2003), 174–176.

32. Ibid., 176.

33. Potter to Martin Van Buren, November 30, 1842. Martin Van Buren Papers, LofC.

34. Charles Newell to TWD, November 17, 1842. RCDC (Box 5, folder 19), JHL.

35. Catharine Williams to TWD, September 6, 1842. RCDC (Box 5, folder 5), JHL.

36. Abby Lord to TWD, October 2, 1842. RCDC (Box 5, folder 10), JHL.

37. TWD to William Simons, October 18, 1842, and TWD to Parmenter, October 21, 1842. RCDC (Box 5, folders 12 and 14), JHL.

38. Patrick T. Conley, *Democracy in Decline: Rhode Island's Constitutional Development, 1776–1841* (Providence: Rhode Island Historical Society Publications, 1977), 372.

39. George S. Boutwell, *Reminisces of Sixty Years in Public Affairs* (New York, 1902), 182–183. See also Arthur Darling, *Political Changes in Massachusetts, 1824–1848* (New Haven, CT: Yale University Press, 1925), 286–287.

40. Jonathan Earle, *Jacksonian Antislavery and the Politics of Free Soil, 1824–1854* (Chapel Hill: University of North Carolina Press, 2004), 104.

41. John Pitman to Joseph Story, November 6, 1842. Pitman-Story Correspondence, WCL.

42. See *Bay State Democrat*, September 2, 1842. See Catharine Williams to TWD, December 28, 1842. RCDC (Box 5, folder 26), JHL.

43. *Bay State Democrat*, July 20, 1842.

44. *Norfolk Democrat*, July 15, 1842. "Kilby" also appears in newspaper coverage as "Kelby."

45. *Bay State Democrat*, August 29, 1842.

46. *Providence Morning Courier*, August 19, 1842. See also See Walter Danforth to Woodbury, August 30, 1842. Levi Woodbury Papers, LofC.

47. *Providence Express*, November 8, 1842. See also Ronald P. Formisano, "The Role of Women in the Dorr Rebellion," *Rhode Island History* 51 (August 1993): 89–104, and Formisano, *For the People: American Populist Movements from the Rev-*

olution to the 1850s (Chapel Hill: University of North Carolina Press, 2007), 174–176. See also Mark S. Schantz, *Piety in Providence: Class Dimensions of Religious Experience in Antebellum Rhode Island* (Ithaca, NY: Cornell University Press, 2000), 207–211.

48. Quoted in Graham, "'Call Me a Female Politician, I Glory in the Name,'" 133.

49. TWD to Mrs. Ida Russell, June 21, 1851. RCDC (Box 13, folder 10), JHL.

50. *Providence Express*, October 26, 1842.

51. Graham, "'Call Me a Female Politician,'" 283–284.

52. Lord to TWD, November 12, 1842, and Williams to TWD November 27, 1842. RCDC (Box 5, folders 18 and 20), JHL.

53. See, for example, Mary Jane Campbell to TWD, October 8, 1842, and William Smith to TWD, October 26, 1842. RCDC (Box 5, folders 11 and 15), JHL.

54. Catharine Williams to TWD, December 28, 1842. RCDC (Box 5, folder 26), JHL.

55. Young Ladies Suffrage Association of Providence to TWD, September 5, 1842. RCDC (Box 5, folder 4). For a description of female suffrage associations in Providence, see Catharine Williams to TWD, October 9, 1842. RCDC (Box 5, folder 12), JHL.

56. *Bristol County Democrat*, August 25, 1842; *Boston Post*, August 29, 1842; *Providence Journal*, August 22, 1842.

57. *Republican Herald*, August 20, 1842.

58. See Erik J. Chaput, "'Let the People Remember!': Rhode Island's Dorr Rebellion and Massachusetts Politics, 1842–1843," *Historical Journal of Massachusetts* 39 (Summer 2011): 108–143.

59. "The Address of Henry Dearborn to the Committee of the House of Representatives," *Massachusetts Governor Council Records* 20 (July 1842–April 1843). Massachusetts State Archives.

60. Massachusetts House Report, February 8, 1843. *Governor Council Records*, July 1842–April 1843.

61. Ibid., 17.

62. Man to Simmons, January 3, 1843. JFS Papers (General Correspondence, Box 17), LofC.

63. See Potter to Francis, November 29, 1842. Henry A. L. Brown Deposit (Box 7, folder 106), RIHS.

64. A copy can be found in the JFS Papers (General Correspondence, Box 17), LofC.

65. *Providence Journal*, January 3, 1843.

66. Conley, *Democracy in Decline*, 354.

67. Ibid., 352–353.

68. See the note of Augustus Coddington describing Dorr's arrival in Pawtucket dated March 25, 1842, in misc. manuscripts (MSS 9003), RIHS; Joseph Holbrook to TWD, March 28, 1842, RCDC (Box 7, folder 6); Franklin Pierce to TWD, April

1, 1843, RCDC (Box 7, folder 7), JHL; and Russell J. DeSimone, *Rhode Island's Rebellion: Robert Abell, Massachusetts Dorrite* (Middletown, RI: Bartlett Press, 2009), 15–16. RIHS.

69. Marvin Gettleman, *The Dorr Rebellion: A Study in American Radicalism, 1833–1849* (New York: Random House, 1973), Appendix B, 235.

70. John Pitman to Joseph Story, April 8, 1842. Joseph Story Papers, LofC.

71. *Burke's Report*, 730–771.

72. For more on Dorr's treason trial, see Erik J. Chaput, "'The Rhode Island Question' on Trial: The 1844 Treason Trial of Thomas Wilson Dorr," *American Nineteenth Century History* 11 (June 2011): 205–232. Special thanks to Susan Mary Grant for help with this article.

73. TWD to Simons, October 18, 1842. RCDC (Box 5, folder 14), JHL.

74. TWD to David Parmenter, October 21, 1842. RCDC (Box 5, folder 21), JHL.

75. Wright to TWD, February 7, 1844. RCDC (Box 8, folder 3), JHL.

76. White to TWD, June 10, 1843, RCDC (Box 7, folder 13), JHL.

77. See the December 7 and December 14, 1842, issues of the *Providence Express* and the *New Age and Constitutional Advocate*, December 3, 9, 16, and 23, 1842.

78. Unknown author to Robert Hale Ives, May 3, 1844. Ives-Gammell-Safe Papers, MSS 509, RIHS.

79. Burke to TWD, April 7, 1844. RCDC (Box 8, folder 9), LofC.

80. Edmund Burke to James Rix, July 25, 1844. Boston Public Library, special collections. ch.E.12.68.

81. *Congressional Globe*, 28th Cong., 1st sess. (March 13, 1844), 379.

82. TWD to Edmund Burke, February 26, 1844. Edmund Burke Papers, LofC.

83. *Burke's Report*, 4. "Memorial of the Democratic Members of the General Assembly of Rhode Island," February 1, 1844. RCDC (Box 8, folder 2), JHL.

84. Burke to TWD, February 25, 1844. TWD Papers (Box 1, folder 6), and Burke to TWD, February 4, 1844. RCDC (Box 8, folder 2), JHL.

85. *Congressional Globe*, 28th Congress, 1st sess. (April 16, 1844), 523.

86. *Appendix to the Globe*, 28th Congress, 1st sess. (March 14, 1844), 464.

87. *Appendix to the Globe*, 28th Congress, 1st sess. (March 14, 1844), 463–464. On New York see George William Van Cleve, *A Slaveholders' Union: Slavery, Politics, and the Constitution in the Early American Republic* (University Press of Chicago, 2009), 263–264.

88. TWD to Burke, February 26, 1844. Edmund Burke Papers, LofC.

89. *Congressional Globe*, 28th Congress, 1st sess. (March 9, 1844), 363.

90. *Congressional Globe*, 28th Congress, 1st sess. (March 16, 1844), 419.

91. See Edmund Burke to Walter Burges, April 20, 1844. TWD Papers (Box 1, folder 8), JHL.

92. *Congressional Globe*, 28th Congress, 1st sess. (March 16, 1844), 394.

93. Adams referred to Tyler as a "slave monger" after the president gave a speech dedicating the Bunker Hill monument in Boston in 1843. See Joseph J. Ellis, *The Founding Couple: John and Abigail Adams* (New York: Alfred A. Knopf, 2010), 75.

94. *Congressional Globe*, 28th Congress, 1st sess. (April 10, 1844), 504.

95. Aaron White to TWD, May 12, 1844. RCDC (Box 8, folder 14), JHL. See also Joel Silbey, *Storm over Texas: Annexation Controversy and the Road to Civil War* (New York: Oxford University Press, 2005).

96. Silbey, *Storm over Texas*, 31, 43.

97. William James Cooper, *The South and the Politics of Slavery* (Baton Rouge: Louisiana State University Press, 1978), 190–194.

98. Silbey, *Storm over Texas*, 68–69. Tyler signed the Texas statehood bill into law on the first day of March 1845, just three days before leaving office.

99. On Dorr's resolutions see TWD to Walter S. Burges, May 23, 1844. RCDC (Box 8, folder 15), JHL.

100. John Ashworth, *The Republic in Crisis, 1848–1861* (New York: Cambridge University Press, 2012), 48.

101. *Burke's Report*, 84.

102. Ibid., 86.

103. There were two editions of the report. The first was created in June 1844 and a second, with minor revisions, in January 1845.

104. Charles Francis Adams, ed., *The Diary of John Quincy Adams* (Boston, 1877), 12:49–50 (June 7, 1844).

105. *Congressional Globe*, 28th Congress, 1st sess. (April, 16, 1844), 523. Surprisingly, Elizabeth Varon's recent history of the idea of disunion from the Revolution to the eve of the Civil War makes no mention of the Dorr Rebellion. See *Disunion! The Coming of the American Civil War, 1789–1859* (Chapel Hill: University of North Carolina Press, 2008).

106. *House Report* #581, 28th Congress, 1st sess. (June 17, 1844), 18.

107. William Goodell, *Views of American Constitutional Law in Its Bearing upon American Slavery* (Utica, NY, 1844); Lysander Spooner, *The Unconstitutionality of Slavery* (Boston, 1845).

108. Spooner, *The Unconstitutionality of Slavery*, 125, 134.

109. *Congressional Globe*, 28th Congress, 2nd sess., 81. See also *Appendix to the Congressional Globe*, 28th Congress, 2nd sess., 260–262.

110. *Journal of the House of Representatives*, 28th Congress, 2nd sess. (January 8, 1845), 181–182.

111. *Journal of the Senate of the United States*, 28th Congress, 2nd sess. (January 6, 1845), 71.

112. *Journal of the House of Representatives*, 28th Congress, 2nd sess. (January 8, 1845), 181–184. See also John Ashworth, *Agrarians and Aristocrats: Party Political Ideology in the United States, 1837–1846* (London: Cambridge University Press, 1987), 231.

113. Yonatan Eyal, *The Young America Movement and the Transformation of the Democratic Party, 1828–1861* (New York: Cambridge University Press, 2007), 204.

Chapter 8: The People's Sovereignty in the Courtroom

1. Michal Belknap, ed., *American Political Trials* (Westport, CT: Greenwood Press, 1994), xxii. See also Erik J. Chaput, "'The Rhode Island Question' on Trial: The Treason Trial of Thomas Wilson Dorr," *American Nineteenth Century History* 11 (June 2010): 205–232.

2. Charles and Tess Hoffman, *Brotherly Love: Murder and the Politics of Prejudice in Nineteenth-Century Rhode Island* (Amherst: University of Massachusetts Press, 1995), 65–66. See also Patrick T. Conley, *Rhode Island in Rhetoric and Reflection* (Providence: Rhode Island Publications Society, 2002), 223–227.

3. See TWD to Lydia Dorr, March 6, 1845, in which Dorr relates how he over-heard Gordon maintaining his innocence to the warden. Gordon was executed on February 14, 1845. TWD Papers (Box 1, folder 12), JHL.

4. John Pitman, *The Treason Trial of Thomas Wilson Dorr* (Providence, 1844), 24.

5. TWD to Robert Walker, August 20, 1845. Thomas Wilson Dorr Collection, Vault A, Box 38, folder 6, NHS.

6. In his 1849 opinion in *Luther v. Borden*, Chief Justice Roger Taney went out of his way to make this precise point about the absurdity of trying Dorr under a law and constitution that were subsequently made null and void. See *Luther v. Borden*, 48 U.S. 7 (1849), 40.

7. Pitman, *The Treason Trial of Thomas Wilson Dorr*, 72.

8. *New England Democrat*, February 8, 1844. See also James C. Garman, *Detention Castles of Stone and Steel: Landscape, Labor and the Urban Penitentiary* (Knoxville, TN: University of Tennessee Press, 2005), 70.

9. A number of these beautiful hand fans have survived and are at the Rhode Island School of Design. See the gallery page at the Dorr Rebellion project website: http://library.providence.edu/dorr.

10. See "Debate on Petition of Sullivan Dorr, June 26, 1844" in TWD Papers (Box 3, folder 24). See also Sullivan Dorr to Richard K. Randolph, June 22, 1844, Alfred Updike Collins Family Papers (Box 2, folder 47), MSS 1065, series 3, RIHS.

11. Allen to James Fenner, June 26, 1844. Zachariah Allen Papers, MSS 254, (Box 1, folder 4), RIHS. Even Dorr's friend, Nicholas Brown, Jr. thought he was "deranged." See Brown to John Brown Francis, May 28, 1842. Private collection of Henry A. L. Brown.

12. Frances Whipple Greene to Lydia Dorr, December 8, 1844. RCDC (Box 8, folder 21), JHL.

13. See the notebook containing "Documents of the Dorr Liberation Society, 1844–1845" in the Dorr Rebellion manuscripts (reel A), JHL.

14. Treadwell to Abby Lord, February 21, 1845, and John Windt to Ms. Thomas Reid, April 1, 1845. Dorr Rebellion manuscripts (reel A), JHL.

15. See *Workingman's Advocate*, August 3 and September 28, 1844, *Republican Herald*, November 19, 1844, and January 8, 1845, and John Harris to Walter Burges, January 2 and 3, 1845, in TWD Papers (Box 1, folder 18), JHL. See also George

M. Dennison's insightful article, "Thomas Wilson Dorr: Counsel of Record in *Luther v. Borden*," *St. Louis University Law Journal* 15 (1970–1971): 414–417.

16. TWD to George Turner and Walter S. Burgess, December 23, 1844 in TWD Papers (Box 1, folder 12), JHL.

17. *Workingman's Advocate*, July 27, 1844.

18. John Commerford to Dorr, July 26, 1844. RCDC (Box 8, folder 18), JHL. See also Sean Wilentz, *Chants Democratic: New York City and the Rise of the American Working Class, 1788–1850* (New York: Oxford University Press, 1984), 340–343. Evans published several of Luther's political tracts including his 1833 manifesto, *An Address to the Workingmen of New England*.

19. Jamie Bronstein, *Land Reform and Working-Class Experience in Britain and the United States* (Stanford, CA: Stanford University Press, 1999), 2. On Evans's early life, see 119–121.

20. *Workingman's Advocate*, August 17, 1844.

21. The *Workingman's Advocate*, July 13, 1844, and August 3, 1844.

22. *Workingman's Advocate*, August 10, 1844.

23. *Workingman's Advocate*, September 14, 1844.

24. Quoted in Mark Lause, *Young America: Land, Labor, and the Republican Community* (Chicago: University of Illinois Press, 2005), 23.

25. Quoted in Bronstein, *Land Reform and Working-Class Experience*, 69.

26. On the Spartan Association, see Wilentz, *Chants Democratic*, 328–329.

27. *Subterranean*, June 21, 1845.

28. Edward L. Widmer, *Young America: The Flowering of Democracy in New York City* (New York: Oxford University Press, 1999), 59.

29. See, for example, *Young America*, April 5, 1845.

30. *Workingman's Advocate*, March 1, 1845.

31. Reeve Huston, "Popular Movements and Party Rule: The New York Anti-Rent Wars and the Jacksonian Political Order," in Jeffrey L. Palsey, Andrew W. Robertson, and David Waldstreicher, eds., *Beyond the Founders: New Approaches to the Political History of the Early Republic* (Chapel Hill: University of North Carolina Press, 2004), 364; Huston, *Land and Freedom: Rural Society, Popular Protest, and Party Politics in Antebellum New York* (New York: Oxford University Press, 2000), 210–211.

32. Quoted in Harold M. Hyman and William M. Wiecek, *Equal Justice under Law: Constitutional Development, 1835–1875* (New York: Harper and Row, 1982), 5.

33. Memoranda August 16, 1847. TWD Papers (Box 3, folder 6), JHL.

34. *Providence Gazette*, December 24, 1844. *Subterranean United with the Workingman's Advocate*, December 21, 1844.

35. TWD to Lydia Dorr, January 1, 1845. TWD Papers (Box 1, folder 13), JHL. See also Catharine Williams, *The Life of Thomas Wilson Dorr*, 39–40, unpublished manuscript, JHL.

36. Harris to Burges, December 20, 1844. TWD Papers (Box 1), JHL.

37. *Ex Parte Dorr*, 3 Howard (1845), 103–104, *Providence Journal*, January 1,

1845, and *Weekly Globe*, December 31, 1844, and January 4, 1845. For a summary of Treadwell's argument, see *Subterranean United with the Workingman's Advocate*, December 21, 1844.

38. Edmund Burke to Walter Burges, January 15, 1845. TWD Papers (Box 1, folder 8), JHL.

39. Dennison, "Thomas Wilson Dorr: Counsel of Record in *Luther v. Borden*," 424.

40. See *Benjamin F. Hallett of Boston on Bunker Hill, July 4, 1844* (Boston, 1844), 4. RIHS. See also *Republican Herald* (extra), July 8, 1844.

41. Bradford to Polk, October 5, 1844, in Wayne Cutler, ed., *The Correspondence of James K. Polk*, 12 vols. (Knoxville: University of Tennessee Press, 1993), 8:154.

42. *New England Democrat*, January 4, 1844.

43. John McKeon to James K. Polk, November 2, 1844, in Culter, ed., *Correspondence of James K. Polk*, 8:259–260. See also *The Liberator*, November 22, 1844, and Burges to TWD, September 21, 1844. RCDC (Box 8, folder 20), JHL.

44. *Subterranean United with the Workingman's Advocate*, October 12, 1844.

45. TWD to Burges, October 1, 1844. Dorr Rebellion manuscripts (microfilm, reel A), JHL.

46. *Niles' Register*, September 14, 1844.

47. Ibid. See also Draft of a letter from Edmund Burke to organizing committee for the September 4, 1844, clambake in Providence. Edmund Burke Papers, LofC.

48. *Workingman's Advocate*, September 7, 1844.

49. *Democratic Review* (August 1844), 127. O'Sullivan cared little for Evans's land reform efforts. He was also generally contemptuous of the Anti-Renters. On the latter point, see Robert D. Sampson, *John L. O'Sullivan and His Times* (Kent, OH: Kent State University Press, 2003), 171.

50. Sampson, *John L. O'Sullivan and His Times*, 126.

51. Charles Sellers, "Election of 1844," in Gil Troy, Arthur M. Schlesinger, Jr., and Fred Israel, eds., *History of American Presidential Elections, 1789–2000*, 3 vols. (New York: Facts on File, 2012), 1:366.

52. George Smith to TWD, June 6, 1851. RCDC (Box 13, folder 7), JHL.

53. TWD to John C. Rivers, October 24, 1845. RCDC (Box 9, folder 16), JHL.

54. *Subterranean*, June, 21, 1845. By June 1845, Walsh had broken with Evans.

55. Polk to John Gellet, December 26, 1844. Thomas Wilson Dorr Collection, Vault A, Box 38, folder 6, NHS.

56. Man to Simmons, January 22, 1845. JFS Papers (General Correspondence, Box 17), LofC. For Dorr's views on Simmons's liberation efforts, see TWD to Walter S. Burges and TWD to Lydia Dorr, both April 6, 1845. TWD Papers (Box 1, folder 13), JHL. See also Patrick T. Conley, *Democracy in Decline: Rhode Island's Constitutional Development, 1776–1841* (Providence: Rhode Island Historical Society Publications, 1977), 367–369, and Marvin Gettleman, *The Dorr Rebellion: A Study in American Radicalism, 1833–1849* (New York: Random House, 1973), 169–173.

57. TWD to Walter Burges, January 18, 1845. TWD Papers (Box 1, folder 13), JHL.

58. Aaron White, Jr., to Walter S. Burges, May 15, 1845. Dorr Rebellion manuscripts (Reel A), JHL.

59. *Rhode Island Acts and Resolves*, June 27, 1845. Rhode Island State Archives. See also "Record of Thoughts upon Being Released from Prison," June 27, 1845. TWD Diary, 1845–1854, JHL.

60. Ladies of the Benevolent Suffrage Association to TWD, July 1, 1845. RCDC (Box 9, folder 4), JHL.

61. Van Buren to William Simons, August 30, 1845. Dorr Rebellion manuscripts (Reel A), JHL.

62. Conley, *Democracy in Decline*, 368–369.

63. TWD to Walter Burges, December 17, 1844. TWD Papers (Box 1, folder 12), JHL, and TWD to Robert Walker, August 25, 1845. Thomas Wilson Dorr Collection, Vault A, Box 38, folder 6, NHS. See also Dorr's notes on the *Luther* cases in the TWD Papers (Box 3, folder 6), JHL.

64. TWD to George Turner, January 24, 1846. Thomas Wilson Dorr Collection, Vault A, Box 38, folder 6, NHS.

65. See Dennison, "Thomas Wilson Dorr: Counsel of Record in *Luther v. Borden*," 415–428.

66. TWD to Estwick Evans, April 12, 1848. Thomas Wilson Dorr Papers, RIHS.

67. Notes of Daniel Webster's oral argument in *Luther v. Borden* (1849). Henry J. Raymond Papers, New York Public Library, manuscripts division.

68. See Dennison, "Thomas Wilson Dorr: Counsel of Record in *Luther v. Borden*," 402.

69. In the *Luther v. Borden* file at the National Archive, there is a plea for the defendants dated November 1842 for *Martin Luther v. Luther Borden* and *Rachel Luther v. Luther Borden*. The case of *Rachel Luther v. Luther M. Borden* was not heard until April 1844.

70. See Hallett's argument as excerpted in Edmund Burke, *Interference of the Executive in the Affairs of Rhode Island*, 29th Cong., 1st sess., 1844, House Report No. 546, 375. Hereafter cited as *Burke's Report*.

71. Ibid., 373–377.

72. "Defendants Plea" (November 1842) and "Evidence in Support of the Defendants' Plea" (November 1843). *Luther v. Borden* case file. National Archives, Waltham, MA.

73. See the bill of exceptions filed by Benjamin Hallett, November 1843 in the *Luther v. Borden* case file.

74. See *Burke's Report*, 375, and *Providence Journal*, November 22, 1843. A formal writ of error was filed on March 1, 1844.

75. *House Report* #581, 28th Congress, 1st sess. (June 17, 1844), 160.

76. Ibid., 159.

77. Ibid., 165.

78. *Providence Journal*, April 19, 1844, for report of the mistrial in Rachel Luther's case. See also the "Agreement of plaintiffs and defendants to use certain documents in the trial before the U.S. Supreme Court" (June 30, 1844). *Luther v. Borden* case file. A formal division of opinion in Rachel Luther's case was entered on June 7, 1845.

79. TWD to Turner and Hallett, February 2, 1847. RCDC (Box 11, folder 4), JHL. See also TWD to Turner, February 3, 1842. Thomas Wilson Dorr Collection, Vault A, Box 38, folder 6, NHS.

80. George Turner to TWD, February 19, 1847. RCDC (Box 11, folder 6), JHL.

81. William M. Wiecek, *The Sources of Antislavery Constitutionalism in America, 1760–1848* (Ithaca, NY: Cornell University Press, 1977), 256–258.

82. Charles Woodhouse to TWD, June 11, 1848. RCDC (Box 12, folder 9), JHL.

83. William M. Wiecek, *Liberty under Law: The Supreme Court in American Life* (Baltimore: Johns Hopkins University Press, 1988), 76.

84. TWD to Benjamin Hallett, January 12, 1848. RCDC (Box 12, folder 3), JHL.

85. Ibid.

86. Edmund Burke to TWD, December 19, 1845. RCDC (Box 9, folder 18), JHL.

87. Clifford confined his argument exclusively to the martial law issue. See *Luther v. Borden*, 48 U.S. 7 (1849), 34.

88. TWD to Clifford, January 24, 1848. RCDC (Box 12, folder 3), JHL.

89. Hallett to TWD, February 11, 1848. RCDC (Box 12, folder 5), JHL.

90. Benjamin F. Hallett, *The Right of the People to Establish Forms of Government* (Boston, 1848), 17.

91. *Luther v. Borden*, 48 U.S. 7 (1849), 20–21.

92. Hallett, *The Right of the People*, 51–52.

93. *Luther v. Borden*, 48 U.S. 7 (1849), 20.

94. TWD to Clifford, January 24, 1848. RCDC (Box 12, folder 3), JHL.

95. Webster agreed to argue the *Luther* cases, which he labeled a case of "transcendent importance," in November 1845 for a fee of $1,000. See Andrew J. King, ed., *The Papers of Daniel Webster: Legal Papers, The Federal Practice* (Hanover, NH: University of New England Press, 1989), 750.

96. Patrick T. Conley, *The Makers of Modern Rhode Island* (Charleston, SC: History Press, 2012), 83.

97. See King, ed., *The Papers of Daniel Webster: Legal Papers, The Federal Practice*, 738.

98. Webster's notes of Daniel Webster's oral argument in *Luther v. Borden* (1849). Henry J. Raymond Papers, New York Public Library, manuscript division.

99. *The Rhode Island Question: Mr. Webster's Argument in Supreme Court of the United States in the Case of Luther Borden v. Martin Luther* (Washington, DC, 1848), 9.

100. Ibid., 11.

101. *Luther v. Borden*, 48 U.S. 7 (1849), 33.

102. Benjamin Hallett to TWD, February 11, 1848. RCDC (Box 12, folder 5), JHL.

103. Edmund Burke to TWD, March 5, 1848. RCDC (Box 12, folder 6), JHL.

104. TWD to Estwick Evans, April 12, 1848. Thomas Wilson Dorr Papers, RIHS.

105. *Luther v. Borden*, 48 U.S. 7 (1849), 34.

106. Hallett, *The Right of the People*, 9. Justices Catron, Daniels, and McKinley were absent due to illness.

107. *Luther v. Borden*, 48 U.S. 7 (1849), 41.

108. Ibid., 43–45.

109. Ibid., 45.

110. *Luther v. Borden*, 35.

111. Ibid., 47.

112. Aaron White to TWD, February 17, 1849. RCDC (Box 12, folder 8), JHL.

113. *Luther v. Borden*, 48 U.S. 7 (1849), 47.

114. Ibid., 39.

115. Wiecek, *The Guarantee Clause of the United States Constitution* (Ithaca, NY: Cornell University Press, 1972), 119.

116. *Luther v. Borden*, 48 U.S. 7 (1849), 43.

117. Ibid., 29–31.

118. Ibid., 41.

119. *Luther v. Borden*, 48 U.S. 7 (1849), 44.

120. Ibid.

121. Michael A. Conron, "Law, Politics, and Chief Justice Taney: A Reconsideration of the *Luther v. Borden* Decision," *American Journal of Legal History* 11 (October 1967): 383.

122. *Luther v. Borden*, 48 U.S. 7 (1849), 42. For a differing view on the holding of *Luther v. Borden*, see Bruce Ackerman, *We the People: Transformations* (Cambridge, MA: Harvard University Press, 1998), 442–443. Ackerman argues that the actual holding in *Luther* comes in a discussion of presidential not congressional power.

123. In a separate paragraph on *Rachel Luther v. Luther Borden*, Taney chastised Story and Pitman for manufacturing an artificial division of opinion. Taney remanded the case back to the circuit court. No action, however, was ever taken on the case because in his opinion in *Martin Luther v. Luther Borden* Taney had essentially settled the matter.

124. *Luther v. Borden*, 48 U.S. 7 (1849), 45.

125. TWD to Hallett, January 15, 1849. RCDC (Box 12, folder 17), JHL.

Chapter 9: The Legacy of the People's Sovereignty

1. See Williams's handwritten biography of Thomas Wilson Dorr at the JHL.

2. Williams to TWD, October 12, 1850. RCDC (Box 12, folder 32), JHL. See also Williams to TWD, October 20, 1852. TWD Papers (Box 1, folder 31), JHL. Williams was living in Brooklyn with Frances Whipple Greene McDougall, the author of the 1844 pro-Dorr political tract, *Might and Right*.

3. Stephen Chambers, "'Neither Justice nor Mercy': Public and Private Executions in Rhode Island, 1832–1833," *New England Quarterly* 82 (September 2009): 430–451, and *Rhode-Island Republican*, May 20, 1835.

4. TWD Diary, 1844–1849, p. 1. TWD Papers (Box 3), JHL.

5. See TWD to Mrs. Ida Russell, June 21, 1851. RCDC (Box 13, folder 8), JHL. In 1854, the Rhode Island General Assembly reversed Dorr's treason conviction. However, as Patrick Conley writes, "in a move both tragic and ironic, the [state] Supreme Court, still under Algerine control, responded by asserting its independence—for which Dorr had fought—by denying the power of the General Assembly to reverse its judgment." Conley, *Democracy in Decline: Rhode Island's Constitutional Development, 1776–1841* (Providence: Rhode Island Historical Society Publications, 1977), 371. See also TWD to Lewis Cass, June 21, 1854, and Aaron White to TWD, June 30, 1854. RCDC (Box 14, folders 37 and 38), JHL.

6. See Conley, *Democracy in Decline*, 369, and Patrick T. Conley, "Death Knell for the Death Penalty: The Gordon Murder Trial and Rhode Island's Abolition of Capital Punishment," in Patrick T. Conley, ed., *Liberty and Justice: A History of Law and Lawyers in Rhode Island, 1636–1776* (Providence: Rhode Island Publications Society, 1998), 282.

7. See, for example, TWD to David Dudley Field, December 8, 1849, and TWD to Tilesten A. Barker, May 29, 1850. RCDC (Box 12, folders 27 and 28), JHL.

8. Edmund Burke to TWD, June 28, 1850. RCDC (Box 12, folder 28), JHL. Burke served as co-editor of the *Washington Union* with Thomas Ritchie.

9. For mention of Dorr as editor of the *Herald*, see *Semi-Weekly Eagle*, June 5, 1851.

10. See Catharine Williams to TWD, July 12, 1851. RCDC (Box 13, folder 10), JHL.

11. In 1859, Dorr's old friend Dan King from South Kingstown wrote a superficial biography called *The Life of Thomas Wilson Dorr*.

12. TWD to Israel Chapman, January 8, 1851. RCDC (Box 13, folder 2), JHL.

13. Harold M. Hyman and William M. Wiecek, *Equal Justice under Law: Constitutional Development, 1835–1875* (New York: Harper & Row, 1983), 126–127.

14. For more on the Wilmot Proviso, see Christopher Childers, *The Failure of Popular Sovereignty: Slavery, Manifest Destiny, and the Radicalization of Southern Politics* (Lawrence: University Press of Kansas, 2012), 102–134, Gerald Leonard, *The Invention of Party Politics: Federalism, Popular Sovereignty, and Constitutional*

Development in Jacksonian Illinois (Chapel Hill: University of North Carolina Press, 2002), 254, and Eric Foner, "The Wilmot Proviso Revisited," *Journal of American History* 56 (September, 1969): 262–279.

15. See TWD to Samuel Bayard, January 18, 1851. RCDC (Box 13, folder 2), JHL.

16. TWD to Edmund Burke, April 9, 1851. Edmund Burke Papers, LofC.

17. See *Republican Herald*, "The Slavery Question—The True Compromise—Duty of Democrats—The Prospect," August 7, 1850. The second part of the essay was published on August 10. Dorr revealed his authorship to C. C. Hazewell in a letter dated August 12, 1850. RCDC (Box 12, folder 30), JHL.

18. TWD's notes on Anti-Slavery (1834) in TWD Papers (Box 2, folder 15), JHL.

19. See TWD Papers (Box 3, folder 6), JHL.

20. TWD Diary, 1848–1854, p. 37, JHL.

21. TWD to Israel Chapman, January 8, 1851. RCDC (Box 13, Folder 2), JHL.

22. TWD to Hopkins Holsey, June 14, 1853. RCDC (Box 14, folder 22), and TWD to Israel Chapman, January 8, 1851. RCDC (Box 13, Folder 2), JHL.

23. TWD Diary, 1848–1854, p. 37, JHL.

24. See *Benjamin F. Hallett of Boston on Bunker Hill, July 4, 1844* (Boston, 1844), 6–8.

25. On Hallett's antislavery activism, see Albert von Frank, *Trials of Anthony Burns: Freedom and Slavery in Emerson's Boston* (Cambridge, MA: Harvard University Press, 1998), 129–130.

26. John Ashworth, *Slavery, Capitalism and Politics in the Antebellum Republic: The Coming of the Civil War, 1850–1861* (New York: Cambridge University Press, 2007), 353.

27. I draw here from Peter Wallner, *Franklin Pierce: Martyr for the Union* (Concord, NH: Plaidswede Publishing, 2007), 72–73, 375–376.

28. TWD Diary, 1848–1854, p. 37, JHL.

29. The flip-flop was not lost on Dorr's contemporaries. See, for example, the *New Hampshire Statesman*, February 6, 1846, in which the editors reprinted Dorr's 1837 public letter condemning the western expansion of slavery and the Slave Power, along with more recent remarks linking the acquisition of Texas with the doctrine of Manifest Destiny.

30. Robert Sampson, *John L. O'Sullivan and His Times* (Kent, OH: Kent State University Press, 2003), 156.

31. Sean Wilentz, *The Rise of American Democracy: Jefferson to Lincoln* (New York: W. W. Norton, 2005), 617–631.

32. Joel H. Silbey, *Party over Section: The Rough and Ready Presidential Election of 1848* (Lawrence: University Press of Kansas, 2009), 123.

33. TWD to Whittier, November 6, 1848. RCDC (Box 12, folder 15), JHL. In the early 1850s, many Democrats in the National Reform Association also began to advocate for Free Soil. While Dorr agreed that the "the best and most appropriate

mode in which the great public domain held by the general government could be disposed of was by throwing it open in moderate portions to actual settlers, without money and without price," he urged the NRA not to follow the Democratic Party line and to avoid the "free soil" frenzy. See TWD to John H. Kesyer, June 2, 1851. RCDC (Box 12, folder 7), JHL.

34. See TWD to Lewis Josseyln, November 15, 1849, RCDC (Box 12, folder 23), and TWD Diary, 1848–1854, p. 39, JHL.

35. TWD Diary, 1848–1854, p. 39, JHL.

36. TWD to Hopkins Healsey, June 14, 1853. RCDC (Box 14, folder 22), JHL.

37. TWD to Lewis Cass, July 20, 1848. RCDC (Box 12, folder 10), JHL.

38. See Willard C. Klunder, *Lewis Cass and the Politics of Moderation* (Kent, OH: Kent State University Press, 1996), JHL.

39. "The Rhode Island Question—Sovereignty of the People," *Democratic Review* (March, 1848): 193–199.

40. TWD to John O'Sullivan, March 30, 1848. RCDC (Box 12, folder 6), JHL. See Jonathan Sperber, *The European Revolutions, 1848–1851* (New York: Cambridge University Press, 2005), JHL.

41. See Dorr's proposed resolutions in the RCDC (Box 12, folder 7), JHL.

42. Quoted in Joseph G. Rayback, *Free Soil: The Election of 1848* (Lexington: University of Kentucky Press, 1970), 116.

43. Philip Fendall to Henry Clay, May 31, 1848, in Melba Porter Hay, ed., *The Papers of Henry Clay*, 12 vols. (Lexington: University Press of Kentucky, 1991), 10:478.

44. Ashworth, *Slavery, Capitalism, and Politics in the Antebellum Republic*, 424. See also White to TWD, January 11, 1853. RCDC (Box 14, folder 2), JHL.

45. Quoted in Childers, *The Failure of Popular Sovereignty*, 110.

46. Quoted in Silbey, *Party over Section*, 119.

47. Michael F. Holt, *The Rise and Fall of the American Whig Party: Jacksonian Politics and the Onset of the Civil War* (New York: Oxford University Press, 1999), 319.

48. Douglas R. Egerton, *Year of Meteors: Stephen Douglas, Abraham Lincoln, and the Election That Brought on the Civil War* (New York: Bloomsbury Press, 2010), 20.

49. Quoted in Michael A. Morrison, *Slavery and the American West: The Eclipse of Manifest Destiny and the Coming of the American Civil War* (Chapel Hill: University of North Carolina Press, 1997), 84. See also Childers, *The Failure of Popular Sovereignty*, 135–138, and Rayback, 116–118.

50. Don E. Fehrenbacher, *The Slaveholding Republic: An Account of the United States Government's Relations to Slavery* (New York: Oxford University Press, 2001), 269.

51. Yonatan Eyal, *The Young America Movement and the Transformation of the Democratic Party, 1828–1861* (New York: Cambridge University Press, 2007), 207–208, 194.

52. TWD to George Pearson (Young Men's Democratic Union Club, Chicago), October 15, 1852. RCDC (Box 13, folder 24), JHL. See also Silbey, *Party over Section*, 119–121.

53. Quoted in Leonard L. Richards, *The Slave Power: The Free North and Southern Domination, 1780–1860* (Baton Rouge: Louisiana State University Press, 2000), 16. See also Childers, *The Failure of Popular Sovereignty*, 136.

54. Childers, *The Failure of Popular Sovereignty*, 164–165.

55. See Fergus Bordewich, *America's Great Debate: Henry Clay, Stephen A. Douglas, and the Compromise That Preserved the Union* (New York: Simon and Schuster, 2012).

56. See Steven Lubet, *Fugitive Justice: Runaways, Rescuers, and Slavery on Trial* (Cambridge, MA: Harvard University Press, 2010), 42–45, and Childers, *The Failure of Popular Sovereignty*, 166–199. For a succinct summary of the Compromise of 1850 see Ashworth, *Slavery, Capitalism, and Politics in the Antebellum Republic*, 17–44.

57. TWD to John H. George, August 17, 1852. New Hampshire Historical Society (emphasis added).

58. See *Republican Herald*, August 7, 1850.

59. TWD Diary, 1848–1854, p. 34, JHL.

60. Rafia Zafar, ed., *God Made Man, Man Made the Slave: The Autobiography of George Teomoh* (Macon, GA: Mercer University Press, 1990), 9–10. Dorr died shortly after Teomoh was hired.

61. Woodhouse to TWD, April 15, 1851. RCDC (Box 13, folder 4), JHL.

62. See Leonard Levy, *Law of the Commonwealth and Chief Justice Shaw* (New York: Oxford University Press, 1957), 72–108.

63. TWD Diary, 1848–1854, p. 40, JHL.

64. Ibid., 37.

65. TWD to George Rees, September 27, 1852. RCDC (Box 13, folders 23), JHL. See also TWD to Edmund Burke, April 9, 1851. Edmund Burke Papers, LofC.

66. James Oakes, *Freedom National: The Destruction of Slavery in the United States, 1861–1865* (New York: W. W. Norton, 2012), 29.

67. TWD to William Wait, February 27, 1851. RCDC (Box 13, folder 3), JHL.

68. Oakes, *Freedom National*, 33.

69. Quoted in *Liberator*, March 6, 1851.

70. Edmund Burke to TWD, May 7, 1851. RCDC (Box 13, folder 5), JHL.

71. Quoted in Morrison, *Slavery and the American West*, 132.

72. TWD to Israel Chapman, January 8, 1851. RCDC (Box 13, folder 2), JHL and TWD Diary, 1848–1854, p. 32, JHL.

73. TWD Diary, 1848–1854, p. 32, JHL.

74. Burke to TWD, May 19, 1851. RCDC (Box 13, folder 6), JHL.

75. Burke to Franklin Pierce, June 24, 1852, quoted in Peter Wallner, *Franklin Pierce: New Hampshire's Favorite Son* (Concord, N.H.: Plaidswede Publishing,

2004), 207. See also Eyal, *The Young America Movement*, 190–194, and Burke to TWD, January 4, 1852. RCDC (Box 13, folder 13), JHL.

76. TWD to George Pearson (Young Men's Democratic Union Club, Chicago), October 15, 1852. RCDC (Box 13, folder 24), JHL.

77. These points are all outlined in TWD to John H. George, August 17, 1852. New Hampshire Historical Society.

78. TWD to William Rice and others, July 2, 1851. RCDC (Box 13, folder 9), JHL.

79. TWD to R. Kneass, September 1, 1852. RCDC (Box 13, folder 20), JHL. See also TWD to J. W. Bradbury, September 20, 1852. RCDC (Box 13, folder 21), JHL.

80. Ashworth, *Slavery, Capitalism, and Politics in the Antebellum Republic*, 486–487.

81. Elizabeth Varon, *Disunion! The Coming of the American Civil War, 1789–1859* (Chapel Hill: University of North Carolina Press, 2008), 223–224, 227.

82. Holsey to TWD, December 14, 1852, RCDC (Box 13, folder 30), JHL; Varon, *Disunion!*, 229, and Ashworth, *Slavery, Capitalism, and Politics in the Antebellum Republic*, 480–483.

83. TWD to Samuel Bayard, January 18, 1851, and TWD to J. W. Bradbury, September 20, 1852. RCDC (Box 13, folders 2 and 22), JHL.

84. *Republican Herald*, July 21, 1852.

85. For Dorr's support of Cass see, for example, *Republican Herald*, May 22, May 29, and June 2, 1852.

86. Quoted in Roy Franklin Nichols, *Franklin Pierce: Young Hickory of the Granite Hills* (Philadelphia: University of Pennsylvania Press, 1958), 202.

87. Wallner, *Franklin Pierce: New Hampshire's Favorite Son*, 195.

88. Quoted in Allan Nevins, *Ordeal of the Union: A House Dividing, 1852–1857* (New York: Charles Scribner's Sons, 1946), 16.

89. Quoted in Larry Gara, *The Presidency of Franklin Pierce* (Lawrence: University Press of Kansas, 1990), 35.

90. See Eyal, *The Young America Movement*, 209–212.

91. *Weekly Raleigh Register*, August 11, 1852.

92. TWD to Chairman of Committee of Correspondence for the Young Men's Democratic Union Club in New York City, August 31, 1852, and TWD to the Democratic Central Committee of Pennsylvania, September 1, 1852. RCDC (Box 14, folder 20), JHL.

93. Thomas Ritchie to TWD, October 26, 1852. RCDC (Box 13, folder 26), JHL.

94. TWD to John H. George, August 17, 1852. New Hampshire Historical Society. See also TWD to E. A. Hibbard, October 21, 1852. RCDC (Box 13, folder 25), JHL.

95. TWD to G. W. Reese, September 27, 1852. RCDC (Box 13, folder 23), JHL.

96. TWD to A. B. Ingalls, September 22, 1852. RCDC (Box 14, folder 23), JHL.

97. TWD to John Morrison, October 1, 1852. RCDC (Box 13, folder 23), JHL.

98. Eyal, *The Young America Movement*, 214–215. The best discussion of the 1852 presidential election is Wallner, *Franklin Pierce: New Hampshire's Favorite Son*, 205–231.

99. TWD to Ira B. Davis (chairman of committee of Young Men's Democratic Union Club), November 12, 1852. RCDC (Box 13, folder 28), JHL.

100. John Ashworth, *The Republic in Crisis, 1848–1861* (New York: Cambridge University Press, 2012), 85.

101. TWD to Pierce, February 6, 1853. RCDC (Box 14, folder 2). On July 13, 1853, Dorr wrote an equally moving and religious letter to the daughters of Burrington Anthony after the passing of their father. See RCDC (Box 14, folder 24), JHL.

102. Wallner, *Franklin Pierce: Martyr for the Union*, 7.

103. Ibid., 86.

104. Quoted in Nevins, *Ordeal of the Union*, 22.

105. Wallner, *Franklin Pierce: Martyr for the Union*, 24, 43–48, 93.

106. TWD to Hopkins Holsey, June 14, 1853. RCDC (Box 14, folder 22), JHL.

107. Holsey to TWD, July 2, 1853. RCDC (Box 14, folder 23), JHL. For more on the use of the 1798 Kentucky and Virginia Resolutions in this period, see Varon, *Disunion!*, 229–230.

108. Davis to TWD, December 13, 1853. RCDC (Box 14, folder 31), JHL and Davis, "Speech on the Kansas-Nebraska Bill," 33rd Congress, 1st sess. (Appendix), 637. On Thomas Davis and his wife Paulina Kellogg Wright, see Patrick T. Conley, *The Makers of Modern Rhode Island* (Charleston, SC: History Press, 2012), 177–182.

109. See TWD to Hopkins Holsey, June 14, 1853. RCDC (Box 14, folder 22), JHL; Eyal, *The Young America Movement*, 226; and Morrison, *Slavery and the American West*, 141–142.

110. Quoted in Harold Holzer, *Lincoln at Cooper Union: The Speech That Made Abraham Lincoln President* (New York: Simon and Schuster, 2004), 37. See also Allen Guezlo, *Lincoln-Douglas: The Debates That Defined America* (New York: Simon and Schuster, 2008), 281–314.

111. Morrison, *Slavery and the American West*, 148.

112. Ibid., 143. See also 137–140.

113. Ashworth, *The Republic in Crisis*, 81.

114. Ibid., 92.

115. Childers, *The Failure of Popular Sovereignty*, 236, 239, 243.

116. Wallner, *Franklin Pierce: Martyr for the Union*, 94–96.

117. Ibid., 98.

118. Davis to TWD, January 14, 1854. RCDC (Box 14, folder 32), JHL.

119. *National Era*, January 24, 1854. See also Eric Foner, *Free Soil, Free Labor, Free Men: The Ideology of the Republican Party before the Civil War* (New York: Oxford University Press, 1970), 94–95, and Jonathan Earle, *Jacksonian Antislavery*

and the Politics of Free Soil, 1834–1854 (Chapel Hill: University of North Carolina Press, 2004), 193–194.

120. Davis, "Speech on the Kansas-Nebraska Bill," 33rd Congress, 1st sess. (Appendix), 638.

121. *Nebraska and the Rights of the People in Territorial Government* (Boston, 1854), 3.

122. Morrison, *Slavery and the American West*, 144. See also Ashworth, *The Republic in Crisis*, 83–91.

123. Dorr's views are summarized in a letter from Rhode Island Senator Thomas Davis, June 22, 1854. RCDC (Box 14, folder 38), JHL.

124. Leonard, *The Invention of Party Politics*, 262; Earle, *Jacksonian Antislavery*, 192.

125. Fehrenbacher, *The Slaveholding Republic*, 276.

126. White to Dorr, March 13, 1854, RCDC (Box 14, folder 35), JHL.

127. Ibid.

128. Thomas Davis to TWD, May 26 and June 22, 1854. RCDC (Box 14, folders 37 and 38), JHL.

129. For the Burns affair, see von Frank, *Trials of Anthony Burns*.

130. Ibid., 352, note 3. For Dana's views on the Dorr Rebellion see Robert F. Lucid, ed., *The Journal of Richard Henry Dana, Jr.*, 3 vols. (Cambridge, MA: Harvard University Press, 1968), 1:67.

131. Wallner, *Franklin Pierce: Martyr for the Union*, 124.

132. Wilentz, *The Rise of American Democracy*, 677.

133. Quoted in Eric Foner, *The Fiery Trial: Abraham Lincoln and American Slavery* (New York: W. W. Norton, 2010), 68. See also Nicole Etcheson, "'A Living, Creeping Lie': Abraham Lincoln on Popular Sovereignty," *Journal of the Abraham Lincoln Association* 29 (Summer 2008); http://hdl.handle.net/2027/spo.2629860.0029.203.

134. Nicole Etcheson, *Bleeding Kansas: Contested Liberty in the Civil War Era* (Lawrence: University Press of Kansas, 2004), 91–92, 126.

135. See Tony Horwitz, *Midnight Rising: John Brown and the Raid That Sparked the Civil War* (New York: Henry Holt, 2011).

136. John P. Hale, *Wrongs of Kansas* (Washington, DC, 1856), 11. See also *Speeches of Hon. A. C. Barstow, Rev. Geo. T. Day, Rev. A. Woodbury, Hon. Thomas Davis . . . On the Occasion of the Execution of John Brown* (Providence, 1859), 29.

137. *New York Tribune* as quoted in *Liberator*, October 16, 1857.

138. *Address of the Hon. B. F. Hallett to the Democrats of Cheshire County at Keene, New Hampshire, July 4, 1856* (Boston, 1856), 25. RIHS.

139. Nevins, *Ordeal of the Union*, 153–154.

140. Childers, *The Failure of Popular Sovereignty*, 250.

141. See M. W. Cluskey, ed., *The Speeches, Messages, and Other Writings of Albert Gallatin Brown* (Philadelphia, 1859), 564–565. See also Ashworth, *Slavery, Capitalism, and Politics in the Antebellum Republic*, 119.

142. Childers, *The Failure of Popular Sovereignty*, 255.

Coda

1. See Douglas R. Egerton, *Year of Meteors: Stephen Douglas, Abraham Lincoln, and the Election That Brought on the Civil War* (New York: Bloomsbury Press, 2010), 51–82, 149–175.

2. Sarah Jacobs to TWD, December 21, 1854. RCDC (Box 14, folder 39), JHL.

3. White to TWD, June 3, 1842. RCDC (Box 4, folder 2), JHL. See also George M. Dennison, "Republican Form of Government—The Dorr War and Political Questions," *The Supreme Court Historical Society Yearbook* (1979), 47, http://www .supremecourthistory.org/wp-content/themes/supremecourthistory/inc/schs _publications-1979.pdf.

4. Brian McGinty, *The Body of John Merryman: Abraham Lincoln and the Suspension of Habeas Corpus* (Cambridge, MA: Harvard University Press, 2011), 109–115. See also George Dennison, "Martial Law: The Development of a Theory of Emergency Powers, 1776–1861," *American Journal of Legal History* 18 (January 1974): 52–79.

5. See Akhil Reed Amar, "The Lawfulness of Section 5—and Thus of Section 5," *Harvard Law Review* 109 (2013): 112–113.

6. On McDougall, see Patrick T. Conley, *The Makers of Modern Rhode Island* (Charleston, SC: History Press, 2012), 139–142.

7. The speech is reprinted and annotated in Harold Holzer, *Lincoln at Cooper Union: The Speech That Made Abraham Lincoln President* (New York: Simon and Schuster, 2004), 249–284, quote at 284.

8. Nicole Etcheson, "'A Living, Creeping Lie': Abraham Lincoln on Popular Sovereignty," *Journal of the Abraham Lincoln Association* 29 (Summer 2008); http:// hdl.handle.net/2027/spo.2629860.0029.203.

Selected Bibliography

Manuscripts

American Antiquarian Society
Political Papers of John Davis
Diary of Mary White
Diary of Levi Lincoln Newton
Abby Kelley Foster Papers

Boston Public Library
Diary of John Park
William Lloyd Garrison Collection
Dorr Rebellion letters

Connecticut Historical Society
John M. Niles Papers

Connecticut State Library
Executive Council Journal
Governor Correspondence

Cornell University Library
James McCall Papers

Gilder Lehrman Collection, New York Historical Society
Thomas Wilson Dorr Correspondence

Historical Society of Pennsylvania
James Buchanan Papers

John Hay Library, Brown University
Charles Newcomb Papers

Thomas Wilson Dorr Papers
Dorr Rebellion manuscripts (microfilm)
Sidney S. Rider Collection, Dorr Correspondence
Sidney S. Rider Papers
Jonah Titus Papers
Private Letters from Prominent Rhode Island Men to Samuel F. Man

Library of Congress
Levi Woodbury Papers
Thomas Wilson Dorr Papers
Edmund Burke Papers
Martin Van Buren Papers
James Fowler Simmons Papers
Daniel Webster Papers
Records of the States of the United States (microfilm)
Joseph Story Papers

Massachusetts Historical Society
George Bancroft Papers
Diary of John Quincy Adams
Diary of Edmund Quincy
John Quincy Adams's Letter Book

Massachusetts Judicial Archives
Case file for *Commonwealth v. Blodget*

Massachusetts State Archives
Governor Council Records
Election Returns
Unpassed legislation files (House and Senate)
Massachusetts General Laws
Journal of the House of Representatives
Journal of the Senate
Acts and Resolves Passed by the General Court of Massachusetts

National Archives (Waltham, MA Division)
Luther v. Borden files

New Hampshire Historical Society Library
Daniel Webster Papers
John George Papers

New Hampshire State Archives

Executive Council Records
Journal of the Senate

Newport Historical Society
Thomas Wilson Dorr Correspondence

New York Public Library, Manuscript Division
The Writings of Henry A.S. Dearborn (six volumes)
Henry J. Raymond Papers

North Smithfield Heritage Association
Metcalf Marsh Papers

Old Colony Historical Society
Diary of Nathaniel Morton
Diary of Aurilla Moffitt

Providence City Archives
Thomas M. Burgess correspondence
Providence City Council records

Rhode Island State Archives
Records of the Adjutant General
Records of the Quartermaster General
Executive Correspondence
Acts and Resolves of the Rhode Island General Assembly
Journal of the House
Journal of the Senate
Petitions to the General Assembly
Unpassed legislative files

Rhode Island Historical Society Library
Thomas Wilson Dorr Collection
Elisha R. Potter, Jr., Papers
Thomas Mawney Potter Papers
Dorr War Microfilm
Joseph Peace Hazard Papers
Henry A. L. Brown Deposit
William M. Bailey Papers
Joshua Spooner Papers
Albert C. Greene Papers
New England Women and Their Families, 18th- and 19th-century series
    (microfilm)

Elijah Walters Family Papers
James W. C. Ely Family Papers
Power-Whitman Papers
James McKenzie Papers
Hiram Hill Diary (microfilm)
Edward Carrington Papers
Sullivan Dorr Papers
Samuel Ward King Papers

University of Rochester
William Henry Seward Papers

Vermont State Archives
Journal of the House of Representatives
Journal of the Senate

Walter Clements Library, University of Michigan
Joseph Story–John Pitman Correspondence

Private Collections
Russell J. DeSimone: Broadsides, Pamphlets and Correspondence relating to Dorr
    Rebellion
Richard Slaney: Correspondence relating to the Dorr Rebellion

Published Papers

Cutler, Wayne, ed. *The Correspondence of James K. Polk*. 10 vols. University of Tennessee Press, 1969–.
Hamilton, J. G. de Roulhac, ed. *The Papers of William Alexander Graham*. Raleigh, NC: State Department of Archives, 1959.
Hopkins, James, ed. *The Papers of Henry Clay*. 11 vols. University of Kentucky Press, 1959–1992.
Wilson, Clyde, ed. *The Papers of John C. Calhoun*. 28 vols. University of South Carolina Press, 1959–2003.
Wiltse, Charles, ed. *The Papers of Daniel Webster*. Series 1, 7 vols. University of New England Press, 1974–1988.

Newspapers and Magazines

Albany Evening Journal
Bay State Democrat

Boston Atlas
Boston Daily Advertiser
Boston Post
Bristol County Democrat
Bristol Phenix
Brownson's Quarterly Review
Charleston Courier
Charleston Mercury
Cincinnati Weekly Herald and Philanthropist
Daily Enquirer (Cincinnati)
Daily Evening Chronicle (Providence)
Democratic Republican New Era
Emancipator and Free American
Hartford Daily Courant
Herald of Freedom
Hill's New Hampshire Patriot
Liberator
The Madisonian
Manufacturers' and Farmers' Journal
National Anti-Slavery Standard
National Intelligencer
New Age and Constitutional Advocate
New England Democrat
New Hampshire Patriot
Newport Mercury
New York Commercial Advertiser
New York Daily Plebian
New York Express
New York Herald
New York Tribune
Niles' Weekly Register
Norfolk Democrat
Northern Star and Constitutionalist
Pawtucket Gazette and Chronicle
Portsmouth Journal
Providence Chronicle
Providence Express
Providence Journal
Republican Herald
Rhode Island Constitutionalist
Southern Patriot
Subterranean
Suffrage Examiner

United States Magazine and Democracy Review
Voice of the People
Washington Globe
Washington Union
Working Man's Advocate

Congressional Reports

Burke, Edmund. *Interference of the Executive in the Affairs of Rhode Island*. 28 Cong., 1st Sess., House Report No. 546 (1844).

Causin, John. *Minority Report of the Select Committee to Whom Were Referred the Memorial of the Democratic Members of the Rhode Island Legislature*. 28 Cong. 1 Sess., House Report No. 581 (1844).

Published Pamphlets

Adams, John Quincy. *The Social Compact Exemplified in the Constitution of Commonwealth of Massachusetts*. Providence, 1842.

Balch, William. *Popular Liberty and Equal Rights: An Oration Delivered before the Convention of the Rhode Island Suffrage Association, July 5, 1841*. Providence, 1841.

Bolles, Augustus. *Affairs of Rhode Island*. Boston: Benjamin Mussey, 1842.

Bowen, Francis. *The Recent Contest in Rhode Island*. Providence, 1844.

Chief Justice Job Durfee's March 1842 Charge to the Bristol Grand Jury. Providence, 1842.

Curtis, George. *Merits of Thomas W. Dorr and George Bancroft as They are Politically Connected*. Boston, 1842.

Dorr, Thomas Wilson. *Aristides— "Political Frauds Exposed . . . the Junto of Providence*. Providence, 1838.

Durfee, Job. *Charge of the Hon. Chief Justice Durfee, Delivered to the Grand Jury at the March Term of the Supreme Judicial Court, at Bristol, Rhode Island, 1842*. N.P., 1842.

Frieze, Jacob. *A Concise History of the Effort to Obtain an Extension of the Suffrage in Rhode Island from the year 1811 to 1842*. Providence, 1842.

Goodell, William. *Lessons of a Single Day*. Pawtucket, 1842.

———. *The Rights and Wrongs of Rhode Island*. New York, 1842.

———. *Views of American Constitutional Law in Its Bearing upon American Slavery*. Utica, NY, 1844.

Green, Harriet Whipple. *Might and Right*. Providence, 1844.

Hale, John P. *Wrongs of Kansas*. Washington, DC, 1856.

Hallett, Benjamin F. *July Fourth Speech at Bunker Hill*. Boston, 1844.

————. *Nebraska and the Rights of the People in Territorial Government.* Boston, 1854.

————. *The Right of the People to Establish Forms of Government.* Boston, 1848.

Jewett, Charles. *The Close of the Late Rebellion in Rhode Island.* Providence, RI: B. Cranston & Co., 1842.

Letters of the Hon. C. F. Cleveland and Hon. Henry Hubbard, Governors of Connecticut and New Hampshire to Samuel Ward King, Refusing to Deliver Up Thomas Wilson Dorr. Fall River, 1842.

Luther, Seth. *An Address on the Right of Free Suffrage.* Providence, 1833.

————. *The Garland of Gratitude: Respectfully Dedicated to the Constitutional Suffrage Ladies of Rhode Island.* Providence, 1842.

Pitman, John. *A Reply to the Letter of the Hon. Marcus Morton, Late Governor of Massachusetts, on the Rhode-Island Question, by One of the Rhode Island People.* Providence, 1842.

————. *To the Members of the General Assembly of Rhode Island.* Providence, 1842.

Pitman, Joseph. *Report of the Trial of Thomas Wilson Dorr for Treason.* Boston, 1844.

Potter, Elisha R., Jr. *Considerations on the Questions of the Adoption of a Constitution and Extension of Suffrage in Rhode Island.* Boston, 1842.

————. *Speech of Mr. Potter of Rhode Island.* Washington, DC: Globe Office, 1844.

Randall, Dexter. *Democracy Vindicated and Dorrism Unveiled.* Providence, 1846.

The Rhode Island Question: Mr. Webster's Argument in Supreme Court of the United States in the Case of Luther Borden v. Martin Luther. Washington, DC, 1848.

Speeches of Hon. A. C. Barstow, Rev. Geo. T. Day, Rev. A. Woodbury, Hon. Thomas Davis . . . On the Occasion of the Execution of John Brown. Providence, 1859.

Spooner, Lysander. *The Unconstitutionality of Slavery.* Boston, 1845.

Story, Joseph. *Charge Delivered to the Grand Jury of the Circuit Court of the United States Holden at Newport on the Law of Treason.* Providence, 1842.

Treadwell, Francis. *The Conspiracy to Defeat the Liberation of Governor Dorr.* New York, 1845.

Tucker, Mark. *A Discourse Preached on Thanksgiving Day, July 21, 1842.* Providence, 1842.

Turner, George, and Walter S. Burges. *The Report of the Trial of Thomas Wilson Dorr for Treason Against the State of Rhode Island.* Providence, 1844.

Wayland, Francis. *The Affairs of Rhode Island.* Providence, 1842.

————. *A Discourse Delivered in the First Baptist Church.* Providence, 1842.

Webster, Daniel, and John Whipple. *The Rhode Island Question.* Boston, 1848.

Unpublished Primary Sources

Allen, Zachariah. *Dorr Rebellion Manuscript.* Rhode Island Historical Society.

Williams, Catharine R. *Recollections of the Life of and Conversations of Thomas Wilson Dorr.* Providence, 1854. John Hay Library.

Secondary Sources

Ackerman, Bruce. *We the People: Transformations*. Cambridge, MA: Harvard University Press, 1998.

Adams, Charles Francis, ed. *The Diary of John Quincy Adams*. Boston, 1877.

Adams, Peter. *The Bowery Boys: Street Corner Radicals and the Politics of Rebellion*. Westport, CT: Praeger Press, 2005.

Ashworth, John. *Agrarians and Aristocrats: Party Political Ideology in the United States, 1837–1846*. London: Cambridge University Press, 1987.

———. *The Republic in Crisis, 1848–1861*. New York: Cambridge University Press, 2012.

———. *Slavery, Capitalism, and Politics in the Antebellum Republic: Commerce and Compromise, 1820–1850*. London: Cambridge University Press, 1995.

———. *Slavery, Capitalism, and Politics in the Antebellum Republic: The Coming of the Civil War, 1850–1861*. London: Cambridge University Press, 2007.

Baker, Jean. *Affairs of Party: The Political Culture of Northern Democrats in the Mid-Nineteenth Century*. New York: Fordham University Press, 1983.

Bamberg, Cherry Fletcher. "Dorcas Lippitt of Providence, Rhode Island, and Her Descendants." *New England and Genealogical Register* (January 2008): 22–36.

Bassett, John Spencer, ed. *Correspondence of Andrew Jackson*. 6 vols. Washington, DC: Carnegie Institution, 1933.

Belknap, Michal, ed. *American Political Trials*. Westport, CT: Greenwood Press, 1994.

Blassingame, John, ed. *The Frederick Douglass Papers, 1841–1846*. New Haven, CT: Yale University Press, 1979.

Bordewich, Fergus. *America's Great Debate: Henry Clay, Stephen A. Douglas, and the Compromise That Preserved the Union*. New York: Simon and Schuster, 2012.

Botelho, Joyce M. *Right and Might: The Dorr Rebellion and the Struggle for Equal Rights*. Providence: Rhode Island Historical Society, 1992.

Bronstein, Jamie. *Land Reform and Working-Class Experience in Britain and the United States*. Stanford, CA: Stanford University Press, 1999.

Chambers, Stephen. "'Neither Justice nor Mercy': Public and Private Executions in Rhode Island, 1832–1833." *New England Quarterly* 82 (September 2009): 430–451.

Chaput, Erik J. "A Governor in Exile: New Hampshire and the 'Rhode Island Question.'" *Historical New Hampshire* 66 (Winter 2012–2013): 91–119.

———. "'Let the People Remember!': Rhode Island's Dorr Rebellion and Massachusetts Politics, 1842–1843." *Historical Journal of Massachusetts* 39 (Summer 2011): 108–143.

———. "Proslavery and Antislavery Politics in Rhode Island's 1842 Dorr Rebellion." *New England Quarterly* 85 (December 2012): 658–694.

———. "Reform and Reaction: Populism in Early America." *Common-Place* 9, no. 2 (January 2009); http://www.common-place.org/vol-09/no-02/reviews/chaput.shtml.

———. "'The Rhode Island Question': The Career of a Debate." *Rhode Island History* 68, no. 2 (Summer/Fall, 2010): 46–75.

———. "'The Rhode Island Question' on Trial: The 1844 Treason Trial of Thomas Wilson Dorr." *American Nineteenth Century History* 11, no. 2 (June, 2010): 205–232.

Chaput, Erik J., and Russell J. DeSimone. "Strange Bedfellows: The Politics of Race in Antebellum Rhode Island." *Common-Place* 10, no. 2 (January 2010); http://www.common-place.org/vol-10/no-02/chaput-desimone/.

Chaput, Erik J., and Raymond J. Lavertue. "'The Instigation of the Devil': Sex, Lust, and Murder in Nineteenth-Century Rhode Island." Talk delivered at the Providence Athenaeum, November 23, 2012.

Childers, Christopher. *The Failure of Popular Sovereignty: Slavery, Manifest Destiny, and the Radicalization of Southern Politics.* Lawrence: University Press of Kansas, 2012.

Chudacoff, Howard P., and Theodore C. Hirt. "Social Turmoil and Governmental Reform in Providence, 1820–1832." *Rhode Island History* 31 (Winter 1971): 21–33.

Cole, Donald B. *Jacksonian Democracy in New Hampshire, 1800–1851.* Cambridge: Harvard University Press, 1970.

———. *Martin Van Buren and the American Political System.* Princeton, NJ: Princeton University Press, 1984.

———. *Vindicating Andrew Jackson: The 1828 Election and the Rise of the Two Party System.* Lawrence: University Press of Kansas, 2009.

Coleman, Peter. "The Dorr War and the Leviathan State." *Reviews in American History* 4 (December 1976): 533–538.

———. *The Transformation of Rhode Island, 1790–1860.* Providence, RI: Brown University Press, 1963.

Conley, Patrick T. *Democracy in Decline: Rhode Island's Constitutional Development, 1776–1841.* Providence: Rhode Island Historical Society, 1977.

———. "The Dorr Rebellion and American Constitutional Theory: Popular Constituent Sovereignty, Political Questions, and *Luther v. Borden,*" in Patrick T. Conley, ed., *Liberty and Justice: A History of Law and Lawyers in Rhode Island, 1636–1998.* Providence: Rhode Island Publications Society, 1998.

———. "No Tempest in a Teapot: The Dorr Rebellion in National Perspective." *Rhode Island History* 50 (August 1992): 67–100.

———. "Popular Sovereignty or Public Anarchy: America Debates the Dorr Rebellion." *Rhode Island History* 60 (Summer 2002): 71–91.

———. "Tom Dorr: Up Close and Personal." In Patrick T. Conley, *People, Places, Laws and Lore of the Ocean State: A Rhode Island Historical Sampler.* Providence, RI: Rhode Island Publications Society, 2012.

————, ed. *Constitution Day: Reflections by Respected Scholars*. Providence, RI: Rhode Island Publications Society, 2010.

————, ed. *Liberty and Justice: A History of Law and Lawyers in Rhode Island, 1636–1998*. Providence: Rhode Island Publications Society, 1998.

————, ed. *Rhode Island in Rhetoric and Reflection*. Providence: Rhode Island Publications Society, 2002.

Conley, Patrick T., and Paul Campbell. *Providence: A Pictorial History*. Norfolk, VA: Donning, 1986.

Conley, Patrick T., and Robert Flanders. *The Rhode Island State Constitution: A Reference Guide*. Westport, CT: Greenwood Press, 2007.

Conley, Patrick T., and Matthew Smith. *Catholicism in Rhode Island: The Formative Era*. Providence, RI: Diocese of Providence Press, 1976.

Conron, Michael A. "Law, Politics, and Chief Justice Taney: A Reconstruction of the *Luther v. Borden* Decision." *American Journal of Legal History* 11 (October 1967): 377–388.

Cottrol, Robert J. *Afro-Yankees: Providence's Black Community in the Antebellum Era*. Westport, CT: Greenwood Press, 1982.

Crapol, Edward. *John Tyler: The Accidental President*. Chapel Hill: University of North Carolina Press, 2006.

Darling, Arthur B. *Political Changes in Massachusetts, 1824–1848: A Study of Liberal Movements in Politics*. New Haven, CT: Yale University Press, 1925.

Dennison, George M. *The Dorr War: Republicanism on Trial, 1831–1861*. Lexington: University Press of Kentucky, 1975.

————. "Martial Law: The Development of a Theory of Emergency Powers, 1776–1861." *American Journal of Legal History* 18 (January 1974): 52–79.

————. "Republican Form of Government—The Dorr War and Political Questions." *The Supreme Court Historical Society Yearbook* (1979): 45–62.

————. "Thomas Wilson Dorr: Counsel of Record in *Luther v. Borden*." *St. Louis University Law Review* 15 (1970): 398–428.

DeSimone, Russell J. *Rhode Island's Rebellion*. Vols. 1–9. Middletown, RI: Bartlett Press, 2009.

DeSimone, Russell J., and Daniel Schofield. *Broadsides of the Dorr Rebellion*. Providence: Rhode Island Supreme Court Historical Society, 1992.

Earle, Jonathan. *Jacksonian Antislavery and the Politics of Free Soil, 1834–1854*. Chapel Hill: University of North Carolina Press, 2004.

————. "Marcus Morton and the Dilemma of Jacksonian Antislavery in Massachusetts, 1817–1849." *Massachusetts Historical Review* 4 (2002): 61–88.

Egerton, Douglas R. *Year of Meteors: Stephen Douglas, Abraham Lincoln, and the Election That Brought on the Civil War*. New York: Bloomsbury Press, 2010.

Ernst, Howard R. "A Call to Arms: Thomas Wilson Dorr's Forceful Effort to Implement the People's Constitution." *Rhode Island History* 66, no. 3 (Fall 2008): 59–80.

Ernst, Robert. "One and Only Mike Walsh." *New York Historical Society Quarterly* 36 (January, 1952): 43–65.

Etcheson, Nicole. "'A Living, Creeping Lie': Abraham Lincoln on Popular Sovereignty." *Journal of the Abraham Lincoln Association* 29 (Summer 2008); http://hdl.handle.net/2027/spo.2629860.0029.203.

Eyal, Yonatan. *The Young America Movement and the Transformation of the Democratic Party, 1828–1861*. New York: Cambridge University Press, 2007.

Faulkner, Carol. *Lucretia Mott's Heresy: Abolition and Women's Rights in Nineteenth-Century America*. Philadelphia: University of Pennsylvania Press, 2011.

Feller, Daniel. *The Jacksonian Promise: America, 1815–1840*. Baltimore, MD: Johns Hopkins University Press, 1995.

Fehrenbacher, Donald E. *The Slaveholding Republic: An Account of the United States Government's Relation to Slavery*. New York: Oxford University Press, 2001.

Foner, Eric. *The Fiery Trial: Abraham Lincoln and American Slavery*. New York: W. W. Norton, 2010.

———. *Free Soil, Free Labor, Free Men: The Ideology of the Republican Party before the Civil War*. New York: Oxford University Press, 1970.

———. *Politics and Ideology in the Age of the Civil War*. New York: Oxford University Press, 1980.

———. "The Wilmot Proviso Revisited." *Journal of American History* 56 (September 1969): 262–279.

Formisano, Ronald P. *For the People: American Populist Movements from the Revolution to the 1850s*. Chapel Hill: University of North Carolina Press, 2008.

———. "The Role of Women in the Dorr Rebellion." *Rhode Island History* 51 (August 1993): 89–104.

———. *The Transformation of Political Culture: Massachusetts Parties, 1790s–1840s*. New York: Oxford University Press, 1983.

Fritz, Christian G. *American Sovereigns: The People and America's Constitutional Tradition before the Civil War*. New York: Cambridge University Press, 2008.

———. "America's Unknown Constitutional World." www.Common-Place.org (October 1, 2008).

Gara, Larry. *The Presidency of Franklin Pierce*. Lawrence: University Press of Kansas, 1990.

Garman, James C. *Detention Castles of Stone and Steel: Landscape, Labor and the Urban Penitentiary*. Knoxville: University of Tennessee Press, 2005.

Gates, Henry Louis, Jr., ed. *Douglass: Autobiographies*. Washington, DC: Library of America, 1994.

Gersuny, Carl. "Seth Luther—The Road from Chepachet." *Rhode Island History* 33 (May 1974): 47–55.

Gettleman, Marvin. *The Dorr Rebellion: A Study in American Radicalism*. New York: Random House, 1973.

Gettleman, Marvin, and Noel Conlon, eds. "Responses to the Rhode Island Workingmen's Reform Agitation of 1833." *Rhode Island History* 28 (August 1969): 75–94.

Gilkeson, John. *Middle-Class Providence, 1820–1940.* Princeton, NJ: Princeton University Press, 1986.

Graham, D. Kurt. *To Bring Law Home: The Federal Judiciary in Early National Rhode Island.* DeKalb: Northern Illinois University Press, 2010.

Graham, Susan H. "'Call Me a Female Politician, I Glory in the Name': Women Dorrites and Rhode Island's 1842 Suffrage Crisis." Ph.D. diss., University of Minnesota, 2006.

———. "A Warm Politician and Devotedly Attached to the Democratic Party": Catharine Read Williams, Politics, and Literature in Antebellum America." *Journal of the Early Republic* 30 (Summer 2010): 253–278.

Grimsted, David. *American Mobbing, 1828–1861: Towards Civil War.* New York: Oxford University Press, 2003.

Hartz, Louis. "Seth Luther: The Story of a Working Class Rebel." *New England Quarterly* 13 (September, 1940): 401–418.

Hayman, Robert W. *Catholicism in Rhode Island and the Diocese of Providence, 1780–1886.* Providence, RI: Diocese of Providence Press, 1982.

Hodges, Almon D., ed. *Almon Danforth Hodges and His Neighbors: An Autobiographical Sketch of a Typical Old New Englander.* Boston, 1909.

Hoffman, Charles, and Tess Hoffman. *Brotherly Love: Murder and the Politics of Prejudice in Nineteenth-Century Rhode Island.* Amherst: University of Massachusetts Press, 1995.

———. *North by South: The Two Lives of Richard James Arnold.* Athens: University of Georgia Press, 1988.

Holt, Michael F. *Franklin Pierce.* New York: Time Books, 2010.

———. *The Rise and Fall of the American Whig Party: Jacksonian Politics and the Onset of the Civil War.* New York: Oxford University Press, 1999.

Horwitz, Tony. *Midnight Rising: John Brown and the Raid That Sparked the Civil War.* New York: Henry Holt, 2011.

Howe, Daniel Walker. *The Political Culture of American Whigs.* University of Chicago Press, 1979.

———. *What Hath God Wrought: The Transformation of America, 1815–1848.* New York: Oxford University Press, 2007.

Huston, Reeve. *Land and Freedom: Rural Society, Popular Protest, and Party Politics in Antebellum New York.* New York: Oxford University Press, 2000.

Hyman, Harold M., and William M. Wiecek, *Equal Justice under Law: Constitutional Development, 1835–1875.* New York: Harper and Row, 1982.

Johnson, Reinhard O. *The Liberty Party, 1840–1848: Antislavery Third-Party Politics in the United States.* Baton Rouge: Louisiana State University Press, 2009.

———. "The Liberty Party in Massachusetts, 1840–1848: Antislavery Third Party Politics in the Bay State." *Civil War History* 28 (Summer 1982): 237–265.

Jones, Daniel P. *The Economic and Social Transformation of Rural Rhode Island, 1780–1850*. Evanston, Ill.: Northeastern University Press, 1992.

Kasserman, David. *Fall River Outrage: Life, Murder and Justice in Early Industrial New England*. Philadelphia: University of Pennsylvania Press, 1986.

King, Daniel. *The Life and Times of Thomas Wilson Dorr*. Boston, 1859.

Klunder, Willard C. *Lewis Cass and the Politics of Moderation*. Kent, OH: Kent State University Press, 1996.

Lampe, Gregory P. *Frederick Douglass: Freedom's Voice, 1818–1845*. East Lansing: Michigan State University Press, 1998.

Lancaster, Jane. "The Battle of Chepachet: An Eyewitness Account." *Rhode Island History* 64 (Summer 2004): 17–24.

Landscape of Industry: An Industrial History of the Blackstone Valley (edited by the staff at the Worcester Historical Museum). Lebanon, NH: University Press of New England, 2009.

Lause, Mark. *Young America: Land, Labor, and the Republican Community*. Chicago: University of Illinois Press, 2005.

Lemons, J. Stanley, and Michael A. McKenna. "Re-enfranchisement of Rhode Island Negroes." *Rhode Island History* 30 (February 1971): 2–13.

Leonard, Gerald. *The Invention of Party Politics: Federalism, Popular Sovereignty, and Constitutional Development in Jacksonian Illinois*. Chapel Hill: University of North Carolina Press, 2002.

Lerche, Charles O. "The Dorr Rebellion and the Federal Constitution." *Rhode Island History* 9 (January, 1950): 1–9.

Lubet, Steven. *Fugitive Justice: Runaways, Rescuers, and Slavery on Trial*. Cambridge, MA: Harvard University Press, 2010.

Lucid, Robert F., ed. *The Journal of Richard Henry Dana, Jr.* 3 vols. Cambridge, MA: Harvard University Press, 1968.

MacAllister, Craig. "New England Calhounites: The Henshaw Faction of the Massachusetts Democratic Party, 1828–1850." Ph.D. diss., University of Michigan, 2009.

Magrath, Peter C. "Optimistic Democrat: Thomas W. Dorr and the Case of *Luther v. Borden*." *Rhode Island History* 29 (October, 1970): 94–112.

Malone, Christopher. *Between Freedom and Bondage: Race, Party and Voting Rights in the Antebellum North*. New York: Routledge Press, 2008.

May, Gary. *John Tyler*. New York: Times Books, 2008.

McGiffen, Steven. "Prelude to Republicanism Issues in the Realignment, 1835–1847 of Political Parties in New Hampshire." Ph.D. diss., University of Manchester, Great Britain, 1984.

Melish, Joanne Pope. *Disowning Slavery: Gradual Emancipation and "Race" in New England, 1780–1860*. Ithaca, NY: Cornell University Press, 1997.

———, ed. *The Life of William J. Brown of Providence, RI with Personal Recollections of Incidents in Rhode Island*. Hanover: University of New Hampshire Press, 2006.

Merrill, Walter, ed. *Letters of William Lloyd Garrison: No Union with Slaveholders.* Cambridge, MA: Harvard University Press, 1974.

Molloy, Scott, Carl Gersuny, and Robert Macieski, eds. *Irish Titan, Irish Toilers: Joseph Bannigan and Nineteenth-Century New England Labor.* Lebanon, NH: University of New Hampshire Press, 2008.

———. *Peaceably If We Can, Forcibly If We Must! Writings by and about Seth Luther.* Providence, RI: Rhode Island Labor History Society, 1998.

Monroe, Dan. *The Republican Vision of John Tyler.* College Station: Texas A&M University Press, 2003.

Morgan, Robert. *A Whig Embattled: The Presidency under John Tyler.* Lincoln: University of Nebraska Press, 1954.

Morison, Samuel Eliot. "The Great Rebellion at Harvard College." *Transactions of the Colonial Society of Massachusetts* 27 (1928): 54–113.

———. *Three Centuries at Harvard, 1636–1936.* Cambridge, MA: Harvard University Press, 1936.

Morrison, Michael A. *Slavery and the American West: The Eclipse of Manifest Destiny and the Coming of the American Civil War.* Chapel Hill: University of North Carolina Press, 1997.

Moses, Wilson J. *Alexander Crummell: A Study of Civilization and Discontent.* Amherst: University of Massachusetts Press, 1989.

Mowry, Arthur May. *The Dorr War: Constitutional Struggle in Rhode Island.* 1901; New York: Chelsea House Publishers, 1970.

———. "Tammany Hall and the Dorr Rebellion." *American Historical Review* (January, 1898): 292–301.

Myers, John. "Antislavery Agencies in Rhode Island, 1832–1835." *Rhode Island History* 29 (Summer 1970): 82–92.

———. "Antislavery Agencies in Rhode Island, 1835–1837." *Rhode Island History* 30 (Winter 1971): 21–30.

Nevins, Allan, ed. *The Diary of George Templeton Strong.* New York: Macmillan, 1953.

———. *The Diary of Phillip Hone, 1828–1851.* 2 vols. New York: Dodd, Mead and Company, 1927.

O'Dowd, Sarah C. *A Rhode Island Original: Frances Harriet Whipple Green McDougall.* Hanover, NH: University Press of New England, 2004.

Palsey, Jeffrey L., Andrew W. Robertson, and David Waldstreicher, eds. *Beyond the Founders: New Approaches to the Political History of the Early Republic.* Chapel Hill: University of North Carolina Press, 2004.

Pease, Jane. "The Freshness of Fanaticism: Abby Kelley Foster: An Essay in Reform." Ph.D. diss., University of Rochester, 1969.

Rae, John B. "Democrats and the Dorr Rebellion." *New England Quarterly* 9 (September 1936): 476–483.

———. "The Great Suffrage Parade." *Rhode Island History* 1 (July 1942): 90–94.

Raven, Rory. *The Dorr War: Treason, Rebellion, and the Fight for Reform in Rhode Island*. Charleston, SC: The History Press, 2010.

Renda, Lex. *Running on the Record: Civil War–Era Politics in New Hampshire*. Charlottesville: University of Virginia Press, 1997.

Richards, Leonard. *"Gentleman of Property and Standing": Anti-Abolition Mobs in Jacksonian America*. New York: Oxford University Press, 1970.

———. *The Life and Times of Congressman John Quincy Adams*. New York: Oxford University Press, 1986.

———. *The Slave Power: The Free North and Southern Domination, 1780–1860*. Baton Rouge: Louisiana State University Press, 2000.

Richardson, James D. *A Compilation of the Messages and Papers of the Presidents*. 20 vols. Washington, DC: Bureau of National Literature and Art, 1897–1917.

Rider, Sidney S. *Bibliographical Memoirs of Three Rhode Island Authors: Joseph K. Angell, Francis W. McDougall, and Catharine R. Williams*. Providence, 1880.

Robertson, Stacy. *Parker Pillsbury: Radical Abolitionist, Male Feminist*. Ithaca, NY: Cornell University Press, 2000.

Sampson, Robert. *John L. O'Sullivan and His Times*. Kent, OH: Kent State University Press, 2003.

Schantz, Mark S. *Piety in Providence: Class Dimensions of Religious Experience in Antebellum Rhode Island*. Ithaca, NY: Cornell University Press, 2000.

Schlesinger, Arthur M., Jr. *The Age of Jackson*. Boston: Little, Brown, 1945.

Schuchman, John. "The Political Background of the Political Question Doctrine: The Judges and the Dorr War." *American Journal of Legal History* 16 (1972): 111–125.

Seager, Robert. *And Tyler Too: A Biography of John and Julia Gardiner Tyler*. New York: McGraw-Hill Book Company, 1963.

Seward, Frederick, ed. *William H. Seward: An Autobiography from 1801–1834 with a Memoir of His Life and a Selection of His Letters from 1831–1846*. New York, 1891.

Shalhope, Robert E. *The Baltimore Bank Riot: Political Upheaval in Antebellum Maryland*. Urbana: University of Illinois Press, 2009.

Sharp, James Roger. *American Politics in the Early Republic: The New Nation in Crisis*. New Haven, CT: Yale University Press, 1993.

———. *The Jacksonians versus the Banks: The Politics in the States after the Panic of 1837*. New York: Columbia University Press, 1970.

Silbey, Joel. *Party over Section: The Rough and Ready Presidential Election of 1848*. Lawrence: University Press of Kansas 2009.

———. *Storm over Texas: The Annexation Controversy and the Road to Civil War*. New York: Oxford University Press, 2005.

Sperber, Jonathan. *The European Revolutions, 1848–1851*. New York: Cambridge University Press, 2005.

Sterling, Dorothy. *Ahead of Her Time: Abby Kelley and the Politics of Antislavery*. New York: W. W. Norton, 1994.

Sterne, Evelyn Savidge. *Ballots and Bibles: Ethnic Politics and the Catholic Church in Providence.* Ithaca, NY: Cornell University Press, 2004.

Stewart, James Brewer. *Holy Warriors: The Abolitionists and American Slavery.* New York: Hill and Wang, 1976.

Stokes, Melvin, and Stephen Conway, eds. *Market Revolution in America: Social, Political, and Religious Expressions, 1800–1880.* Charlottesville: University Press of Virginia, 1996.

Story, Walter, ed. *The Life and Writings of Joseph Story.* Boston: Charles C. Little & James Brown, 1851.

Sullivan, Joseph W. "Reconstructing the Olney's Lane Riot: Another Look at Race and Class in Jacksonian Rhode Island." *Rhode Island History* 65 (Summer 2007): 49–60.

Sweet, Edward F. "The Origins of the Democratic Party in Rhode Island, 1824–1836." Ph.D. diss., Fordham University, 1971.

Sweet, John Wood. *Bodies Politic: Negotiating Race in the American North, 1730–1830.* Philadelphia: University of Pennsylvania Press, 2003.

Tew, John D. "Echoes from the Dorr Rebellion: The 1842 Aplin/Carpenter Correspondence." *American Ancestors* 12 (Fall 2011): 37–40.

Thompson, Paul M. "Is There Anything Legal About Extralegal Action?: The Debate Over Dorr's Rebellion." *New England Law Review* 36 (2001–2002): 385–431.

Troy, Gil, Arthur M. Schlesinger, Jr., and Fred Israel, eds. *History of American Presidential Elections, 1789–2000,* 3 vols. New York: Facts on File, 2012.

Tyack, David. *George Ticknor and the Boston Brahmins.* Cambridge, MA: Harvard University Press, 1967.

Tyler, Lyon Gardiner, ed. *The Letters and Times of the Tylers.* Richmond, VA: Whittet and Shepperson, 1885.

Varon, Elizabeth R. *Disunion! The Coming of the American Civil War, 1789–1859.* Chapel Hill: University of North Carolina Press, 2008.

Van Broekhoven, Deborah B. "'A Determination to Labor': Female Antislavery Activity in Rhode Island." *Rhode Island History* 44 (May, 1985): 35–45.

———. *The Devotion of These Women: Rhode Island in the Anti-Slavery Network.* Amherst: University of Massachusetts Press, 2002.

Vile, John R. "John C. Calhoun on the Guarantee Clause." *South Carolina Law Review* 40 (1988–1989): 667–692.

von Frank, Albert. *Trials of Anthony Burns: Freedom and Slavery in Emerson's Boston.* Cambridge, MA: Harvard University Press, 1998.

Wallner, Peter. *Franklin Pierce: Martyr for the Union.* Concord, NH: Plaidswede Publishing, 2007.

———. *Franklin Pierce: New Hampshire's Favorite Son.* Concord, NH: Plaidswede Publishing, 2004.

Warshauer, Matthew. *Andrew Jackson and the Politics of Martial Law: Nationalism, Civil Liberties, and Partisanship.* Knoxville: University of Tennessee Press, 2007.

Watson, Harry. *Liberty and Power: The Politics of Jacksonian America*. New York: Hill and Wang, 1990.

Widmer, Edward. *Young America: The Flowering of Democracy in New York City*. New York: Oxford University Press, 1999.

Widmer, Ted. "Brief Life of a Harvard Demagogue, 1805–1854: Thomas Wilson Dorr." *Harvard Magazine* 93, no. 3 (1991).

———. *Martin Van Buren*. New York: Time Books, 2005.

Wiecek, William M. *The Guarantee Clause of the U.S. Constitution*. Ithaca, NY: Cornell University Press, 1972.

———. *Liberty under Law: The Supreme Court in American Life*. Baltimore: Johns Hopkins University Press, 1988.

———. "'A Peculiar Conservatism' and the Dorr Rebellion: Constitutional Clash in Jacksonian America." *American Journal of Legal History* 22 (July 1978): 237–253.

———. "Popular Sovereignty in the Dorr War — Conservative Counterblast." *Rhode Island History* 32 (May 1973): 35–51.

———. *The Sources of Antislavery Constitutionalism in America, 1760–1848*. Ithaca, NY: Cornell University Press, 1977.

Wilentz, Sean. *Chants Democratic: New York City and the Rise of the American Working Class, 1788–1850*. Oxford University Press, 1984.

———. *The Rise of American Democracy: From Jefferson to Lincoln*. New York: W. W. Norton, 2005.

Wiltse, Charles. *John C. Calhoun: Sectionalist, 1840, 1850*. New York: Bobbs-Merrill, 1951.

Wood, Gordon S. *Empire of Liberty: A History of the Early Republic, 1789–1815*. New York: Oxford University Press, 2009.

Wright, Conrad E., and William Pencak, eds., *New York and the Rise of American Capitalism: Economic Development and the Social and Political History of an American State 1780–1870*. New York: New York Historical Society Publications, 1989.

Zboray, Ronald J., and Mary S. Zboray, *Voices without Votes: Women and Politics in Antebellum New England*. Hanover, NH: University Press of New England, 2010.

Zuckerman, Michael B. "The Political Economy of Industrial Rhode Island, 1790–1860." Ph.D. diss., Brown University, 1981.

Index